POSITIVE REGARD

POSITIVE REGARD

Carl Rogers and Other Notables
He Influenced

Melvin M. Suhd, Editor

SCIENCE AND BEHAVIOR BOOKS, INC.
Palo Alto, California

Printed in the United States of America.

Library of Congress Card Number 93-087337

ISBN 0-8314-0081-1

In chapter 9, material is reprinted with the permission of Macmillan College Publishing Company from *Freedom To Learn for the 80s* by Carl Rogers. Copyright ©1983, 1969 by Macmillan College Publishing Company, Inc.

Cover design by Tony Aguila
Editing and interior design by Rain Blockley
Proofing and indexing by Judy Palen
Typography by TLC Graphics
Printing by Haddon Craftsmen

Contents

Preface

This book grew out of the idea for a "bioanthology"—a mosaic of biographies that connect one noted person to some of the people who drew notable inspiration from him or her. Focusing on a principal person or charismatic leader, this format recognizes others as part of a whole—a *gestalt*—and as part of a human continuum that spans continents and disciplines.

Aside from acknowledging and honoring the central figure, this format helps change the way we understand and write about people, their work, and their effect on the rest of us. I believe we can pay homage to special people without deifying them on unattainable pedestals. We need not perpetuate history as a description of elitists who acted alone, created great ideas in a vacuum, and were unreachable. Ideas do not have to die with a single person or freeze because others saw that person's master scheme as impenetrable.

The persons we honor can be human beings who walked with us and helped us reach higher levels of consciousness. We can advance the "good life" by paying respect to more of our peers and showing how our lives and ways of thinking are interwoven. Showing our uniqueness as well as our togetherness, we can develop a sense of interdependence that moves our world to greater peace and love.

I wanted to help create a book about Carl Rogers and people in his "extended family" because so much of their work is about interconnectedness. Each life story in this book represents someone who has made his or her own contribution to the greater community, and all are connected in that they acknowledge Carl's influence.

Our world thrives according to whether and how we recognize our interconnectedness as people in the human family. Without denying our differences with each other, we may do well to experiment with new perspectives about our conflicts and our unity. On a global scale, as Robert Spitzer has said, an extraterrestrial anthropologist viewing Earth from millions of miles away might see us as billions of homogenous creatures moving together, connected in some unheard rhythm of rising, moving around, and relaxing again in the course of a day. We might be called the Dancing Planet.

On a more personal scale, we find another part of our human connectedness when we look at how one individual's life and work touch, change, and inspire other lives—and how those people repeat the cycle with their own ideas, energies, and human interplay. This enlarges the context in which we consider another person, emphasizes our mutual influence, and underlines the evolution of our regard—for each other and ourselves as well.

Conventionally narcissistic biographies do little to enhance the belief that life is a *gestalt,* that we are all interconnected, and that we are part of a universe that has been evolving for millions of years. We fail to recognize that notable people are influenced by—and, in turn, influence—others across disciplinary and cultural paths.

Without a sense of community or family of people, the life and works of a notable person become "history" rather than a part of generational evolution. Each generation sees its own creations as original, and it writes history to verify the revolutionary rather than evolutionary process of life. Rugged individualism prevails over cooperation and sharing. We may thus attribute an entire movement or major event to a person we believe acted alone. We glorify the superstar. The team becomes a blur and is soon forgotten.

Too often, the contribution also fades when the designated star retires or expires. That creative process or idea becomes rigidified because followers have no precedent for understanding that the work of a pioneer is a conglomerate of those before and those who were a part of its creation.

It does not have to be this way. Edison and his community not only turned on the incandescent lamp but also enhanced the light of reason, logic, and "messing about." Influenced by him and aided by his work, other people did notable things in politics, social sciences, religion, philosophy, and so on. Sojourner Truth and her extended family not only advanced the cause of emancipation but also influenced persons who then promoted self-empowerment, improved social systems, and developed multicultural value systems.

So it is my hope that, in reading this book, you will come into a new way of appreciating yourself, your part in evolving the world's well-being, and your mutual influence with other people—past, present, and future.

Acknowledgments

There are two editors of this book. I take responsibility for assembling the notables who appear. This was the most enjoyable part, for I had the opportunity to meet with persons who have influenced my life, and to interview special persons who helped me contact the many individuals who could be considered for inclusion. My co-editor, Rain Blockley, helped me take a concept and turn it into a book that I believe will make a significant contribution to literature. Her editorial suggestions dramatically improved the text and caused the anthology to reflect a cohesiveness without denying the individuality of the contributors.

I researched over fifty notables who could have been included in *Positive Regard*. I interviewed thirty-two persons. The difficult part of my editorial role was narrowing the selection to the eight persons who appear in this book. This was a personal decision. I believe every reader will appreciate those who appear. I can certainly be faulted for not adding others who rightfully merited inclusion.

Among those who offered me special assistance were Karl Linn, who through his meetings concerning the life of Lawrence K. Frank inspired me to come up with the idea of a "family" biography, or bioanthology. All the people at the Center for the Study of the Person went out of their way to meet with me and share their knowledge and materials to make my search possible. Nel Kandell, Gay Swenson, Maria Bowen, and Valerie Henderson were especially helpful. Without Suzanne Spector's help, Haruko Tsuge might not have appeared in this book. Suzanne made a special effort to act as my spokesperson when visiting in Japan, and in encouraging Haruko to participate. David Russell, at the University of California, Santa Barbara, spent much time with me going over his extensive resources to help locate individuals. And I thank Natalie Rogers—my friend, my sister—who in her way, without judgment but with congruence, relieved my anxiety over the decisions that I finally made.

Then there are all the friends and relatives who assisted me and supported me throughout this chaotic three-year period. Sharon Markham and David Schwartz, especially, were there for me during these trying moments.

Finally, I want to honor a special brother, Bob Spitzer, publisher of Science and Behavior Books. To me, Bob is one of the most creative persons in the world. He also has a genius for remaining behind the scenes. While I believe he should be the root person for another bioanthology, his elusiveness may make such a task extremely difficult. Without his grasp of my concept, this book most likely would not have happened. His patience and support, both morally and financially, permitted me to work through this enormous project.

—Mel Suhd

Carl Rogers

by Howard Kirschenbaum

Carl Ransom Rogers was born in Oak Park, Illinois, on January 8, 1902, fourth among the six children of Walter and Julia Rogers. Walter was in the heavy construction business, building roads and bridges across the country. As his family had grown, his business had prospered—enough to purchase the fine home in Chicago's exclusive suburb where Carl spent his childhood.

Childhood and Boyhood: 1902–19

The Rogers were devout, conservative Protestants who led the children in lengthy prayers each morning, forbade them from dancing or playing cards, and stressed the values of hard work and family responsibilities. Two of Carl's mother's favorite biblical phrases were typical of their strict attitudes: "Come out from among them and be ye separate" and "All our righteousness is as filthy rags in Thy sight, o Lord." To Carl, "The first expressed her conviction of superiority, that we were of the 'elect' and should not mingle with those who were not so favored; the second her conviction of inferiority, that at best we were unspeakably sinful."[1]

Carl did, indeed, "come out from among them" and, in fact, spent most of his childhood isolated from his peers. All through grade school, he came home immediately after school to do chores. Then, when he was thirteen, the family moved to a 300-acre gentleman's farm and manor house twenty-five miles west of Chicago. Living on the farm, far from his classmates, Carl lacked opportunities to mingle freely with boys and girls his own age, and instead fell back upon his two younger brothers for companionship. Within the limits of the family, however, the boys had great fun and adventures—Carl making up stories and fantasies which the boys would act out: playing cowboys and Indians in the woods behind their house, shooting pigeons, playing pioneers, trying unsuccessfully to ride the heifers, and getting into as many forms of trouble as their imaginations allowed.

They were also a teasing family. As Rogers later put it, "You just took digs at everybody, and everybody took digs at you."[2] Among the siblings, Carl seemed to be the most sensitive to this form of banter. While he held his own on the surface, inside his feelings were often hurt, and he regularly went off by himself, reading, losing himself in the adventure and nature stories of James Fenimore Cooper, Jean Stratton-Porter, and other popular writers of the time. His parents barely tolerated his reading. "There you are again with your nose in a book" was a frequent reproof.[3]

The Rogers much preferred the children to occupy themselves with more practical pursuits, such as family chores and working on the farm. As a six-year-old in Oak Park, Carl fed and cared for the chickens behind their house and sold the eggs to his mother and their neighbors. It was the traditional business enterprise for the Rogers children. He had to make out invoices, keep records, and do most everything required of a small-business proprietor. On the farm, he arose at five, milked a dozen cows each morning, and then took the train to the next town to attend high school. In the winter, his predawn chores included stoking coal into the large furnace. In the summers, he drove the horse-drawn milk wagon to town, or was in charge of all the pigs on the farm, or had complete charge of one section of the farm, where he rode the cultivator, cared for the team of horses, repaired the equipment, tested the soils, and did whatever else was required. While much of this work was arduous, he came to love the outdoor work. Working and playing on the farm fed a love of nature that lasted his whole life.

As a boy he also developed a permanent interest in science. In Oak Park, this first took the form of an impressive collection of moths and other insects, which he collected around the neighborhood, classified, and mounted. On the farm, he and his brothers were given two acres to cultivate on their own, which became another small business operation. Hearing his father and the foreman discuss scientific agriculture led Carl to read up on the subject himself, including Morison's *Feeds and Feeding*, a major scientific tome on the subject. "The design of a suitable experiment, the rationale of control groups, the control of all variables but one, the statistical analysis of the results—all of these concepts were unknowingly absorbed through my reading at the age of 13 to 16."[4] Carl and his brothers applied the scientific method to their own plot, comparing the yields from their experimental crops of oats, barley, corn, and various vegetables with their control groups, achieving good results, and even selling some of their surplus produce to the local market. By the time Carl finished high school, although his excellent academic performance qualified him to pursue any career direction, he was convinced that he wanted to be a farmer.

College Years: 1919–24

Carl attended the University of Wisconsin in Madison, because they had an excellent agriculture program and because Rogers family members had always attended that university. As sincere as his love of farming was, he soon found that campus social and religious activities held greater interest for him than agriculture. Given his religious background and eagerness to make new friends, it was natural that he would join the "Ag-Triangle," a group of agricultural students meeting under the auspices of the YMCA. The young men set up their own curriculum, organized social and educational activities, conducted business in a parliamentary fashion, discussed topics deeply, and became a closely knit group.

The Ag-Triangle was an extremely important experience for Carl. Here he was able to interact on a deep and trusting level with other young men from many different backgrounds. Summing up his first semester at college in his journal, he wrote, "As I look back it seems to me that it has been the best and richest five months I have ever had. I have learned more from the hearts and lives of men. I have made the first friend I have ever had and hosts and hosts of fine acquaintances." He also assumed leadership roles in the Ag-Triangle and the Boys Club, organizing and directing boys' activities both in Madison and at summer camp in Sturgeon Bay, Wisconsin.

Through the YMCA and related activities, Carl had many opportunities to explore and deepen his religious convictions. At church services, retreats, and revival meetings, he heard prominent campus and national speakers proclaim the "good news," and his sensitive imagination soon became inflamed with spiritual images and yearnings which caused him to reevaluate his career direction. After one Fellowship meeting, where "Dad" Wolfe spoke on "Selecting a Life Work," Carl wrote, "Oh, it's wonderful to feel that God will really lead me to my life work, and I *know* He will, for never has he deserted me.[5] Months later he wrote, "During Eddy's morning speech I almost made up my mind to go into Christian work and during his afternoon speech I made my final decision. God help me keep it!"[6]

Moments of certainty were followed by further doubt about his calling. Then, while still deciding whether to enter the ministry, Rogers had the unusual privilege of being selected as one of ten United States youth delegates to the World Student Christian Federation's conference in Peking, China in March 1922. The five-month trip affected Rogers' religious and social outlook significantly.

On the three-week Pacific voyage the students, scholars, and religious leaders on board had endless discussions exploring many questions of faith and commitment. Five days at sea, he wrote, "We have had many discussions already on lots of the doubtful points, and I am thankful beyond words that we are with a group of leaders who are forward-looking, young minded people, who are still building their own faiths, not dogmatists who are sure that their own interpretation is the only one."[7] They discussed whether one needed to believe in the deity of Christ to be a Christian and what it meant to be a Christian. The more Carl questioned the doctrine he had been taught and the more he developed his own views on Christianity, the closer he felt to God, but the further he felt from his parents' theological views.

The conference itself was an exciting week of forums, committee meetings, general sessions, speeches, debates, and informal meetings and discussions among the two hundred foreign and six hundred Chinese delegates, devoted to understanding one another, discussing their mutual problems, and "binding together in a real and vital fellowship the Christian students of the world." As Carl wrote home, "It has been an education for a narrow, provincial middle westerner like myself to find what splendid men may be hidden behind different labels of nationality, or wrapped up in packages of different color."[8]

After the conference, Rogers spent almost three months traveling around China with other students, missionaries, and experts on China and the Orient. Hosted by local YMCA representatives in each area they visited, he not only viewed the usual tourist spots, but had many opportunities to meet the people of the land of China in a more intimate fashion. He gave dozens of formal speeches and informal talks to groups of hundreds of students and adults around China and then in stops in Korea, Hong Kong, Japan, the Philippines, and Hawaii. So eager was he to cram every experience possible into the trip that, while most of his companions were asleep, Rogers spent all night climbing the 12,368-foot Mount Fujiama on his final night in Japan, arriving at the top just in time to see the magnificent sunrise.

Throughout the entire five-month trip, Carl kept up a voluminous correspondence with family and friends back home. His parents read his letters, describing his new beliefs about Christianity and social issues, with consternation. The transcontinental and transpacific mails were so slow, however, that their reactions might take two months to reach Carl. By then, two more months of living had ensued, and whatever imminent changes he had discussed in the earlier correspondence were all but solidified. By the time he returned home in August, there was an intellectual and emotional gap between him and most of his family that would never be bridged. The next few years were not without their conflicts and heated discussions in the Rogers home; but, as he later wrote, "from the date of this trip, my goals, values, aims, and philosophy have been my own."9

Inspired by his trip to China, Rogers returned home committed to join the ministry. While he had been an excellent student all along and was elected to Phi Beta Kappa while away in China (an unusual honor for a junior), during his first two years of college he still had found his extracurricular activities more engaging than his courses. Now he threw himself into his studies, determined to accumulate all the scholarly knowledge possible to aid him in his ministerial vocation. In long papers on "The Pacifism of Wyclif," "The Soul of a Troubadour," and "The Development of Luther's Idea of Authority in Religion: 1518," for example, Rogers argued the irreconcilability of Christianity and war, explored how St. Francis of Assisi emphasized that doing good works and following the example of Christ was more important than a mystical union with God, and described the evolution of Luther's revolutionary idea that each person could interpret the scriptures personally rather than rely exclusively on external authority.

The combination of Rogers' academic excellence and ongoing campus involvements received high grades from his professors and excellent recommendations to graduate school. One professor described him as "one of a very small group of the most promising men I know in the present student generation who are headed for the ministry. . . . To unusual qualities of mental keenness and fearlessness, he adds still rarer qualities of heart and spirit that, in my judgment, qualify him unusually for religious leadership in the coming generation."

Rogers joined the Alpha Kappa Lambda fraternity, noted for its scholastic excellence, and lived at the fraternity house during his junior year. He also joined the college debating society and gained considerable confidence when he realized he could tackle a subject on which he knew nothing and quickly master it to the point of holding his own in formal debate. In addition to these activities and his classes, Rogers also pursued a business venture he established after returning from China. He imported and sold Chinese jewelry and small crafts on campus, earning several thousand dollars profit, with which he helped put himself through college and pay for his first year of graduate school.

While Rogers' academic courses and extracurricular activities were time consuming enough, the pursuit that most engaged him emotionally was his courtship with Helen Elliott. He and Helen had been childhood friends in Oak Park and had renewed their friendship when they both attended the University of Wisconsin. As an aspiring commercial artist, Helen had transferred to the Chicago Academy of Fine Arts, but she and Carl continued to pursue their relationship ship on vacations and occasional weekends, and through correspondence. Usually ill at ease with women, Carl enjoyed being with Helen and found her to be an intelligent, honest, practical, and attractive young woman. She liked him but was not sure she was cut out to be a minister's wife. Eventually, a few months after his return from China, Helen accepted Carl's proposal of marriage. For the next two years, through intermittent visits and dates and an exchange of over two hundred letters, their love deepened and their passion, bridled by the strict Victorian morals of the time, grew stronger.

In his senior year, Rogers applied to and was accepted at Union Theological Seminary in New York City. He and Helen had every intention of going together. Although the families approved of the match, they disapproved of the early marriage. Married people, they felt, ought to be settling down, with the man holding a steady job and the woman raising a family. The idea of four years of schooling *after* marriage seemed preposterous. Besides, Carl's studies would be demanding enough without adding to them the obligations and distractions of marriage and possibly children. Both families strongly advised the young people to wait.

The couple, deeply in love, would not wait. Although Helen was reluctant to give up the promising career she had just begun as a commercial artist, she agreed with Carl that since so much was likely to happen to him during his four years in New York, unless they could share these experiences together, they would very likely grow in different directions. Against their parents' advice, they were married on August 28, 1924, at the Elliott home in Oak Park. For their honeymoon, they piled all their belongings into Carl's new Model-T coupe and drove east to New York City.

The New York City Years: 1924–28

Rogers chose Union Theological Seminary because it was "the most liberal in the country and an intellectual leader in religious work."[10] His parents were so unhappy about his choice that Walter Rogers tried, unsuccessfully, to bribe his son with an offer to pay his way in full if Carl attended the conservative Princeton Seminary instead.

Carl and Helen found a small apartment on West 123rd Street in Morningside Heights, practically across the street from Union and a few short blocks from Columbia University. The two young Midwesterners found New York City extremely exciting with its theaters, art museums, Bohemian life in Greenwich Village, and many social and cultural opportunities. Helen attended art classes in the city and audited many of Carl's classes at Union.

Rogers found his courses, many of which were taught by outstanding theologians and educators, to be very exciting intellectually. Arthur Cushman McGiffert, the head of the seminary, taught many of the classical philosophers and theologians but encouraged his students to think for themselves and not accept any particular orthodoxy. Harry Emerson Fosdick gave them "a feeling for modern and liberal religion." Through exchange teaching programs with Teachers College and the Columbia University graduate school, Rogers also became intrigued with the field of psychology. A course with Harrison Eliott and Grace Loucks and another with psychologist Goodwin Watson and psychiatrist Joseph Chassell, called "Working with

Individuals," exposed Rogers to various methods for working with people in professional helping relationships.

That summer, as a "replacement pastor" in Dorset, Vermont, Rogers delivered scholarly sermons to his rural congregation and learned first hand of the psychological problems in many of the families to whom he ministered. During the year, he also helped pay his way through seminary by working weekends as director of religious education at the First Congregational Church in Mount Vernon, New York.

In his second year at Union, Rogers pursued his growing interest in psychology by taking some courses at Teachers College, including his first actual clinical psychology course with Leta Hollingworth and an education class with William Heard Kilpatrick, America's leading proponent of John Dewey's progessive education philosophy. Impressed by this philosophy, Rogers came to view religious education as equivalent to social education—a process of helping people learn to identify questions or problems (be they spiritual, personal, or social questions), to pursue truth in investigating those questions, and to develop their own solutions to their questions or problems. Meanwhile, as he continued to explore his own religious questions, he came to feel that Jesus was not a deity, but one of history's greatest ethical teachers and social activists. Thus Rogers' religious views were becoming secularized as he was becoming enthralled by the world of psychology and education. Soon the inevitable implications of this transition became apparent to him. He left Union Theological Seminary and moved across Broadway to enroll in Teachers College, Columbia University to pursue a career in psychology.

Teachers College, at the time, was a leader in the testing and measurement movement in psychology. One of Rogers' professors was E. L. Thorndike, a pioneer in intelligence testing. To help support himself in graduate school, Rogers worked on a major public opinion survey project, taking charge of the statistical analysis and presentation of the data. At the same time, in a second clinical psychology course with Leta Hollingworth, he had his first opportunities to interview and attempt to help troubled children. Then, as a major part of his training, he was awarded a fellowship at the newly formed Institute for Child Guidance in New York City, which represented many "different shades of psychoanalytic thinking and other psychiatric and psychological views." Here he made lengthy case studies of children, using a combination of intelligence, personality, achievement, and psychodynamic testing and interviewing techniques. He was exposed to Freudian thought, a lecture by Alfred

Adler, Rorschach testing, and various psychoanalytic and psychiatric approaches. Rogers' formal training in psychology, then, followed two divergent lines: that of evaluating children from the outside, using objective tests and statistical measurements; and that of attempting to understand the complex inner world of children through sensitive questioning techniques and careful listening. The former enhanced Rogers' appreciation and understanding of the scientific method, while the latter increased his insight into and fascination with the psychological dynamics within each person.

Attempting to reconcile these two approaches to understanding human behavior, Rogers developed a new instrument for his dissertation, *Measuring Personality Adjustment in Children Nine to Thirteen Years of Age.* Adapting questions that psychologists and psychiatrists might ask children in clinical interviews, he constructed a paper-and-pencil test that helped reveal the child's attitude toward (1) himself and his abilities, (2) his relationship to his companions, (3) his family, and (4) all of these, as revealed by the content of his daydreams and fantasies.* There were separate forms of this "Personality Adjustment Inventory" for boys and girls. The test was published in 1931 by the YMCA's Association Press and remained in publication for the next half century, selling some half million copies.

Having completed his doctoral course work in 1926 and his clinical training by 1928, Rogers was now ready to search for his first full-time professional position. The field of clinical psychology was just emerging from the shadow of testing and measurement and laboratory psychology, and jobs for clinical psychologists were few and far between. With a wife, a two-year-old son named David, and another child on the way, he could not wait to pick and choose. So, when a job became available in upstate New York, Rogers applied and was hired as a psychologist in the Child Study Department of the Rochester Society for the Prevention of Cruelty to Children.

The Rochester Years: 1928–39

Many of Rogers' New York friends and colleagues feared the Rochester position would be a dead end for the promising young psychologist. Instead, it turned out to be the laboratory in which Rogers would gain invaluable experience working with thousands of trou-

---

* My solution to the perennial pronoun problem is to use the male form in the first half of this chapter and the female form in the second half.

bled youth and adults and which would form the basis for his pioneering work in counseling and psychotherapy.

Each year, some six to seven hundred children came or were sent to the Society for help. Their presenting problems represented every behavior and personality disorder imaginable: enuresis, stealing, lying, sex perversions, sadism toward animals or younger children, extreme withdrawal or aggressiveness, incest, stammering, eating dirt and worms, and numerous comparable problems. Intake workers would route the children to some combination of the Medical Department, Protective Department, Child Placing Department, and the Child Study Department, which Rogers joined in 1928 and was the director of by 1929.

At this time, the professions of clinical psychology, psychiatry, and clinical social work were still in their infancy. For Rogers, this was both a problem and an opportunity. A problem because there was so little practical guidance in effective treatment methods with children. An opportunity because, out in the field, away from the orthodoxies of any particular university or school of professional training and faced with problems that went far beyond *his* training, he was forced to experiment widely, develop and evaluate his own solutions to problems, and learn from his own experience. The principle that guided his efforts was *pragmatism*. Will this work? Is it effective? Any method of helping children was worthy of consideration if it seemed potentially helpful. The theoretical basis of a helping approach was far less important to him than the results that approach yielded. Whether the professional was a psychologist, psychiatrist, or social worker mattered little if that person had insights or techniques that could be of help.

Rogers' own training had emphasized the importance of forming an initial diagnosis to precede treatment, but he was concerned that each profession and professional seemed to have a favorite, often divergent, diagnostic approach. Freudians, for example, gave enormous weight to early childhood influences. Sociologically inclined workers gave greater weight to the neighborhood, school, and peer groups. Other psychologists relied almost entirely on psychological testing. In an attempt to cut across ideological boundaries and take into consideration *all* the factors that could significantly be influencing the child's present behavior, Rogers developed a new method of diagnosis called the *component factor method*. This approach considered eight factors influencing the child's development and present behavior: heredity, physical factors, mentality, self-insight, family emotional tone, economic and cultural factors, social experience, and education and supervision. Children were rated on a seven-point scale for each factor. The method required caseworkers to consider all these aspects of a child's history and present situation. It also enabled the staff to predict and measure the success of different types of treatment for children with different component factor profiles.

Diagnosing children was one thing; treating them was quite another. To deal with the hundreds of troubled children they saw, Rogers and his colleagues employed the full panoply of techniques at their disposal. Their recommendations very often involved a *major change* in the child's environment: moving the child from his or her own home into a foster home, from one foster home to another, from foster home to an institution, from the institution back home. In many other instances, the staff suggested *modifying* the child's current environment: educating or helping the parent, changing the school program, or encouraging involvement in appropriate camps, groups, or clubs. In about one-fifth of the cases, Rogers' department employed actual treatment interviews or *direct therapy*. Although Rogers went on to make his contribution in the latter area, he still had great respect for the efficacy of environmental treatments. "We shall not," he wrote, "be inclined to look down upon treatment involving the manipulation of the environment, if we recall the fundamental axiom upon which it is based, namely, that most children, if given a reasonably normal environment which meets their own emotional, intellectual, and social needs, have within themselves sufficient drive toward health to respond and make a comfortable adjustment to life."[11]

For those children for whom direct therapy was warranted, Rogers spent years experimenting with various forms of treatment. These included the "less deep" approaches of educational therapy, persuasion or suggestion, and release or expressive therapy to the "deeper therapies" of psychoanalysis, interpretive therapy, and relationship therapy. He found educational therapy, in which the helper shared pertinent information with the child, to be helpful in a limited number of cases. He observed that persuasion or suggestion by the therapist had, at best, short-term benefits, or none at all when the suggestions ran counter to the child's emotional needs and resistances. For example, it had a great impact on Rogers when he observed a skilled hypnotist meet increasing resistance from a bed-wetting youngster, who eventually could not even be induced into a trance state when the therapist's posthypnotic suggestions asked the boy to alter his nighttime behavior. On the other hand, Rogers found release or expressive therapy, particularly expressive play therapy, to be of true cathartic value in helping children release and accept deep-seated feelings. However, he found the method wanting in helping them work through conflicts enough to make a satisfactory adjustment in the real world.

Aside from the theoretical and scientific problems he found with psychoanalysis, Rogers saw that this method, which might require a hundred hours per patient for a thorough analysis, was impractical for an agency with a small staff who saw many hundreds of children each year. It was *interpretive therapy* that initially impressed him as having the greatest potential for effecting real change in attitudes and behavior. For a number of years, Rogers brought all his skill and psychological insight to bear in helping children and their parents accept his interpretations of the causes and meaning of their behavior. Sometimes it worked. Sometimes it only seemed to work. The interpretation was "accepted" by the child or parent who, at the time, also seemed to "feel" the interpretation was true. Yet, weeks or months later, the child or parent would seem to forget or be unable to act on the new insight. Rogers often described two incidents that helped him gradually move away from interpretation in therapy.

Using the theories and methods of William Healy, one of the outstanding authorities at the time on delinquent and problem behavior in children, Rogers began working with a young pyromaniac. Following Healy's view that delinquency was often associated with sexual conflict, he held numerous treatment interviews with the boy in the detention home, tracing back the causes of the boy's behavior to his sexual impulses about masturbation, and gradually interpreting this understanding to him. The boy appeared to accept the interpretation, so the treatment was terminated. Feeling very proud of his skill in handling the case, Rogers was shortly thereafter amazed to find out that the boy, on probation, had been arrested again for setting fires. Rogers was incredulous. As he sought to explain the experience, he began to recognize the limits of interpretation and realize that authorities in the field could be wrong and that there was new knowledge yet to be discovered.

On another occasion, Rogers recalled, "I had learned to be more subtle and patient in interpreting a client's behavior to him, attempting to time it in a gentle fashion which would gain acceptance. I had been working with a highly intelligent mother whose boy was something of a hellion. The problem was clearly her early rejection of the boy, but over many interviews I could not help her to this insight. I drew her out, I gently pulled together the evidence she had given, trying to help her see the pattern. But we got nowhere. Finally

I gave up. I told her that it seemed we had both tried, but we had failed, and that we might as well give up our contacts. She agreed. So we concluded the interview, shook hands, and she walked to the door of the office. Then she turned and asked, 'Do you ever take adults for counseling here?' When I replied in the affirmative, she said, 'Well, then, I would like some help.' She came to the chair she had left, and began to pour out her despair about her marriage, her troubled relationship with her husband, her sense of failure and confusion, all very different from the sterile 'case history' she had given before. Real therapy began then, and ultimately it was very successful."[12]

"This incident," he summarized, "was one of a number which helped me to experience the fact—only fully realized later—that it is the *client* who knows what hurts, what directions to go, what problems are crucial, what experiences have been deeply buried. It began to occur to me that unless I had a need to demonstrate my own cleverness and learning, I would do better to rely upon the client for the direction of movement in the process."

Of all the methods Rogers experimented with during the Rochester years, it was *relationship therapy* that had the greatest appeal and most influenced his subsequent thinking. With theoretical roots in the *will therapy* of Otto Rank, Freud's associate and disciple, and practical adaptations developed by Rank's students Jessie Taft and Frederick Allen and, later, Virginia Robinson, relationship therapy stressed the patient's positive will as the source of growth in therapy, and it shifted emphasis from the analysis of past content to the patient's self-insight and self-acceptance within the therapeutic relationship. Rogers called Taft's 1933 book, *The Dynamics of Therapy in a Controlled Relationship,* "a small masterpiece of writing and thinking." Describing this type of therapeutic relationship with parents, Rogers wrote, "The [social] worker endeavors to provide an atmosphere in which the parent can come freely to experience and realize his own attitudes. The worker creates this atmosphere by her acceptance of the parent, by her failure to criticize, by her refusal to impose on the parent any program or recommendations, and by her refusal to answer questions except when the parent genuinely desires an answer and is unable to answer for himself. . . . The effect of this relationship upon the parent may be characterized by the terms 'clarification of feelings' and 'acceptance of self.'"[13]

As Rogers' experience and knowledge of the child guidance field deepened, he began to communicate his insights in a variety of forums. In the Rochester area, he became a leading authority on child psychology and was often asked to address parent, school, and community groups on this topic and to join the boards of various community agencies. When the Child Study Department was reorganized in 1939 into a more all-encompassing Child Guidance Center for the community, Rogers was appointed as director of the new venture, in spite of opposition from the psychiatric community, which argued that a physician should fill this role. Beyond local recognition, Rogers published his work in leading professional journals, including several original research studies on the diagnosis and treatment of children's problems. For example, after he delivered papers at the American Association of Orthopsychiatry in Cleveland, the National Council of Social Work in Indianapolis, and the New York State Association of Applied Psychology at Cornell University, his addresses were published as articles in those organization's professional journals. While he remained involved in the psychology profession during these years, Rogers found an even more congenial group of colleagues in the social work field. He served on the executive committee of the American Association of Social Workers and was the first chairman of New York State's chapter of the national organization.

Summarizing a decade of learning in Rochester, Rogers wrote his first book, *The Clinical Treatment of the Problem Child*. It was a thorough and scholarly work that reviewed the various methods for helping children, from environmental change to direct forms of therapy. With vivid case studies from Rogers' own experience to describe each treatment method and a summary of the pertinent research, including his own, the book advanced the child guidance field and enhanced its author's reputation.

As a result, when Ohio State University had an opening for a clinical psychologist in 1940, Rogers was invited to apply and was offered the position. He hesitated to accept, as he did not really want to leave Rochester, where he was deeply involved in the community and the new Child Guidance Center. David, now fourteen, and Natalie, twelve, were also involved in their school and peer group activities; Helen enjoyed her friends and community activities; and the whole family loved its summer cottage on nearby Seneca Lake. As a final inducement, Ohio State offered Rogers a full professorship—too good an offer to refuse. Later, he wrote, "I heartily recommend starting in the academic world at the top level. I have often been grateful that I have never had to live through the frequently degrading competitive process of step by step promotion in university faculties, where individuals so frequently learn only one lesson—not to stick their necks out."[14]

The Ohio State Years: 1940–45

In his first quarter at Ohio State, Rogers taught a course called "Techniques in Psychotherapy." Following the outline of *The Clinical Treatment of the Problem Child,* he surveyed the various approaches for conducting counseling and psychotherapy. Eventually his students asked the inevitable question: which approach do *you* prefer? This caused Rogers to clarify his own views on effective counseling more explicitly than before. He clearly favored what he called the "newer therapies" that emphasized release, self-acceptance, insight, and the importance of the therapeutic relationship over the "older therapies" that employed suggestion, interpretation, psychometric testing, and an emphasis on past history. In this, Rogers did not feel particularly in the vanguard; rather, he believed this was the general trend among modern, enlightened practitioners.

Always of a practical bent, Rogers not only lectured on effective practices but also demonstrated these approaches to his students and then had them practice what they had observed. Later that year, he offered a practicum on advanced clinical treatment, possibly the first such supervised therapy ever conducted in a university setting. Each student conducted at least one case of intensive therapy, and there were ongoing discussions of the progress of each case. Such practical training of therapists was aided by a major innovation which Rogers helped develop and popularize at that time: the phonographic recording of therapeutic interviews.

Although some earlier experiments in recording therapy had taken place, transcripts were generally unavailable. Rogers believed that readily accessible recordings and transcripts of therapy would be of enormous help in training therapists and conducting research on therapy, so he and his doctoral student Bernard Covner set up a recording studio in the Psychology Clinic at Ohio State. It was a formidable task. The voices from the counseling room were transmitted to the adjoining room where two alternating machines cut grooves in the recording disks. The shavings would have to be brushed off continually and the records changed every three minutes. Within a year, however, they had recorded over eight hundred disks, including several complete therapy cases.

This invaluable tool enabled Rogers to study and understand the therapeutic process more carefully. In analyzing thousands of counselor and client responses, he and his students documented how the therapist's "acceptance, reflection and clarification of feelings" hastened the client's "expression of feelings, insight, and positive actions based on this insight."[15] The technique of *accepting and reflecting feelings* is illustrated by this excerpt from a later interview with a high school student.[16]

ROGERS: But, uh, part of what really makes for difficulty is the fact that your relationship with your stepfather is not completely rosy.
MIKE: M-hm. Let just put it this way: I hate him and he hates me, and it's that way.
ROGERS: You *really* hate him and you feel he *really* hates you.
MIKE: Well *(thinking about it)*, I don't know if he hates me or not, but I know one thing. I don't like him whatsoever.
ROGERS: M-hm. You can't speak for sure about his feelings, cause only he knows exactly what those are; but as far as you're concerned . . . .
MIKE: He knows how I feel about him.
ROGERS: You don't have any use for him.
MIKE: Not whatsoever. . . . And that's been for about eight years now.
ROGERS: So, for about eight years, you've lived with a person whom you have no respect for and really hate.
MIKE: Oh, I respect him——
ROGERS: *(simultaneously)* Oh, I got that wrong.
MIKE: ——I don't have to but I do. But I don't love him. I hate him. I can't stand him.
ROGERS: There are certain things you respect him for, but that doesn't alter the fact that you definitely hate him and don't love him.
MIKE: That's the truth. . . .

This exchange occurred only a few minutes into their first meeting, before an audience of several hundred school counselors. Experiencing the psychological safety which Rogers' accepting method fostered, Mike continued to explore his feelings and, a few minutes later, revealed a much deeper concern: that he had recently considered suicide and thought he might be going insane. Conversely, Rogers observed that the therapist's more *directive* behaviors— asking highly specific questions, explaining, discussing, informing, indicating topics of conversation, suggesting, interpreting, and proposing client activities—appeared frequently to cause resistance and defensiveness and to transfer the responsibility for growth from the client to the therapist. Using the recorded interviews to gather data on counselor techniques, Rogers and his students found that the more directive counselors used *six times* as many words as the nondirective ones, and that most counselors were far more directive than they realized they were.

Still Rogers did not fully realize the implications of what he was learning until the end of his first year at Ohio State, when he was asked to address the psychological honor society at the University of Minnesota. "The aim of this newer therapy," he said, "is not to solve one particular problem, but to assist the individual to *grow,* so that he can cope with the present problem and with later problems in a better integrated fashion . . . it relies much more heavily on the individual drive toward growth, health, and adjustment. . . . In the second place, this newer therapy places greater stress on the emotional elements, the feeling aspects of the situation, than upon the intellectual aspects. . . . In the third place, this newer therapy places greater stress upon the immediate situation than upon the individual's past. . . . Finally this approach lays stress upon the therapeutic relationship itself as a growth experience."[17]

He thought he was reporting an increasingly widespread viewpoint. Goodwin Watson had said more or less the same thing earlier in the year at a conference at Teachers College in which Rogers participated. Therefore, Rogers was totally unprepared for the furor his talk aroused. "I was criticized, I was praised, I was attacked, I was looked on with puzzlement. By the end of my stay in Minneapolis it really struck me that perhaps I was saying something new that came *from me;* that I was not just summarizing the viewpoint of therapists in general. . . . It would seem quite absurd to suppose that one could name a day on which client-centered therapy was born. Yet I feel it is possible to name that day and it was December 11, 1940."[18]

It was not a new idea which Rogers stated that day, but a change in his professional self-concept and a determination to study and advocate this newer perspective. To further clarify and communicate his viewpoint, Rogers began working on his second book, *Counseling and Psychotherapy,* which was published in 1942. It soon became one of the most influential books ever written in that field. In it, Rogers used numerous, vivid examples from recorded interviews to outline his conception of effective *nondirective* or *client-centered* counseling and psychotherapy. It was significant that he intermingled the latter two terms so easily. In his view, there was no clear distinction between adjustment *counseling* and in-depth *psychotherapy.* The same nondirective approach would be of help whatever the depth of the client's psychological problems.

Also significant was his use of the word *client* to describe the recipient of therapy. This departed from the medical, psychiatric model in which the patient is usually viewed as a "sick" person, who expects the doctor to cure him, to do something *to* him, to assume much of the responsibility for his well-being. In contrast, the term *client* implies a more egalitarian relationship, as with a lawyer or an accountant. One consults a professional who has some particular skills, but the locus of control remains with the client who will make his own decisions. Call a client a patient, and he is liable to act like one. While Rogers was certainly not the first to use the word in this context, with the publication of *Counseling and Psychotherapy,* the word *client* achieved widespread, common usage.

With this book, then, Rogers introduced a new model of therapy—not new in its concepts or techniques, but in its collection of already existing ideas and practices into a clear, consistent, and extreme counseling approach. He supported his model with page after page of examples based on his own experience, with forceful polemical writing, and with the beginnings of empirical research. And he did one more thing in *Counseling and Psychotherapy.* He included "The Case of Herbert Bryan," the first complete psychotherapy case ever to be recorded, transcribed, and published. Comprising the last 170 pages of the book, the case included every counselor and client response in all eight interviews, plus Rogers' running commentary on the counselor's behavior. For example,

C26. Why did the counselor interrupt here? This seems to be a quite unnecessary directive question breaking into the flow of feeling. It leads to brief client responses ending in a pause (S28), which the counselor has to break with another rather directive question. This in turn leads to a repetition of the symptoms originally described (S29), and it is only following this that a fresh start in recognition of feeling is made. This is a minor example of the way in which clumsy handling by the counselor can delay progress.

C43, S43, C44. Adequate recognition of attitudes brings the flow of feeling around again to the same point which was poorly recognized at C18, C19. The phonographic recordings indicate that this frequently occurs. If the client expresses some attitude which has significance for him, and this is misunderstood or inadequately

recognized by the counselor, the same attitude is likely to
be expressed later. Adequate recognition, on the other
hand, tends to lead to further and deeper expression.

It was almost impossible for the reader of these interviews to
remain aloof. Vicariously each reader became the counselor of
Herbert Bryan, wondering, "Now, how would I respond at this
point?" In fact, Rogers advocated just that: that readers cover up the
counselor's response and formulate their own responses before reading further. In critiquing Herbert Bryan's counselor, then, Rogers was
critiquing all counselors; for all counselors sometimes do what this
one counselor got praised or blamed by Rogers for doing.

Thus Rogers became the conscience of thousands of counselors
and therapists across the country, as well as one of their models, for
it was not hard to figure out that Herbert Bryan's counselor was
Rogers himself. Whether or not one agreed with Rogers' nondirective philosophy, it was impossible to ignore it, for he had drawn the
battle lines so clearly. On the one hand, his national reputation as a
leader in the field was immediately established, and students from
within the university and outside it flocked to his classes and asked
him to be their graduate or dissertation advisor. On the other hand,
his nondirective method was denounced throughout academia as
being superficial and unrealistic. While *Counseling and Psychotherapy*
became a professional best seller—virtually gospel to many psychologists, counselors, social workers, pastoral counselors, and other
helping professionals across the country—it was not reviewed in
any major journal of the psychological or psychiatric professions.
He was soon honored with national offices in the social work and
psychology professions including vice-president of the American
Association of Orthopsychiatry, president of the American
Association for Applied Psychology, and member of a distinguished
panel of the American Psychological Association attempting to
reunite the splintered field of psychology. At the same time, he was
an outcast in his own department at Ohio State, relegated to a small
office, assigned to courses at odd hours, and given little cooperation
on the research projects he wished to undertake.

Given this lack of support at his own institution, when Ralph
Tyler invited him in the summer of 1944 to set up a new counseling
center at the University of Chicago, with a *carte blanche* to undertake serious research on psychotherapy, Rogers accepted. Although
he loved working with his graduate students at Ohio State—including

Victor Raimy, Virginia Axline, Arthur Combs, Thomas Gordon, Charles Curran, William Snyder, and others who went on to make important professional contributions in their own right—and although he and Helen regretted leaving their lovely home in Columbus, David and Natalie were now on their own, and this made leaving much easier.

Before moving to Chicago, however, Rogers accepted a one-year assignment with the United Service Organization to assist in the war effort. He had already trained government personnel in nondirective interviewing techniques and worked with returned Air Force gunnery officers who were having adjustment problems. Now he took on the responsibility for teaching counseling skills to several thousand USO staff and volunteers to help them meet the psychological needs of the millions of soldiers who had begun returning home. He spent that academic year continuously leading the same workshops across the country and writing a short book with John Wallen, a graduate student from Ohio State, entitled *Counseling with Returned Servicemen*. Published by McGraw-Hill, it was a pithy introduction to nondirective therapy for the layperson and used widely, if briefly, for its intended purpose.

Rogers spent the summer of 1945 recuperating from the year's ordeal and from an operation. Then he and Helen moved to Chicago, where they rented a large, airy apartment overlooking Lake Michigan, within walking distance of the university's new Counseling Center.

The Chicago Years: 1945–57

As a member of the Psychology Department at the University of Chicago, Rogers taught graduate courses and served as advisor to many graduate students working on their advanced degrees. Simultaneously, at the Counseling Center, he played the various roles of administrator, supervisor, researcher, and counselor.

Rogers was but one of the many counselors and therapists working in the new center. A combination of full-time staff, part-time staff, visiting fellows, graduate students, and other employees and associates all worked with clients. From four thousand therapeutic interviews the first year, the number grew to over eleven thousand client interviews several years later. Clients were of all ages, backgrounds, and professions and represented all degrees of psychological problems, from minor maladjustments to serious mental illness.

In quantity and breadth of practice, the Counseling Center soon became one of the country's largest university settings for counseling and psychotherapy.

By all accounts, it was an extraordinarily exciting place to work. Counseling, training sessions, observations, case conferences, supervisory meetings, seminars, classes, practica, professional discussions, recordings, and research projects were going on at all hours. Faculty and students interacted freely, discussing and critiquing one another's counseling sessions, analyzing the data from the latest research study, debating points of psychological theory. Students were encouraged not simply to write papers to show their mastery of a subject and impress their teachers, but rather to expand the professional knowledge base by engaging in original research projects and writing up their results for professional publication. As an administrator, true to his counseling style, Rogers believed the staff and students could be trusted to make many of the decisions regarding Counseling Center operations. Therefore, he turned over much of the responsibility to them, choosing the title of Executive Secretary for himself, instead of Director.

A staff member of the Center from 1947 to 1953 remembered how "Carl provided a genuine, thoroughgoing climate of democracy in Center government. There was diffusion of responsibility in both day-to-day administration and in basic policy making. Staff members could exert major influence on policies in terms of their ability to persuade or influence other staff members. A concomitant of this power diffusion was the fact that Carl did not offer strong emotional support or protection to staff members. They had to make it on the power of their ideas. Carl did not play papa. This is not to say that staff members never perceived him in that way or that they did not want that kind of support. It is simply that Carl didn't behave in those terms."[19]

Unlike other pioneers in the history of psychotherapy, Rogers had no desire to achieve unanimity of thought and practice among his associates. One student, Rex Reed, recalled "a seminar which met at the Rogers' apartment near the university. The class (about 20 graduate students) met from 7:30 p.m. until all hours. Rogers, with the others in the group, was a student too. Members of his staff, counselors (Bill Kell, Ollie Bown, etc.), came and read a paper to us. All of us commented on the paper when it was finished. Then we'd divide into groups of three or four and go into separate rooms where we discussed the 'meat' of the paper. After 30 or 45 minutes we would reassemble, make comments in the group again and have a supper. It was then—

during these 'moments' in the seminar—when I learned more definitely to assess the man's simplicity, brilliance, acceptance. . . . He always appeared to have time to listen to any of us. He never imposed his ideas. Always he joined us as . . . a learner."[20]

The combination of Counseling Center structures, which encouraged equality, freedom and autonomy among staff and students, and Rogers' own presence as a trusting and concerned leader who modeled high standards of achievement, seemed to have the effect of freeing students and staff to follow their own lights and to engage in highly productive and creative work. The experience of Manual Vargas was typical of many students and staff who worked with him then. "During my first two years at the Counseling Center, I felt that I had one of my most personally creative cycles of my life. . . . I was, as usual with Carl, given the freedom to try and do exactly as I pleased and what I liked, and at the same time, encouraged to explore and discuss completely openly with my peers at the Center whatever it was that I was doing. . . . I was in a constant period of deep inner creativity, and I look back to those years as one of the most satisfying periods of my life. I think that the credit for that can be given very much to the personality that Carl was."[21]

In his counseling role, Rogers maintained a steady stream of clients. On average, he saw seven to ten individuals for a total of fifteen or more counseling hours per week. Some of these typically were graduate students who wished both to work on personal problems and to experience "the master" at work. They were rarely disappointed. His colleague at Chicago, Rosalind Dymond (Cartwright), described him as "the most acute listener I have ever known."[22] Norman Brice, a graduate student, wrote, "At the end of the first [counseling] session with Carl, I came out to Virginia Hallman, his secretary, and practically shouted, 'Now I know the secret ingredient!' She was kind of low-key and gave me a 'What's with you?' response. I told her I have never felt so deeply and fully understood and so completely respected in all my life, and that the effect on me was electrifying."[23]

Brice's reference to the "secret ingredient" not only highlights Rogers' ability as a gifted counselor, but suggests the next stage in the evolution of Rogers' thought and practice. At Ohio State, and in *Counseling and Psychotherapy*, Rogers had emphasized the *technique* of reflecting feelings as the key ingredient in successful psychotherapy. While he acknowledged the importance of the counselor's accepting *attitude*, he nevertheless emphasized the nondirective *method* in his teaching and writing. Then, the more he taught this approach to others, and continued to work with clients himself, he came to understand that the "secret ingredient" was not the technique after all. As he wrote:

> It is common to find client-centered therapy spoken of as a method or a technique. No doubt this is due in part to earlier presentations which tended to overstress technique. It may more accurately be said that the counselor who is effective in client-centered therapy holds a coherent and developing set of attitudes deeply imbedded in his personal organization, a system of attitudes which is implemented by techniques and methods consistent with it. It has been our experience that the counselor who tries to use a "method" is doomed to be unsuccessful unless this method is genuinely in line with his own attitudes. On the other hand the counselor whose attitudes are of the type which facilitate therapy may be only partially successful, because his attitudes are inadequately implemented by appropriate methods and techniques.[24]

The therapeutic attitude itself stemmed from what Rogers called a "basic hypothesis" about human growth. At its core, the hypothesis stated that people are capable of making their own responsible choices—something Rogers came to believe about political self-determination on his China trip, about education at Teachers College, and about therapy in Rochester and Columbus. In Chicago, he began to state it more explicitly and frequently as the starting point for his whole conception of therapy.

> Client-centered therapy operates primarily upon one central and basic hypothesis which has undergone relatively little change with the years. This hypothesis is that the client has within himself the capacity, latent if not evident, to understand those aspects of his life and of himself which are causing him pain, and the capacity and the tendency to reorganize himself and his relationship to life in the direction of self-actualization and maturity in such a way as to bring a greater degree of internal comfort. The function of the therapist is to create such a psychological atmosphere as will permit this capacity and

this strength to become effective rather than latent or
potential.[25]

How does the therapist create this psychological atmosphere?
Primarily by conveying to the client two attitudes: *acceptance* and
understanding. "It would seem that when the individual is deeply
accepted as he is, when the private world of his own reality is genuinely understood and genuinely accepted by another, without evaluation, and when this understanding and acceptance is communicated
to the individual, this optimum atmosphere exists."[26]

By *understanding*, Rogers meant "the therapist's willingness
and sensitive ability to understand the client's thoughts, feelings,
and struggles from the client's point of view. This ability to see completely through the client's eyes, to adopt his frame of reference, has
seemed to be an important way of implementing the fundamental
hypothesis and is the basis for the use of the term 'client-centered.'
To receive completely what the client is trying to communicate of his
feelings even when his communication is confused or incoherent or
fragmentary—to be able to enter into the client's private world and
see it from *his* point of view—that is what we mean by adopting the
client's frame of reference."[27] Rogers increasingly began to use the
word *empathy* to describe this type of understanding. While the
term had been used in the fields of psychology and psychotherapy for
some years, Rogers popularized it. He often emphasized that empathy meant seeing the world *as if* one were the client, but never so
totally identifying with the client that the "as if" quality was lost. The
examples in his writing show that Rogers was becoming increasingly
empathic himself.

MRS. OAK: Uh, I caught myself thinking that—that—that during
these uh, sessions, uh, I've been sort of singing a song.
Now that sounds uh–uh, vague, and—and—and uh–uh,
not actually singing . . . sort of a song without any music.
A—a, uh, probably a kind of poem coming out (M–hm .)
And uh, I like the idea, I mean it's sort of come to me
with—without anything built out of—of—anything. And
in . . . following that, it came, it came this other kind of—
of—of a uh, feeling. Well, I s—s—found myself sort o–of
asking myself uh, is that the shape that cases take?
(M–hm.) A, uh–uh, is it possible that I—I—I am just
verbalizing and, and—and uh, at times of becoming

intoxicated with my own—own, u–uh, verbalizations? (M–hm). And then uh, following this, came, well, am I just taking up your time? Uh . . . then a doubt, a doubt . . . (M–hm.) Then something else occurred to me. Uh, from whence it came I—I don't know, no actual logical kind sequence of the thinking. The thought struck me: We're [two words missing] uh, overwhelmed or uh, doubtful, or—or uh, we can show concern or, or an–a–any uh, uh, interest when—when the, when blind people uh, learn to read with their fingers, uh, Braille. And I don't know, it—it may be just sort of—of . . . it's all mixed up . . . it may be that's something that I'm uh, uh, eg–experiencing.

ROGERS: M–hm. Let's see if I can get some of that "uh–uh," that sequence of feelings. First, sort of as though you're . . . and I gather that the first one is a fairly positive feeling . . . as though maybe you're kind of creating a poem here . . . uh, a song without music somehow but something that might be quite uh, quite creative, and then the—the feeling of a lot of skepticism about that. "Maybe I'm just saying words, uh, just being carried off by words that I, that I speak, and maybe it's all a lot of baloney, really." Uh . . . and then a feeling that uh . . . perhaps you're almost learning a—a new type of experiencing which would be just as radically new as for a blind person to try to make sense out of what he feels with his fingertips.

MRS. OAK: M–hm. M–hm.

Ironically, as Rogers began to realize that it was the *attitudes* of acceptance and empathic understanding, rather than the *method* of nondirective therapy which was the key ingredient in therapeutic progress, his and his colleagues' methods became increasingly nondirective. A study by Seeman compared counselor behavior over a six-year period and found that the client-centered therapists in Rogers' group had steadily increased the frequency of their nondirective, reflection-of-feeling responses to the point where these constituted eighty-five percent of the counselor's statements![29] For Rogers and his associates, then, the fully empathic, nondirective response remained the most effective way they knew to convey the attitudes of acceptance and understanding to the client—attitudes that allowed the client to accept himself, freely explore his feelings, and make his own responsible choices.

In 1951, Houghton Mifflin published Rogers' third major book, *Client-Centered Therapy*. In addition to describing the changes in his thinking and practice, Rogers devoted a major section of the book to applications of the client-centered approach to other fields. He wrote: "The individual who comes to rely upon this hypothesis in his therapeutic work finds almost inevitably that he is driven to experiment with it in other types of activity."[30] His graduate student Elaine Dorfman and staff members Nicholas Hobbs and Thomas Gordon respectively wrote chapters on "Play Therapy," "Group-Centered Psychotherapy," and "Group-Centered Leadership and Administration." Rogers wrote other application chapters on "Student-Centered Teaching" and "The Training of Counselors and Therapists." The kernels for some of Rogers' later books are contained in several of these chapters.

The final section of the book contained a lengthy "Theory of Personality and Behavior," intended to place the client-centered approach within a broader understanding of human psychology. Scientific research might increasingly demonstrate *that* client-centered therapy works, but only psychological theory could explain *why* it works. Rogers set forth a "self theory" that built upon the work of his former students Victor Raimy and Arthur Combs, which in turn built upon the Gestalt and phenomenological movements in psychology. The theory contained nineteen propositions which Rogers elaborated at some length. These included:

> 1. Every individual exists in a continually changing world of experience of which he is the center. . . . 2. The organism reacts to the field as it is experienced and perceived. This perceptual field is, for the individual, "reality". . . .. 4. The organism has one basic tendency and striving—to actualize, maintain, and enhance the experiencing organism. . . . 5. Behavior is basically the goal-directed attempt of the organism to satisfy its needs as experienced, in the field as perceived. . . . 8. A portion of the total perceptual field gradually becomes differentiated as the self.. . . 9. As a result of interaction with the environment, and particularly as a result of evaluational interaction with others, the structure of the self is formed—an organized, fluid, but consistent conceptual pattern of perceptions of characteristics and relationships of the "I" or the "me," together with values attached to these concepts.. . . 10. The values attached to experiences,

and the values which are a part of the self-structure, in
some instances are values experienced directly by the
organism, and in some instances are values introjected or
taken over from others, but perceived in distorted
fashion, as if they had been experienced directly. . . .
12. Most of the ways of behaving which are adopted by
the organism are those which are consistent with the concept of self. . . . 16. Any experience which is inconsistent
with the organization or structure of self may be
perceived as a threat, and the more of these perceptions
there are, the more rigidly the self-structure is organized
to maintain itself.. . . 17. Under certain conditions,
involving primarily complete absence of any threat to the
self-structure, experiences which are inconsistent with it
may be perceived, and examined, and the structure of self
revised to assimilate and include such experiences.[31]

Although more theoretical than anything he had written to
date, his clear presentation and the various examples he provided to
illustrate his propositions made Rogers' theory of self one of the most
accessible such theories in psychology. That an approach to therapy,
together with the beginnings of scientific research on that approach,
were built upon the theory added to its importance. Consequently,
Rogers' self theory was and continues to be included in a number of
texts on personality theory. Unlike the client-centered *method,*
which received little acclaim in academia, Rogers' theory of self was
given more respect. Ironically, when Rogers continued to develop the
theory and, in 1959, published a much longer and more elaborate "theory of therapy, personality, and interpersonal relationships as developed in the client-centered framework," little attention was paid to
it—a fact that always puzzled and disappointed Rogers, who believed
that client-centered theory, method, and research were all of a piece.

In *Client-Centered Therapy,* meanwhile, he also tentatively initiated a personal style of writing which would come increasingly to
characterize his speaking and writing style throughout his career. In
the preface he wrote:

This book is about the highly personal experiences
of each one of us. It is about a client in my office who sits
there by the corner of the desk, struggling to be himself,
yet deathly afraid of being himself—striving to see his

experience as it is, wanting to *be* that experience, and yet deeply fearful of the prospect. The book is about me, as I sit there with that client, facing him, participating in that struggle as deeply and sensitively as I am able. It is about me as I try to perceive his experience, and the meaning and the feeling and the taste and the flavor that it has for him. It is about me as I bemoan my very human fallibility in understanding that client, and the occasional failures to see life as it appears to him, failures which fall like heavy objects across the intricate, delicate web of growth which is taking place. It is about me as I rejoice at the privilege of being a midwife to a new personality—as I stand by with awe at the emergence of a self, a person, as I see a birth process in which I have had an important and facilitating part. . . . The book is, I believe, about life, as life vividly reveals itself in the therapeutic process.

Not simply a stylistic innovation, this first-person form of communication, so different from typical academic writing, reflected an important personal change Rogers was then going through. It also illustrated the next stage of development of the client-centered approach. In 1949–51, Rogers went through a period of intense personal distress. The precipitating cause was a difficult case with a schizophrenic client. Rogers said later that he mishandled the case by vacillating between warmth and aloofness toward her. She demanded more than he felt he could give and shrewdly exploited his ambivalence and vulnerability until he was uncertain whether her view of the relationship or his was real. This, in turn, resulted in a profound loss of Rogers' confidence in himself, his therapeutic ability, his worth as a person, and even his grasp of reality.

One day he felt he absolutely had to get away, lest he suffer a complete mental breakdown. He and Helen were on the road within an hour and stayed away for two or three months on what he later called his "runaway trip." Upon returning, his continuing distress was apparent to Ollie Bown, one of the therapists at the Counseling Center, who offered Rogers a therapeutic relationship. Rogers wrote, "I accepted in desperation and gradually worked through to a point where I could value myself, even like myself, and was much less fearful of receiving or giving love. My own therapy with my clients has become consistently and increasingly free and spontaneous ever since that time."[32]

There it was. Rogers, like the vast number of clients he had helped over the years, down deep, did not feel adequate. His parents had never accepted him for who he was, nor had he. His fundamentalist background, which had told him he was "as filthy rags in Thy sight, o Lord," had stayed with him. Growing up in a home where expressions of feeling were viewed as a sign of weakness, isolated from friends until college, he had had difficulty sharing his feelings and giving and receiving love ever since. While he overcame these influences to a degree, on the most basic level his sense of self-worth remained vulnerable, no matter how much he accomplished, no matter how many people cared for and admired him. As Rogers plumbed the difficult emotions and memories, as he came to accept himself more, not only did his empathy for clients deepen, but he began to feel more comfortable sharing his own feelings and accepting others' positive feelings toward him. This happened gradually, over many years, and was not necessarily apparent to his friends and colleagues in Chicago, for he remained generally shy and reserved. But inside, Rogers experienced a profound change, and this came out in his evolving description of the ingredients of effective therapy.

Some of Rogers' colleagues at the Center, as well as Carl Whitaker and his associates in Atlanta, were exploring the possibilities of the therapist sharing his positive or negative feelings, as appropriate, with clients in therapy. Rogers applied the term *congruence* to this phenomenon, based on the geometric concept of congruent triangles. He wrote, "It appears essential that the therapist be genuine, or whole, or congruent in the relationship. What this means is that it is important for the therapist to be what he is in his contact with the client. To the extent that he presents an outward facade of one attitude or feeling, while inwardly or at an unconscious level he experiences another feeling, the likelihood of successful therapy will be diminished. It is only as he is, in that relationship, a unified person, with his experienced feeling, his awareness of his feelings, and his expression of those feelings all congruent or similar, that he is most able to facilitate therapy. It is only as the therapist provides the genuine reality which is in him, that the other person can successfully seek the reality in himself."[33]

On the other hand, congruence did not mean that the therapist interrupts the client to say, "I feel hungry" or "I wonder what my wife is doing fight now," whenever such thoughts occur. Rather, it is when feelings in the therapist occur persistently and, particularly, are problematic to the relationship that the therapist would do well to express them. Otherwise they will surely be communicated anyway and are likely to interfere with the therapist's ability to continue to accept and empathize with the client. In addition, when such a message is not communicated clearly, it is likely to confuse the client, who has to guess what the therapist is feeling. Uncharacteristically, Rogers provided few case study examples of congruence, probably because he was just beginning to understand this phenomenon and would continue to explore and internalize the concept for many years to come.

Another important concept Rogers borrowed from a colleague during the Chicago years (always giving credit for the source) and then popularized was that of *unconditional positive regard.* His doctoral student Stanley Standal helped Rogers further clarify the meaning of acceptance. Rogers wrote:

> To the extent that the therapist finds himself experiencing a warm acceptance of each aspect of the client's experience as being a part of that client, he is experiencing unconditional positive regard. This concept has been developed by Standal . . . .. It means that there are no *conditions* of acceptance, no feeling of "I like you only *if* you are thus and so." It means a "prizing" of the person, as Dewey has used that term. It is at the opposite pole from a selective evaluating attitude—"You are bad in these ways, good in those." It involves as much feeling of acceptance for the client's expression of negative, "bad," painful, defensive, abnormal feelings as for his expression "good," positive, mature, confident, social feelings . . . .. It means a caring for the client, but not in a positive way or in such a way as simply to satisfy the therapist's own needs. It means a caring for the client as a *separate* person, with permission to have his own feelings, his own experiences.[34]

With the introduction of unconditional positive regard, Rogers solidified his concept of the therapist's role. Back in 1946, he had said the counselor's role was best described by the terms "warmth, permissiveness, acceptance, understanding, and nondirectiveness." During the next decade at Chicago, little by little, he augmented, abridged, and modified this description. Warmth and acceptance became acceptance and liking. Acceptance and liking became "a warm regard for the client as a person of unconditional self-worth," which became unconditional positive regard. Understanding became empathy. "A nondefensive genuineness," later called congruence, was added to the list. Though permissiveness and nondirectiveness were maintained in practice as effective ways of implementing the three key attitudes, Rogers no longer saw them as essential conditions for effective therapy.

When one concentrates on the single steps in a long staircase, he may neglect to notice that whole floors are passing by. So it was with Rogers' changes during this period. All the subtle modifications of terms and concepts and techniques could easily obscure the major changes in thinking and practice that had occurred. In the twelve years in Chicago, Rogers moved from the *method* to the *attitudes* to the *relationship* as the key ingredients in the therapeutic process. Although he and his colleagues in Chicago favored the nondirective or client-centered techniques as the most effective ways for creating a relationship characterized by congruence, empathy, and unconditional positive regard, Rogers believed and often stated that therapists of many different schools could be effective in creating such a relationship. In fact, he was quite fond of quoting several studies by one of his students, Fred Fiedler, which showed that experienced therapists of different schools of thought were more similar in their actual practices than experienced and inexperienced therapists of the same school of thought.[35, 36] Moreover, some of the qualities the experienced therapists had in common were some of the very conditions Rogers had identified as essential for therapeutic change, namely, "the therapist's ability to understand, to communicate with, and to maintain rapport with the client."[37]

The Fiedler research suggests that, somehow, Rogers and his colleagues had found ways to actually measure the therapist's ability to understand and communicate with the client. They did much more than that. They developed ways to measure almost every aspect of the therapeutic relationship. Rogers remained a committed scientist. He believed that "psychotherapy may become a science, applied with art, rather than an art which has made some pretense of being a science."[38] He noted that "adherents of any clinically effective procedure tend to become dogmatic. If client-centered counseling does not provide sufficient examples, psychoanalysis or Rorschach will be glad to oblige. As the clinician's emotional security becomes tied up with dogma, he also becomes defensive, unable to see new and contradictory evidence. But when research is persistently undertaken, the security which all of us must have tends to become lodged, not in dogma, but in the process by which truth is discovered, in scientific method."[39]

Thus, from the beginning of his time in Chicago, Rogers established the Counseling Center as a site for research on counseling and psychotherapy. When Rogers came to Chicago, only a handful of research studies existed on client-centered therapy. By the time he left, there were perhaps two hundred. He and his associates continued to make phonographic recordings of therapeutic interviews. By 1947 they had a half dozen complete therapy cases that had been recorded and transcribed. In a few years the number had grown to thirty, and by 1956 Rogers wrote that "thousands of therapeutic interviews had been electrically recorded and studied"—all still before tape recorders!

Beginning in Ohio, Rogers and his colleagues had studied the actual behavior of therapists and clients in the counseling interviews, to sharpen their understanding of what actually takes place in therapy. They found reliable ways of measuring therapist directive and nondirective behavior, and client expressions of feeling, insight, and defensiveness. This enabled them to document how acceptance and understanding by the therapist consistently led to further exploration and insight by the client. But did such insight lead to any significant changes in the client's personality or subsequent behavior?

At Chicago, they set about to answer that all-important question. First they used many accepted tests and measures which had already been correlated with mental health criteria: the Rorschach test, the Thematic Apperception Test, tests of dogmatism, the Minnesota Multiphasic Personality Inventory (MMPI), and tests of anxiety, attitudes toward self and others, perceptual acuity, and even galvanic skin response and heart rate. As these accepted instruments showed that clients had changed for the better during and after therapy, it became more difficult to dismiss the client-centered approach as ineffective or superficial, as many academicians were wont to do.

Still there remained the question of *controls*. How could one be certain that any changes brought about during therapy were the result of the therapy itself, rather than the added motivation of clients who come for therapy, or the repeated test taking, or other factors? Research on psychotherapy utilizing adequate controls would be an expensive undertaking. Rogers' prominence in the psychology and social work professions, however, and the Counseling Center's reputation as a leader in psychotherapy research opened doors. When Rogers submitted grant proposals to the Rockefeller, Ford, and other foundations to establish a major research project on psychotherapy, with larger populations and more elaborate controls than ever employed before, the money was forthcoming. Rogers raised over $650,000 in the late forties and fifties to support their research at Chicago, an astronomical sum in those days.

Such sums were needed for the complicated and sophisticated *program design* Rogers and his associates implemented. It entailed twenty-five clients in the first group, another twenty-five added a few years later, plus their control groups; several "test points" at which clients and their controls (the *subjects*) were repeatedly tested; thirteen different measurement tools used from once to several times each to assess the subjects' progress (everything from standardized psychometric tests to ratings by counselor, subject, and two friends of the subject); and a major new "Q-sort" instrument they created to measure the client's perception of himself as he was, as he would like to be, and how he viewed other people. Seven hundred hours, outside of the counseling hours, went into gathering and recording all the test data in a single, forty-session case. It is staggering to contemplate the investment of time and energy required to complete this project.

Rogers and his group soon began to share the results of their research with the scientific community. A 1949 issue of the *Journal of Consulting Psychology* contained an introductory article by Rogers and six research reports by his students. In 1950, the *Yearbook* of the *Encyclopedia Britannica* reported: "These first efforts of Rogers to subject his methods of non-directive therapy to scientific test constituted a landmark for clinical psychology." In 1954, the University of Chicago Press published Rogers and Rosalind Dymond's book, *Psychotherapy and Personality Change,* including five chapters by Rogers and others by Dymond, Thomas Gordon, and other staff and students, each reporting different aspects of their research with the first group of clients. The *Library Journal* called it "the first thoroughly objective study of outcomes of psychotherapy in which adequate controls have been utilized," and the American Personnel and Guidance Association selected the book as the outstanding research work in the field.

Even before establishing his research project at Chicago, Rogers had enjoyed a solid national reputation. Partly as a result of his role in reintegrating the American Association for Applied Psychology, of which he was president, back into the American Psychological Association, Rogers was elected president of the APA for the 1946–47 term. Thereafter he remained active in the APA, usually delivering one, two, or three papers at its annual convention, serving as president of the Division of Clinical and Abnormal Psychology, and acting in other leadership capacities. From 1956 to 1958, he served as the first president of the newly formed American Academy of Psychotherapists.

Students continued flocking to his classes at the University of Chicago. One student, Theron Alexander, later a psychology professor himself, recalled:

> I took several classes under him—and most of the time there were three or four hundred people in them—that met in a large auditorium. People came from all over the world, and the University did not feel it could make any restrictions on who could come in. So they just kept getting a larger and larger auditorium until it accommodated the people. . . . He would start out to discuss some topic and maybe discuss it for ten or fifteen minutes and then open it up to discussion. People were very anxious to discuss and it was never a dragging discussion. Most of the time it was very interesting. . . . The people were so excited, either by great hostility for the ideas or enamored with the ideas; but there were enough who were either way to have arguments not only with Rogers but with each other across the auditorium. . . . In his heyday he was probably the most talked about person in psychology.[40]

Five visiting professorships during this period—including ones at Harvard, the University of California at Berkeley, and the University of Wisconsin—an honorary degree, academic awards, and even an article about his work in *Time* magazine in 1957 reflected and added to his national esteem. Yet what Rogers cherished most was the American Psychological Association's first Distinguished Scientific Contribution Award, which he received in 1956 along with Kenneth Spence and Wolfgang Kohler, two other prominent psychologists. As stated in his citation, Rogers had been selected to receive the profession's highest honor

> for developing an original method to objectify the description and analysis of the psychotherapeutic process, for formulating a testable theory of psychotherapy and its effects on personality and behavior, and for extensive systematic research to exhibit the value of the method and explore and test the implications of the

theory. His imagination, persistence, and flexible adaptation of scientific method in his attack on the formidable problems involved in the understanding and modification of the individual person have moved this area of psychological interest within the boundaries of scientific psychology.

Years later Rogers described this award as having had "greater personal meaning than all the honors which have followed since." Eugene Gendlin, then a graduate student of Rogers, later recalled a story that illustrated the sincerity of Rogers' commitment to science. A study by Kirtner appeared to contradict some of the views held by Rogers and the Counseling Center staff. Consequently, "most of the staff of the Counseling Center were outraged and sought to argue one loophole or another against the study. Only Rogers welcomed the findings and cited them in his next publication. Rogers sought to argue with all the rest, saying, 'Don't you see, facts are always friendly. This will lead us to some further step.' When the retort was, 'But perhaps thus-and-so would account for the findings differently . . . ,' Rogers would say, 'And perhaps you will be the person to find that in your next study.'"

The data yielded by the voluminous research at the Counseling Center continued to impress Rogers so much that, just before leaving Chicago, he formulated his clearest and most extreme statement on the therapeutic process. Entitled "The Necessary and Sufficient Conditions of Therapeutic Personality Change," this 1957 essay was couched in the form of an "if/then" scientific hypothesis. In essence, Rogers' hypothesis stated that, *if* (1) a client is experiencing a state of psychological malaise or dissatisfaction, (2) the person is in contact with a therapist, (3) the therapist is congruent or integrated in the relationship, (4) the therapist experiences unconditional positive regard for the client, (5) the therapist experiences an empathic understanding of the client's internal frame of reference and endeavors to communicate this experience to the client, and (6) the communication to the client of the therapist's empathic understanding and unconditional positive regard is to a minimal degree achieved, *then* positive therapeutic change will occur. "If these six conditions exist," he wrote, "and continue over a period of time, this is sufficient. The process of constructive personality change will follow." He further described what he meant by "constructive personality change" and how such change and the therapist's levels of congruence, empathy, and unconditional positive regard might be measured.[42]

Such an extreme and specific statement had many implications, and Rogers was quick to spell out many of them: "It is *not* stated that these conditions apply to one type of client, and other conditions are necessary to bring about psychotherapeutic change with other types of client. . . . It is *not* stated that these six conditions are the essential conditions for client centered therapy, and that other conditions are essential for other types of psychotherapy.. . . It is *not* stated that psychotherapy is a special kind of relationship, different in kind from all others which occur in everyday life. . . . It is *not* stated that special intellectual professional knowledge—psychological, psychiatric, medical, or religious—is required of the therapist. . . . Intellectual training and the acquiring of information has, I believe, many valuable results—but becoming a therapist is not one of those results. . . . It is *not* stated that it is necessary for psychotherapy that the therapist have an accurate psychological diagnosis of the client. . . ."[43]

In effect, Rogers was putting in the form of a scientific hypothesis a profoundly important belief about human beings. Provide the conditions of congruence, empathy, and unconditional positive regard and people will become healthier. In layman's terms, surround people with honesty, understanding, respect, and trust, and they will flourish. We can trust people to become healthier, more self-enhancing, more constructive individuals if we provide them a psychologically nurturing environment in which to grow.

As Rogers came to understand the implications of this hypothesis, which he did throughout the fifties, he began applying these insights to other fields, and other fields recognized the applicability of the client-centered approach to their own work. Thus, articles by Rogers appeared in publications as varied as: *Marriage and Family Living, Teachers College Record, Pastoral Psychology, American Journal of Nursing, Harvard Educational Review, Educational and Psychological Measurement, Annals of Allergy, Scientific American, Management Record, ETC.* (the journal of the Society for General Semantics), and the *Harvard Business Review,* to name a few. This was the beginning of Rogers' extending his work and influence into many disciplines and areas of human experience.

One reason Rogers was able to think and write about the relationship of his work to so many different fields was that, during the years in Chicago, he and Helen had developed the routine of taking a two- or three-month vacation each year. Their long winter breaks typically included about two months in the Caribbean and Mexico, with visits on the way to David and Natalie and their growing families. The children were well launched in their careers, David in medicine and medical research and Natalie in art therapy—career choices that clearly reflected their parents' values. They were each married, and by 1957 each had three children. Aside from seeing them, Rogers' winter vacations gave Carl a period away from the daily routine of teaching, counseling, and supervision; a time to reflect on his work; to read widely in philosophy, science, and other disciplines; and to consider the implications of his work and its relation to various areas of living.

Rogers' several visiting professorships provided this sort of perspective as well. In the spring of 1957, he spent a semester at the University of Wisconsin at Madison. Aside from teaching, he used this time to listen to many hours of taped interviews and to formulate his "process conception of psychotherapy"—a sophisticated analytical tool for describing how the client's experience and expression of himself is changed throughout the therapeutic process.

It was a successful visiting experience for everyone, but when his supporters at Wisconsin asked him to move there permanently, Rogers had little initial interest in accepting. The Counseling Center at Chicago had achieved an international reputation as one of the leading, if not *the* leading, centers for training and research in psychotherapy. It was his creation, and he was fully immersed in all aspects of the work there, including the large, ongoing research project. On the other hand, he recognized that he had probably made his major contribution at Chicago and that to remain there would mean more of the same sort of work. At Wisconsin he recognized the potential for a new type of impact.

Having stated his hypothesis so clearly—that these conditions in therapy would produce positive change in *any* clients—he became eager to test the hypothesis with extremely disturbed individuals and with so-called "normal" populations—groups with which he had worked before but that had not constituted a major part of his practice. So he told his sponsors at Wisconsin that he would consider coming if he could have joint appointments in the departments of psychology and psychiatry, the opportunity to train both psychologists and psychiatrists together, and full access to the state mental hospital to work with and conduct research on psychotherapy with hospitalized schizophrenics. It seemed like an impossible order to fill, but after considerable effort, all his wishes were granted.

In a letter to all his colleagues and students at Chicago, explaining how he had probably been at the Counseling Center long enough and how, in Wisconsin, he hoped he might have the opportunity to make a new and significant contribution to the mental hygiene field, he closed with these two paragraphs:

> P. S. As I think over what I have dictated, I realize that in one respect it does not quite express my feeling. Because I fear that my decision will cause temporary pain and upset, I have soft-pedaled my own feeling of enthusiasm. I tried once to tell staff in a memo—you may remember it—what a large streak of pioneering spirit there is in me. I really am kin to the old frontiersmen, and my feeling at the present time is that I can hardly wait to throw my pack on my back and leave the settlement behind. I itch to get going! In my feelings I am already in the excitement of meeting the new problems, new challenges, and the broad horizon of new opportunities I see here. The thought of new wilderness to explore, with all that I believe it will mean to me and to others in the way of significant learnings and fresh developments, is like wine in my blood. I feel ten years younger.
>
> So if what I am saying in this memo seems to you as if I am talking to you from a distance, halfway up the ridge on the trail of a new adventure, you are right, for that is the way it is. What I hope you will realize is that this in no way alters my affection for you, but is simply my need to keep on going.

Freud, Skinner, and Rogers: The Growth of Humanistic Psychology

Abraham Maslow, in the 1950s, often spoke of a growing "third force" in psychology. This loose movement, known variously as holistic, existential, or humanistic psychology, was in stark contrast to the psychoanalytic and behaviorist traditions in modern psychology. Although Rogers had received some training in psychoanalytic thinking, it was but one of his early influences, one that made little impact on the practical Midwesterner. He often spoke scornfully of what he described as the psychoanalysts' almost mystical constructs and their unwillingness to submit their theories and methods to the rigorous testing of empirical research. On the other hand, he had enormous respect for Sigmund Freud (1856–1939), although he never met him. He believed that Freud, unlike many of his disciples, was more of a genuine scientist, a keen observer who was continually willing to change and enlarge his theories to incorporate new evidence and experience.

Yet Rogers was puzzled that he and Freud, both having entered so deeply into the world of troubled individuals, had reached such different conclusions about human nature. They both recognized full well the depth of the internal struggles that can exist within each personality, yet these internal psychodynamics had a different meaning to each of them. For Freud, the struggle between the *id* and the *superego* was mediated by the *ego,* which helped the individual relate realistically to the outside world. But make no mistake about it, the id was the basic force which, left to its own devices, would lead the individual and the society to ruin. In this idea—that underneath the civilized facade of each person was a ravenous beast, intent only on fulfilling its selfish desires for sexuality, acquisitiveness, and domination—Freud's view of human nature paralleled the traditional religious concept of humans being basically sinful or evil.

Rogers had a different view. He acknowledged the powerful destructive forces within people but saw no evidence to suggest that these were *primary.* He saw negative *and* positive impulses existing side by side within the individual. Over many years of counseling and research, he saw that when the therapist could provide the conditions of congruence, empathy, and unconditional positive regard, this helped the individual learn to accept both the positive and negative feelings within himself. Once the individual could understand and accept all parts of himself and his inner experience more fully, that person tended to chose more constructive courses of action.

This did not mean that people were "basically good"—Rogers never put it that way—but that human beings were basically "reliable" and "trustworthy" members of the species. He pointed out that all species have their different characteristics. Lions are more aggressive, mice more timorous, sheep more gregarious than other species.

Since the lion has the most pronounced reputation for being a "ravening beast" let us choose him. What are the characteristics of his common nature, his basic nature? He kills an antelope when he is hungry, but he does not go on a wild rampage of killing. He eats his fill after the killing, but there are no obese lions on the veldt. He is helpless and dependent in his puppyhood, but he does not cling to the dependent relationship. He becomes increasingly independent and autonomous. In the infant state he is completely selfish and self-centered, but as he matures he shows, in addition to such impulses, a reasonable degree of cooperativeness in the hunt. The lioness feeds, cares for, protects, and seems to enjoy her young. Lions satisfy their sexual needs, but this does not mean they go on wild and lustful orgies. His various tendencies and urges come to a continually changing balance in himself, and in that sense he is very satisfactorily self-controlled and self-regulated. He is in basic ways a constructive, a trustworthy member of the species *Felis leo.* His fundamental tendencies are in the direction of development, differentiation, independence, self-responsibility, cooperation, maturity. In general the expression of his basic nature makes for the continuation and enhancement of himself and his species.

We wince to see the lion kill the antelope; we are annoyed when the sheep eats our garden, we complain when the mouse eats the cheese we are saving for our picnic. I regard the dog as destructive when he bites me, a stranger; but surely none of these behaviors justifies us in thinking of any of these animals as basically evil. If I endeavored to explain to you that if the "lion-ness" of the lion were to be released, or the "sheep-ness" of the sheep, that these animals would then be impelled by insatiable lusts, uncontrollable aggressions, wild and excessive sexual behaviors, and tendencies of innate destructiveness, you would quite properly laugh at me. Obviously, such a view is pure nonsense.[45]

Humans, like all animals, have their species characteristics, and all of Rogers' experience led him to believe that humans, when given a definable, nurturing climate in which to grow, could be relied on to grow in self-enhancing *and* socially constructive directions. This was not merely a theoretical nuance in an academic discussion. Coming out of the depth of his clinical and research experience, and coming from one of the country's most respected psychologists of that period, Rogers' more optimistic description of human nature represented a new model for answering one of the oldest philosophical and religious questions: the nature of man.

Rogers' thinking became a prototype for answering other perennial philosophical questions and contemporary social questions as well, such as the matter of free will versus determinism and the uses of the behavioral sciences to predict and control human behavior. On these matters, his views were clarified and expressed in debate with the leading figure in the "second force" in psychology, the behaviorist B. F. Skinner.

Early in the century, Ivan Pavlov in Russia and E. L. Thorndike in the United States pioneered in laboratory experiments on animal behavior. They were not interested in the internal world of their experimental subjects; they focused exclusively on the organism's observable behavior. Pavlov observed how different stimuli led to different responses and how an animal's responses could be influenced by manipulating the stimuli, an approach known as *classical conditioning*. Thorndike demonstrated that rats learned certain tasks through repetition, and many psychologists and educators eagerly used this to justify classroom learning by repetitive drill. In the 1930s, Burrhus Frederick Skinner (1910–90), a contemporary of Rogers, began working in this behaviorist tradition.

Skinner focused on how, if a particular response was rewarded, or *reinforced*, it was more likely to occur again. It did not matter what stimulus produced the original response. Most of Skinner's experimental work was done with pigeons. By reinforcing with food certain behaviors of pigeons, Skinner was able to teach the birds to dance, play table tennis, and even keep guided missiles on their proper course. By varying the timing and consistency of the reinforcement, Skinner showed how the animals' behavior could be either strengthened or extinguished.

This appealed to American psychology. As with testing and measurement in psychology, the behaviorists' work was concrete. The results could be measured. And the concepts were readily understandable. Almost everyone has been reinforced by parents or teachers for "good" behavior, or punished for the opposite, or has tried to "shape" a pet's behavior through praise or other rewards. So we readily accept the commonsense correctness of Skinner's principles. His school of operant conditioning soon became, and still is, the most widely taught learning theory in colleges across the country.

Like Rogers, who eventually applied his psychotherapeutic learning principles to other related fields, Skinner also began to apply his principles of learning to spheres other than the laboratory. He spoke and wrote frequently about child-rearing and education. In his widely read novel *Walden Two,* he describes his ideal society, built upon the principles of operant conditioning. *Programmed learning,* which is based on operant conditioning, became an important new educational technology. Behavior therapy emerged as a major new form of therapy and eventually spawned as much research as had the client-centered model.

As they were the leading researchers in their field, psychologists of international renown, and prolific spokesmen for their different viewpoints, it was inevitable that Rogers and Skinner would eventually meet. When they finally did speak directly to one another, the "Rogers–Skinner debate" soon became the most widely popularized discussion of the differences between behaviorist and humanistic psychology.

Their first meeting was the same 1956 American Psychological Association convention where Rogers received the Distinguished Scientific Contribution Award. Their "Symposium on the Prediction and Control of Human Behavior" included a paper by Skinner, a paper and rebuttal by Rogers, and a final rebuttal by Skinner. Published shortly thereafter in *Science* magazine, this exchange has become one of the most widely reprinted essays in the behavioral sciences. A second meeting between the two occurred at a 1960 closed conference sponsored by the American Academy of Arts and Sciences in which twenty-nine leading psychologists were invited to discuss issues regarding psychology and society. Their personal interaction here was minimal. Finally, in June 1962, Rogers and Skinner came together for a two-day conference at the University of Minnesota at Duluth, in which the two men engaged in over five hours of genuine dialogue. Although this was the richest encounter between them, filled with frequent humor and eloquence by both protagonists, this exchange was not available in printed form until Rogers' dialogues with Skinner, Martin Buber, Paul Tillich, Gregory Bateson, Rollo May, and other intellectual giants were published in 1989.[46]

In their exchanges, Skinner brilliantly argued the case for determinism in human behavior. He illustrated how all behavior can be explained by a combination of our genetic makeup and the particular history of reinforcement we each experience. Rogers did not deny the importance of such reinforcement; he just did not believe that this was a sufficient explanation for all behavior. As he had written and emphasized, as early as 1946, "The clinical experience could be summarized by saying the behavior of the human organism may be determined by the influences to which it has been exposed; *but it may also be determined by the creative and integrative insight of the organism itself.*"[47] Skinner accepted that people do have an inner life, including the perception of having free choice, but denied that such a feeling or belief had any causal efficacy. Rogers countered with Victor Frankl's example of his and others' experience in the concentration camps.

> It would be very interesting to try and tell him [Frankl] that the freedom of choice which remained to himself was completely unreal. He knew it was real, because he saw people who did not exercise that, who felt that they were completely controlled, die like flies. For the ones who had the best chance of survival were the ones who still retained the concept that "I am a person. I choose." And so for me, this is an entirely different dimension which is not easily reconcilable to the deterministic point of view. I look at it as being similar to the situation in physics, where you can prove that the wave theory of light is supported by evidence; so is the corpuscular theory. The two are contradictory. They're not at the present state of knowledge reconcilable; but I think one would only be narrowing his perception of physics to deny one of these and accept only the other. And it is in this same sense . . . that I regard these two dimensions as both real, although they exist in a paradoxical relationship.[48]

Rogers did not object so much to Skinner's desire to more effectively predict and control human behavior, but he argued that he and Skinner differed over the questions of: "Who will be controlled? Who will exercise control? What type of control will be exercised? Most important of all, toward what end or what purpose, or in the pursuit of what value, will control be exercised?" He characterized Skinner's utopia as a static one in which people were "happy and well-behaved" and maintained that "at a deep philosophic level" *Walden Two* and *1984* are "indistinguishable." Rogers would have people become "self-directing, self-actualizing, creative, and adaptive" and enlist science toward these ends.

"It saddens me to hear Rogers say that 'at a deep philosophic level' *Walden Two* and George Orwell's *1984* seem 'indistinguishable,'" replied Skinner. "They could scarcely be more unlike—at any level. The book *1984* is a picture of immediate aversive control for vicious selfish purposes." Walden Two, on the other hand, is a community where no person or group exerts current control over others. It is "a world in which there is food, clothing, and shelter for all, where everyone chooses his own work and works on the average of only 4 hours a day, where music and the arts flourish, where personal relationships develop under the most favorable circumstances, where education prepares every child for the social and intellectual life which lies before him, where—in short—people are truly happy, secure, creative, and forward-looking. What is wrong with it? Only one thing: someone 'planned it that way.' . . . And this, to the child of the democratic tradition, spoils it all."

To which Rogers replied that Skinner underestimated the problem of power. "To hope that the power which is being made available by the behavioral sciences will be exercised by the scientists, or by a benevolent group, seems to me a hope little supported by either recent or distant history. It seems far more likely that behavioral scientists, holding their present attitudes, will be in the position of the German rocket scientists specializing in guided missiles. First they worked devotedly for Hitler to destroy the USSR and the United States. Now, depending on who captured them, they work devotedly for the USSR in the interest of destroying the United States, or devotedly for the United States in the interest of destroying the USSR. If behavioral scientists are concerned solely with advancing their science, it seems most probable that they will serve the purposes of whatever individual or group has the power." Rogers concluded one of their exchanges in a passionate comparison of the two approaches to the behavioral sciences, as he saw them:

> It is my hope that we have helped to clarify the range of choices which will lie before us and our children in regard to the behavioral sciences. We can choose to use our growing knowledge to enslave people in ways never dreamed of before, depersonalizing them, controlling them by means so carefully selected that they will perhaps never be aware of their loss of personhood. We can choose to utilize our scientific knowledge to make men happy, well-behaved, and productive, as Skinner earlier suggested. Or we can insure that each person

learns all the syllabus which we select and set before him, as Skinner now suggests. Or at the other end of the spectrum of choice we can choose to use the behavioral sciences in ways which will free, not control; which will develop creativity, not contentment; which will facilitate each person in his self-directed process of becoming; which will aid individuals, groups and even the concept of science to become self-transcending in freshly adaptive ways of meeting life and its problems.

These excerpts only begin to suggest the variety of subjects and the richness of expression in Rogers and Skinner's two major encounters. Nor do they suggest some of the ways that Rogers suggested and others have actually attempted to reconcile these two divergent approaches to psychology and human behavior.

Aside from its inherent interest, the ongoing Rogers–Skinner debate propelled Rogers still further into the forefront of the growing movement toward a humanistic psychology. Along with Abraham Maslow, Gordon Allport, Rollo May, Kurt Goldstein, the Gestalt psychologists, Kurt Lewin and the phenomenologists, those associated with the National Training Laboratories and the new field of human relations training, and others, Rogers was promulgating a new paradigm in psychology.

First, this psychology gave much more emphasis and credence to the individual's *phenomenal field:* for example, the client-centered therapist's trying to understand the client's frame of reference rather than evaluating or diagnosing from the outside, or the existential psychotherapist's helping the patient find *meaning* in his life. Second, this psychology focused not just on the remediation of psychological problems, but on psychological *health, creativity, self-actualization,* or what Rogers called "the fully functioning person." It was concerned with helping people not only "adjust," but to experience their human potential to the fullest. Third, it was a psychology interested in those factors that distinguish humans from other species: choice, will, freedom, values, feelings, goals. In its focus on the potential and uniqueness of human beings, it was, indeed, a *humanistic* psychology.

While there were several important leaders within this growing orientation, Rogers was arguably the most prominent. He was the most serious researcher among them. He was probably the most prolific as a writer and speaker. And he was certainly the most active in the leadership of many national professional organizations. When the Association for Humanistic Psychology was formed in 1961, aside from being a founding sponsor, Rogers was invited to be president. He declined, feeling he had already had enough of that sort of responsibility; but he was active in the organization for many years. Until his death, Rogers would continue to be a pioneer and leader in the humanistic psychology movement.

The Wisconsin Years: 1957–63

Many people are familiar with Carl Rogers' landmark work at the University of Chicago and his subsequent years of innovative work in California. But the seven-year interim is a time of which little is known, even by Rogers' followers, and a time that Rogers himself often wished he could forget. He once called this period "the most painful and anguished episode in my whole professional life." His dream in moving to the University of Wisconsin was never fulfilled. The hope of having psychologists and psychiatrists working together on joint training and research projects never materialized to any significant degree. No great precedents were set in the education and training of psychologists and psychiatrists. His joint appointment in Psychology and Psychiatry enabled him to work in both realms, but it helped little in bringing the two together.

This is not to say he didn't make a valiant effort. Again attaining over a half million dollars in outside funding, he set up a pioneering research project on the treatment of schizophrenia through the therapeutic relationship. Subjects with schizophrenia included both acute cases who had been at the Mendota State Hospital for less than eight months and chronic patients who had been there for many years. A control group of "normal" subjects, without schizophrenia, received the same treatment. Rogers and his staff developed new scales to measure the therapeutic "conditions," i.e., congruence, empathy, and unconditional positive regard. He also developed an important new "process scale" to measure the client's movement toward psychological health.[49]

This scale was based on Eugene Gendlin's theory of experiencing.[50] Gendlin, formerly a student at Chicago, now hired by Rogers to initiate and coordinate their "Psychotherapy Research Project," had developed a theory about how people perceive, interpret, and describe their *inner experiencing,* that is, their sensations, emotions, cognitions, and their sense of self. Using Gendlin's basic concepts, Rogers formulated a seven-point "process conception of therapy," which played an important role in their research.

On the lower ends of this scale, the individual does not recognize or express her feelings and personal meanings; she is remote from or unaware of her inner experiencing; where there is incongence between what the person is experiencing and what she is expressing, she is unaware of the incongence; there is a lack of communication of self; experience is construed rigidly, and the person sees her constructions not as her own perception or generalization but as facts; she does not recognize her problems or her responsibility in relation to her problems or there is no desire to change; she avoids close relationships as being dangerous. The paranoid schizophrenic, for example, would be at the extreme low end of this scale. She is sure "they" are out to get her. Her failures are never her own; "they" are responsible. Sometimes she has these strange feelings inside her, but they are not "her own." They are being sent into her through the people on the television. She does not want to get close to anyone on the ward or even the therapist, for such exposure would make her vulnerable and be very dangerous.

On the other end of the process scale, at stages six and seven, the individual fully experiences her feelings and personal meanings; she frequently tunes into her inner experiencing and uses it as a major referent to understand herself; any incongruence is temporary only, because she is constantly referring to her inner experiencing. Because she is so in touch with her inner experience, her communication of self is rich and varied; her constructs and generalizations about herself and her world are tentative, flexible, subject to change as new data emerges in her experiencing; she accepts responsibility for her problems; she relates to others openly and freely on the basis of her immediate experiencing. In effect, the process scale exemplified one of the characteristics of humanistic psychology by describing mental health in concrete terms, by moving from a conception of sickness or disturbance or maladjustment to its implied opposite: Rogers' "fully-functioning person."

The Psychotherapy Research Project used the new constructs and rating scales to explore the relationships between three sets of variables: the therapist's three *conditions,* the various dimensions of the *process* scale, and many different *outcomes* of therapy. The outcomes were determined on the basis of traditional psychological tests, evaluations by ward personnel, release from the hospital, and the like. The main hypothesis was that high therapist conditions would lead to movement along the process scale which, in turn, would lead to positive outcomes of therapy. The world of psychology and, for the first time in Rogers' career, psychiatry eagerly awaited the results.

They waited for many years. At Wisconsin, as at Chicago, Rogers delegated responsibility to the research team, but this time he was away so often—for speeches, workshops, visiting professorships and extended vacations—that he never succeeded in building a truly group-centered, trusting, effective team. Then, when one of the team members, Charles Truax, began to engage in some very suspicious and unethical behavior, Rogers vacillated in his response. By the time he decided to fire Truax, most of the team's data analyses in Truax's possession had mysteriously disappeared, and the legal situation became so complicated that Rogers could not fire Truax. Years were added to the project as all the raw data had to be reanalyzed. Meanwhile, serious disputes between the principal researchers over authorship of the final product led to further recriminations and legal threats. The book was finally published years after Rogers left Wisconsin. Rogers and his colleagues, except Truax, repaired their relationships. The latter, following a history of mental illness, committed suicide a decade later.

By the time *The Therapeutic Relationship and Its Impact: A Study of Psychotherapy with Schizophrenics* was published in 1967, the results were anticlimactic. The research outcomes were mixed. The experimental group of patients did no better than the control group as a whole; but on closer examination, those patients whose therapists demonstrated higher levels of congruence, empathy, and unconditional positive regard *did* do significantly better than subjects in the control group. Many other results were of interest, and excellent chapters by Rogers, Gendlin, and others were valuable contributions to the field. But no one cared. Given the timing, the lack of fanfare over its release, and the fact that the project had long since ended and Rogers had moved on to other areas of interest, the 625-page book sold few copies and made little or no impact on the field. No wonder Rogers regarded this seven-year period as the most unsatisfying episode in his career.

On the other hand, personal life in Madison was very satisfying for Carl and Helen Rogers. They found a beautiful home on the shore of Lake Monona, of which Helen wrote "I felt 'my cup runneth over.' This was surely a spot in which I could spend the rest of my days." Helen made many friends in Madison, continued to paint, and pursued her lifelong interest in the Planned Parenthood movement. Although only a five-minute drive from the university, they were definitely out in country. Rogers was able to garden and pursue his other hobbies of photography and making mobiles. They also had a speedboat, and Rogers liked to tow the grandchildren on water skis and take them snorkeling.

They also did a great deal of entertaining. A former colleague from the Rochester years, Louise Johnson, remembered spending the weekend at the Rogers' home. "I was impressed with the telephone calls from former students and the dropping in for a social call by two former students who were passing through on vacation, one bringing his wife and children. From the conversations I could sense the warmth of the friendly relationships which existed between the man and those whose lives he had touched and the high regard and affection felt for him."

The Rogers continued their pattern of taking extended winter vacations. Now they went not only to the Caribbean, but to Hawaii and to the Philippines, where Natalie and Larry Fuchs and their children were living while Larry was head of the Peace Corps there; or to Nashville, where David was a professor and chairman of the Department of Medicine of Vanderbilt University, and a prolific researcher and writer in the field of medicine. Carl and Helen regularly took vacations with one of their children's families, and all twelve of them occasionally got together for holidays at one of their homes.

In addition to family holidays and vacations, the Rogers spent a great deal of time away from home on various professional trips. Among the most memorable in this period were a six-week professional tour of Japan in the summer of 1961 and nine months as a Fellow at the Center for Advanced Study in the Behavioral Sciences at Stanford University in California. Japan, still transitioning from its feudal past to democracy, was fascinated with Rogers' client-centered approach. Apparently his ability to convey genuine caring and unconditional acceptance spanned cultural and even language barriers. On one occasion he conducted a demonstration counseling session, without a translator, with a Japanese man who spoke no English. Rogers' warm attention, "uh-huh's," and nonverbal communication was enough to have the man express great appreciation for the help he felt he had received. Another Japanese counselor said Rogers' importance to him was "to teach me the basic way of becoming to be democratic and not authoritative." Within a few years, a Japanese publisher had brought out a seventeen-volume collection of Rogers' work. The year after being in Japan, Rogers had much time for reflection and writing at Stanford. He particularly enjoyed his contacts with British philosopher of science Michael Polyani, psychoanalyst and author Erik Erikson, and future Nobel Prize-winning physicist Richard Feynman, who similarly expressed their pleasure in their encounters with Rogers.

Other sources of satisfaction for him, which were some compensation for his unpleasant experiences at the University of Wisconsin, were his professional activities and his writing. As the founding president of the American Academy of Psychotherapists, he made another significant contribution to the field by encouraging the creation of a tape library, in which his own and others' therapy sessions, representing different schools of thought, were made widely available to interested professionals. He continued to be prolific throughout the entire period, with many new articles appearing in the journals or in book chapters each year. But by far the most significant publication of this period came in 1961 with his seventh book, *On Becoming a Person*. A collection of unpublished and previously published essays, this was Rogers' first book aimed not exclusively at counselors and therapists. His publisher Houghton Mifflin had some concern, because it was not apparent for whom the book *was* intended.

There were chapters on the process of psychotherapy, characteristics of a helping relationship, and even some of the research on therapy. But there were also chapters on the process of "becoming a person," of growing toward psychological health and well-being. There were chapters exploring the philosophical implications of his approach to psychology, including "A Therapist's View of the Good Life: The Fully Functioning Person." Other chapters explored the nature of science and "The Place of the Individual in the New World of the Behavioral Sciences."

"The good life," Rogers wrote, "is a *process,* not a state of being. It is a direction, not a destination." The more fully functioning person is "open to his experience," that is, aware and accepting of her feelings, perceptions, and thoughts. She has a "trust in his [her] organism," a confidence that, when she is open to *all* of her inner and outer experience and not blocking or defensively distorting it, then her inner directions and promptings are a trustworthy guide to action. She has an *internal locus of evaluation:* that is, although she is aware of and sensitive to the "oughts" and "shoulds" and expectations of others, she trusts her own judgment as the most important guide to right and wrong, desirable and undesirable, in a given situation. There is an "increasingly existential living," in which "the self and personality emerge *from* experience, rather than experience being translated or twisted to fit preconceived self-structure." Such a person, said Rogers, seems to move away from facades and toward congruence in her daily living. There is an increase in spontaneity and creativity.

A major section of *On Becoming a Person* applied Rogers' client-centered approach to other fields: education, family life, interpersonal relationships, intergroup communication, and creativity. Whatever the relationship, he pointed out, the teacher's, parent's, leader's, or individual's congruence, empathy, and unconditional positive regard will unleash improved communication, personal growth, and learning in others. Here was a way of helping, or better yet *a way of living* that had profound implications for all human relationships.

As usual, Rogers used vivid case study examples from his experiences in therapy to illustrate his points, and he wrote with a clarity and personal style that communicated to the lay reader and professionals alike. In fact, his opening chapter, "This Is Me," was a highly personal and effective introduction in which he shared with the reader something of his early background and how he slowly came to adopt his client-centered philosophy.

The book was an instant success. Counselors, therapists, social workers, ministers, teachers, other helping professionals, students of psychology, and the vast number of individuals who were just starting to become engaged in the growing humanistic psychology movement found in it an inspiring professional treatise, a prescription for personal growth, and a personal encounter with a wise, engaging, and affirming author. Some three-quarters of a million copies were sold (the book is still in print), and for decades Rogers continued to receive several letters per week from grateful readers.

With the success of *On Becoming a Person,* his many speaking engagements, his trip to Japan, his year at Stanford, and his other extracurricular experiences in the early sixties, Rogers soon soured on university life. He found the politics of academia increasingly frustrating. He hated the system of departmental requirements for psychology students, which he said kept them in fear throughout their graduate careers, placed undue emphasis on statistics and methodology, and discouraged creativity and originality. He believed that, rather than constituting a true community of scholars, academics at Wisconsin and other universities resisted new ideas, jealously guarded their own turf, engaged in petty battles, and abused their tenured positions. They certainly resisted *his* ideas, no matter how credible the research.

Rogers' success and influence, on the other hand, were occurring primarily *outside* the university, through his writing, speeches, workshops, and professional activities. The implications soon became clear to him. In January 1964, at the age of sixty-two, Rogers once again surprised the profession by leaving Wisconsin and moving to La Jolla, California to join the staff of the Western Behavioral Sciences Institute.

From New York City to Rochester, to Ohio, to Chicago, to Wisconsin, each of his previous westward moves had taken him farther into new territory in his profession. Now he had reached the West Coast. Where was there left to go professionally?

The Early California Years: 1963–72

Western Behavioral Sciences Institute (WBSI) was founded in 1959 by Richard Farson, one of Rogers' students from Wisconsin, and Paul Lloyd, a wealthy California Institute of Technology physicist who was impressed with the potential of the behavioral sciences to enhance business, government, and human relationships. When Rogers was on leave at the Center for Advanced Study at Stanford, he accepted Farson's invitation to join the board of WBSI. His subsequent decision to leave Wisconsin was certainly tied to the attractiveness of being able to continue his work in the congenial atmosphere of the new institute and the temperate weather and relaxed life style of southern California.

The Rogers purchased a relatively small, modern, one-story home high on a hill in La Jolla, an exclusive section of San Diego. Through the floor-to-ceiling glass walls of their large, airy living room, they had a spectacular view of the Pacific coastline stretching north to the horizon, as well as the coastal mountains to the northeast. Here Helen enjoyed her painting and Carl his gardening. In a small shop out back, Carl had a workbench for minor repairs and for making mobiles. Later he used the shop as an office. His garden was filled with lemon trees, cacti, succulents, tuberous begonias, and many other exotic plants which he nursed with exquisite care over the years. It was a far cry from the farm in Illinois, but his love of growing things never left him.

A ten-minute drive down the hill and along Torrey Pines Avenue led to the offices of WBSI. The Institute was a combination think tank and research and training organization, devoted to furthering humanistic approaches to the behavioral sciences and applying these to business, government, education, and society. It was initially an informal, nonhierarchical organization, where the staff members typically generated their own projects and income. Rogers chose Resident Fellow as his title. In spite of the institute's nontraditional structure, Rogers and many of the staff had solid reputations in their fields and obtained a good number of large contracts, particularly with government agencies, to work on issues involving human relations, human resources, training, and education.

After a number of years, the very success of WBSI led to a formalization of the organization's structure and a less democratic style of governance. Carl and many of his colleagues tried to reverse this pattern, without success. After a good deal of political infighting, emotional agony, and damaged relationships, Rogers and about twenty-five colleagues split off in 1968 to form their own organization, Center for Studies of the Person (CSP), which continues to this day.

Rogers and his colleagues affectionately described CSP as a "nonorganization." Though it was legally a corporation, its eventually forty-five or so members had equal voices in its governance. Its "non-director," a position that rotated among the members, served as the organization's spokesperson and coordinator. No one except the secretaries received a salary. Individually or in groups, the members established their own "projects" to carry out work that interested them and to generate their own income. These included the Educational Innovation Project, the Adolescent Drug Abuse project, the La Jolla Program (for training group-facilitators), the Conference Planning Service, the Research Design Center, the project for Developing Awareness Through Interracial Encounters, the Institute for Drug Education, and many others.

It was at WBSI and then CSP that Carl Rogers both found and created the supportive organizational setting and personal relationships that sustained and stimulated him for another quarter century of productive and creative work. He had spent the previous thirty-five years administering major projects, counseling large caseloads of clients, teaching full loads of courses, and/or conducting large and complex research projects. Once he moved to California, he gave up most of that. He still taught courses from time to time (and for a few years had an ongoing, part-time teaching position at nearby United States International University); he still saw the occasional client for a few more years; he still showed great respect for empirical research and often quoted research findings and encouraged others in their research, and he still initiated innovative projects on occasion;

but none of these were primary activities for him. What he did mostly, for many years, was to write, speak to audiences of all sizes, and conduct scores of workshops and small, intensive group learning experiences.

In this nontraditional role of free-lance professional writer, teacher, and consultant, he was not alone. The 1960s saw the beginning of a large industry of workshops, conference centers, training institutes, and consulting on a wide array of topics in education, psychology, human relations, and personal growth. Major corporations, the armed services, the nonprofit sector, as well as individuals interested in personal growth recognized value in the behavioral sciences and humanistic psychology. Seriously or frivolously, they became involved, attended workshops, organized group retreats, and brought in speakers and consultants. As a respected national figure whose interests and talents spanned many disciplines, Rogers was a popular figure to invite to present a keynote address, consult with CEOs or professional staff, or feature as a workshop leader at one's conference. Although he never profiteered nor grew wealthy from these activities, he always had plenty of work—in fact, many more offers than he chose to accept.

Income from speeches, workshops, and consulting, combined with royalties from his growing number of publications, combined with his and Helen's family investments, allowed the Rogers to live quite comfortably. For many years there were still twenty to thirty thousand dollars left over after meeting their own needs, which Rogers donated to causes and projects he believed in, including professional projects, social causes, and helping young colleagues with their various projects. One year Helen helped the infant San Diego chapter of Planned Parenthood become established by donating ten thousand dollars to help it win a large matching grant.

The picture of Rogers during his sixties and seventies, then, is that of an active, healthy man enjoying the good life, both in the traditional sense of material and family success, and also in his own meaning of continuing personal and professional growth and innovative and productive work. Freed from the pressure to focus singlemindedly on counseling, teaching, or research responsibilities, he found, without planning it, that his interests took him in many new directions— all based on his life's work to date, but all venturing into new and creative applications of his basic philosophy of human growth, learning, and relationships.

One of the first such applications was the attempt to formulate a "more human science." Although Rogers' credentials as a serious scientist were impeccable, he was generally dissatisfied with the fruits of the traditional "logical positivist" approach to science when applied to psychology and human relationships. He believed that the most important questions were rarely asked, the research focused too narrowly on easily tested outcomes, and the subjects of research were too rigidly objectified and dehumanized. On the other hand, he was excited by the type of science being practiced at WBSI: tackling major problems of human relationships, learning, and productivity; learning about helping people by working with people; trying to change the traditional model of the detached researcher to one of the involved, committed researcher; and learning from experiences in the real world instead of the laboratory.

In 1966, he and William Coulson established a WBSI project with four goals:

> to examine the current assumptions on which the
> behavioral sciences are built, and the model of science
> currently held in this field; to consider the various points
> of view which bear on this problem, and the
> contributions each has made; to hold small conferences—
> in which the individuals would be from different
> sciences, and would hold different orientations in the
> philosophy of science; to assist in formulating a philoso-
> phy of science and a model of science more appropriate
> for present-day behavioral sciences.[51]

As in many of the remaining projects in which Rogers became deeply involved, his role was that of its leading intellectual light, a primary speaker or leader at the actual events, and the national spokesperson and interpreter. His younger colleagues and partners generally handled the details of design, implementation, and day-to-day management.

This project was relatively short-lived. Its main accomplishment was an invitational conference in which Rogers, British philosopher of science Michael Polyani, and Drs. Jonas Salk and Jacob Bronowski *(The Ascent of Man)* were leading participants. Other philosophers and scientists from England, France, Israel, and the United States also participated. Many of the sessions were designed as presentations and discussions among the participants only, although an all-university lecture by Dr. Polyani at the University of California at San Diego and a televised dialogue between Rogers and Polyani were also included in the program. The major addresses, the dialogue, and many segments of the discussions were then published in a book entitled *Man and the Science of Man,* edited by Coulson and Rogers under the imprint of Charles Merrill Publishers. It was the first of a "Studies of the Person" series which Coulson and Rogers would edit for a number of years.

This first volume was a flop, selling under 3,000 copies and making practically no dent in any field. Some of the presentations and discussions were interesting and provocative, but as a whole, the book failed to further the project's real goal: to formulate a new model and philosophy of science. The discussion was too theoretical. There were practically no case study examples of this new model of science at work. Without the practical examples that had always character-ized Rogers' writing, the abstract discussion lacked readability and applicability for practitioners in most disciplines. Although a few books in the subsequent series tried to fill this gap, the "science project" and Studies of the Person series (with the exception of one book by Rogers on education) would have to be considered one of the least impactful ventures in Rogers' career.

This was in stark contrast to the "encounter group" movement which Rogers helped initiate, rejoined in 1964, and was in the fore-front of for many years.

In 1946 and 1947, Kurt Lewin and his colleagues were experi-menting with a new form of small group learning experience. This evolved into the training groups or *T-groups* that were conducted by the National Training Laboratories (NTL) in Bethel, Maine and Washington, DC. In these groups of some dozen participants, the leader did not set the agenda; rather, the group members set the direction, vied for leadership, developed group norms, and explored issues of concern to them. The leader facilitated communication and helped the group understand its own development. In the process, participants discovered much about themselves and their strengths and weaknesses in human relations and group participation. Participants could put these insights to work back in their own organizations, work settings, and personal lives.

Also in 1946 and 1947, Rogers and his colleagues at the Counseling Center of the University of Chicago were themselves experimenting with the small, intensive group. Rogers had developed a teaching style that had much in common with later encounter groups. He didn't teach. He provided resources but let the class decide what it wanted to do, attempting to clarify students' thoughts and feelings as these emerged. In this leadership vacuum, conflict was not uncommon—nor was closeness, as members finally began taking the responsibility for the group on their own shoulders and started sharing resources and helping one another. Thus, quite naturally, Rogers began developing his own style as group *facilitator,* as he called it. He, Thomas Gordon, and their colleagues then found other opportunities to put this model to work, using it to train large numbers of counselors in the Veterans Administration and in other settings.

The NTL groups and the Chicago groups had different aims. The major focus at the NTL was on the professional training of leaders and managers, with the personal growth of the participants being a secondary gain. The Chicago groups concentrated on the personal growth of the participants, with the expectation that this growth would enable people to be more effective in their helping relationships. NTL went on to become the major practitioner of human relations training in the world, while Rogers, whose priority was still research on psychotherapy, used the small, intensive group approach only in some of his courses and occasional workshop settings.

His former students and colleagues Thomas Gordon and Richard Farson, however, continued to experiment with uses of the small, unstructured, "group-centered" model for personal and professional growth. Beginning in 1958, they invited Rogers to join them in occasional workshops that used this model. By the time Rogers joined the staff of WBSI in 1964, that organization was already using the small, intensive group extensively in their work. One staff member, Jack Gibb, was a national leader in this field. Rogers joined right in and quickly became convinced that this approach, which he came to call the *encounter group,* was "the most rapidly spreading *social* invention of the century and probably the most potent."[52]

What exactly happens in an encounter group? This varies depending on the group's purpose, the participants, and the style of leadership. One description by Rogers, though, tried to encompass most of the group of which he was a part:

> The basic encounter group is relatively unstructured, which provides a climate of maximum freedom for personal expression, exploration of feelings, and interpersonal communication. Emphasis is on interaction among the group members, in an atmosphere which encourages each to drop his defenses and facades and thus enables him to relate directly and openly to other members of the group. Individuals come to know themselves and each

other more fully than is possible in the usual social or
working relationships; the climate of openness, risk-
taking and honesty generates trust which enables the participant to recognize and change self-defeating attitudes,
to test out and adopt more innovative and constructive
behaviors and subsequently relate more adequately and
effectively to others in his everyday life situation.[53]

In such groups, many positive and negative emotions often
came to the surface. In one taped encounter group, in which Rogers
and Farson were the facilitators, Jerry, a competent business executive, said in an early session: "I look at myself with some strangeness
because I have no friends, for example, and I don't seem to require
friends." Rogers described how, in a later session, when Jerry "heard
Beth, a married woman, talking of a remoteness she felt between herself and her husband and how much she craved a deeper and more
communicative relationship, his face began to work and his jaw to
quiver. Roz, another member of the group, seeing this, went over and
put her arm around him and he broke into literally uncontrollable
sobs. He had discovered a loneliness in himself of which he had
been completely unaware and from which he had been well defended
by an armor-plated shell of self-sufficiency."[54]

In another filmed encounter group, in which eight participants
expressed different perspectives on drugs, a young man named
"George" angrily accused Rogers of taking all the credit for the discoveries of others. Saying "This is stupid and superficial and I am
going to go out into the real world," George walked out of the
group. Amy began crying after witnessing such hostility. Tony Rose,
Rogers' cofacilitator, crossed the circle to hug and comfort her. After
George left, Russ said, "My mother reached out but my dad has no
compassion whatsoever. He never held me, nor cried with me. [By
now Russ, Amy, and Joe were crying.] You need at least one person
to hold you. I couldn't talk when George was here. He's like my
dad—so sure he's right. I could never be violent. I know how it
feels to get kicked and hit." Rogers put his arm around Russ' shoulder and told him he had heard very clearly his deep need for a father.
Russ put his head on Rogers' shoulder and said, "If my father had held
me for just one minute . . . .." He sobbed as he said this, feeling it very
deeply. A little later Randy said that he would rather die than go to
prison again (he was scheduled to be sentenced a few days after the
group. Later Rogers tried to intervene with the judge on his behalf),

and Russ said, "That's why kids take drugs—because they can die to get away from the horrors of life. We have to be ashamed of feelings in our culture. We can't express them."⁵⁵

What attracted Carl Rogers to all this? When he left Wisconsin in 1963, he was a sixty-two-year-old man who had made an enormous contribution to many fields and could easily rest on his laurels. Moreover, he was a rather levelheaded individualist, a conservative when it came to fads and movements, a product of Midwestern reserve and inhibition, financially established, a husband for almost forty years, a grandfather of six—in short, one of the least likely candidates to start a whole new phase of his career by entering the young, energetic, and erratic "human potential movement" which seemed to be growing so fast in popularity across the nation. True, this was his opportunity to test his theories of therapeutic growth with a "normal" population, one of his research goals which had not materialized in Wisconsin. The vast majority of participants in human relations training and encounter groups were normally functioning, reasonably successful individuals. Encounter groups were the perfect occasion for Rogers to be himself—accepting and understanding— and to see how these therapeutic conditions might help normal individuals in their own quest for growth.

Accepting, understanding . . . and *congruent,* that is. Herein lay another reason for his entering the encounter group field. Earlier we saw Carl Rogers as a shy boy, sensitive, liking people but awkward in social settings. When he was a young man, it was primarily through church-related work that he made contact with others his age. His later colleagues described him as a man who appeared reserved, even aloof at times, but who entered readily into deep emotional contact with people when he had the opportunity. His own counseling approach indicated a gradual recognition of the importance of the congruent therapist, a whole person, in the relationship. This recognition coincided with his own therapy, in which he came to trust his own feelings more and to value himself more. At the same time, his writing became more personally expressive. The composite portrait is that of a man striving in different ways throughout his life to communicate more of himself, to come into closer contact with people around him. Where the setting encouraged this, as in therapy, he was capable of extremely close relationships and delighted in them. But in most other situations it was rarely easy. There was always the reserve to overcome. He lacked a natural spontaneity, although he strove always to be genuine and usually inspired great trust in those who knew him. For Rogers, then, encounter groups provided not only a realm of further professional interest, but a vehicle for his own personal growth, a chance to move along the same process continuum that his clients did, toward a greater trust in and openness to his feelings and a greater willingness to risk himself in relationships.

Helen Rogers had always been much more spontaneous and open with her feelings than her husband. Now friends and family frequently commented on the changes they saw in him resulting from his encounter group experiences. Natalie said, "I've seen a tremendous change in him. I just can't get over it. He . . . could help other people open up about themselves but not say anything about himself. The group experiences he has had have changed him into being much more self-revealing, much more open about his needs for affection and being affectionate or demonstrative." For example, "being physical—the way he gives me a hug or kiss or the way he will come sit down and put his arm around me, particularly if I may be in some emotional pain, or the way I see him in groups talk about himself or move—take himself out of a place and move toward somebody. I don't think it ever would have occurred to him to get up and move physically closer to somebody before he'd been in encounter groups, that that would matter, that that feels good to him as well as to the other person."

Whatever his motives for becoming involved with encounter groups, he became deeply involved. During the five-year period from 1964 through 1968 he served as facilitator in dozens of groups lasting from one day to eight days, not including the short groups and the brief demonstrations of encounter groups he did before live audiences. He led groups for corporate presidents, college administrators and faculty, nurses, religious workers, interracial groups of health care providers and consumers, mental health workers, couples, adolescents, teachers and students, and other populations. This continued well into the 1970s, although not quite so frequently. During this period, Rogers' colleagues at Center for Studies of the Person formed the La Jolla Program to train hundreds of encounter group leaders, working with thousands of participants, and Rogers had an ongoing involvement with this project.

In 1971, Orienne Strode of CSP invited Carl and David Rogers to help her begin a Human Dimensions in Medical Education project, which would use encounter groups to help medical educators become more aware of their own, their students, and their patients' feelings. David was just moving from being dean of The Johns Hopkins University School of Medicine and medical director of The Johns Hopkins Hospital to becoming president of the Robert

Wood Johnson Foundation, the second largest private foundation in the United States sponsoring medical research. With father and son both quite involved in the early stages, the Human Dimensions project went on for many years and had a major impact on thousands of medical professionals around the country.

As usual, Rogers soon began writing about his experiences, describing the encounter group phenomenon to both professional and popular audiences. Published by Harper and Row in 1970, *Carl Rogers on Encounter Groups* was among the clearest, most accessible accounts of the small, intensive group experience. True to form, it included some of the research on encounter groups, which Jack Gibb had compiled, as well as some of the movement's abuses. The book, which was Rogers' first "trade" publication, sold an impressive quarter million copies and augmented his stature in the humanistic psychology field. The popular magazine *Psychology Today* called Rogers the "grand master," and an article in *Look* magazine described him as "an elder statesman of encounter groups." In addition to describing encounter groups in speeches, interviews, articles, and a book, he also participated in several filmed encounter groups for educational television and mass distribution. One of them, "Journey into Self," which included the exchange with Jerry and Roz described earlier, was made into a sixty-minute documentary. Produced by Bill McGaw, it was nominated for an Academy Award and actually won an Oscar for the best feature-length documentary of 1968.

Once again, Rogers' own experience and the research he cited seemed to support his basic hypothesis. Given a climate of congruence, understanding, and acceptance, people grow in predictable and positive ways. With respect to encounter groups and human relations training, this assertion appeared to have enough face validity, anecdotal support, and research evidence that, at least for a period, a great deal of national attention focused on the use of small, intensive groups in myriad personal and professional development settings. Rogers, in the pursuit of his own scientific and professional goals and his desire to grow personally and be closer to others, became a national leader in the movement. But being a prominent leader was not what Carl Rogers was about. The whole thrust of his philosophy of helping relationships was not to lead, but to empower others to lead themselves. So when Harper and Row, eager to publicize *On Encounter Groups,* got Rogers an invitation to appear on Dick Cavett's nationally televised interview show, they were amazed when Rogers was reluctant to accept. "But one show will lead to another," they said incredulously. "That's what I'm afraid of," he answered and declined the invitation.

Although most of Rogers' views on the subject of education were formulated before 1963, they were not widely known nor very influential until his California years. Ever since his Teachers College course with William Heard Kilpatrick in 1925, Rogers had appreciated the basic premise of John Dewey's educational philosophy: that the primary avenue for education is and should be *experience*. His therapeutic approach emphasized the client's experiencing her inner world fully and experiencing the therapist's congruence, empathy, and unconditional positive regard. His own teaching emphasized experiential learning, whether it was training counselors by having them do counseling or teaching courses by making students responsible for their own learning. As early as 1951, in *Client-Centered Therapy*, he described his educational views in a lengthy chapter, including the statement: "We cannot teach another person directly; we can only facilitate his learning."

In 1954, Rogers gave a short, five-minute talk at the Harvard Business School. Designed to kick off a demonstration of student-centered teaching, "Some Personal Thoughts on Teaching and Learning" went even further: "I realize increasingly that I am only interested in learnings which significantly influence behavior. . . . It seems to me that anything that can be taught to another is relatively inconsequential, and has little or no significant influence on behavior. . . . I have come to feel that the only learning which significantly influences behavior is self-discovered, self-appropriated learning. . . . As a consequence of the above, I realize that I have lost interest in being a teacher. . . . When I try to teach, as I sometimes do . . . it seems to cause the individual to distrust his own experience, and to stifle significant learning. Hence I have come to feel that the outcomes of teaching are either unimportant or hurtful."[56] He went on in this vein, explaining that "I am only interested in being a learner." He described the sort of learning he valued, and listed the implications of this viewpoint, which included the abandonment of examinations, grades, credits, degrees, diplomas, and other artifacts of what he viewed as "insignificant learning." Realizing that such views would be considered outrageous by most people, he did not seek to have this presentation published for several years.

In 1959, in an essay called "Significant Learning: In Therapy and in Education," he stated his educational views in a somewhat more acceptable form, though still radical in their implications. First he reminded the reader of his years of research in therapy, which demonstrated how a client who had a real problem she wished to work on could be greatly helped by a therapist who demonstrated congruence, empathy, and unconditional positive regard. Similarly, the teacher who wishes to facilitate significant *student* learning will help the students find problems and subjects that have meaning to them and will demonstrate realness and genuineness, acceptance and trust, and empathic understanding in her relationship with them. Finally—and this condition is somewhat different in education than in therapy— the teacher will endeavor to provide *resources* to assist the students in their self-directed learning. These include more than the traditional resources of books, articles, audiovisual material, and the like. The teacher herself is a resource whose knowledge, skills, and experiences are available to help students achieve their own learning goals.

When he included these two essays in *On Becoming a Person* in 1961, Rogers' thoughts on education began to reach a much wider audience. As the "open classroom" movement, imported from England, was rapidly gaining popularity and as various approaches to "humanizing education" were beginning to catch on around the country, Rogers' concepts gave a philosophical and psychological depth to the discussion of these new educational methods. He could speak with authority about the real, accepting, understanding teacher, helping students set their own learning goals and evaluate their own progress. Once again Rogers became an intellectual leader, a father-figure, a model for a young and vigorous movement, this time attempting to revolutionize education. Once again, he brought his scientific attitude to bear in an area where many were carried away with the apparent success or popularity of their methods but could not really substantiate their approach's validity with objective data. Encouraged by Rogers, researchers such as David Aspy, Flora Roebuck, and others in the United States, and Reinhard and Ann-Marie Tausch in Germany, began to turn out significant amounts of high quality research that supported student-centered learning.

Rogers wrote articles, gave interviews, conducted demonstrations of student-centered teaching before large audiences, taught workshops, and eventually compiled all his ideas on education into a new book called *Freedom To Learn: A View of What Education Might Become,* published by Charles Merrill in 1969. Describing traditional schools, he wrote in the introduction, "When we put together in one scheme such elements as a *prescribed curriculum, similar assignments for all students, lecturing* as almost the only mode of instruction, *standardized tests* by which all students are externally evaluated, and *instructor-chosen grades* as the measure of learning, then we can almost guarantee that meaningful learning will be at an absolute minimum. . . . But there *are* alternatives."[57]

The book described the alternatives, including the provision of resources, learning contracts to help students set their own goals, helping students learn how to conduct an inquiry and discover things themselves, simulation activities to provide experiential learning, programmed instruction to help the student learn something she wants to learn more efficiently (Rogers even quoted Skinner without sarcasm), the basic encounter group, and self-evaluation. Of course, as in therapy, these techniques had little value unless accompanied by the teacher's facilitative *attitudes:* congruence, empathy, and "prizing, acceptance and trust" (comparable to unconditional positive regard). Three long case studies—of an elementary school teacher, a college teacher, and Rogers himself—showed how teachers could combine these attitudes with various methods to facilitate significant learning in the classroom. Other chapters explored the applications of his views specifically to graduate education, the philosophical and values ramifications of this approach to learning, and a plan for self-directed change for an entire educational system.

The response to *Freedom To Learn* was typical in Rogers' experience It was panned by academics and heralded by real-world practitioners. Critics called it superficial. Edgar Friedenberg wrote, "Like another American philosopher, Huckleberry Finn, Carl Rogers can get in almost anywhere because the draft of his vessel is so terribly shallow." Others called it warmed-over John Dewey, and in a sense they were correct. Consider Rogers' basic arguments: The most significant learning occurs when the content has meaning to the student. We must help students learn to set their own goals and achieve them. We must facilitate, not direct, the learning process. Democratic structures are better than authoritarian. Education of this sort strengthens the student psychologically, enables her to deal more effectively with life, and helps her continue to learn and solve problems as she grows older. The primary goal of school should be to "grow persons," not merely to teach subject matter.

These concepts *were* all basic to progressive education. And now a new generation was ready to hear them—not in the language of the twenties and thirties, but that of the sixties and seventies. If Rogers was standing on Dewey and Kilpatrick's shoulders, it was his own vision he was expressing, infused with the new insights of a humanistic psychology, years of experience, solid research on therapeutic change, and his own philosophical perspective and personal writing style.

It was a vision that appealed to numerous educators in a wide range of settings. *Freedom To Learn* sold over 300,000 copies from 1969 through the seventies, at the same time when *On Becoming a Person* and *On Encounter Groups* were near or at the height of their popularity. Rogers' prominence as a famous psychologist, psychotherapist, *and* educator spread more widely than ever. Because of this prominence, he was able to embark on a series of experiments in system-wide educational change that, until then, he had only imagined.

For a number of years, Rogers had circulated the idea of a bold experiment in education that he wished to undertake. He wanted to involve large segments of an entire school system in encounter groups. It was his belief that, as teachers, administrators, students, and parents experienced the positive effects of encounter groups, this would release an excitement about learning and educational innovation that would dramatically change the entire system. In the late sixties, the Immaculate Heart school system in Los Angeles accepted Rogers' invitation. This Catholic school system consisted of a college, several high schools, and over twenty elementary schools. Rogers and twenty of his colleagues from CSP spent a number of years conducting encounter groups and working with the Immaculate Heart system in a variety of consulting capacities. In a similar project, not initiated by Rogers, Newman Walker and Car Foster in the Louisville, Kentucky public schools initiated a project to unleash self-directed change in that failing urban school system. They based much of their work on Rogers' thinking, purchased 500 copies of *Freedom To Learn* for the teachers, and invited Rogers to visit Louisville several times to meet with faculty, administrators, and students.

In *Freedom To Learn for the 80s,* a new (1983) edition of the original 1969 publication, Rogers summarized the findings from the Immaculate Heart and Louisville projects, as well as four other experiments he was aware of, but not directly involved in, of systemwide educational change. With considerable candor, he described the ultimate outcomes of these experiments as "a pattern of failure." In all cases, it appeared that the six institutions or systems did, indeed, go through a revitalizing change process that produced some exciting and successful results—along with a good deal of controversy, turmoil, and sometimes a conservative backlash. The initial results, which sometimes lasted for years, seemed to justify Rogers' belief in democratic, self-directed learning systems, as well as in encounter groups as an effective change strategy. However, in none of these cases did the innovations last over time. Critics have pointed out that Rogers and his colleagues' use of encounter groups was naive, that a much more sophisticated organizational development process was warranted in trying to effect profound, long-term changes in large systems.

In other instances, however, the change agents' intervention was not the main problem. The Louisville experiment, for example, was going along very well; it had all the potential of becoming a landmark case of revitalizing a decaying urban school system. Then, to achieve court-ordered desegregation, the Louisville city schools were combined with the surrounding suburban school districts, and all hell broke loose with anti-busing riots, violence, hatred, and controversy over the politics and funding of the schools. In the process, the experiment was dismantled. For reasons that had nothing to do with educational philosophy or methods, the successful venture in innovative, self-directed learning was abandoned.

Sobered by the political realities of changing large systems, Rogers nevertheless retained his belief in the value of student-centered education and the usefulness of encounter groups as a potent vehicle for personal growth and institutional change. While his personal involvement with the topic of education and changing educational systems tapered off in the seventies, he continued to speak and write articles on the subject until the early 1980s. *Freedom To Learn for the 80s* contained a much fuller treatment of the accumulating objective data supporting his views. He wrote, "research provides convincing evidence—from two teams based on two continents—showing that students *learn more, attend school more often,* are *more creative,* more capable of *problem solving,* when the teacher provides the kind of human, facilitative climate that has been described in this book."[58]

Leaving Wisconsin and the intense pressures of university teaching, counseling, research, writing, and speaking to become a resident fellow at WBSI and CSP did not mean moving to a laid-back, southern California lifestyle. We have already seen how the 1960s were a period of highly productive and creative work for Rogers, including a simultaneous focus on science, culminating in *Man and the Science of Man* (1968); education, culminating in *Freedom To Learn* (1969); and intensive small group work, culminating in *On Encounter Groups* (1970). Rogers published two other books during this period, as well: *Person to Person: The Problem of Being Human* (Rogers and

Stevens, 1967) and *Becoming Partners: Marriage and Its Alternatives* (1972).

The first was the product of a woman named Barry Stevens, who had lived a long and interesting life and had found Rogers' writings of great importance to her at a difficult period. She asked Rogers for permission to use several of his essays in a book of readings she wanted to put together. He agreed but also encouraged her to write of *her* experiences and psychological struggles and to contribute to the book herself. She took four essays previously written by Rogers and three by Rogers' former colleagues Gendlin, Shlien, and Van Dusen, and then very skillfully wove her own experiences around these essays. Her free-flowing memories and associations came across with a great deal of power and often served as a vivid case study of what the professionals were talking about. Rogers thought Stevens' name should be listed first, but she convinced him to be first author for publicity reasons. Even so, it was such an unusual book that she found it difficult to find a publisher. Finally her son, John Stevens, set up a small publishing company to publish this book and a few others: by Frederick "Fritz" Perls (the Gestalt psychologist), Barry Stevens, and the poet Hugh Prather (whose popular book *Notes to Myself* is dedicated to Carl Rogers, "who showed me where to look"). Eventually, these books were selling so well that Pocket Books, one of the biggest paperback publishers, bought the rights to some of them. *Person to Person* then reached an even wider audience, and Rogers' name became still better known by the layperson interested in psychology.

Becoming Partners was the indirect result of Rogers' interest in and relationships with younger people. He had long entertained the question of how the fully functioning person would behave in the world. He believed that, from the viewpoint of psychological health, the optimum person is a "person in process," someone who is always "becoming," a person who is open to her inner experiencing, trusts the wisdom of her organism, and is willing to grow beyond outdated self-concepts or institutional strictures when these no longer reflect her current experience, needs, or reality. This was the ideal toward which Rogers himself strived, and now he began to notice more and more people like that around him. He saw these qualities emerging in participants in encounter groups as they dropped their defenses, discovered and expressed their fuller range of feelings, and became more flexible in their self-concepts and behavior. He saw it in the young activists of the civil rights, peace, and women's movements of the sixties and seventies, who were skeptical of authority, trusting their own experience, pursuing their own potential, and rejecting out-moded social stereotypes and limitations.

And, especially, he saw these qualities in his younger colleagues at WBSI and CSP. Here were forty or so men and women who were all involved in cutting-edge projects and explorations, who admired Rogers greatly but still treated him as an equal. As one CSP member said, "most people here feel free to tell him things, both positive and negative. I can remember at the annual meeting this year, there were a couple of times that people got mad at him and felt free about doing that. I think there are few places he can really go where he's treated pretty much like other people, where he's not put on a pedestal. In effect, if we think he's full of shit, one of us will say that."

Rogers appreciated this. He often spoke and wrote of his affinity for younger people. "Probably the major factor in keeping me alive as a growing therapist is a continuing association with young people on a thoroughly egalitarian basis. I have always worked with young staff members; I have never found people my own age stimulating except for rare and fortunate exceptions. I find that younger people are full of new ideas, exploring the boundaries of our disciplines and raising questions about any sacred cows which I hold dear. This keeps me stimulated, moving, and I hope growing."[59]

There was mutual admiration. Whenever Rogers spoke with younger audiences, an immediate rapport arose. As one young man wrote to his girlfriend, the evening after he accidentally stumbled upon a group of psychology students at his college meeting with Rogers:

> I think that I love him. Now my only problem is how to explain why I feel this way after being with the man for only six hours in a large group. I guess what it is about him that makes him so instantly charming is that he represents the finest of human beings at a time in my life when the need for "real" people is so desperate. Here I am trying to understand myself and the world and as a result in an emotional state varying (from minute to minute) between ecstasy and dread-filled depression; I walk into this strange room and discover a man so *deeply* human that you want to cry for joy. Yes, Mrs. Robinson, there is a Colonel Sanders! He had the kind of overflowing warmth and compassion that makes you feel like going over to him, telling him all of your problems, and then lying on his lap . . . He is the father that every child wishes he had. . . . Rogers makes you feel important

because he listens to you with a genuine concern. And more important, he does this in a completely natural way; no technique was perceptible to me. Like I said, you feel like you're talking to the guy next door, or better yet—to your best friend, as opposed to feeling like you're talking to an authority figure, a therapist, a teacher, a wise man, etc.[60]

Perhaps Rogers' affinity for young people is best symbolized by the commencement address he delivered at Sonoma State University in June 1969. He began by explaining to the audience of some 1500 graduates, faculty, and family members that, "As an undergraduate I majored in medieval history. I have enormous respect for the scholars of the Middle Ages and their contributions to learning. But I want to speak to you as Carl Rogers, in 1969, not as a medieval symbol. So I hope I will not offend you if I remove these medieval trappings— this nonfunctional cap, this handsome but useless hood, and this robe, designed to keep one warm even in the rigors of a European winter." As he spoke, he removed each piece of academic regalia and then proceeded to address the graduating class, in his shirtsleeves, on "The Person of Tomorrow."

He had called this person "The New Man," until the women's movement raised his awareness. Later he would use "The Emerging Person" as the phrase that summarized a number of characteristics he saw and admired in younger and older people in increasing numbers. First was a "desire for authenticity," a freedom from facades, an aversion to "hypocrisy, deceit, mixed messages . . . doublethink and doubletalk." Second was a belief that "institutions exist for people," an opposition to "all highly structured, inflexible, bureaucratic institutions." Beyond these two major qualities, he noted (in his words): the *unimportance of material things; a nonmoralistic caring; the wish for intimacy; a skepticism about science;* a fascination with *the universe within* the person—from one's feelings to *esoteric and transcendental religious experience;* a desire to live in *balance with nature;* being *a person in process,* always changing; and finally, living by *the authority within:* having *a trust in her own experience and a profound distrust of all external authority.* Was Rogers describing a temporary social phenomenon or fad, or was this truly a character portrait of the person of tomorrow? Clearly he hoped it was the latter, and for several years became something of a publicist for this emerging person.

One of the areas in which Rogers saw this striving for authenticity, intimacy, nonmoralistic caring, and distrust for formal institutions was in the area of love, sex, and marriage. When Scott, Foresman and Company asked him to write a modern psychology textbook reflecting his humanistic viewpoint, his early chapters included three on the subject of marriage. The more he wrote about marriage, the less interested he was in completing the text. Plans changed and the next year Delacorte Press published Rogers' thirteenth book, *Becoming Partners: Marriage and Its Alternatives.* Coming out shortly after the O'Neills' best seller, *Open Marriage,* it was easy to see Rogers' book, as some did, as simply another paean to nontraditional intimate relationships, a requiem for monogamy. It was much more than that, although Rogers did say that traditional marriages were, indeed, becoming only one of many viable options for the future.

What made the book unique was Rogers' perspective on changing marriage norms. In working on the book, he had interviewed many couples who shared with him openly the details, struggles, and joys of their various marriage relationships, whether traditional, second or third marriages, open marriages, living-together committed relationships, interracial marriages, or communal marriages. Their words and case studies provided vivid, realistic examples throughout the book. Rogers also included a lengthy, risky, and touching description of his and Helen's own forty-six-year marriage, including how they learned to communicate honestly about sex early in their marriage, how Helen stood by him during a year he was impotent in his forties, how he stood by Helen during an agonizing six-year period of her mother's dying, and other important events, issues, and problems in their life together. "And while our sex life is not quite the same as in our twenties or thirties," he concluded, "our physical closeness, our 'snuggling,' and our sex relationships are somewhat like a chord which is beautiful not only in itself, but also for its many, many overtones which enrich it far beyond the simple chord."

Alongside the rich case study material was Rogers' ongoing commentary, focusing less on the *form* of each partnership, but rather on the place of *feelings* and *communication* in the relationship. In one case he wrote, "what impresses me is that Joan . . . experiences no trust in her own feelings. . . . She is dimly aware of the doubts she has about the relationship, of the lack of a feeling of deep love, of her unreadiness to commit herself to this man. But these are only 'feelings.' *Only feelings!* It is not until after marriage, and after having a child, that she realizes what reliable guides her gut reactions were, if she had only *trusted* them enough to *listen* to them." This was

Rogers at his best: listening to the couples so carefully that they shared deeply of their relationships, empathically capturing the meaning that their statements and their relationships seemed to have to them, and then commenting with compassion and insight about what he had spent a lifetime studying—how people recognize and communicate their feelings in relationships.

Working in so many different areas, Rogers continued to receive numerous awards and recognitions. The first several of seven honorary degrees were bestowed on him during this period. He served on the editorial boards of several journals. Among other honors, in 1967 he received the Distinguished Contribution Award from the American Pastoral Counselors Association, in 1968 the Professional Achievement Award from the American Board of Professional Psychology, and in 1972 the American Psychological Association's Distinguished Professional Contribution Award, thereby becoming the first psychologist in history to receive the APA's highest award for *both* scientific and professional contributions. Explaining the reason for this latest tribute, the citation read:

> His commitment to the whole person has been an example which has guided the practice of psychology in the schools, in industry and throughout the community. By devising, practicing, evaluating, and teaching a method of psychotherapy and counseling which reaches to the very roots of human potentiality and individuality, he has caused all psychotherapists to reexamine their procedures in a new light. Innovator in personality research, pioneer in the encounter movement, and respected gadfly of organized psychology, he has made a lasting impression on the profession of psychology.

At age seventy, Rogers had achieved almost every honor and award possible in his own profession and a good many in other professions as well. Surely it was now time to retire.

The Later California Years: 1972–87

Although Rogers had always recognized the radical implications of his theories and methods in therapy, education, group leadership, and other areas—even marriage—he never thought of his work as having a particularly *political* meaning. This changed in the 1970s, as he entered the final stage in the evolution of his life's work.

In 1972, Rogers and Bill McGaw collaborated on another documentary film of an encounter group, this one composed of Irish and British citizens, both Protestants and Catholics, involved in the bitter disputes and violence in Northern Ireland. Rogers and Pat Rice, a Catholic priest, conducted the encounter group in the studios of WQED in Pittsburgh. Although the degree of emotional honesty and closeness was not as great as often occurs in encounter groups, some real communication and improved understanding definitely took place. In fact, the participants valued the experience so highly that, at some risk to their own lives, they went back to England and Ireland and worked in teams, showing the documentary in movie theaters and leading discussions among the viewers.

For decades Rogers had believed that intergroup tensions could be lessened in a facilitative climate of genuineness, understanding, and trust. In encounter groups, he often experienced this personally as he saw how individuals and subgroups gradually relaxed their defenses and allowed themselves to really listen to others whose views they previously abhorred. As they listened, they began to move beyond their stereotypes and preconceptions and achieve a gradual recognition of their common humanity and common goals. Rogers was much impressed with the potential of honest, person-to-person communication to reduce interpersonal and intergroup tensions. After the Camp David accords of 1978, he often wrote and spoke of the role President Jimmy Carter played in facilitating communication between Menachim Begin and Anwar Sadat, leading to an historic peace treaty between Israel and Egypt.

Beyond recognizing the potential of his theories and methods to enhance communication between hostile or politically opposing groups, Rogers had a concerned citizen's interest in politics. He kept reasonably well informed on the news, contributed to political and social causes, and in the seventies began to speak out on "Some Social Issues Which Concern Me," including his opposition to the war in Vietnam.[61] Yet, for all this, when a psychologist named Alan Nelson asked him in 1973 about "the politics of the client-centered approach," Rogers answered that there were no politics in the

approach, meaning that no partisan or liberal or conservative political agenda was involved. Nelson laughed at this answer, arguing that
a client-centered philosophy was revolutionary in how it turned
traditional power relationships topsy-turvy, seeking to give clients and
students unprecedented power and control over their lives in therapy
and educational settings. If that wasn't political, what was?

This clicked for Rogers. While humanistic psychology was pro-
liferating in the sixties and now the seventies, so were many important political and social movements. The civil rights movement, the
peace movement, the student movement, and now the women's movement were all speaking the common language of *empowerment.* They
rejected the concept of top-down control, of artificial limitations on
the ability of blacks, Vietnamese, students, and women to achieve their
full potential. They sought to return "power to the people," to enable
them to make the decisions that affected their lives. Rogers realized
that his life's work represented a psychological foundation for these
political movements, and these movements suggested a political
dimension to his work that he had never recognized. Somewhat
embarrassed, likening himself to the man who in his first literature
course realized he had been "speaking prose" all his life but never knew
it, Rogers now admitted, "I've been practicing and teaching politics
all my professional life and never realized it fully until now."

As Rogers applied the term *politics* to human relationships, he
now meant "the process of gaining, using, sharing or relinquishing
power, control, decision-making. It is a process of the highly complex interactions and effects of these elements as they exist in relationships between persons, between a person and a group, or between
groups." He wrote,

> this new construct has had a powerful influence on
> me.. . . It has caused me to take a fresh look at my profes-
> sional life work. I've had a role in initiating the person-
> centered approach. This view developed first in
> counseling and psychotherapy, where it was known as
> client-centered, meaning a person seeking help was not
> treated as a dependent patient but as a responsible client.
> Extended to education, it was called student-centered
> teaching. As it has moved into a wide variety of fields, far
> from its point of origin—intensive groups, marriage,
> family relationships, administration, minority groups,
> interracial, intercultural and even international

relationships—it seems best to adopt as broad a term as possible: person-centered.[62]

After several years of working with this concept of the "person-centered" approach, Rogers wrote *Carl Rogers on Personal Power: Inner Strength and Its Revolutionary Impact,* published by Delacorte Press in 1977. (His name in the title was the publisher's idea.) In separate chapters, he explored the political dimensions of the person-centered approach in many fields: the helping professions, the family, marriage and partnerships, education, administration, working with the oppressed, and resolving intercultural tensions. As always, he included many case studies and examples of how people in all these areas of interest, in different countries, were able to achieve positive outcomes by empowering clients, students, staff, poor people, and groups in conflict to solve their own problems and make their own decisions in a facilitative climate characterized by genuineness, understanding, and trust. Another chapter explored a theoretical foundation for the person-centered approach: what Rogers called the *actualizing tendency* of all organisms to move toward their own enhancement and independence from external control. Several chapters discussed the person-centered approach in action.

In many ways, the book was Rogers' most complete statement to date of his philosophy. The person-centered approach was not simply an approach to therapy or teaching or any other particular relationships, but an approach to *all human relationships,* be they helping relationships, personal relationships, or political relationships. For this contribution, Richard Farson described Rogers as "a man whose cumulative effect on society has made him one of the most important social revolutionaries of our time."

One of the chapters in *On Personal Power* described a particular workshop format utilizing the person-centered approach. It had originated when Natalie Rogers, a therapist herself, expressed some regret to her father that they had never really worked together and suggested they do so. This evolved into a series of workshops, lasting for seven years, in which Rogers, Natalie, and a number of the CSP staff undertook to give participants an in-depth experience of the person-centered approach. The workshops were usually one to two weeks in length and had from sixty to several hundred participants, although about one hundred was a typical number. Originally, the workshop structure employed a variety of learning formats, with time blocks set aside for encounter groups, special interest groups, and relatively unstructured whole community meetings. The staff served as encounter group facilitators and also contributed to the special-interest sessions and community meetings. Rogers sometimes conducted a demonstration therapy session in front of the group or spoke about his work and recent interests.

Most of this initial workshop format was familiar to Rogers and the staff. The unusual piece was the group-centered community meetings, in which the staff did not attempt to set the direction for the group. The community meetings became, in effect, large-group encounter sessions. Eventually, after a period of confusion and some frustration, the large group seemed to develop a way of working— an organic, flexible structure that facilitated meaningful encounters, experiences, and learnings.

Intrigued with the power of these open-ended, large-group experiences, the staff gradually introduced less and less initial structure in subsequent workshops. Eventually all they did was convene the first community meeting, introduce themselves, and let the participants know that this workshop could be anything the community wished it to be. This left participants with the responsibility for meeting their own needs. One after another, and without much initial success, community members would try to get the group to participate in a particular activity, urge the community to adopt a new focus or format, ask for help on personal or professional issues, and ask—in fact, frequently *demand*—that the staff, particularly Rogers, play a more active role. This period of jockeying about, attempting to establish group purposes, leadership, and ways of working and being together would often go on for days. It produced enormous frustration, anger, and cognitive dissonance, as well as excitement, meaningful encounters, and deep personal learnings for many or most of the participants. Eventually the large group would find its collective voice and develop a way of working. This often involved establishing a time-structure that included encounter groups, special-interest groups, demonstrations, and the like. Once it was clear that the group had truly taken responsibility for its own direction, then Rogers and the staff felt comfortable sharing more of themselves as persons and professionals without having to worry that they would be taking the leadership back from the group.

Was all the *sturm und drang* worth it? Were all the hours and days of anguishing power struggles and soul searching necessary for participants to really understand the person-centered approach? The staff seemed to think so, believing that the *political* implications of the person-centered community experiences were critically important. Here were groups of sometimes several hundred individuals from different backgrounds, often different countries, demonstrating and experiencing the proposition that they could be trusted to organize their own living and learning structures. In one large group, an Israeli and a Palestinian participant had a powerful encounter, moving from deep anger and stereotyping to considerable understanding. Other groups saw similar, important rapprochments between blacks and whites, middle-class and working-class people, different nationalities and subgroups of all sorts, including between participants who wanted to have free time in the early afternoon and who wanted to have it in the late afternoon, and those who had been fighting for supremacy as though their lives depended on it. In all these situations, almost invariably, the group worked out their conflicts. In doing so without artificial rules and structures imposed from above, they developed a real sense of community, humanity, and affection that included a healthy respect for one another's differences. To Rogers and the staff, this was a powerful metaphor and model which needed to be demonstrated as widely as possible. Democracy, *real* democracy, works! For them, the open-ended, person-centered community became the epitome of learning structures and the logical extension of the person-centered approach.

Dozens of person-centered workshops were conducted around the United States and abroad by Rogers and the CSP staff, and through other projects that spun off from the La Jolla group. Rogers was involved, to differing degrees, in most of these spin-offs, such as the Center for Interpersonal Growth in New York and the Center for Cross-Cultural Communication in Europe. In some of the foreign countries, the political implications of the person-centered approach were even clearer. Brazil was not a real democracy in 1977, when Rogers and his colleagues convened three short workshops in Recife, Sao Paulo, and Rio de Janeiro. Some six to eight hundred people attended each. Speaking publicly about individual freedom, self-actualization, and self-determination was not typical in this society, and secret police were present at least one of the meetings. Even with the time delays of translation and interpretation, these workshops and others like them in Brazil had an enormous impact on the participants and, arguably, a subsequent impact on the society.

For all their potency, the strictly community-centered workshops did not catch on to any major degree. After a number of years, Rogers, the La Jolla group, and the Long Island group all virtually abandoned the model, although some of the CSP staffers continued to use it on occasion in their own projects. Rogers, in spite of his infatuation with the approach, eventually recognized that this extreme model of group-centeredness was not necessarily the most productive way of conducting large workshops. It was *one* valuable model, but not the only one. In fact, there was a continuum of choices as to how much structure to introduce in a person-centered learning experience. Approaching his eighties, Rogers came to prefer a modus operandi that was a little less volatile and which allowed him to share more of himself with groups. He developed a way of working that served him well throughout the rest of his life.

He still occasionally delivered formal presentations at conferences and sat on professional panels. Where possible, however, he much preferred a workshop format that was more typical of the initial person-centered workshops: an eclectic mix of presentations, demonstrations, whole-group interaction and, when feasible, small-group encounters. He typically conducted such workshops with one co-leader, although he occasionally joined the staff of a larger program someone else had organized. Whether the workshop topic was "An Introduction to the Person-Centered Approach," a favorite, or "Transitions" or "Education for the '80s and Beyond" or some other focus, the same basic elements tended to be present. Participants got to hear Rogers discussing the client-centered approach to helping relationships; they watched him conduct a live, unrehearsed therapeutic interview with a member of the audience; they experienced a bit of student-centered teaching or an encounter group in the way Rogers and his co-leader facilitated the discussion period; they heard about and perhaps experienced something of Rogers' work in applying the person-centered approach to intergroup and international problems; and perhaps they experienced a short version of a person-centered community.

This format seemed ideal for Rogers to communicate his ideas, his work, his current interests, and *himself*—a lifelong need which, if anything, seemed to increase in his final years. It was as though he had a sense of urgency about sharing the person-centered philosophy with a world that appeared to be teetering on the brink between self-destruction and self-actualization. From 1977 to 1985, aside from dozens of workshops and presentations he gave in the United States, Rogers traveled to Brazil three times, Mexico five times, Spain twice, England three times, Italy twice, Austria four times, West Germany three times; Finland, Venezuela, South Africa, Japan, Switzerland, Hungary, and Ireland to spread the person-centered approach. Many of these trips were several weeks in duration and involved two or more workshops in each country. He also made personal side trips to

China, Sweden, Kenya, and Zimbabwe. In 1986, at age eighty-four, he and his colleague Ruth Sanford undertook a four-week journey to South Africa, with person-centered workshops in Johannesburg and Capetown; a three-week trip to the Soviet Union, with two intensive workshops and several large, public meetings in Moscow and Tbilisi; and a week-long trip to Hungary for a workshop in Szeged, near Budapest.

In the South Africa workshops, Rogers and Sanford gave formal presentations. Rogers also conducted demonstration therapy session and a demonstration encounter group which, dramatically, included black, white, and colored South Africans—all before audiences of six hundred people! Again, in the Soviet Union, he spoke and demonstrated the person-centered approach before large audiences. In both countries, he and Sanford also involved the audience in extensive interaction and discussions, which at times followed a question-and-response format and at other times took on some of the characteristics of a person-centered community encounter. The risk he was taking was obvious to everyone. What if the client did not open up and begin to explore her feelings? What if the encounter group or the person-centered community went nowhere or, worse yet, blew up in an expression of hostility that could not be mitigated or resolved? Rogers, on stage in the enormous auditorium, appeared oblivious to such fears. Instead he attended with incredible focus, empathy, and concern to the client and her deepening expressions of feeling; or he sat with the audience, patiently accepting their various expressions of frustration or confusion, believing they would eventually recognize and experience the potency of the person-centered approach to learning and building community.

Even when the workshops were conducted through interpreters, participants were invariably moved to see Rogers at work. His ability to establish an immediate rapport with his client in therapy, to engender enough trust for encounter group participants to share meaningful feelings, and to reach a large audience with his personal style of presenting and responding to them were all impressive at any stage in his career. For this legend in psychology, now eighty-four years old, to have traveled halfway around the world to be with them and to share so much of himself was an experience they would never forget. Interest in Rogers, client-centered therapy, and the person-centered approach continued to grow on five continents as a result of his globe-trotting endeavors. "The impact we had on Soviet psychologists was profound," wrote Rogers. "I say that with some assurance, because many members of the Moscow workshop spoke publicly of their experience, two days after the workshop, to a most prestigious Scientific Council. To hear them tell others of the personal and professional changes resulting from the workshop was for me a magnificent reward."[63]

If Rogers was evangelizing during this period, it was not for the person-centered approach alone, although that was a big part of it. There was a larger cause. The older he was, and the more experience he had in facilitating communication and community among diverse groups, the more committed he became to reducing international and intergroup tensions and achieving world peace. His presentations and workshops—while still highlighting his ideas and methods for enhancing mental health, learning, and individual development—always returned to the importance of applying person-centered approaches to important social and world problems. These were not always theoretical propositions or small experimental attempts to demonstrate these principles by leading encounter groups, such as in Ireland or South Africa. In 1985, Rogers and his colleagues convened fifty international leaders in Austria, including the former president of Costa Rica and ambassadors, legislators, and high-level representatives of many countries, for a workshop on resolving problems in Central America. Using the person-centered community model, modified for the occasion, they did indeed help these leaders achieve real movement toward addressing important and complex issues. In the Soviet Union, just as Mikael Gorbachev was coming to power, Rogers' personal contact with high officials and his work with over two thousand Soviet professionals was another important step in the nongovernmental "citizen diplomacy" movement that was so important in encouraging and supporting Glastnost, the movement toward openness and democracy that dramatically altered Soviet and world history.

Rogers remained realistic about the net effect of his work toward conflict resolution and world peace. "I do not believe I deceive myself as to the significance of these efforts. Certainly we had no obvious influence on the total situation in any of these countries. But I derive much satisfaction from knowing that, on a small scale, we were able to demonstrate in each of these tension-filled groups, that meaningful dialogue could be established, that conflicts could be reduced, that a more realistic mutual understanding could emerge. We worked only on a test-tube scale, but we showed what was possible. Now the question is whether there is the social will to multiply these efforts."[64]

The question remains, but the work *was* noticed. For his latest efforts, and for a lifetime of work dedicated to fostering human understanding, Rogers was nominated in 1987 for the Nobel Prize for Peace.

In an essay entitled "Growing Old—Or Older and Growing," seventy-five-year-old Carl Rogers described the *previous* ten years as "the most satisfying decade of my life." Part of this stemmed from his considerable productivity, including five books, his leadership in the fields of encounter groups and education, and his beginning work on the political implications of the person-centered approach. But much of his satisfaction derived from more personal reasons: close collegial relationships, a growing closeness to his children and grandchildren, and deepening friendships with men and women—in short, intimacy. He wrote:

> In the past few years, I have found myself opening up to much greater intimacy in relationships. I see this development as definitely the result of workshop experiences. I am more ready to touch and be touched, physically. I do more hugging and kissing of both men and women. I am more aware of the sensuous side of my life. I realize how much I desire close psychological contact with others. I recognize how much I need to care deeply for another and to receive that kind of caring in return. I can say openly what I have always recognized dimly: that my deep involvement in psychotherapy was a cautious way of meeting this need for intimacy without risking too much of my person. Now I am more willing to be close in other relationships and to risk giving more of myself. I feel as though a whole new depth of capacity for intimacy has been discovered in me. This capacity has brought me much hurt, but an even greater share of joy.[65]

It also brought him "deeper and more intimate relationships with men" and with a number of women with whom I have, "platonic but psychologically intimate relationships." Only in his college days in Wisconsin had Rogers had such friendships with men, and never with women except for Helen. Now, he wrote, "With these close friends, men and women, I can share any aspect of my self—the painful, joyful, frightening, crazy, insecure, egotistical, self-deprecating feelings I have. I can share fantasies and dreams. Similarly, my friends share deeply with me. These experiences I find very enriching."[66] Similarly,

Carl and Helen's relationships with their children and grandchildren became increasingly open and close, including cleaning up some old hurts and "unfinished business" from their earlier years as a family, supporting David and Natalie through difficulties in their marriages, and sharing in the grandchildren's struggles and joys over identity, sexuality, and careers. Rogers wrote of the joy he and Helen felt over their children being "two of our best and closest friends, with whom we share our inner lives." Their golden wedding anniversary in 1974, which the whole family spent together in a resort setting, symbolized not so much the idealized picture of family stability and serenity, but of a commitment to share themselves as fully as possible with one another and, if that produced problems or hurt feelings, to deal openly with the consequences.

This commitment to ongoing growth and change was more difficult for Helen than for Rogers as they entered their seventies, when Helen's health began to deteriorate and she became more dependent on him. Although he recognized signs of aging in himself, including some arthritic pain and vision problems, Rogers remained in excellent health and good physical condition. The years were not as kind to Helen, who experienced a number of serious health problems and hospitalizations. At various times, Rogers took over a great deal of responsibility for her care, but beyond a certain point was unwilling to curtail his own professional activities and personal relationships. This produced considerable stress for them both. In 1977, Rogers wrote of Helen:

> She has met her pain and her restricted life with the utmost of courage. . . . She is making remarkable progress in fighting her way back, often by sheer force of will, to a more normal life, built around her own purposes. But it has not been easy. She first had to choose whether she wanted to live, whether there was any purpose in living. Then I have baffled and hurt her by the fact of my independent life. While she was so ill, I felt heavily burdened by our close togetherness, heightened by her need for care. So I determined, for my own survival, to live a life of my own. She is often deeply hurt by this, and by the changing of my values. On her side, she is giving up the old model of being the supportive wife. This change brings her in touch with her anger at me and at society for giving her that socially approved role. On my part, I am angered at any move that would put us back in

the old complete togetherness; I stubbornly resist
anything that seems like control. So there are more
tensions and difficulties in our relationship than ever
before, more feelings that we are trying to work through,
but there is also more honesty, as we strive to build new
ways of being together.[67]

Helen died peacefully in March of 1979, in the hospital, with
Carl, Natalie, and several close friends around her. In the period of
her dying, she and several people close to her had a number of experiences that left Rogers much more open to the possibilities of paranormal phenomena and some form of life after death. Living in
California, surrounded by many young people who were involved in
spiritual and psychic explorations, it was inevitable that Rogers
would be exposed to theories, anecdotes, and even experiments on
psychic phenomena. But as a scientist and agnostic, he had remained
skeptical and disinterested for many years. In his seventies, through
reading and close friends, he heard and personally observed some
occurrences that led him to wonder about there being "more things
under heaven and earth" than he had previously imagined. He even
wrote an essay entitled "Do We Need 'A' Reality?" in which he
explored how new advances in science and the experience of a number of writers raised some interesting questions about our normal view
of reality. But, on the whole, this area still held relatively little interest for him. Then, around Helen's death, some experiences occurred
which affected him more directly and intrigued him further. In
describing one such occasion, he wrote,

Helen was a great skeptic about psychic phenomena and
immortality. Yet, upon invitation, she and I visited a
thoroughly honest medium, who would take no money.
There, Helen experienced, and I observed, a "contact"
with her deceased sister, involving facts the medium
could not have possibly known. The messages were
extraordinarily convincing, and all came through the tip-
ping of a sturdy table, tapping out letters. Later, when the
medium came to our home and *my own table* tapped out
messages in our living room, I could only be open to an
incredible, and certainly nonfraudulent experience.[68]

Other highly unusual experiences occurred around this time and in subsequent years, but Rogers was reluctant to write about them. As a distinguished scientist himself, he knew full well how traditional science and the professions view paranormal phenomena. Whether psychic occurrences or life-after-death existed or not and, if they *did* exist, how to explain them were certainly of interest of him; but these matters were not among Rogers' priorities. He had no intention of undermining his professional contributions or international work by leaving himself, or Helen, or to ridicule. So, publicly, he shared only a brief anecdote or two, hinted that there might be more to come (which at some point there probably will), and left it at that.

However, a fresh nuance began to appear in Rogers' description of the therapeutic process. In his last years, Rogers spoke of the intuitive, transcendental, even spiritual aspects of the client-centered relationship. A bit earlier in his encounter group experiences, he had come to trust his intuition more. If he had a strong urge to put his arm around someone, even though they appeared to be saying, "Keep away from me," he might do so. If he suddenly had a fantasy of a participant sitting on a throne and wanting all the group members to be her subjects, he might voice that fantasy, not as the truth, but simply as his own fantasy. Very often these intuitive reactions turned out to unleash "a surprising depth of reaction and profound insights." He found himself trusting his intuition much more in small groups, in individual therapy, and in person-centered communities.

Trusting and expressing himself more than ever in therapy and group settings, he found himself often concentrating so fully on the other person, entering into the client's world with such deep empathy, that at times it felt as though he were hardly a separate person at all. Certainly on one level of consciousness he remained separate. But when he was most in tune with the other person, he, Rogers, no longer seemed to matter. He was not Carl Rogers *attempting to be empathic* with the other person. He was *with* this other person. It was as though they were so much on the same wavelength that they were no longer separate. He did not have to take a split second cognitively to frame his responses; his responses *happened.* But if he was not *willing* these empathic responses, where were they coming from? It was as though the words were coming on their own, as though some unseen force was working through him, as though he were the willing medium through which larger forces were working. Were he a more religious person, he might have credited some divine force or holy spirit for guiding his words. That was not Rogers' inclination;

still, he could not deny his *feeling* that something was happening here, at special moments in therapy and in intensive groups, which could not be fully explained by his previous formulations.

So he tried using other words to describe it, recognizing that while congruence, empathy, and unconditional positive regard "have been investigated and supported by research . . . recently my view has broadened into a new area that cannot as yet be studied empirically." He went the furthest in trying to capture this "one new characteristic" of a growth-promoting relationship in 1986, when he wrote, "When I am at my best . . . when I am closest to my inner, intuitive self, when I am somehow in touch with the unknown in me, when perhaps I am in a slightly altered state of consciousness in the relationship, then whatever I do seems to be full of healing. Then simply my *presence* is releasing and helpful. . . . At those moments it seems that my inner spirit has reached out and touched the inner spirit of the other. Our relationship transcends itself and becomes a part of something larger. Profound growth and healing and energy are present."[69]

He quoted a participant in a recent workshop who said, "I found it to be a profound spiritual experience. I felt the oneness of spirit in the community. We breathed together, felt together, even spoke for one another. I felt the power of the 'life force' that infuses each of us—whatever that is. I felt its presence without the usual barricades of 'me-ness' and 'you-ness'—it was like a meditative experience when I feel myself as a center of consciousness. And yet with that extraordinary sense of oneness, the separateness of each person present has never been more clearly preserved." Rogers then acknowledged, "I realize that this account partakes of the mystical. Our experiences, it is clear, invoke the transcendent, the indescribable, the spiritual. I am compelled to believe that I, like many others, have underestimated the importance of this mystical, spiritual dimension."

Intuitive . . . altered state of consciousness . . . inner spirit . . . mystical . . . transcendent . . . spiritual? Was this *Carl Rogers* speaking? Had he lost his objective marbles? Or had he finally come to his senses? Although these late-in-life changes or speculations of his were not widely known, reactions seem to reflect the bias of each commentator. The more scientifically inclined say, "Tsk, Tsk. As sharp as he may have remained in other respects, he sure went off the deep end on this score," while the more spiritually inclined breathe a sigh of relief and congratulate him for remaining open to new learning and for returning to his spiritual roots. Unfortunately, he never got to explore this new dimension in relationships much further. Whether it would have led to new insights and major contributions to various disciplines or whether it would have encouraged all sorts of pernicious practices in the name of healing cannot be known. In the end, perhaps it will be regarded as an interesting addendum to a long career, the value of that career remaining the same whatever one thinks of this last foray into new territory.

Helen Rogers' death in 1979 freed both partners: she from her physical suffering, he from the tension between meeting his independent professional and personal needs *and* remaining committed to Helen and their relationship. Their parting had been caring and complete. Now he was on his own again, for the first time in over half a century. Never really having ceased, he threw himself back into work and life with gusto. In his late seventies, he not only found that he still retained his great capacity for work but discovered new wells of energy for play and for relationships.

Rogers' remarkable travel schedule while working for conflict resolution around the world has been noted. He learned how to pace himself, taking time to relax in each country before and after his workshops and taking a couple of hours to rest each afternoon when he was working. Valerie Henderson, a younger CSP associate, recalled, "When we would come back from a trip, I'd be exhausted while he'd bounce right back and be ready to start again."[70] He also continued to write, although failing eyesight made this more difficult. In 1980, Houghton Mifflin published Rogers' fifteenth and final book, *A Way of Being,* a collection of essays touching on the various subjects that had interested him in recent years.

He also *played* a great deal more. This included travel, always a great love. Typically he added days or weeks to each international workshop to sightsee and travel in the host and neighboring countries. He also prized and took time to be with his many close friends in La Jolla and elsewhere. The professional and personal relationships with his CSP colleagues and others continued to nourish him intellectually and emotionally, as they had for years—helping him to remain on the cutting edge professionally and to enjoy life more fully than ever. He even stopped protesting about people making a fuss over his birthday. He wrote, "a large group of friends came to my home, bringing food, drink, songs, and surprises to celebrate my seventy-eighth birthday. It was a wild, wonderful, hilarious party—with love, caring, fellowship, and happiness—which I will never forget."[71] At his eighty-fifth birthday, celebrated with scores of friends who had rented a hall for the occasion, he basked unabashedly in their many expressions of affection and, visibly moved, responded to them, "There isn't anything I could possibly say to all this, except *I feel very much loved. I* thank you. Thank you."[72]

Loving and being loved were a major theme of Rogers' final years. In his essay on "Growing Old—Or Older and Growing," discussing the physical changes he experienced at seventy-five, Rogers had written, "I feel as sexual in my *interests* as I was at thirty-five, though I can't say the same about my ability to perform. I am delighted that I am still sexually alive, even though I can sympathize with the remark of Supreme Court Justice Oliver Wendell Holmes upon leaving a burlesque house at age eighty: 'Oh to be seventy again!'"[73] As it turned out, Rogers' identification with Justice Holmes' wistful remark was premature. In an addendum to the same essay, written after Helen's death, he added, "As the year drew to a close, I was increasingly aware of my capacity for love, my sensuality, my sexuality. I have found myself fortunate in discovering and building relationships in which these needs can find expression. There has been pain and hurt, but also joy and depth."[74]

This brief description only hinted at the whole picture, intentionally and appropriately so. After getting married as a virgin and now single again, following almost fifty-five years of monogamy, Rogers had joined the younger generation. At age seventy-eight, he developed intimate, loving, sexual relationships with three women and maintained all three relationships *simultaneously* for the next six or seven years. They were older, mature, professional women who understood and accepted the situation and cherished their relationship with Rogers, as he did with them. Finding time with each of them, around some of his road trips and on their periodic visits to La Jolla, he managed to maintain each partnership as a discrete, discreet, and precious relationship.

When Rogers had described the previous decade as the most satisfying of his life, little could he foresee what lay ahead in the next one. His letters to friends in the 1980s, which often included the line "I'm having a great time," barely conveyed the reality. His work, his family, his love relationships, and his friendships were all giving him the deepest satisfaction. But this did not simply occur on its own, as a reward for having lived a good life. He continued to work and stretch himself to make it happen. Whether conducting therapeutic interviews before audiences of hundreds of professionals around the world, or bringing hostile groups together to reduce international and intergroup tensions, or trying to maintain honest and intimate relationships in his personal life, he remained a pioneer and a risk-taker until the end.

A few weeks past his eighty-fifth birthday, after a long work session, Rogers suggested to his companion that they go to Las Vegas for the weekend, just for the fun of it. He had never been there; in fact, he had shunned that kind of glitz all his life. But, now, he thought it might be fun to see what it was all about. So they went. They visited the nightclubs, danced, gambled a bit, and had a grand time. Later, back in La Jolla, they put on a phonograph album and sang show tunes together. In the middle of the night, Rogers fell on the way to the bathroom and was rushed to the hospital with a broken hip. He came through the operation fine, but the next night suffered a heart attack and went into a coma. He often said he did not fear death but did fear a long, undignified dying. Following his wishes, artificial life support systems were disconnected after three days, on February 4, 1987. Carl Rogers died with family and loved ones around him.

A prediction he had affirmed ten years earlier had come true. "As a boy," he wrote, "I was rather sickly, and my parents have told me that it was predicted I would die young. This prediction has been proven completely wrong in one sense, but has come profoundly true in another sense. I think it is correct that I will never live to be old. So now I agree with the prediction: I believe that I will die *young*."[75]

References

[1] Rogers, C. R. Autobiography. In Boring, E. G. and Hilgard, E. (Eds.). *A history of psychology through autobiography, Vol. 3*. Reading, MA: Addison-Wesley, 1965, p. 344.

[2] Interview between Wesley Westman and Carl R. Rogers, September 15, 1962, unpublished.

[3] Interview between Howard Kirschenbaum and Carl R. Rogers, March 1971, unpublished.

[4] Reference 1, p. 347.

[5] Rogers, C. R. Diary, unpublished.

[6] Rogers, C. R. Diary, unpublished.

7 Rogers, C. R. *China diary,* February 25, 1922, unpublished.

8 Reference 7, April 10, 1922.

9 Reference 1, p. 351.

10 Reference 1, p. 353.

11 Rogers, C. R. *The clinical treatment of the problem child.* Boston: Houghton Mifflin, 1939, p. 5.

12 Rogers, C. R. *On becoming a person.* Boston: Houghton Mifflin, 1961, p. 11.

13 Rogers, C. R. and Hart, J. T. A conversation with Carl Rogers, August 5, 1966. In Hart, J. T. and Tomlinson, T. M. (Eds.). *New Directions in Client-Centered Therapy.* Boston: Houghton Mifflin, 1970, p. 515.

14 Reference 1, p. 361.

15 Rogers, C. R. *Counseling and psychotherapy: Newer concepts in practice.* Boston: Houghton Mifflin, 1942.

16 Rogers, C. R. Mike. Taped interview. Philadelphia, PA: American Academy of Psychotherapists.

17 Reference 15, pp. 28–30.

18 Rogers, C. R. Remarks on the future of client-centered therapy. Presented at a symposium on the future of client-centered therapy, American Psychological Association, September 1964.

19 Seeman, J., personal communication, April 1972.

20 Reed, R., personal communication, November 10, 1971.

21 Vargas, M., personal communication, May 1971.

22 Cartwright, R., personal taped communication, May 1971.

23 Brice, N., personal communication, April 13, 1972.

24 Rogers, C. R. The attitude and orientation of the counselor in client-centered therapy. *Journal of Consulting Psychology,* 1949, *13,* p. 82.

25 Rogers, C. R., A current formulation of client-centered therapy. *Social Service Review,* 24, 1950, p. 443.

26 Reference 24, p. 84.

27 Reference 25, p. 444.

28 Rogers, C. R. and Dymond, R. F. (Eds.). *Psychotherapy and personality change.* Chicago: University Press, 1954, p. 313.

29 Seeman, J. A study of the process of nondirective therapy. *Journal of Consulting Psychology,* 13, 1949, 157–168.

30 Rogers, C. R. *Client-centered therapy: Its current practices, implications, and theory.* Boston: Houghton Mifflin, 1951, 384.

31 Reference 30, pp. 483–517.

32 Reference 1, p. 367.

[33] Rogers, C. R. Client-centered therapy: A current view. In Fromm-Reichmann, F. and Moreno, J. L. (Eds.). *Progress in psychotherapy.* New York: Grune and Stratton, 1956, pp. 199–200.

[34] Rogers, C. R. The necessary and sufficient conditions of therapeutic personality change. *Journal of Consulting Psychology,* 21, 1957, p. 98.

[35] Fiedler, F. E. A comparison of therapeutic relationships in psychoanalytic, nondirective and Adlerian therapy. *Journal of Consulting Psychology,* 14, 1950, 436–45.

[36] Fiedler, F. E. Factor analyses of psychoanalytic, nondirective and Adlerian therapeutic relationships. *Journal of Consulting Psychology,* 15, 1951, 32–38.

[37] Reference 30, p. 55.

[38] Rogers, C. R. Recent research in nondirective therapy and its implications. *American Journal of Orthopsychiatry,* 16, 1946, p. 588.

[39] Rogers, C. R. A coordinated research in psychotherapy: A nonobjective introduction. *Journal of Consulting Psychology,* 13, 1949, 152.

[40] Alexander, T., taped interview with Howard Kirschenbaum, May 1971, unpublished.

[41] Gendlin, E. personal communication, May 1971.

[42] Reference 34, p. 96.

[43] Reference 34, pp. 100–101.

[44] Rogers, C. R. A process conception of psychotherapy. *American Psychologist,* 13 1958, 142–149.

[45] Rogers, C. R. A note on "the nature of man." *Journal of Counseling Psychology,* 4, 1957, 220–201.

[46] Kirschenbaum, H., and Henderson, V. (Eds.). *Carl Rogers: Dialogues.* Boston: Houghton Mifflin, 1989.

[47] Rogers, C. R. Significant aspects of client-centered therapy. *American Psychologist,* 1, 1946, 422.

[48] Rogers, C. R., and Skinner, B. F. (1962). Dialogue on education and the control of human behavior. See reference 46, p. 132.

[49] Rogers, C. R. A tentative scale for the measurement of process in psychotherapy. In Rubinstein, E. A. and Parlof, M. B. (Eds.). *Research in psychotherapy.* Washington, DC: American Psychological Association, 1959.

[50] Gendlin, E. T. *Experiencing and the creation of meaning.* New York: The Free Press of Glencoe, 1962; Gendlin, E. T. *Focusing.* New York: Bantam Books, 1978.

[51] Coulson, W. R., and Rogers, C. R. (Eds.). *Man and the science of man.* Columbus, OH: Charles E. Merrill, 1968, p. 5.

[52] Rogers, C. R. *On encounter groups.* New York: Harper and Row, 1970, p. 1.

53 From an advertising flyer for Carl Rogers and Richard Farson's filmed encounter group, "Journey Into Self," 1968.

54 Reference 52, p. 109.

55 McGaw, W. H. (Director). "Because That's My Way," a taped encounter group produced by station WQED, Pittsburgh.

56 Roger, C. R. Some personal thoughts on teaching and learning. *Merrill Palmer Quarterly,* 3, 1957, 241–243.

57 Rogers, C. R. *Freedom to learn: A view of what education might become.* Columbus, OH: Charles E. Merrill, 1969, p. 5.

58 Rogers, C. R. *Freedom to learn for the '80s.* Columbus, OH: Charles Merrill, 1983, p. 197.

59 Rogers, C. R. From a typed page in his files, entitled "Grass Roots Contacts," unpublished, undated.

60 Anonymous. Unpublished letter, October 17, 1970.

61 Rogers, C. R. Some social issues which concern me. *Journal of Humanistic Psychology,* 12, 1972, 2, 45–60.

62 Rogers, C. R. *Carl Rogers on personal power.* New York: Delacorte Press 1977, pp. 4–5.

63 Rogers, C. R. On reaching 85. *Person-Centered Review 2:* 2, May 1987, p. 151.

64 Reference 63, pp. 151–52.

65 Rogers, C. R. Growing old: Or older and growing. In Rogers, *A Way of Being.* Boston: Houghton Mifflin, 1980, pp. 83–84.

66 Reference 65, p. 84.

67 Reference 65, pp. 85–86.

68 Reference 65, p. 90.

69 Rogers, C. R. A client-centered/person-centered approach to therapy. In Kutash, I. and Wolf, A. (Eds.). *Psychotherapist's casebook.* Jossey-Bass, 1986, pp. 198–99. Also in Kirschenbaum, H., and Henderson, V. (Eds.). *The Carl Rogers Reader.* Boston: Houghton Mifflin, 1989, pp. 137–138.

70 Henderson, V. Phone interview with Howard Kirschenbaum, December 14, 1991.

71 Reference 65, p. 95.

72 From a videotape shown at the memorial service for Carl Rogers, at Sherwood Auditorium, La Jolla (CA) Museum, February 21, 1987.

73 Reference 65, p. 71.

74 Reference 65, p. 95.

75 Reference 65, p. 89.

Author's Note

I was prepared to write a typical, short, third–person "About the Author" blurb to accompany my biographical chapter on Carl Rogers, when Mel Suhd, the editor, asked me to undertake a more personal essay. I questioned him on this, suggesting that the readers would not care about me and my life, but rather would only be interested in what I had to say about Carl Rogers. He disagreed, saying that readers are interested in the person behind the keyboard, that my relationship with Carl is relevant to the theme of the book and, besides, I was a "notable" in my own right. Sensing that his flattery was working, he gave me free reign to tell my own story as I saw fit, or to describe my relationship with Carl Rogers, or to do both. He even generously allotted me five pages for the endeavor. Against my better judgment, I proceeded. l just want to go on record that this was Mel's idea.

My first exposure to Carl Rogers was as a doctoral student at Temple University in 1969. I found his short, radical essay on "Some Personal Thoughts on Teaching and Learning" to be stunning. It appealed to every iconoclastic bone in my body and immediately led me to read *On Becoming a Person* and the just-published *Freedom To Learn*. Enchanted with Rogers, personally and professionally, I wanted to know more about the man and his work and wondered if there were a biography. Discovering that there was not, the idea struck me to write Rogers' biography myself, both for its own sake and to serve as my doctoral dissertation. I immediately sat down and wrote, "Dear Dr. Rogers, My name is Howard Kirschenbaum, and I would like to write your biography."

I was that son of brash young man. Raised by loving, intelligent, liberal, middle-class parents in Long Beach, New York, I was a relatively indulged member of my generation. My mother's unconditional positive regard gave me an enormous reservoir of self-esteem, while my father's more conditional acceptance and high but fair standards led me to feel the necessity to achieve in order to feel good about myself. So I achieved—Eagle Scout, A-student, summer jobs, sports, senior class president, you name it. I ended high school with the belief that I personally could do most anything I wanted in this world, the objectivity to recognize that many were not so fortunate, and the compassion to care.

Where could such attitudes lead a young person, coming of age and attending college in the early sixties? I became deeply involved in the civil rights movement—for all the good and altruistic reasons, along with a measure of rebellion, self-righteousness, and search for identify. My first arrest occurred when I was a sophomore at John Hopkins University in Baltimore, when we attempted to integrate a roller-skating rink in Catonsville, Maryland. The second was in Mississippi in 1964, the day after our coworkers Goodman, Schwerner, and Chaney were murdered by the Klan. In my junior and senior years at the New School for Social Research, in New York City, organizing against the Vietnam War became a major focus of my energies, as well as studying literature.

Becoming a teacher, for me, seemed a good way to further the cause of peace and justice. I wanted to encourage young people to move beyond middle-class complacency and materialism and become involved in the great social movements of the day, to help build participatory democracy at home and around the world. As a future teacher, I was inspired by Sidney Simon and Merrill Harmin, two leaders in the new "values clarification" movement in education. We became friends and colleagues; and while earning a masters degree in education at Temple University and teaching high school English and history for three years, I began working with them, leading workshops and writing professional articles for educational journals. Wanting to pursue my career as a teacher, educator, and consultant, I returned to Temple for a doctoral program in educational psychology.

By the time I wrote to Carl Rogers, then, to inquire about writing his biography, I was able to send along several articles I had coauthored, as well as the manuscript by Sid Simon, Rodney Napier, and me of the forthcoming book *Wad-Ja-Get? The Grading Game In American Education.* Rogers wrote back that, although he had received a few such inquires before in which he had not been interested, he would consider cooperating with me on such a project. That summer of 1970, I drove out to La Jolla to meet him. We hit it off, and he agreed to work with me. His help consisted of spending many hours with me in taped interviews about his life and work, providing complete access to his files, allowing me to accompanying him to various workshops and meetings and writing a cover letter that I sent to hundreds of his former students, colleagues, family, and friends, soliciting their letters, tapes, and reminiscences about Rogers. The next year I completed my doctoral course work, did my library research on Rogers, and then moved to the Adirondack Mountains in upstate New York.

I bought and lived in a cabin in the woods, with no phone or electricity, a mile from the closest neighbor. It was here that I planned to finish my dissertation, while simultaneously founding what came to be called the National Humanistic Education Center at a nearby farm that Sid Simon and I purchased for that purpose. By now I was more deeply involved in consulting and writing, not only in the area of values education, but also human relations training, affective education, personal growth workshops, and other approaches that were sometimes grouped under the umbrella of "humanistic education." I became deeply involved in leading workshops and consulting all around North America (and eventually Sweden, Venezuela, Israel, Australia, Philippines, etc.), publishing *The Humanistic Education Quarterly,* and establishing a mail-order clearinghouse of materials in the field. Over the following six years, I kept working on the dissertation and biography, but only sporadically, sandwiched as it was between eight new books, mostly coauthored, including *Values Clarification: A Handbook of Practical Strategies for Teachers and Students,* which sold 600,000 copies; *Developing Support Groups;* and *Skills for Living,* a 300-page curriculum used with over a million high school students nationwide. I also cut up trees that fell across our road and, if no one else was around, fixed broken toilets at our sixty-person conference center in Upper Jay, New York. I was a whiz with a magic marker, newsprint, chain saw, and monkey wrench.

My consulting trips often provided good occasions to interview family and associates of Rogers in far-flung places around the country. Throughout the seventies, I stayed in touch with Carl: visiting him in La Jolla; meeting him at a conference in Montreal, where he had given a keynote address to the Association for Humanistic Psychology, and driving him to our cabin in the woods, where he spent the night and the next day addressed a group at the conference center; reading the articles and manuscripts he regularly sent me; and checking out factual questions with him as I worked on the biography. I eventually finished the 600-page dissertation on "Carl Rogers: A Case Study of a Psychologist and Educator" and received my doctoral degree in 1975. I then continued to revise and shorten the manuscript for trade publication.

If I had followed Thoreau's example and "moved to the woods to live deliberately," it did not quite turn out as planned. Outgrowing our first conference center, we located a new facility in the southwestern Adirondacks. Sagamore Lodge and Conference Center was the former vacation estate of the Alfred Vanderbilt family. It had accommodations for a hundred guests, exceptional rustic architecture (including bark-covered exteriors and twenty-five fireplaces), meeting rooms, a two-lane covered bowling alley, a tennis court, and was the only property on a mile-long lake, surrounded by state-owned wilderness. The very first event we held at Sagamore, in the summer of 1977, was a workshop on the "Person-Centered Approach," led by Carl and six of his colleagues from Center for Studies of the Person. The week-long staff preparation and the two-week workshop gave me another three weeks of close contact with Carl and with Helen Rogers, who accompanied him, and with Natalie Rogers, who was one of the workshop leaders. I got to experience the *sturm und drang* of a 100-person, person-centered workshop as both a participant and an innkeeper, witnessing the staff and participants' personal and interpersonal dynamics at all hours: in sessions, in the dining room, and in the sleeping quarters. This was particularly helpful, as I was just finishing up the biography, which was published as *On Becoming Carl Rogers* by Delacorte/Delta Press in 1979.

A few months after we purchased Sagamore, the former J. P. Morgan family estate, a slightly smaller version of Sagamore, on its own secluded lake nearby, came up for sale. For a number complicated reasons, it, like Sagamore, cost the equivalent of a typical suburban home at the time, although the value of both increased tenfold in ensuing years. As the owner or director of two major Adirondack "Great Camps," as they are known, both listed on the National Register of Historic Places, I gradually began an entirely new vocation in the field of historic preservation. It has involved leading two extensive political campaigns, including amending the New York state constitution, to save two important historic sites in the Adirondacks; founding and serving as president of the nonprofit Adirondack Architectural Heritage organization; creating and directing a living history museum; serving as board member of the Adirondack Nature Conservancy and. Adirondack Land Trust; and other nonprofit and entrepreneurial ventures related to environmental conservation and historic preservation in an area as large as the state of Massachusetts. But that's another story.

Although I cut back somewhat on my professional activities in the 1980s, I continued to write and consult on a regular basis. From 1981 to 1984, I organized and served as executive director of the National Coalition for Democracy in Education, a federation of a dozen organizations (with forty thousand members) and a thousand individual members who joined together to respond to some of the fundamentalist right-wing attacks on church–state separation, public education in general, and humanistic education in particular. Carl was fully supportive of this project. lending his name and contributing financially to it.

One year I visited him in California and, at a time when he felt inundated with and burdened by commitments, persuaded him to take a day off, just for the fun of it. We drove out to the new San Diego animal park (a rural extension of the famous zoo) and spent the day enjoying the animals, the drive, and one another's company. It was the closest I ever felt to being Carl's friend, as opposed to his biographer or geographically distant colleague. In 1985, he and Ruth Stanford led a week-long workshop at Sagamore on "Education for the 1980s and Beyond," in which I assisted in a limited staff capacity.

On January 20, 1987, Carl wrote and invited me to work with him on editing a "Carl Rogers Reader," a collection of articles and book chapters spanning his life's work. He wrote, "I think of you because you have in the past had such close familiarity with all of my work— more so than any other one person—and also because you have a sufficient distance from my work that you are probably less biased than some might be." Returning from a two-week trip, on February 5, I immediately wrote Carl that I would be delighted to work with him on this project. I did not know that he had died the night before.

With Natalie and David Rogers' support, Valerie Henderson (a close associate of Carl) and I went on to edit two volumes of Rogers' work: *The Carl Rogers Reader* and *Carl Rogers: Dialogues,* the latter being a collection of his personal dialogues or correspondence with some of the leading intellectual figures of the twentieth century—

Martin Buber, Paul Tillich, B. F. Skinner, Gregory Bateson, Rollo May, and Reinhold Niebuhr. When the published copies arrived from Houghton Mifflin and I sat down with pleasure and excitement to peruse my latest books, I felt a wave of horror and mortification as I read the first sentence of our introduction to *The Reader:* "Carl Ransom Rogers (1902–1987) was the most influential psychologist in American history." It was supposed to say "influential *psychotherapist.*" To this day, I don't know how that embarrassing error occurred. Carl was certainly *one* of the most influential psychologists, but to suggest that he was *the* most influential is a bit of a stretch.

In recent years, in addition to occasionally lecturing or presenting short workshops on Carl Rogers' life and work, I have become more involved in my earlier field of values and moral education. Times have changed, and many of us have grown and matured over the years. While I believe as strongly as ever that young people must be given the opportunity and skills to think for themselves and clarify their own values, I also recognize the importance of parents', educators', and other adults' teaching and modeling basic moral and civic values for our youth. My latest book, *One Hundred Ways To Enhance Values and Morality in the Schools and Youth Settings,* published by Allyn and Bacon, presents a practical model for combining traditional approaches to teaching values and morality with contemporary approaches for helping young people learn the skills and values for responsible autonomy. I have also begun to teach graduate courses on the subject at the State University of New York at Brockport and, to get back in closer touch with teenagers today, I taught a semester course on "American Values" in one of the Rochester, New York public high schools.

So at this stage of life, at forty-eight, with a wide array of professional and personal interests, I am not sure which of several directions I will pursue in the years ahead. I take each new book or course or project as it comes, or as I conceive it—trying to say yes to those options that will feel satisfying and enjoyable to me and hopefully be of some use to others. I look forward to just about every day, whether it involves writing on the word processor, attending a meeting, giving a lecture, or renovating an historic building. I am comfortable living this way, which Carl once described as letting "the flow of my experience carry me, in a direction which appears to be forward, toward goals of which I am but dimly aware."

Perhaps less relevant to this essay, but just as important to me, has been the personal side of my life. This has included: a cherished relationship with my parents, now in their eighties, and our large extended family; a first marriage of ten years with many valued memories; the adoption and raising of a wonderful daughter. now fifteen; a divorce; and a very happy remarriage of ten years, with a fine expanded family in the bargain. Now I move back and forth between *two* homes in the woods: the secluded, lakeside, log home in the Adirondacks; and a secluded house adjoining a large wild park, only fifteen minutes from downtown Rochester. I feel very grateful for it all.

While the foregoing autobiographical sketch conveys an overview of my *association* with Carl Rogers, it barely reveals our *relationship*. As Rogers' biographer, it has been a privilege to have had scores of people who knew him over the years discuss their relationship to him with me. In many cases, former students and colleagues have used this occasion as an opportunity to clarify unresolved feelings or unfinished business in their association with Carl. One such individual, a successful psychologist in his own right, shared with me a long and detailed account of how Rogers failed to be as warm and interested in him as he felt their relationship warranted. A part of my response to him, with a little editing, begins to explore my relationship with Carl and Carl's relationships with others.

"It didn't surprise me to hear how a series of attempts to get closer to Carl over the years met with politeness, cordiality, and a solidly distancing wall. Nor was I really surprised at how Rogers did not, in rejecting your overtures, offer counterproposals of his own. Without defending him, I think, especially in the last fifteen years or so, he has come to feel he doesn't owe anybody a particular response. If he's not interested in meeting your family at that moment, he'll politely decline and that's that. He has plenty to do—many projects, a good number of friends, hobbies; he's really quite self-sufficient— so he has no particular desire to offer to get together on another occasion. That's got to offend, hurt, and disappoint people, sometimes mildly, sometimes deeply. When Rogers is cooler to people than they would like, there is a tendency to conclude that he is at fault, that he's not doing right by them, that he's not being 'Rogerian' or 'humanistic,' that maybe he is not all he purports to be.

"Let me explore this a little further. I get mixed messages from Carl. Sometimes he communicates to me that he really cares for me, likes me, appreciates me and my work, is a real friend and colleague. Sometimes I feel treated as though I'm only a business associate, a biographer, who is answered politely, yet from a distance. I think both are true, although paradoxical. I mean, how can I be a close friend, an intimate, one month and a mere professional associate the next?

It would seem that if he really regards me as a friend in January, he'll feel the same way in February.

"I have two responses to my own wonder about this. One is that I've gotten to know him relatively late in his life, and I think he has less of a stake now in being consistent. He's more comfortable in going with his present moods. I don't think he even remembers previous contacts and conversations with a person over time as well as he used to (he can still listen brilliantly in the moment). So this is a combination of aging, and trying to be congruent, and not feeling like he has to be consistent in order to maintain a particular image.

"The other factor, I think, is that I and others come to expect an affective expression on his part all the time, in every conversation or letter. Yet there are many times when he simply wants to answer a question or send me something, and that's all he's focused on then. So I might just as well be a stranger writing to him; I would get the same sort of response. I can accept that, because I look at the big picture and realize that through his actions, through the time he has often taken in writing to or being with me, in his financial contributions to my various causes, in a lovely unsolicited gift he once sent me, that he damn well *is* communicating to me that he values me and my work; lest why would he give up his valuable time for it? I think to some extent that could be said about your relationship with him, too; his letters of recommendation and his intellectually engaging correspondence with you must have indicated his care and respect for you at one point. Then time and distance made your relationship less important to him. Still later, trying to analyze or figure out where your relationship went wrong probably wasn't important to him at all, although it was to you.

"I know many people who are still trying to come to terms with their experience with and feelings about Carl. In spite of all the positive things they report about his humanity and effectiveness, they still have an unresolved issue, a hurt feeling or two, perhaps even a wonder, as you expressed it, whether Carl's 'personality may have a basic flaw' which might explain whatever was unsatisfying about their relationship with him.

"I don't think so. Most of all, I think of Carl as being very human. Some days he's hot, some days cool. He's got lots going on, and depending on the day will respond warmly or more businesslike. As I look over his letters to me, his closing line varies from 'Affectionately' to 'Cordially,' from 'Hastily' to 'Love.' I much prefer love to cordiality, and I could confront him and ask for more; but frankly, I don't think he gives a damn. I love him as he is. My fantasy is, if I asked him about you, he'd say: 'Oh, yeah, ———. Nice guy. Bright. Seems to me he had some feelings about me and our relationship that he was never quite able to work out.' And there would be a tone of acceptance rather than evaluation in his voice. I suspect that when we can accept ourselves, then we can accept Carl for who he is —pretty much the person that meets the eye—a good and caring man, who has a great deal to give to others and who also has learned to take care of himself."

I'm not exactly sure why it was easy for me to accept Carl as he was. It helped that, by the time I got to know him, he had become more congruent and therefore, to me, more real. If he was angry he said so, and that was that. When I neglected to return some photographs to him in a timely manner, he wrote to me, "I want those albums returned! It troubles me a good deal that I don't hear from you about that," then went on to another matter, then signed off "Affectionately, Carl." If he was tired, he got up and said he was going to bed. If he was ready for a change of venue, or topic, he said so. If, occasionally, he felt like referring to somebody as a jerk—strong language for him—he would. Never to the person's face, of course, and he didn't really mean to dismiss anyone so thoroughly. If he met the person, he would be genuinely humane and empathic; it just felt good to blow off some steam or momentary frustration. At one time he would not have allowed himself that luxury. Now he let himself be human.

I remember the first time I met him, at Carl and Helen's home in La Jolla. I was a young whipper-snapper, hoping he would consent to assist me in writing his biography. Helen was occupied, so I first met with Carl for forty-five minutes in his study. Then we rejoined Helen, and Carl gave her an impressive summary of all that I had said to him. I remember thinking, with amazement, "My god, this man is an incredible listener!" Then I laughed at myself for being so surprised; after all, that was why I was there.

He *was* an incredible listener, but there was nothing superhuman about it. I was an excellent listener, too. All of Carl's outstanding qualities were readily accessible to me and others. He was a fine person— caring, considerate, honest, intelligent, committed. If he was more so than most of us in these respects, it was only a difference of degree, not of quality. As far as I was concerned, that was his genius: he explained in his writings and demonstrated in his personal and professional example the best qualities of being which we all have within us. There was nothing esoteric about Carl. What you saw was what you got, and what you were capable of yourself.

He wasn't perfect, of course. In spite of his genuine humility, I often thought his ego was quite tied up in his work and his accomplishments. I sometimes found him old-fashioned and quirky. He was uninterested in some new developments in psychology and education that I thought he should have shown an interest in. I thought he sometimes oversimplified and was naive. He sometimes appeared to forget things he told me previously. So what's new? All this confirmed that he was human. Whether these characteristics could in some objective sense be termed "flaws," or whether he simply failed to meet my expectations one hundred percent of the time, my conclusion was the same. So what? Who *is* perfect? Who *does* meet our expectations all the time? If we held to that standard, there would be no heroes, no one to admire.

Not that Carl was a hero to me. Heroes are bigger than life, while Carl's dimensions were quite human. He was neither a guru nor a demigod, but rather a fine *model,* an excellent *example,* then and now. He occupies one part of my conscience. When I am trying hard to be true to myself, I sometimes think of Carl. When I am wondering about the pros and cons of the scientific method and experimental research to help further some work I am interested in, I think of Carl and his involvement with research. When I am wondering how long I will have the energy and vigor to keep on being a change agent, or an activist, or a pioneer, I think of Carl at sixty-five . . . and seventy-five . . . and eighty-five.

To the extent I had worked through emotional issues and developed a positive relationship with my own father; to the extent that my experiences participating in and leading human relations groups and doing counseling had taught me that all people—even famous ones—are vulnerable human beings; to the extent I had come to accept and like myself; to that extent, I was able to understand and accept Carl for who he was. Just as he accepted me for who I was, I accepted and cherished him.

✛

When I first met Maureen O'Hara, she had just been elected president of the Association for Humanistic Psychology. She followed the tenure of Liz Campbell, who had set the stage for changing the organization's image. In two short years under Maureen and Liz, AHP came to life as a truly androgenous institution dedicated to expanding humanistic psychology to include the diversity its name implies.

Maureen is a genius who also knows how to interact with her peers and to share center stage. She is prolific, capable of handling a number of projects at the same time. I find her to be a warm, effervescent person. We immediately established a sister–brother relationship that continues to enrich my life. She is also a brilliant writer whose works will continue to expand our understanding of social, political, and humanistic thought.

✛

2

Streams

On Becoming a Postmodern Person

by Maureen O'Hara

For years, whenever I wrote a resumé I would have the uneasy sensation of writing about more than one person. When anyone asked me to write an autobiographical statement, I would need to know the purpose of it so I could choose which "me" to write about. As I face this task now, my experience is different. I have a greater sense of inner coherence than I have ever had, and I have increasing clarity about such issues as identity, self, and being. It is not, however, the sort of coherence I searched for during my early days in psychology—not the perfectly integrated, self-actualized, focused, "personhood" promised by either of the two systems of psychotherapy I adopted for my work: client-centered theory and Gestalt therapy theory. Rather, my sense of psychological coherence comes from understanding my life in terms of the contexts, relationships, connections, commitments, and passions that I inhabit and that inhabit me, woven or cobbled together into a grand, ever-changing quilt or collage. I will get to how that happened a little later. First the basics.

I was born in 1943 in Shipley, Yorkshire, a small wool town in the industrial north of England. My parents, Ethel and Jim, were both from families that had eked out an existence at the very bottom of the economic scale. Dad had picked coal from the railway tracks as a boy and worked in unskilled jobs as an adult. Because her sister had become ill, my mother had been pulled from a very good British grammar school to enter domestic service at fourteen. Even though she was a survivor and made the best of her lot, she has always grieved the loss of a life of the mind. Her loss drove her insistence that my life would be different. Even if it meant working herself to the edge of endurance, she would find the money to keep me in school.

My brother was eight years older. Even though our age difference meant we were never really friends, nonetheless I adored him. When he went to do his National Service as a sailor at eighteen, I cried for weeks at the loss of my first love.

My earliest memory reveals a great deal about my temperament. I was two years old and going to nursery school on the bus for the first time. The school bus arrived, a big blue double-decker trolley full of wriggling, screaming kids. For an instant I was poised between the security of my mother's grasp and the excitement and drama of the teeming trolley. I pulled my hand from hers and leapt onto the bus, ready for anything.

I excelled all through primary school, especially in science. I was always the class monitor, prefect, teacher's helper, that sort of thing. By age eleven, I had earned entrance to one of England's direct-grant grammar schools, an elite private school founded in the 1600s at which local authorities made available a few scholarships for very bright poor children.

I had a harder time of it there. Standards were higher and the school culture was mercilessly class-conscious. From the first day, I was singled out, humiliated in public, and taunted by classmates for the ways in which my vocabulary, dress, limited cultural knowledge, and even posture signified my "non U" (not upperclass) origins.

Interestingly—and significantly—absent from the school was one dimension of prejudice: sexism. An all-female faculty covered subjects from physics to domestic science to engineering to languages, creating the sense in my young mind that women could excel and succeed in any area that tickled their fancy. By the time I learned that this was not the opinion of most of the rest of the world, I had already discovered a passion for science and scholarship.

Family financial realities meant I left high school at sixteen. I had passed my "O" Levels with enough distinction to get a good job working in a hospital laboratory. My educational aspirations now focused on the vocational training required for the work in the lab. To earn extra money, I worked overtime taking blood samples from infants and helping out at autopsies. I spent my seventeenth birthday in the morgue.

That might have been the end of my academic life but for John Bates, the pathologist who directed the lab. Very quickly he recognized that I was different from the other kids in the lab, and he decided to act as my mentor. One day he drove me home and, after a couple of hours' conversation with my parents (to which I was not privy), he persuaded them to let me quit vocational school and start taking "A" Levels in order to enter the university.

For the next two years, I went to classes five nights every week. My social life—what little of it there was—was limited to the weekends. I gained entrance to the local Polytechnic, now the University of Bradford. Because Bradford wasn't yet a fully chartered university, I opted to sit as an external student for the examinations offered by the University of London, and in 1966 graduated with an honors degree in biology.

While at Bradford I married Michael Merrett, one of my professors. Thirteen years older than I, he was generally accepted as the high flyer of the department, something that was important to me at the time. He became another mentor. By the time I graduated, I was already involved in his research and was offered a postgraduate position in the Botany Department of Leeds University to continue my work toward a doctorate in botany.

My early biological career was meteoric, I must say. By the end of my first year as a graduate student, I had given three papers at scientific meetings. During the second year, while my supervisor was on sabbatical in the United States, I made an interesting discovery about the relationship between cell structure and the photobiochemistry of a primitive plant. When I showed my results to Professor Irene Manton, a Fellow of the Royal Society, she urged me to get to press at once. With a keen sense of gender politics gained from her lifetime in a predominantly male world, she explained, in no uncertain terms, that a woman should publish her work alone whereever possible. She also shared with me her experiences, pains, and glories as one of a pair of brilliant sisters, both of whom were Fellows of the Royal Society. A lifelong feminist, she once muttered in glee, "Newton would turn over in his grave if he knew that women sat in his chair at the Society!"

It was Professor Manton who first introduced me to the work of philosopher-chemist Michael Polanyi, a friend of hers. My scientific career was thus grounded in what has come to be known as the "new paradigm." I shall never forget the art works that surrounded us on the Botany Department's laboratory walls. In my lab, for

instance, we had an original Matisse, and elsewhere were works that would have been a credit to any art museum.

Dr. Manton was keenly aware and very vocal about the way in which personal aesthetics and sensibilities entered into the interpretative process in science. She was particularly fond of pointing out that she discerned the significance of some newly discovered submicroscopic structure through *indwelling*, a term she got from Michael Polanyi. She once said to me, while helping me pick out the contours of a newly identified chloroplast structure, "You cannot see it unless you *love* it."

It was several more years before I rediscovered Polanyi's work in a psychological context and began to understand the relationships between psychological empathy, Polanyi's indwelling, and the newly emerging interpretative epistemologies. Although Professor Manton was always ambivalent about women who pursued both a scientific career and marriage—she had no such choice, she would point out—she was nonetheless very supportive of my ambitions as a scientist. She had every faith that if I so wished, I too could turn over crazy old Newton some day.

That was not to be. During my third year as a graduate student, with everything virtually completed for my thesis, my husband was offered a fellowship at Michigan State University. He wanted me to interrupt my work and go with him. There really was no discussion. We managed to get a job for me in the same phycology (algae!) laboratory, and the plan was that I would write my dissertation after we returned to England. As we said at the time, the work for the thesis was finished, it was original, and much of it was ready for publication. What could it hurt to spend eight months in one of the best algae labs in the world?

Well, it hurt a great deal. Only after we arrived in East Lansing did we we learn that MSU had an anti-nepotism policy. My husband and I couldn't work in the same lab, so I had to work somewhere else. I took a position as a technician in the Plant Research Laboratory. It was important work, but it was in a field of applied botany not even related to my own area of reseach. I did manage to participate on a couple of publications but I had lost the edge. My marriage suffered. Then I got very sick and during the course of the illness experienced an event that changed everything.

At first I ignored the pain. I was afraid of the American medical system. After several days I collapsed and was rushed to the hospital with a fully developed peritonitis, which almost killed me. While I was unconscious , I had the distinct impression that I was leaving my body and embarking on some new journey. Awarenesses altered. My body was no longer the limit of my consciousness. I felt as if I were filling the entire room, then the hospital, and ultimately the world. I "knew" things I could not know. I felt an overwhelming, expansive, exquisite sweetness—love that was beyond description.

The suggestion came from somewhere that I could remain in this state of bliss for eternity. The choice was mine. I was distinctly aware that I could stay in this bliss, or I could return and encounter embodied life again. To do so would entail pain, grief, and all the travails of both physical and psychological reality.

From somewhere came the recognition that the being I was in this state was not identical to the being-in-the-body I had been up until then. This newly discovered being had never known such love while in Maureen's body, and I realized I wanted to. The choice became clear. I would go back. And with the choice came the awareness that my life was to be about love, about trying to understand and to reexperience, in the flesh, the kind of unconditional love for people and for Creation that I had felt in this state.

I never returned to England with my husband, and I never finished my doctorate in plant science. I divorced Michael and was hired to teach biology at Oberlin College (where I later married another scientist). For a couple of unhappy years I grieved the fact that my male supervisor at Leeds University had refused to recommend a waiver on the residency requirements so that I could complete my Ph.D. while I was in the United States. He insisted I return to England to finish out my residency. This was impossible and he knew it. Even though I was by then married to a U.S. citizen, I could not leave the States until my immigration status had been regularized. This took almost two years. The text of his letter of refusal still burns in my mind. "I recommend that you give up your scientific ambitions and settle to your new domestic life in the United States."

Then a series of unexpected things happened that made the loss of my scientific career less disastrous. First I discovered that my new husband was bisexual. I had no idea what that meant until one day I learned, the hard way, that I was not the only object of his sexual interests. Although a great deal about our life at that time remains a private matter, one aspect of it is quite public. I developed a vital, urgent, and heartfelt interest in human sexuality. I devoured everything I could find that would lead me to understand what was happening to us, to me, and by this time (early 1970) to the whole culture.

The sexual revolution was shaking the foundations of polite society, and as faculty members of one of the country's vanguard institutions, we were confronting its effects every day. Two women students, Sandra Simons and Nancy Stead, asked if I would be willing to be faculty sponsor for an ad hoc course in human sexuality. They were both counselors in the college's Planned Parenthood center, and they had been instrumental in inviting a team of National Training Laboratory trainers to conduct encounter groups campus-wide in the winter of 1970. These groups had generated a great deal of controversy, creating passionate friends *and* foes of affective education.

If I had known more about what they had in mind I would probably have been too timid to try. But fools rush in, and so it was with us. Their plan was to run our class as an experiential encounter group, in which students could encounter themselves and each other in terms of what it meant to be a sexual person. We designed a course in which readings and written assignments followed what were the vital interests of the students. It would be a course about them.

Classes met in campus lounges, in small groups facilitated by trained teams made up of one student and one faculty member. I drew together a multidisciplinary group of faculty whose expertise ranged from modern dance to plant physiology. They had in common an intense interest in holistic education and a willingness to bring themselves as persons into the learning process.

Authentic participation in the course was to form part of the students' developmental journey. They were not simply learning *about* intimacy and sexuality but learning to *be* sexual and intimate. Sessions included massage training, body awareness, sensitivity training, a visit to a gay bar, as well as lively encounters among the students as they struggled with each other's differences in values, experience, sexual orientation, race and ethnicity, and gender. As early as 1970 we had one section that comprised eighteen students: six African-American men and women, four Jewish men and women, and eight assorted WASP. Some of the students were heterosexual, some lesbian, some gay (all closeted until the class). Although most reflected Oberlin's historically liberal attitudes, a few class members were very conservative when it came to sex and gender. During that school year we encountered each other to the heights and depths of our aspirations and prejudices, yelled in each other's faces, cried in each other's wine, and danced in each other's arms. By the end of the year we had a community of committed transformation agents, many of whom are still active on behalf of human emancipation.

I had met gestalt therapist Erving Polster that year and, to better train the group facilitators, I entered a gestalt therapy training program at the Cleveland Gestalt Institute. I also shopped around for a graduate program in which I could study human sexuality, human growth, and education. I finally chose Union Graduate School, a nonaccredited fledgling institution in Yellow Springs, Ohio. Colleagues at Oberlin, most of whom had Ivy League credentials, had serious reservations. One told me, "If you are going to an experimental program, make sure you have someone with a recognizable name on your committee." Inexperienced foreigner that I was, I had no clue as to who that might be. Sandra Simons, my undergraduate cofacilitator, came to my rescue. She brought me a copy of Carl Rogers' book *Freedom To Learn* and suggested I ask Carl to help.

I was amazed when he accepted. Later I discovered that he had first presented the essay "On Becoming a Person" at Oberlin College and he had something of a mission to see Oberlin shaken up by radical new ideas—especially his.

The next few years brought me into contact with another universe. I immersed myself in radical politics and feminism. Together with my husband and other faculty and administrators, I helped found the first gay and lesbian counseling group at Oberlin. I became active in the women's and gay liberation movements and became a trained sex educator and sex therapist. I completed gestalt therapy training and a clinical psychology internship. In 1972 we shook up the campus with a women's conference that featured Gloria Steinem and Flo Kennedy.

Meeting Steinem was both an inspiration and a disappointment. She seemed so uninterested in what we were doing. We were not "politically correct" because we focused on women's and men's personal psychological growth. The feminist party line at the time was that inner psychological reality was merely a reflection of outer political reality. Marxist-influenced feminist ideology considered therapy rather bourgeois and a waste of revolutionary energy. Change the political and economic, and the inner world will take care of itself. We at Oberlin disagreed and ploughed on with our emancipation project which included attention to both inner growth and political freedoms. A year later we shook 'em up even more with a men's conference featuring Joseph Pleck, the African-American poet Stanley Crouch, and radical gay activists.

I also created, and was hired to teach in, a program at Oberlin in humanistic education. This included courses in death and dying, personal narrative, the religious experience, gender roles and

consciousness, women's studies, group dynamics and group facilitation skills, and counseling for dormitory counselors. We took a lot
of flak from more traditional academics who even brought in an
evaluation team to dislodge our program. The team felt we had a terrific program, however. One member, Nevitt Sanford, then of the
Wright Institute, felt he would use some of our approaches at his own
institution.

We were ecstatic at the outcome. We had gone from being an ad
hoc course to a fully staffed academic program and finally to an
academic major, all in about four years. We felt empowered and
dizzy from our David and Goliath victory. I felt my life and my self
were transformed: any remnants of the person I had been in
England—scientist, social conformist, skeptic, and analytical thinker—
were replaced by this openhearted, optimistic, socially noncon-
forming, impassioned evangelist for the human potential movement.
I was a humanistic true-believer, with all—in Yates' words—the
passionate intensity associated with that.

By the time I moved to La Jolla, California in 1975, I could scarcely
recall a time when my life had not been full of intense emotional
engagement with what had become a central question of life. How was
I to be a decent human being, to live life to the fullest, and to tap into
the unlimited potential for creativity and joy which is the human
birthright?

I was bolstered by the fact that Carl Rogers, whose work by this
time I had embraced as my path, had asked me to join his Person-
Centered Approach workshop staff. The work we did together, in several countries and in many different places in the United States,
remains the most fertile learning period of my life. I am still discovering things I learned in the total-immersion learning events we
called person-centered approach workshops.

Although these programs have been described in detail in several places, none of the descriptions has come close to capturing the
full scope of the experience. Staff and participants alike were drawn
to the very edge of our humanness, thrust into some of our darkest
corners, only to be raised up a moment later to taste the best of
ourselves. We danced with angels and devils—we *were* angels and
devils—and through it the "unbearable lightness of being" challenged us to reinvent our respective consciousness, relationships,
and understanding of reality.

In 1977 some of us went to Brazil. I had met Brazilian educator
Lucio Campos in the summer of 1975. When Maria Villas-Boas

Bowen brought Eduardo Bandeira to my house in 1976, I jumped at the chance to take PCA on the road. It would take another volume to describe what happened to me in Brazil; suffice it to say it was love at first sight.

We arrived in Manaus in the middle of the night. As we deplaned the air hit me in the face like a warm, wet wall. The sounds were overwhelming. Even the jet noise could not completely drown out the noise of equatorial ZZZZs. The next day Eduardo rented a launch and we explored the Amazon. We traveled to the place where the rivers Solimões and Negro meet: *O Conjunto das Aguas*. The sight made a primal impression.

For over a thousand miles these two rivers run separate courses. For whatever ecological reason, Solimões is opaque and yellow. Rio Negro, as its name implies, is the color of black tea. Its waters are clear. Both ecosystems reach homeostatic equilibrium hundreds of miles upstream. Near Manaus the two great streams meet to form the mighty Amazon. What is deficient in either ecological system is made up by what is in excess in the other. The mixture becomes recharged with vital possibilities, and the biological results are simply spectacular! The abundance, fecundity, richness, exhuberance of nature right at that convergence of the two rivers were overwhelming. It became a metaphor, which I was to use later on a television interview in São Paulo, for what happened to us as our American psychological thought came together with the people of Brazil. The metaphor and the image was to serve a far deeper significance a couple of years later.

After Manaus, our group, firmly in the thrall of Brazil, went on to conduct three giant one-day workshops in Recife, São Paulo, and Rio de Janeiro. As many as eight hundred people per day participated. Our trip culminated in a three-week residential program in the mountains outside Rio. Almost two hundred psychologists attended.

After the Brazilian trip with the PCA team, I was asked by Lucio Campos and others to return to Brazil to offer training programs in client-centered gestalt therapy. For many Brazilians, client-centered theory was "too nice, too American." Raised on phenomenology, existentialism, psychoanalysis, and Marxism, many Brazilian intellectuals favored the more European and frankly revolutionary stance of gestalt therapy. At the same time, because they were all well aware of the potential for abuse in authoritarian approaches—they were at that time still suffering under government oppression—they valued the Rogerian person-centered position with regard to the power relationships between client and therapist. My work offered them a combination of Rogerian non-authoritarianism and European epistemological complexity.

From 1977 to 1987 I conducted training programs for therapists in client-centered gestalt therapy in every major city in Brazil. In those early years, ours were the only humanistic training programs available, so I had the good fortune to work with some of the very talented and wonderful people who made up Brazil's humanistic leadership. The experience was profoundly enriching for me. I learned far more than I taught, both as a woman and as a psychologist. One occasion exemplifies this.

The name Arcozelo conjures up magical images to this day. The colonial coffee plantation had seen better days. It was owned by Pasqual Carlos Magno, a former Brazilian ambassador who was fanatically dedicated to the arts and to youth. The *fazenda* had been the site of youth art festivals and had a reputation among radical artists, hippies, and idealists as a place where human potential was cherished.

We arrived for our workshop to discover the place was not ready for us. Longer on idealism than business acumen, Pasqual had let the *fazenda* run down. The kitchen was so neglected that it needed two days of scrubbing and disinfecting before we dared prepare food in it. Throughout the program, even when the kitchen opened, we found ourselves treating a steady stream of diarrhea patients. The sleeping rooms too were dirty, many of the foam mattresses infested with sundry tropical creatures. We were forced to purchase, from the receipts of the program, a hundred new ones. Somehow it didn't matter. The spirit of adventure and adversity was putting a luminescent edge to everything, and we took each new obstacle in stride as another puzzle to solve.

I will always remember Niva, a very well-manicured Brazilian psychologist, arriving at the site in a chauffeured Mercedes, with two enormous leather suitcases stuffed to the gunwails with European designer clothing. Demanding to be shown to her room to rest after her trip, she instead received a brief explanation of our predicament. In no time flat, Niva had changed into blue jeans, taken up a broom, and—pulling on what must have been some kind of ancient gender-memory—she put herself to a task no woman of her family had perfomed since they arrived from Portugal. Without once complaining, she swept and mopped the floors of the whole women's domitory. In a later training group, she confessed that in terms of her growth as a person and as a professional, she got more from that experience and the feelings of pitching in with a team than she got from the rest of the program.

The experience I remember most vividly from that first trip to Brazil involved Tio Paulo, the soot-stained cook who served our meals. A couple of days into the second week, word was passed that the *Americanos* John and Maureen had been invited to a special event that night. At about ten we were picked up in an open, ramshackled old truck, along with Eduardo and his new lover Lika, who was to be our translator. We sat packed in the truck, bumping and lurching along in the dark on an unlit dirt road. The stars were unbelievably bright, the Southern Cross visible the whole way. We sang and laughed, Brazilians and Americans traveling on to an undisclosed site.

Eventually we came to a rough, clay-sided hut. The room was lit by oil lanterns and candles. People were packed densely around the walls, about fifty or so poorly clothed *campesinos,* some black, some mulatta, and others distinctly Indian. Drummers were beating out an hypnotic rhythm that sounded like the very soul of Brazil. We had entered a *terreiro,* a dirt-floored building in which Afro-Brazilian religious ceremonies are held, and were about to experience a Macumba service. Macumba is one of the basic animistic Brazilian folk-religious sects which, along with Umbanda and Candomblé, have evolved from African religions brought to Brazil with African slaves.

As the drumming intensified and acrid tobacco smoke was blown around like incense, people began to throb and sway with the music. It was impossible to remain unaffected. Even though it was a little frightening, I nonetheless allowed the boundaries of consciousness to slip farther and farther from their anchors. My ordinarily very gringo fastidiousness yielded as we all drew deeply from the *cachaça* bottle as it was passed. We swayed and vibrated with the drums.

At one point, a young woman next to me was "taken" by a spirit. She keeled over, falling on her face in the dust, her body gyrating and twitching within the chalk circle drawn on the mud floor. Quickly three white-clad women approached her and bustled her into an antechamber, where she was dressed in the white attire and given the correct accoutrements of the "entity" that had taken possession of her. My translator, herself a practitioner of Macumba, explained that the mirror and comb symbolized Yanxã, the goddess of the waterfalls. Exu the diabolical trickster was already present, making mischief, barking out his obscene remarks, and blowing smoke into onlookers' faces.

Then the curtain opened and in swaggered the Pae dos Santos (the "Father of the Saints," the high priest of the *terreiro*). I recognized him at once. It was Tio Paulo, only instead of the dirt-streaked visage I had seen at the stove earlier in the day, here was a man in spotless white clothes, radiant, proud, and dignified. He appeared several inches taller. As he spoke, his voice, not hesitant now, rang out in confident, authoritative tones. I had never seen such a transformation. He was different in every respect. In the place of the downtrodden, desultory servant was an articulate, potent teacher. The people assembled clearly acknowledged him as a leader and guide, and he accepted his role with dignity and compassion.

He proceeded around the circle giving advice to some, herbal concoctions to others, ritual cleansings to others. The mother of one young girl decried her daughter, saying she was possessed. She told Paulo that her daughter scratched her crotch while sleeping—a clear sign she was possessed. She asked Paulo for some incantation or exorcism. He quickly reassurred the girl's mother. He explained that her daughter was not possessed, she merely had an infestation of pinworms which were leaving her intestine at night and making her scratch. He gave her a vermicidal plant, explained how to make the medicine, and told the mother to love her daughter. One after another, Paulo laid his hands on the people. With much ceremony and pomp he offered wisdom and comfort to his small band of co-celebrants, continuing into the early hours of the next day before everyone had been answered and the entitites had been persuaded to return to the other world for another night. He had words for the gringos too. He told both John and me that we were here without guides. We had been sent, he said, to help people find their authentic paths. We were to first find our own! He sounded too much like Carl, for my liking. I was hoping for something more dramatic—at least a goddess or something. I thanked him, anyhow, and realized I had stopped calling him *Tio* Paulo, which I was now aware carried in Portuguese the same mixture of affection and disrespect Harriet Beecher Stowe's "Uncle Tom" carried for North Americans.

At the *fazenda* the next day, I was surprised to find Paulo in his familiar role, unchanged by his or our previous night's adventures. I later asked him if he were conscious of the radical difference between his demeanor in the kitchen and that in his role of Pae dos Santos. Treating me with the kind of patience one reserves for a rather dull child, he explained that he well knew that white society would have an entirely different response to an articulate, authoritative black teacher and leader than to a soot-stained servant. Like many individuals who know persecution, he had learned to hide himself under the guise of servile stupidity to avoid drawing attention to himself as a threat. "To do my work I must remain invisible. You whites are privileged. Use your privilege to enlarge the circle," he charged us. I have never forgotten him.

It was on one of many trips to Brazil that I met R. D. Laing and, thanks to the silver tongue of Eduardo Bandiera and my own narcissism, was talked into organizing a large one-day meeting between the Person-Centered Approach team, including Carl, and Laing and his colleagues. To be held at the Hilton Hotel in London, this meeting was to provide another *"conjunto das aguas."*

This time the streams that met were the currents at work in my own psyche. We arrived at Laing's home a little after seven. We were all very nervous. Natalie Rogers had had an uncomfortable run-in with Laing earlier in the day, and we were beginning to suspect that our understanding about the meeting was rather different from that of Laing and his people. Our team—which was made up of Carl Rogers, Maria Villas Boas Bowen, Natalie Rogers, John K. Wood, Jared Kass, Joanne Justin, and myself—believed we were there because Ronald Laing wanted a chance to work with Carl Rogers. As it turned out later, Laing's team thought we were there on our initiative because Carl wanted to work with them. The archbishops of extraordinary understanding caught in one big mutual projection—*folie aux* everybody!

We were shown out to an office to one side of the main house. It was small for the number of people assembled: eight of us and maybe ten of their people, including Laing, Frances Huxley, and Hugh Crawford (who, if memory serves me, was the director of the famed Philadelphia House at the time). There were others whose names I never heard, including a striking blonde woman who spent the evening taking photographs.

The room seemed to be vibrating already as we entered, breathing in and out with its occupants. The feel and smell seemed strongly masculine. Pipe smoke was heavy; the strong smell of tobacco clung to the clothes of several whose hands I shook. Straight-lipped British smiles revealed the usual tobacco-stained teeth untouched by orthodontics. Colors were dark—blacks, greys, and browns. Our California clothes seemed brash next to the somber tweeds and worsteds. Such was my excitement that time began to slow down and stretch out. I could feel myself slipping into another state of consciousness. Sounds, smells, and sights took on added intensity. As we took our places in the circle and I looked around, my heart rate quickened. I refused the marijuana being passed from hand to hand. I already felt like my mind was in the process of being "blown," and I certainly needed no psychoactive assistance. I did accept the wine that was circulating like a communion cup.

Laing expressed a few words of welcome to Carl and suggested we begin the process of getting to know each other. Carl began in his characteristic way: an opening rite we had performed at the start of every PCA event. He invited us to introduce ourselves. Knowing the ritual from many repetitions, we spoke, one after the other, until everyone in the brightly dressed half of the circle had spoken.

I have little recollection as to what everybody said. I know I said something rather precious about hearing Laing in Belo Horizonte, Brazil and how I had sensed deep correspondences between his thinking and ours. I was probably articulate and undoubtedly very serious. I know I did not reveal anything about the now-mounting apprehension that pounded away beneath my sternum. As we talked, one after the other in our blandness, I could see eyebrows beginning to lift on the tweedy side of circle. Instead of the smiles, nods, and other signs of acceptance we were accustomed to, we were met with cold impassiveness and, in a couple of cases, outright smirks.

After all of us had spoken, there followed a long, loud silence. As we sat waiting for someone to speak, my depth of focus shifted in and out in the rapid-fire fashion of a sports photographer. Click—Laing's face. Click—Carl's. Click, click—Maria, Jared. Click—my own hands shaking. With a shutter speed of milliseconds, I scanned the room and tightened up like a spring. I dared not breathe.

Francis Huxley, nephew of Aldous and author of *The Sacred and Profane,* spoke first. He was puffing on a pipe, as I recall. Not only were his teeth stained but so was his beard. He spoke in a voice that proclaimed his privilege and undoubted erudition. Public schooling, an Oxbridge education, and a lifetime of consort with the intellectual elite of British culture oozed forth with every rich syllable. It was the voice of superiority, unshakeable self-confidence, and absolute indifference to the impact it had on its listeners—beyond, that is, its intention to dominate.

"My God!" he began. His tone feigned naive innocence but dripped with derision. "I can only imagine what kind of reaction you would have obtained from our gang, Ronnie, if you had asked any of us to perform so politely." Laing smiled.

The air hung heavy, Huxley's salvo reverberating around the room. I sat in stunned silence. Carl recovered first. As he began to speak, his voice wavered just a little but quickly took on its familiar fluency as he gracefully articulated our creed about human nature and the nature of relationships. Just as I began to relax, Laing interrupted again with another salvo, this time at Carl directly. "If you and I are to have any kind of meaningful dialogue," he declared, "you are going to have to cut out the Cailifornia 'nice-guy' bullshit and get to something approaching an authentic encounter."

Now my head was swimming. I was feeling very protective of Carl. My California "family" was being ambushed, for god's sake! At the same time, though, unbidden came a much less noble reaction. I had the urge to denounce Californianism and to line up with the Brits. I began to feel like a vile and spineless creature. Suddenly there was no end to my potential for treachery. I imagined standing aside from Jewish friends as pogroms proceeded. I remembered St. Peter and wondered how I had failed to identify with his denial before. After a lifetime of identifying myself with the hero in stories of oppression and persecution, I was brought face to face with a slimy invertebrate cowardice. I said nothing.

When one of my colleagues spoke up, I began to feel better. The eloquent elaboration of the basis of our approach and the self-assured confidence in our grasp of truth calmed my disquiet. I was able to align myself with my comrades once more. But I was mortally shaken and I knew it. As the conversation continued, I would waver back and forth as Laingian followed Rogerian and so on.

As I recall, the basic theme of the conflict seemed to center on whether human beings should be considered fundamentally trustworthy. Could we interpret behavior as manifestations of a universal tendency—the self-actualizing tendency, as Rogers had called it—that propelled us toward self-realization and self-healing? We believed yes, and Laing's folk believed no. Correlary to our credo was the idea that those who denied the self-actualizing tendency were either wrong, misguided, or too afraid to have faith. They needed to be convinced to surrender themselves to the benevolence of the universe. Empathy, nonjudgmental acceptance, warmth, and congruence—key concepts in Rogerian theory—created the conditions wherein people might be so persuaded.

Correlary to their belief was the idea that those who unconditionally trusted human nature and denied that it had a dark side were wrong and probably dangerously so. Such people needed to be convinced that despite their "niceness," their unacknowledged dark side had tremendous power and could be heinously destructive. In particular, middle-class bourgeois values were suspected of covering up unacknowledged repressive violence against the passionate authentic self. In Laing's theory, this was the origin of most mental illness and of social pathologies such as fascism and violence. The antidote was to denounce all attempts to stifle the raw self by brutally and frankly confronting all manner of inauthenticity supposedly revealed in bourgeois sensibilities.

Adding greatly to my inner turmoil was the increasingly troublesome awareness that a good deal of the Laingian position had some ring of truth about it for me. After all, here I was in mortal combat with a very dark side to my own nature. I wanted to hear the Laingian position and I didn't. If I found their ideas convincing, did that mean I must adopt their brutishness, so reminiscent of the bullying I had experienced as a girl growing up in the industrial north of England? And if I rebuffed their assaults, refused to be written off as a California wimp, and stood up for love, gentleness, civility, and gracefulness in human relationships, did that mean I must deny the realities of both my present experience and those of my early life at the hands of the "civilized" middle class?

The encounter continued. I spoke some, listened some; but while the front of me was performing its dance of participation, another deeper reality was unfolding. Another consciousness—almost another Maureen—was awakened. Images began to float into this other being.

I remembered Miss Grange, the very proper spinster landlady of our cold-water slum house. In the 1940s she came every week to collect the rent. We lived in terror that some day she would arrive and we would not have the money. It's not that she would have evicted us. She would have just looked very disappointed, and we would have died of shame. Just the sight of her lizard-skin handbag on our sideboard could spotlight the desperate shabbiness of everything in the room, including the people.

I recalled quiet-spoken Mr. McDonald, the "man from the Pru," who picked up our penny insurance premiums. He used to slip his fingers into my blouse and threatened to tell my parents I'd asked for it if I said a word. He told me he would pay me four times the cost of the monthly premium if I would perform other things with him. "That's a lot of money for a little girl of your kind," he said. He was right, but I declined anyway.

Loud, coarse Elsie, who would have fought off tigers to protect her kids from their drunken father, came to mind. She alone kept her kids from being put into what was euphemistically referred to as "the care of the local authority" by the social worker with the Morris Minor.

I remembered, with vivid shame, the teacher at the elite girl's school who singled me out on the first day. In front of the whole school, she said I needed remedial classes for my "atrocious use of the English language and slovenly posture."

Then there was the male chemistry teacher at evening school, with a voice like Francis Huxley's, who had begun our first class with a witty, satirical invitation to the class's "distaff" members (plural, although I was the only female present) to drop out then, before he had to get rough and we "poor dears, get humiliated. Go home to your fathers," he said with a sneer, "until you find husbands to take you off their hands."

As the instances of shame and humiliation at the hands of the civilized middle class flooded back, the educated, sophisticated "California Maureen" who championed the ideas of my beloved friend and teacher Carl Rogers, became not much more than a patina on the gritty Yorkshire kid who had fought her way out of the slums by virtue of native intelligence, solid family support, welfare-state structures that made it possible for bright poor youngsters to attend elite schools, and who had developed more than the little pugnacity and impudence required to survive it all. My escape had also entailed turning my back on many of my own roots, learning to play the middle-class game, developing the "right" accent, and minimizing my working class affiliations. I was the first of my extended family to go to university and even the first of my newly acquired middle-class social circle to become a gastronomic snob by learning French cuisine. I had survived and I had prospered, but I had been hurt—deeply hurt—in the process. Sitting there in Laing's study, I was aware of the scars for the first time.

Then another series of memories made their appearance: an altogether different picture of my relationships with the middle classes. I remembered John Bates (my pathologist mentor), Dr. Irene Manton, and of course Carl's response to my letter. Then there was Sonia Nevis, my first therapist, who helped me identify the "fragile, tender blossom" that inhabited deeper levels of Maureen and first taught me the meaning of unconditional acceptance.

I remembered, too, numerous experiences in workshops, counseling sessions, and classes when I was opened up to a sweetness, a delicacy, a fineness of spirit that would have been as unsupportable in my early life as mangos in Michigan. Nothing in the bleak nastiness of my West Yorkshire childhood had encouraged me to aspire to anything remotely like the life I now had. I was thirty-five, living in a communal household in Southern California on very little income but enjoying tremendous riches. Spiritually and psychologically, life was gentle, full of love and joy—even ecstasy—and I was not so angry. "Here and now" in California was ever so much easier than England had been "there and then." Images floated in and out of my reverie as, for the first time in my life, perhaps, I pondered the multihued complexity of all my varied experiences.

I was still caught or pulled up into this other place of being when somebody decided we should all leave to go get something to eat. Laing had offered to buy us all dinner and had reserved tables at a Chinese restaurant half a block up the street.

There was considerable animosity by this time. Both groups were muttering and mumbling amongst themselves. I hoped that eating together might serve as some kind of tribal hospitality rite and that we might get closer to each other. On the way over, I struck up a conversation with Hugh Crawford. I seemed to have a greater affinity for his down-to-earth Scottish sensibility than for either my California colleagues or the more contentious of the Laingians.

At the restaurant, one long table was positioned near the wall, along the length of the room. It was set up to hold all of us. Carl sat with his back to the wall, Californians by his side, including his daughter Natalie. Hugh and I sat along that side too. After an awkward, clumsy dance of "who sits where?" Laing took himself off to a separate, unprepared table at the other end of the room. He was joined by a young lieutenant, Stuart I think his name was, and by John Wood and Jared Kass of the California team. The set-up could not have been more suggestive if it had been directed by Hal Prince: a long table with Carl in the center, flanked by people anxious to be in his presence, and over to one side a small, intimate group around Laing. At first no one else was in the restaurant.

As the dinner progressed, Laing's performance intensified. He joked and bantered in his melodic Glasgow style. His wit was sharp and entertaining. I talked with Hugh, who made some apologies for the roughness of our earlier meeting. I got the distinct impression that this was not the first time he had been embarrassed by Laing's behavior and that he personally found the abrasiveness very uncomfortable.

The restaurant door opened. In walked two young men looking for a Chinese meal. As they took in the scene, they began making sport. From their accents it was obvious they also were Glasgwegian, their wit every bit as well honed as our host's. Suddenly Laing was upstaged, and it was clear he didn't like it. Already pretty drunk, he began upping his ante, intensifing the barbs of his comments as if in word-to-word combat.

We were all unprepared for what happened next. Up until now Laing had aimed wide, sending his arrows indiscriminately at both his people and ours. All of a sudden he half stood and pointed his finger in Carl's direction. Carl was looking extremely uncomfortable, no longer sure how to react. Unfamiliar with British humor, he was unsure if these proceedings were funny or not but, like a well-mannered guest in an alien land, he remained polite and noncommittal. Laing yelled to the newcomers, "You see that bald-headed man over there?" And then, with an unmistakeably scornful reference to Carl's most popular book, "Well, he's no' a *man*, he's a *person!*" His alcohol-loosened tongue rolled out the "r" in "person."

Silence fell. Everybody looked stunned. Carl's face turned bright red. The rest of us had a variety of responses from squirmy embarrassment to white-knuckled fury. I was deeply ashamed. Reliving some primitive experience of inappropriateness, I felt entirely responsible for Carl's being in this situation. It was like inviting a well-bred classmate to my home only to have a family member get drunk and be abusive. In my shame I was paralyzed. As the shame turned to fury, I began to tremble. I made some feeble attempts to smooth things out (principally my own dishevelment). It didn't work. Laing had us going and he knew it.

He came over to the table and sat before me, making slurred conversation. He was insulting and teasing and he was enjoying himself. He poured Scotch into my glass—a sign of friendship and goodwill, I thought—and asked if I liked the liquor. To humor him I said I did, although in truth it was not a favorite of mine. Whereupon he leaned over and spat in my glass. "Well, how do you like it now?" he leered. Now beside myself with shame and rage, I picked up the glass and hurled its contents at his face. I believe I missed.

The assembly was breaking up, people milling about and scurrying towards the door. Laing paid the bill and we spilled out onto the damp London pavement. Tempers were close to explosion. As we walked back toward Eton Place, Laing announced that we were not welcome in his house. Alcohol, fatigue, and intense emotion threatened to propel us into a physical encounter right there on the street outside his house. At least one member of our team, dark side surging to the fore, had to be restrained from throwing a punch. Several other people arrived, friends and family members of the California team, including my own intentional family, who had been told they could attend the post-meal meeting. Voices were shrill and confused, but in the middle of it all I heard Carl declare he would not go through with the event the next day. He'd had enough of Laing, and his politeness had given way to anger and indignation.

Carl's announcement seemed to come as a surprise to Laing's team. "What? Back out?" Apparently that had not occurred to them. The next moment someone decided we had to enter the house after all and "get this bloody mess sorted out."

This time we were ushered into a room inside the house. Laing greeted the newcomers like the consummate host, welcoming them in and generously offering them Scotch and wine. My husband remarked later that he felt his mind bend as he juxtaposed our group's obvious extreme distress with Laing's noblesse and grace. The room we entered was absolutely lovely. In the slowed-down vision of heightened arousal, my eyes took in the marvelous, rich colors of the antique Persian carpet, the evocative presences of various masks, effigies, artworks, and symbols collected on global travels by an eye tuned to the luminosity of sacred consciousness. "How could such a boorish bully have such exquisite sensibility?" I wondered. Laing's private study was like a temple.

He started the proceedings with what I took to be his familiar opening ritual. "There are only two rules. Nobody gets hurt and nothing gets broken." People began to talk, both sides trying to say things that might magically heal the gulf between us. Our group was angry. Their group was showing signs of alarm as the reality of the next day's meeting began to impinge on that night's proceedings. Even the more belligerent Laingians were now expressing trepidation about facing a large group with soft plans and hard feelings.

Carl, who had said nothing since we entered, finally asked Laing to give him one good reason why he should go ahead with the next day's event. Laing, suddenly assuming the self-righteous position of guardian of social etiquette, said, "I'll give you a thousand. Those are all the people who have bought a ticket expecting to see both of us tomorrow." Somehow that convinced Carl and the rest of us to once more commit to the next day's event and do whatever it took that night to salvage the program.

I tried to speak. The conversation was somehow dancing over and around Laing's behavior in the restaurant. I began to speak to him, to express my pain and shame. My voice was shrill. I was cut off by someone—I don't recall whom—implying that my feelings were unimportant. The next day's meeting was the agenda now.

At that, my ordinary mind left and what followed was like nothing I had experienced before. I lost my mind. I saw the inside space of my skull expand to engulf ever-widening worlds: the room, the present situation, the continent of Europe with its history and traditions, and the New World, both north and south. Inside this

expanded universe I could see and feel the eternal battles raging—
between old and new, between north and south, between rich and
poor, between light and dark, between oppressor and oppressed,
between madness and sanity, between London and California,
between men and women, between acceptance and rejection, between
love and fear, between good and evil and, ultimately, between being
and nonbeing. My private inner battle raged in the same polarized
duality as the conflicts of external realities. The madness of it was
unbearable—and inescapable.

As the paroxysms took hold of my body, I felt a crumbling of
the dam wall that until then had separated the neatly ordered contra-
dictions of my being. I had no more resistance. The uneasy disquiet
I had felt throughout the planning process to bring my Califonia reality "home" to England now burst through the retaining walls with
maelstromic fury. "I"—whomever that pronoun now referred to—
could only watch as the pieces of shattered reality pulled loose from
their designated places in my psychic landscape and sloshed about like
so much flotsam. Out of my solar plexus emerged a long harping wail.
I yelled, "You son of a bitch!" or some such, at Laing, now the
embodiment of archetypal nemesis. He smiled patronizingly and
encouraged me to "get it all out." As I slipped further into chaos,
Laing seemed interested in me for the first time—the psychological
final straw! The last blocks of the dam fell away and for a time—only
minutes, but it seemed like an eternity—I was engulfed in pure madness. I raged and sobbed as the tidal wave swept everything before it.
As I surrendered to unspeakable terror, the demons of a thousand life-
times laughed in my face. The gargoyles and incubi of countless
humiliations and vanities swirled around me, casting their taunts.
Some wore Laing's face and some wore Carl's. Swept onward, I was
aware only of an anonymous male presence close by. He did not touch
me at first, but the smell of his tobacco-tainted breath, and the rise
and fall of his chest, were reassuring in some way.

I surrendered, further giving myself up to other, kindlier ghosts
and apparitions: madonnas, knights, and delicate maidens. By now
sweetness began to permeate my experience. I leaned into the male-
ness of my companion as oceanic calmness took the place of the tem-
pest. After a few moments of utterly perfect sobbing, I opened my eyes
to find Laing's young lieutenant offering his support and urging me
to "go on through it." Laing had moved closer too. Their earlier
antagonism and derision were gone, and so was Laing's patronizing
air (perhaps I had only imagined it before). In their place was a
steadying but non-interfering accompaniment. I was contained by their

presence, which seemed to have become almost luminous. Neither exploited my fragility—both seemed more comfortable with madness than with rationality. Little by little, the violence left my body and I slipped into a relaxed calm that was at once empty and pregnant. They helped me out of the circle and onto a couch, where a hazy half-sleep cradled me until the meeting ended a couple of hours later.

I think of the Rogers–Laing encounter as being the beginning of my own authentic story. In the madness, all the structures of my psyche—the roles and conceptual schemata with which I navigated life—came unglued. For years, since my earliest interactions with what for me were the repressive demands of middle-class culture, and continuing all the way through to the equally demanding although infinitely "nicer" California human-potential-movement culture, I had been busily accumulating ways of being, thinking, and acting that would make the people I admired like me, accept me and, above all, teach me. I realize as I look back that all that changed after the meeting at Laing's house.

My emancipation did not come overnight, and it did not come without pain and loss. Imperceptibly at first, I gradually slipped into a significant depression. It affected my work and my home life, and it seriously disturbed my intellectual life. The work I was doing with Carl and the others became more problematic. I began to spend more time with John K. Wood, who was also a heretic, although a much more polished one than I. It felt good to have long conversations with John about what he referred to as "Rogerism"—the frankly true-believer feel to writings and programs appearing under the name Person-Centered Approach. My own convictions were in shreds, and I gradually came to believe that what I had previously thought to be grounded in empirical science was actually an ideology, a faith system, which although humane and humanistic, appeared to have no different epistemic status than any other religion.

The crisis deepened. It became difficult to spend much time with Carl or any other members of the team without feeling different, critical, and alienated. There was tremendous loss for me in this. Whereas in the past I had been one of the first to be invited into the inner circle of new projects and programs, I now found myself left out, ostracized even. Since my personal life had been so entirely wrapped up in our work together, disconnection from the Person-Centered Approach folks meant increasing social isolation.

After the British meeting I decided to move to Brazil for a year. Then, after a year of working in translation, I decided that if I were to do any more work in Brazil, I must master Portuguese. Not being one for classroom language study, and intoxicated with what I had already experienced of Brazilan culture and the Brazilian people, I chose to make living and working there my language course.

Being six thousand miles away from both California and Yorkshire, immersed in a cultural setting as different as both are from each other, forced to know life through new symbolic systems, I found Brazil was like a giant cocoon. While I was doing my work, training psychotherapists all over Brazil, my inner world was reconstructing my reality.

Looking back, I see I was in a fairly deep depression for the next few years. I took interpersonal risks which, from this vantage point, seem self-indulgent. Not the least of these were the numerous amorous involvements with unsuitable men, with whom I sought metaphysical escape. It is with great puzzlement and indescribable gratitude that I recall how my beloved partner Bob—or Pook, as we know him—was able to wind himself around my psychological deconstruction and remain alongside.

I lived and learned an enormous amount during those Brazil years. It was as if I wanted to experience all of life again—the pain, the passion, the drama, the joy, everything—with my own eyes open and my own interpretive ears listening to new stories. I recall a number of dreams featuring an infant girl. She was always perfect, always already all-knowing, and I felt from her a tremendous faith in me. At times of anxiety or doubt, she would appear and reassure me and I could go on.

I gradually developed a rhythm of spending five to six months every year in Brazil and the rest of the time in California. This was to last for almost nine years. The longer I was away from Southern California and the work Carl was doing in La Jolla and elsewhere, the more differentiated my own work became from person-centered orthodoxy. In particular, I began to examine American humanistic psychology more from a third-world perspective.

I had been introduced to the work of Brazilian pedagogue Paulo Freire in 1972, while teaching at Oberlin. Even then I had seen the importance of political analysis for understanding the process of human emancipation. As I rediscovered Freire and his work, and as I lived daily life in the culturally different Brazilian context, I was able to examine American humanistic psychology from the critical perspective of Freire's Marxist-Christian humanism. Through conversations with Freire himself and people deeply involved in his work and ideas, in particular Afonso Fonseca, I gradually developed a clearer understanding of how the sociopolitical contexts of life, especially the dimension of privilege and oppression, become internalized into the pychological structures of individuals. I applied this awareness to myself as I processed what had happened at Laing's house, and I applied it to my work. In particular, I began to look at the lives of oppressed people—whether oppressed by dysfunctional families or by large-scale social sytems, such as sexism, racism, or class—through the lens of what is these days referred to as a social-constructivist position.

By this time, through readings and experiences as diverse as Gramsci and Sufism, French Lacanian feminism, Bhagwan Rajneesh, Michael Polanyi, Doris Lessing, and Arthur Koestler, I had embarked on the next stage of my intellectual journey. My writings of that time were attempts to sort out the pieces that had come in my explosion at Laing's house.

In 1985 I decided the six-thousand-mile commute between Southern California and Brazil was taking its toll on my body as well as my finances. I had to try to create a more settled life somewhere and for many reasons chose to remain in Southern California. After several years of following my friend Carl in refusing to enter the "credential game," I realized I needed a license to practice as a therapist. It was another friend, Lois Brien, who convinced me that although Carl, a successful, powerful white male, could make a living independent of any established legitimizing systems, I might not. If my new sociopolitical awareness of the relationship between private choices and public policy taught me anything, it was that marginalized groups and individuals cannot expect the same outcomes from unorthodox choices.

With a healthy dose of my life-saving narcissism intact, I was still unwilling to play the orthodoxy game all the way. I could not bring myself to go back to graduate school to prepare for a clinical psychology licensing examination. I sat for the Marriage, Family and Child Counseling license (which in California permitted most of the scope of practice afforded by a psychology license) and on receiving my license started a private practice near San Diego, California.

Another part of this settling down involved Pook. I was still living in the small community household in which I had lived since we moved out from Oberlin in 1975, although I had divorced bisexual David in 1980. Pook and I had been a solid couple for some time and, precipitated by family events for both of us, we decided to marry. Our decision was based on many factors, not the least of which involved our parents. Pook's father was ailing. In some primal way, the passing of his father signified the need to assume an adult stance in the world. Marriage, dismissed for so long as an unnecessary constriction of our lives as unencumbered and radically free "persons," now seemed to symbolize connection to our roots, to our culture, and to our families. After almost a decade of attention to such psychological themes as individuation, freedom, autonomy, and mastery, we now found ourselves luxuriating in the warmth of our family relationships. Earlier, the narrowness of small-town family life had felt stifling and restrictive. Now, participating in the old family rituals and assuming our places in the burials, baptisms, marriages, and graduations of our respective clans added meaning and depth.

I don't think it an unrelated coincidence that at this point I began to find myself increasingly uncomfortable with the view of human nature that sat at the centre of psychology in general and humanistic psychology in particular. Coming on the heels of the experience at Laing's house and of my examination of larger social issues such as feminism and the aspirations of peoples of color in Brazil and in the United States, my personal rediscovery of the importance of family connections pushed me in new intellectual directions.

Once, in Brazil, I held a training program in a place outside São Paulo with a name it took me the whole time I was there to learn how to pronounce: Itaquaquecetuba. One of the trainees, Zelia, a psychiatrist, invited her old friend Paulo Freire to engage in dialogue with us. In the conversation, Freire challenged Rogers' assertion that Rogerian student-centered learning was in any significant way similar to his own "pedagogy of the oppressed." In particular, he challenged the Eurocentric view of "the person" painted by Rogerian theory. Paulo argued that such a radically individualistic view was possible only in a world where the necessities of life were provided. Rogers' version of personhood was, in Freire's view, both the cause and effect of ways of thinking, feeling, and acting characteristic of dominant groups. As Michael Polanyi had done fifteen years before, Freire challenged me to acknowledge the ways in which knowledge is inseparable from the knowers—in other words, is socially constructed.

I discovered that Freire was skeptical about psychology. He freely expressed the opinion that, because of its preoccupation with the individual, psychology is always in great danger of falling into empty and impotent psychologism looking at a mirage: the individual is abstracted from his or her social context. I remember his response to my assertion that client-centered therapy was based in dialogue. "Dialogue about what?" He wasn't impressed with the North American preoccupation with self. He believed that even the most intimate landscape of inner reality has to be seen as being about the world. If not, he believed, psychotherapy is bound to be an alienating process.

Through these conversations with Freire, I began to clarify some of my own queasiness about Rogerianism. Reading voraciously outside humanistic psychology, I discovered a whole literature challenging some of the givens of the individualistic psychology of our times. Tom Wolfe had coined the label "the 'me' generation." I nodded in silent agreement with Daniel Yankelovich's notion of a "self-fulfillment contradiction," Christopher Lasch's indictment of the "cult of narcissism," and Michael Marien's diagnosis of the "sandbox syndrome"— which collectively charged that we had become too self-absorbed. I was particularly impressed by the research of Robert Bellah and his colleagues at Berkeley, which revealed that although Americans long for a sense of community, they feel isolated and alienated.

All these critics were pointing at least one finger of blame at the human potential movement, reserving special venom for what they saw as the alienating consequences of a psychology such as Rogers', based as it is in a version of the self, abstracted from the world of relationships, economics, social groups, politics, history, and biology.

To some extent I agreed with these critics. Somehow, though— perhaps because my concrete experience of humanistic psychologists (most of whom were my friends) showed me that these were compassionate, socially concerned, and altruistic people—I felt their criticisms, though cogent, were not quite on the money.

Certainly I agreed with Freire that too much retroflexive self-absorption can lead to a tendency to psychologize—seeing all human suffering as originating in the intrapsychic realm of the individual. From my early work in the women's and gay movements, I had been acutely aware that, by focusing on the individual rather than the culture, psychology more often than not blamed the victim for his or her own suffering. It bothered me that people often interpreted Rogers' writings as saying that changes in individual consciousness will be sufficient to humanize society.

For those of us who worked closely with Carl during his later years, it was obvious that he had become somewhat of a contradiction. While he never modified his individualistic core ideas about the nature of consciousness, in the years before his death he nonetheless increasingly focused on broader social questions and pushed his work ever father into frankly political arenas.

It was an odd mix, really. Passionately committed to people in pain, he felt equally passionate that the principles of client-centered therapy had something to offer for the relief of that pain and for the transformation of situations that caused it. He believed in individual empowerment and in the validity of each person's own experience. On the other hand, he surrounded himself with people who fell into what one embittered former Rogerian disciple, Bill Coulson, once called psychosalvationism. This referred to an attitude of, "If only the whole world saw it our way," or the "one-truth fallacy," that lay unexamined at the heart of Rogers' (and Western culture's) view of the universe.

In his last years, Rogers and various colleagues, of which I was one, took the client-centered message to over twenty countries, including: South Africa, where we facilitated encounters between blacks and whites; Latin America, where North encountered South; Europe, where Eastern bloc Marxists met Western humanists; and Ireland, where Protestants met Catholics. Perhaps the most ambitious project was the meeting that Gay Leah Swenson, director and creator of the Carl Rogers Institute for Peace, had organized in Rust, Austria. This meeting occurred while tensions between Sandanistas and Contra rebels were tearing Nicaragua apart. To consider the problems of Central America, it brought together diplomats, politicians, and peace activitists from Nicaragua, the United States, and various Central American and European countries. It remains a landmark event.

Carl also traveled to the then Soviet Union, where participants from all the Republics met each other in new and more open ways. Many in the former Soviet Union and in the United States believe that his visit to the Soviet Union and his influence on the psychological profession of the whole Soviet system played a part in the transformations that followed—at least in the frame through which the human experiences were understood. In conversations with Soviet psychologists since then, I have been told that humanistic psychological concepts are preferable to others, such as psychoanalysis, because they seemed to speak more directly and explicitly to the actual experiences of people.

Participating in these experimental workshop communities, in whatever country and whatever language, takes everyone—participants and facilitators—on intense emotional and conceptual voyages. I often felt that the staff were transformed more than the participants. After all, the participants attended only one; they had their two weeks and then returned to sort through the experience within the contexts of lives as usual. For us, who at that time went from workshop to workshop, PCA *was* life as usual. Gradually, themes and patterns emerged which could not be seen from only one or even two workshops. These patterns forced us to reconsider Rogers' theory of the self in light of our actual practice, and to find ways to answer Freire's and others' criticisms.

Carl, his daughter Natalie, and John K. Wood had originally invented the gatherings, which they called client-centered approach workshops, as a way to test the hypothesis—which originated in Rogers' experience in individual therapy—that under certain conditions not only will individuals move toward self-actualization and growth, but so will communities and groups. I attended the first event in Santa Cruz, California, and was asked to join the staff for the next.

From the outset we were uncomfortable with using the term *client* for participants in these gatherings, so we renamed them person-centered approach workshops. The name stuck and has gradually replaced *client-centered* as the name for Rogerian approaches in general.

It became obvious, through our enormously rich experiences in these events, that we needed to reconsider the meaning of concepts such as person, self, and society, and to rebuild psychological theory. It seemed obvious to me that psychology needed a view of persons that included the individualistic, autonomous aspects of self—so precious to inhabitants of democratic societies—and at the same time understood the ways we participate in larger social realities such as families, groups, and societies.

Human beings, their concerns, aspirations, loves, hates, fears, and achievements can be fully understood only when we acknowledge that whenever someone expresses "self" fully, he or she simultaneously expresses both individuality and belonging. Doing workshops in several different cultural contexts, I began to see that whenever I expressed myself authentically without reservation—presented my whole truth, as I *experienced* it, *understood* it, and *expressed* it—I also expressed my gender, nationality, class, ideology, and cosmology. Along for the ride in such moments are all the subtle cues and clues about my place in the world. The choice of words, the meanings I make, the form and content of my expression are clearly, uniquely mine. At the same time, though, they are part of the intersubjective worlds to which I belong. And whether I am aware of it or not (and mostly I am not), these transindividual aspects of my identiy are recognized by others and have their effects on them.

This was a big bone of contention between Carl and me. He was never able, at least on a conscious level, to acknowledge the ways in which the self-constructs of self-actualizing individuals were part of the cultures that produced them. Nor did he seem to grasp that his own response to people was filtered through and constructed from the cultural biases of white, male, middle-class America. To Carl, paraphrasing Gertrude Stein, a person was a person was a person. He did seem to have had some intimations of the relationship between identity and community—he was fond of saying that "the most personal is the most universal"—but he never seemed to grasp the implication of this.

Carl was the quintessential liberal Romantic. What worried him was the way larger social realities stifled, perverted, repressed, or otherwise exploited the natural subjectivity of individuals. As a feminist, I too was acutely aware of the soul-destroying consequences of the societally imposed restrictions on women's potential, but I could not see it the way Carl did. I had very little enthusiasm for his view of self, which seemed to place the individual's needs irrevocably at odds with those of others. I wanted to discover if it were humanly possible to be free *within* society and not just free *from* it. Could fully authentic and self-actualizing people work together creatively, or were they doomed (as the critics were saying) to isolated lives of competition and alienation? Was it really a choice, as Nietzsche had said, between radical freedom and aloneness or connection and death of the soul?

I began to notice that there are in fact special circumstances in which conflicts between the individual and the group and between conflicting groups become resolved in ways that take nothing from either the individual or the group. It is possible for a group—be it family, team, organization, or community—and the individuals who are part of it to establish a level of mutuality in which a high-order harmony is achieved. That is not to say without conflict. It is not a static harmony in which no discord is ever heard. It is more like a conversation or a piece of orchestral improvisation whose music finds its way between the contributions of individuals. It is as if a resonance exists between the context and the parts. It is as if the group consciousness becomes tuned to the consciousness of the individuals who give it existence. At the same time, the individuals align themselves and their activities to the music of the whole.

This experience is hard to describe. My native language, English, is a language of an individualistic culture. We are rich in words that describe atomic entities, we are poor in the language of relation and connection.

I gradually began to discern, first within these large group processes and later in my individual and family therapy, that there are moments—exquisite moments—when some state of being is reached in which the customary struggle ceases between opposing elements or the separate voices of individual participants and in its place occurs another level of reality altogether.

In these moments it does not matter whether one speaks of someone's individual reality or of the group's reality, because at these moments they are identical. The music and the instruments, the poet and the poem, the players and the game become one. The individual speaks for the whole, the whole lives through and within the individuals. The group becomes conscious. In other words, when the members of a group come to understand how any particular voice bears upon the shared predicament, the group as a whole makes an evoluationary step toward knowledge and expansion of critical consciousness. The wisdom in the group resides in the whole made from the different threads of the parts.

Never was this more evident than at a PCA workshop in Europe where John, an African-American, was having difficulty accepting the views of a coparticipant, a white South African. John eventually exploded into spontaneous and wholehearted verbal rage at racist violence in South Africa. It was a moment of total authentic individuality. Interestingly enough, everyone else felt more connected to John at that moment than they had the whole week. Until then, John had been holding himself out a little from the group; he had plenty of reasons from his own American life to distrust whites. As he surrendered to his existential reality, to his full authentic experience of "I," for the first time he experienced himself and was experienced by others as *part* of the group. There together, moved by his humanity and touched in our own, we all participated in the moment. The separate "I"s became integrated into a "we."

Then Nigel, the white South African, responded in an equally autonomous and authentic manner, expressing the depths of his disappointment and frustration. Sobbing, he told John that in South Africa he had been a lawyer who had defended blacks accused of pass-law violations. He was hurt and angry at blacks because they reacted to him the way John did. He was even angrier at whites who felt he was a traitor. He had been forced from his beloved and tortured homeland, and his loss was overwhelming.

As he too stopped holding back, a sudden shift occurred in the relationship between him and John. Their separateness melted and mutual comprehension replaced the antagonism of a moment before. Both John and Nigel had found an ally where before they had seen an enemy. They experienced a oneness of purpose, not through compromise or leaving their own reality aside and trying to be understanding, but through vigorous, truthful assertion of their uniqueness and separateness. In the safety of the context, they expressed their individual "truths" about apartheid without inhibition, censorship, reservation, or judgment.

Nigel and John were not the only ones who gained. Everyone present became more conscious of apartheid at every level of its evil existence, from the uniquely personal pain to the broadly political costs and consequences. At that moment of truth, even inner subjectivities changed. It will never more be possible for anyone who was present at that moment to react in quite the same way to issues of racism and injustice. Everyone had grown, and the growth was irreversible.

From that moment on, each individual person, the group, and even "society" had a greater grasp of the issues, a more subtle feel for their consequences, and a greater ability to live and function in a world where such situations exist. Both the individuals and the collective had undergone what Freire calls a *pascoa,* or Easter. We had died as we were before the incident, and had been reborn closer to each other and closer to our common humanity.

I realized that a great deal more was going on in these groups than we had been aware of. Not only were people learning to become more fully alive, in touch with their fullness as individual men and women, but they were also developing a more relational consciousness and advancing their relational or participatory competencies. They were learning that although all the group members had a unique reality, point of view, or consciousness that emerged from within their particular time and place in the universe, it was nonetheless *about* the whole. Individual identity and consciousness is created from, and interpenetrated by, the whole. And the identity and consciousness of the community require the contribution of the parts, the people who belong to it. Every voice has something essential to add to the story of the community. Every voice silenced robs the whole of some of its consciousness of itself.

By reading my own consciousness—tuning into myself—I found I could sense what was going on in the group. It brought a whole new perspective on the old feminist adage that "the personal is the political." If I were agitated, then perhaps the group was agitated; if the group were agitated, I discovered I was agitated. But that was not all. I discovered it was possible to "read the group's mind." By paying attention to more subtle clues within myself and within the group, by allowing myself to surrender to the group's moment, I discovered that it was quite easy to tap into wisdoms that were far beyond me as an isolated individual. I became an avid reader of newspaper sports pages, looking for interviews with athletes describing those moments when they played "beyond themselves," pulling up into that special state of group flow that happens when a team is "on." I devoured stories about mothers who knew something was going to happen to a child before it happened, and I collected accounts by musicians describing the ways in which they experienced how it is the music that makes the musician.

At first these notions seemed to suggest to me that if only people could be encouraged to let all their feelings out and to act authentically on their own views of reality, then some New Age utopia was just around the corner. Experiences in the workshops were so overwhelming that it would have been difficult to resist the pull of "true believership," had we not also experienced the potential dangers of such a view.

After our successful trip in 1977, John Wood and I returned to Brazil to conduct a month-long training program in Itapoã, Bahia. The program was very intense, and a good deal of tension arose among the facilitators right from the beginning. Unlike the teams we had put together before, this leadership team had some conceptual disagreements which we had somehow minimized in our enthusiasm to create the program. In particular, the Brazilian facilitator Eduardo Bandeira and I were engaged in some kind of unacknowledged competition. As long as John Wood was present, the threesome was stable and the workshop community remained stable. It was tense, however. Instead of having creativity and energy flowing throughout the process, we came to a tight, frustrating deadlock about many important issues.

John Wood left midway through the program. The group polarized immediately. Some people were attracted to Eduardo's Dionysian exuberance. He was a hard-drinking, nihilistic Zorba of a man who seemed afraid of nothing. I, on the other hand, was a foreigner thousands of miles from home, a woman, and much more Artemis than Psyche. The more ribald Eduardo became, the more spiritual I tried to become. As we tried to decide if the group should spend a day sailing on the bay, I tried to balance Eduardo's insistence on the "need to explore the darker side of human passions" with a call to being more focused on what I (pretentiously) called at the time "higher consciousness." After three days of impasse, half the group forced a decision. In a virtual coup d'état, they opted to go on Eduardo's trip despite the lack of consensus. Those left behind felt betrayed and violated by the abortion of a process to which we had thought everyone was committed.

The group on the boat spent the day in pure, exuberant fun. Those at the retreat center made art, meditated, and spoke to each other about their sense of violation and experience of grief. With the noisier folks out at sea, a contemplative calm came over the group, and we spent the day very quietly.

When the revelers returned, they all seemed pretty agitated. Eduardo apparently had been in an altercation with his new wife, and others had been drawn into the anger. People were distressed and bewildered. They were also tired, hungry, and under the influence of good Brazilian beer.

As we all came together, it was obvious that our community had broken down. We were now two groups, we did not have a shared frame of reference, we were no longer tuned into each other in the way we had been earlier, we were in two completely different consciousness states, and our leaders were in conflict. Neither Eduardo nor I fully realized the implication of that until it was too late. Still believing that the route to harmony was *always* by way of authentic expression of whatever feelings were present, group members began to vent their rage. The words got uglier and uglier, and at one point Eduardo removed his jacket and challenged me to an all-out confrontation. "Até o fim," or "to the finish," he challenged.

Terrified, I did not know what to do. Several of the men who had stayed at the center moved in to subdue Eduardo and stop the process.

Suddenly a young woman, who until then had been the very model of Latin American girlhood—modest, soft-spoken, and conciliatory—screamed in agony and lunged at Eduardo. When someone moved to help her, she released a pair of scissors with which, she said, she had intended to stab Eduardo. One by one, people collapsed in tears. The room looked like a battlefield, people sitting in small groups, rocking and comforting each other. Gradually peace descended, but we were all deeply wounded.

It took me many months to understand what happened at Itapoã. But as the riots raged in Los Angeles over the May Day weekend of 1992, I thought of it all again. One thing is very clear. If the full expression of feelings is to be containable within a group, people need to establish a shared reality, a shared context, a shared commitment to mutual benefit. If groups do not share a frame of reference, then one person's authenticity becomes another's lie. Authentic expression of diverse positions easily drives people apart when not everyone commits to empathic understanding and mutual respect.

Over the years I have come to believe—and the recent riots in Los Angeles have only intensified the urgency I feel about this—that unless we as a people learn to understand the way that social contexts create individual subjectivities and learn how to create shared societal contexts in which people thrive rather than shrink, we are doomed to a long catastrophic period in human history.

I have come to think of such relational or community competence as one of the necessary conditions for democratic life in pluralistic communities. After two centuries of emphasizing the development of individual consciousness in Western culture, it has, in my view, become urgent that we now turn our attention to developing relational and contextual consciousness. That will permit us to live out our individual subjectivities in ways that safeguard the integrity of our communities and can tap into the multiple truths and wisdoms of our larger societies and environments.

Our experiences in these PCA groups seem to suggest that if a community can search for its own truth by listening to the voices of its members, that community may heal itself, may learn, may evolve, and may achieve its own voice with respect to other communities. Freire was right, there was something dangerous in our North American idealization of the unencumbered individual, atomized thinking and glorification of objectivity and abstractionism. We needed to understand more about humans in their contexts.

I had other reasons to explore the new epistemological ideas about reality, truth, and knowledge, as well as psychological concepts such as self, perception, and identity. Sometime after the Laing affair, I noticed that Carl and some of those around us were becoming increasingly fascinated with paranormal phenomena. This ranged from visits to psychics, participation in seances, and consultations with all sorts of folks who claimed to have paranormal powers. From the beginning, this made me very uncomfortable.

On my first trip to Brazil, a group of psychic researchers invited Carl and his team to attend various kinds of supernatural events. These included a psychic reading, a possession by spirits, and a lecture by a Professor Andrade who promised to provide scientific evidence for such paranormal phenomena as reincarnation, poltergeists, and spirit-possession. At the lecture I was first polite, then amused, and finally appalled as I listened to what Professor Andrade tried to pass off as scientific evidence. Ever since my contacts with Michael Polanyi's ideas, I had maintained interest in epistemology, especially in the whole question of pseudoscience and scientism; and here it was, in extreme form. I was appalled because my colleagues, including Carl, seemed to accept the professor's proposition and to find my skepticism irritating. This culminated in my being prevented from participating in a visit to a psychic who said she was going to put Carl Rogers in touch with Carl Jung, who wished to talk to Carl "from the other side." John K. Wood and I were kept from attending the session because it was well known that "spirits won't come down if skeptics are present."

This and other instances like these troubled me intensely. I was personally hurt at being excluded as *persona non grata* from interesting goings on. I also felt that all of our work, including my own, would be weakened if we loosened our commitment to open dialogical investigation of phenomena, para or normal.

Another burr in my saddle came in the form of the young philosopher David Jacobs, who had recently arrived in La Jolla. Like me, David had come to California to study with Carl. David lived in our collective household for awhile after he arrived, so I had ample opportunity to learn of his deep disappointment at what he found at Center for Studies of the Person. As a self-described egghead, he found the anti-intellectualism among its members oppressive. He argued, persuasively to me at least, that the Rogerian position was a credo based on, in Maslow's words, "unproved articles of faith and . . . taken for granted definitions, axioms, and concepts." He felt our behavior more cultlike than investigative and the meetings at CSP more like acts of worship than meetings of critical thinkers.

At first I was defensive and protective. It was all right for me to argue and challenge Carl, but I resented that this interloper should dare. During his several months in our house, however, David funneled to me a whole library of philosophical writings he had read while a doctoral student in the Human Development Program at the University of Chicago.

Carl gradually read less and less from psychology and increasingly turned to writers such as Marilyn Ferguson (who published the *Brain-Mind Bulletin*), Fritjof Capra, Rupert Sheldrake, physicists such as David Bohm and Illyn Prigogine, and New Agers, many of whom frequently crossed the line between science and pseudoscience. Carl became increasingly involved with gurus, psychics, and physicists.

It is difficult here to describe all the levels of the discomfort I felt during these years. Some of them were profoundly personal. My connection with Carl—which had sustained, excited, and challenged me since I first met him through his writings—was now in jeopardy. The person-centered approach team had become my intentional family, and I felt I was losing them too. Yet I just couldn't bear being part of a team that was tilting at an accelerating rate into beliefs I did not share. What was worse, I felt they were dangerous beliefs. I saw my colleagues acritically accepting ideologies that sounded fascistic, enslaving, and dehumanizing. After a decade of commitment to what I thought of as "the emancipation project" in psychology, I felt us moving farther and farther into preaching, exhortation, and true-believership. After forty years of feeling free to speak my mind and name my truth, I had my first experience of feeling silenced.

For years I had read accounts by all manner of oppressed minorities who described being held in worlds of silence by dominating elites. Although parts of these accounts of powerlessness reminded me of the early years of my own life, I never identified with being silenced. Always the feisty chatterbox, I had seen the problems of oppression in terms of structural inequalities. I thought my difficulties were because we were poor and believed that once I was no longer poor, they would disappear. I had focused most of my own thinking on the transformation of political structures, institutions, and economic arrangements to create a more equitable distribution of wealth and freedom of access to power. It was through the experience of finding myself silenced in our person-centered approach team that I came to feel, in every cell of my being, the utter hopelessness of trying to tell your own truth in a world that believes something else.

At first I did try to speak up. My voice would constrict, I would sweat and feel dizzy, but somehow I could squeeze out my disagreement. Gradually I became more strident, more whiny, and less confident. Whereas a few years before I could go to a workshop confident in my skills and knowledge, I gradually found myself obsessing before presentations, overpreparing, and increasingly reading presentations rather than trusting in a more dialogical process. There were occasions when my voice simply would not come out. I remember one in particular. Carl had just responded to a young woman's despair at what she saw as a deteriorating world situation, with the hundredth monkey story and a reference to Bell's Theorum. Whatever the science of the story, the effect of his response was to cajole the woman into having faith that things would be getting better soon. I found my heart pumping out of my chest. The sweat was pouring down my back. When I tried to speak, my voice simply would not come out. Try as I might, I could not speak my disagreement. I shrank back into the shadows and felt utterly alone.

This sense of isolation came to a head for me when Carl and some colleagues from the Center for Studies of the Person organized *Carl*

Rogers and Associates, a learning program in the Person-Centered Approach. It included most of the old PCA team, but I was conspicuously excluded. When I asked Carl about the exclusion, he informed me, sadly and quite embarrassed, that some of those included found my skepticism and criticism unpleasant, and would not work with me. It was them or me, and he chose them. He was emphatic that this was not his choice, but that because of the consensual process, he had gone along. I was to be invited from time to time as a resource person, but my place within the inner circle was denied.

I was furious and very hurt. I felt the betrayal of my personhood, our relationship, and the direction my own intellectual work had taken. As I tried to explain all this to Carl, the feelings got the better of me, and I dissolved into inarticulateness.

I left for one of my Brazilian trips a day or so later. I arrived in Brazil obviously depressed. Encouraged by my dear friend Rachel Rosenberg, Portuguese translator of Carl's books, I decided to write out my frustration. I entitled the article "Stalking the Wild Paradigm Shift" and in it discussed Carl's shift from his original stance as a "pure scientist," by which I meant someone engaged in an open-ended search for truth, to one that was more of an applied technologist in search of behavioral technologies that could bring about certain preestablished goals. I felt this led to epistemological confusion in much of Carl's work.

The words tumbled over each other onto the page. I stayed at it most of the night as idea after idea competed for a hearing. By dawn I was spent. The next morning I mailed the work to Carl without rereading. He was still overseas and by the time he returned, I had already presented the ideas at a Brazilian seminar. Carl's reply, which I still cherish and read once in a while when I feel alone, was swift and characteristically honest.

Dear Maureen,

I have just finished reading your paper on "Stalking the Wild Paradigm Shift." I shouldn't be reading it at all, since there are many, many things to be done, having just arrived home last night. But I wanted to see what you had to say.

I am really vastly educated by reading it. I feel I have learned more about science as a technology. I have learned more about myself. I have learned about changes in myself. I have learned more about you. I understand better the strange alienation that you felt in the PCA group, which was a mystery to me at the time. I have learned a lot about large groups and significant attitudes in dealing with them. Most important of all, I guess for me, is the fact that I like myself best as a pure scientist and realize that each departure from that has been a bit disappointing, in a manner which up to this point has been puzzling and mysterious. I guess the total of what I am saying is that I am very grateful to you for your paper. I thank you for it.

As a paper I think it has one major flaw. I think it tries to cover too much in one paper. I am not quite sure how to resolve this, but would be glad to discuss it with you, or perhaps you've already found one.

I know your paper and the ideas it contains will help me in my next dealings with groups, large or small. It has also reinforced my desire to again find some time for direct involvement, either with individuals or small groups, because that's where I can most successfully "in-dwell." Perhaps it will also help me to have the same attitudes toward large groups, although thus far I haven't learned as profoundly from large groups as from individual or small group contacts.

The fact that I really shifted from the pure science attitude, which I know is a very important part of me, to the applied scientist or technologist, was very revealing to me. I think the analysis was quite correct. I believe now that I can distinguish more clearly when I am one or the other.

I will already have sent you, or will send you with this letter, a copy of the paper I gave in Finland. I think it is a pretty good paper, but it is not based on my own experiences and this troubles me. I have not usually written from borrowed ideas. Nevertheless, I stand by it as being my intuitive sense of the directions we are taking.

In conclusion, I guess I would just say that I wish more of my colleagues were writing papers involving clearly independent and critical thinking in the way your paper does.

I'm glad I wasn't there to hear you deliver it. I might have been embarrassed by parts and the focus might have turned to me rather than your ideas. But I am delighted to have read it and certainly want a copy when it is revised. In this copy there are some faults which I think are purely typographical, but the meaning came through in spite of that. Thanks again.

Very cordially and affectionately,
Carl.

The letter helped ease the pain of being excluded from the learning project. More significantly, it encouraged me to continue thinking my own way through the increasingly muddled terrain that was—and is still—the field of humanistic psychology.

For the next few years, much of my writing was in response to numerous experiences of hearing people in my field, including Carl, play fast and loose with science and epistemology. One day I received a copy of a book entitled *The Hundredth Monkey*, which I was told had been distributed at an AHP meeting, and from which Carl was quoting. In it was reference to a book by Lisle Watson in which he described how monkeys had supposedly transmitted behavioral learning among them in some kind of telepathic, mind-to-mind transfer. Since I had studied the same monkey research while a science undergraduate in England a dozen years before, I knew there was something fishy in the Watson story. It troubled me deeply that these studies were being misrepresented to promulgate some idea that knowledge could pass among human beings via such paranormal mechanisms. It troubled me even more that some folks thought there was something exciting about a notion—heralded as a new paradigm shift by writers such as Ken Kesey, Marilyn Ferguson, Werner Erhardt, and now Carl—that once something becomes a reality for a critical mass it becomes true for everyone.

Unable to bear the rising anxiety provoked by such acritical acceptance of what were in essence fascistic ideas, and feeling that once again it was either silence or marginalization, I cranked out another essay, "The Hundredth Humanistic Psychologist," in which I debunked the monkey story and discussed many of my concerns about the proselytizing turn that humanistic psychology was taking. I made it plain and I made it public that I believed the acritical, anti-intellectual habits of mind widespread throughout much of the human potential movement was at best silly and at worst represented a "dark side" regressive process that might lead people to swallow the kinds of self-congratulatory propaganda that had fueled the Nazi and Fascist successes of the 1930s.

When this article was published, I discovered a whole new community of other skeptical humanists, including Rollo May, Walter Truett Anderson, Don Michael, and many others. They drew me into a new community of learners struggling to understand the way reality, knowledge, and the human mind create and sustain worlds of meaning and experience. Slowly but surely, through bimonthly discussion groups held at Rollo's house in Tiburon, we began to outline a new social-constructivist psychology that would affirm the centrality of human consciousness at the same time as it recognized the inter-subjectivity of human knowing.

During the next three years, I wrote several pieces on science and pseudoscience. I was beginning to attract the attention of a group of skeptical fundamentalists: the *Committee for the Scientific Investigation of Claims of the Paranormal* (CSICOP) whose journal, *The Skeptical Inquirer,* was publishing debunkings of one paranormal claim after another. The group eventually asked me to speak to their annual skeptics' meeting.

This invitation turned into a disaster from one point of view but another intellectual turning point when viewed from another. I was to participate in a panel on debunking the New Age movement. From the preconference banter, I got the impression that the organizers thought it quite a coup to have a New Age "insider" denounce her own colleagues. Treachery makes good drama!

I decided, instead, to debunk debunking. Outlining the social-constructivist arguments, using almost entirely the arguments from folks like Michael Polanyi and Steven Toulmen, as well as my own new thinking about the inseparability of the knower and the known, I challenged the skeptics assembled to become skeptical about skepticism. I suggested that the excesses of the New Age movement were insignificant compared to the excess of positivist science and that the scientific superstition was far more insidious—because it passed for objective truth—than more frankly religious positions such as New

Age pseudoscience. New Agers were simply an idiosyncratic group of nice middle-class folks trying to feel good in an increasingly chaotic world. Because of their relatively insignificant place in the social hierarchy, their belief systems hurt no one but themselves. But science was the belief story held by the powerful elites. Their blindness to constructivist ideas might have global ramifications.

In the presentation, I was careful to honor science as one truth system among many but suggested that more dangerous pseudoscientific dragons for the CSICOP St. George to slay were scientistic "disciplines" such as sociobiology. I used the sociobiological proposition that male sexual violence such as rape is the normal outcome of "selfish genes" as an example of scientism or moral inversion. It typifies cases in which essentially moral or political positions are passed off as scientifically "true."

As I spoke, a deadly silence descended over the group. As I went on, people began to fidgit. There were moments when I couldn't hear myself read. I felt dizzy and my knees felt wobbly. It was the silencing experience I had before, only this time I wouldn't be silenced. I kept going. The venom in the room intensified. People scoffed out loud and shook their heads vigorously enough so that I could see. By the time I sat down, I was light headed, my heart was pounding in my chest, and the dinner I had eaten before the session was lurching uncontrollably in my stomach. I managed to sit through another presentation. When it came time for questions, the lines at the microphones went clear to the back of the room. At least half of them were for me, all but one very hostile.

As my terror intensified, I realized I was experiencing what all heretics must feel. I was suddenly and paradoxically thankful that I was born into a post-enlightenment world in which secular rationality, not religion, framed our public life. I was in the odd position of being thankful for a scientific rationalism I had just got done criticizing, a system committed to arguing with rather than burning its unbelievers.

My feelings got the better of me. I gradually found myself sliding off my chair and onto the floor behind the podium. To my horror and embarrassment, I began to vomit and eventually had to be taken by ambulance to a local Catholic hospital. As I regained my composure, I took in the scene in the emergency room. A white-coiffed sister was holding my hand and reassuring me. Around us was a whole array of high-tech medical equipment beeping away under the watchful eye of Our Lady of Perpetual Care. I doubled up in hilarious laughter as I caught the paradoxical absurdity of the whole scene. I think that was my very first postmodern giggle!

At around the same time, my interest in feminism, in learning, and in teaching landed me in a women's studies department at San Diego State University, teaching psychology of women. It was sometimes hard to read feminist criticisms of humanistic psychology (it was too individualistic, they said) without feeling defensive. Feminist theorists were making the same citicisms of patriarchal world views in general, including humanistic psychology, that I had been *living* in my experience of client-centered therapy. It was very helpful to examine client-centered theory from a vantage point from within an entirely different and largely critical perspective.

In that odd dialectical way that consciousness seems to advance, the raw feminist critique—in its own way just as monolithic as the andocentric, Eurocentric vision it challenged—provided the limiting boundary I needed to understand what profound wisdom there actually was in the person-centered position. I now understood that the error in Rogerian thinking was not in its overall view of the human condition but rather in its insistence that scientific "objectivity" secured its claim for legitimacy. From the feminist margins, I began to take seriously the postmodernist assertions that all truth is socially constructed. It suddenly seemed obvious to me that logical positivism, with its ideal of an impersonal absolute truth, was indeed a failed project, as Michael Polanyi had claimed so long before.

Gradually it became clear that person-centered therapy, psychoanalysis, behaviorism, religions, and all other approaches to questions of human existence should not be compared as rival versions of the truth. Rather, they should be seen as alternative stories *about* human reality, offered by their different framers as their best account of how they understand the human predicament.

Overnight any need disappeared to debunk, challenge, and criticize even the silliest and wildest beliefs some people held. If all we humans have are our belief systems, then who was I to say that ids, egos, and superegos were any more or less real than "inner children," "goddesses within," or "wild men"? There seemed little difference between a belief that dream images came from some collective unconscious and a belief that spirits inhabit one's body and will appear in dreams until they are set free.

A longtime believer in the liberal, humanistic tradition of the European enlightenment, I had always placed my faith in a Voltairian rational universe. Sooner or later, I had believed, all humanity would receive a good liberal education and we would all agree that the best way to conduct our lives would be along the lines prescribed by John

Stuart Mill. It now appeared that such a world was unlikely and probably undesirable.

At first, this was a very disturbing idea. I had nightmarish visions of a world of endless relativity, with collective allegiance going to those with the biggest sticks or the largest bankrolls. But accepting that there might not be impersonally derived universal values does not mean that we are absolved from the need to examine, debate, and make judgments about better or worse value systems. I certainly do not believe that no moral distinctions can be made between a system that endorsed slavery and one that enfranchised everyone, for example. Certainly there are differences between value systems. Making choices about where one stands and taking positions to support or oppose the positions of others cannot be avoided by embracing a post-positivist world. Indeed, one might even, as ever, find cause to fight or die for one system over another. What had changed for me was that I could no longer frame and claim moral superiority of one system over another as a debate between absolute truth and superstition. Disagreements and conflicts would have to be argued in less doctrinaire language. Much more subtle, complex, and subjective valences would have to be weighed. In particular, it meant that we as valuing persons would be forced to assume a much greater personal responsibility for the values we hold. No more hiding our bigotry behind claims of scientific neutrality.

The challenge of our age was not, as many of my humanistic teachers had once believed, the idealized emancipatory progress of some abstracted "man" or even woman, but something far more problematic. It seemed to me that the urgent question facing us as a species was how people with varied world views—people with disparate ideas about who we are and how we should live, people who construe their multiple universes in vastly different ways—could peaceably coexist. And how, if we are to solve the multiple interpenetrated challenges facing the planet in these last years of the twentieth century, can we learn how to cooperate on the urgent issues and tasks that face the whole of humanity?

I had once believed peace between people rested on our ability to liberate some inborn emancipatory tendency common to all of us; on our finding ways to reach to achieve some transcendent oneness. I now came to believe that if we were to make it as a species, to avoid blowing ourselves to smithereens because we had better bombing skills than communication skills, we would have to turn our attention outward. We need to learn ways of organizing ourselves, from the level of the family and the organization, to the level of politics and international relations, in which diverse individuals and diverse communities can be affirmed for their uniqueness as beings-for-themselves, with their own interests, values, and ways of beings. At the same time, we must learn how to create agreements and relationships among these diverse elements that are based on a spirit of mutuality and interdependence rather than on coercion and inequality.

In search of theory that might underpin such a new relational ethic, I began to devour philosophical works that attempted to address that hard-to-describe edge where individual freedom meets the commons. I was looking for metaphors, paradigms, and just plain old cliches capable of holding the tension between the need to be and the need to belong. As I plunged into the postmodern discussion about reality ranging in disciplines as distant as sociobiology and metaphysics, from post-structuralism and critical theory to "goddess feminism" and witchcraft, once again my certainties crumbled. This time, though, the experience was thrilling rather than frightening.

Accompanied by new fast friends who had come together to discuss humanistic psychology theory, I dared dismantle past truths once again. We were all searching and together we constructed, deconstructed, and reconstructed with alacrity. Rollo May brought to the discussions his awesome erudition and psychological wisdom. There seemed no aspect of the human condition that has escaped Rollo's investigation. What a scholar! What a heart! An exemplar of John Donne's affirmation that the glory of God "is a man, fully alive." Walter Truett Anderson added the skeptical political-scientist's eye. Whenever I got inflated by some ungrounded utopianism, Walter would burst the bubble with a gentle reminder of the "real politik" of a planet with five billion people on it. Donald Michael brought a similar, perhaps even more sobering frame. As a twenty-year member of the Club of Rome, his intellectual life is spent with those at the highest levels thinking about the "global problematique." Don provided a global perspective, ensuring that we never forget that the world looks very different through the eye of a Chadian, Bosnian, Bangladeshi, or Peruvian. The macro-level frames of reference that Don and Walt brought, together with Jacqueline Larcomb Doyle's twenty-odd years as a psychotherapist and family specialist, enabled us to explore the intricate contours of human experience in a comprehensive or holistic way.

Needless to say, it was slow going. Reweaving reality is not the stuff of brainstorms and flip charts. Sometimes we would meet for several hours and end up back where we started. Other times we would jump ahead, making a seeming breakthrough, only to find the trail peter out. But gradually and in the most satisfying of manners, we found ourselves really learning new ways to see, new ways to hear, and new ways to understand the human predicament.

As part of this group, I pulled closer to the Association for Humanistic Psychology. Often our discussions would come around to AHP as we would express our frustration about the New Age direction the organization had taken in recent years. We shared a profound skepticism about many unsupported claims of the paranormal as well as sadness and alarm at the cheap hucksterism that was increasingly showing up at AHP meetings and in the human potential movement in general. It sometimes seemed that AHP was becoming choice fishing grounds for anyone with a new brand of snake oil. Annual meetings began to take on the appearance of a fin-de-siecle crank's tea parties, with channelers, mediums, and hypnotists vying for air time with self-styled prophets, gurus, and aerobics instructors. On the other hand, we were all closely aligned with the humanistic position in psychology and were actually rather open-minded about how human beings might expand the limits of consciousness.

One day I realized that my relationship with AHP was rather like that of the adolescent with her family. I was constantly finding fault, always kvetching about the ways in which it failed to live up to my demands for perfection. And, also like the adolescent, I was expecting someone else to fix it for me. Almost as if on schedule, my next growth challenge appeared in the guise of a phone call from Ruben Nelson asking if I would be willing to put my time where my mouth was and serve on AHP's board of directors.

In some ways it was the last thing I should have accepted. I was just starting to establish a good private practice, my writing was flowing, I was deepening my studies in feminist thought, and my husband and I had just adopted a fourteen-year-old boy, Michael.

I was elected and, before I knew it, life changed considerably once again. Until my first board meeting, I was unaware of the dire straits AHP was in. The organization was a hair's breadth away from bankruptcy, and morale was so low our meetings were extremely hard going. It was clear to everyone that in its present state the organization was not viable.

One day about twenty-five people, AHP oldtimers, met at Rollo's house. I do not clearly remember everyone who attended but the group included Rollo, Walt, Don, Jackie, the then Executive Director Paul DuBois, Debbie Swackhammer, Tom Greening, Ruben Nelson, Elizabeth Rifler, Frances Vaughan, Roger Walsh, Jeffrey

Mishlove, Dennis Jaffee, Donald Polkinghorn, Fritjof Capra, and Will McWhinney. The question before us was simple: "Is this the time to pull the plug on the ailing organization?"

The meeting was very emotional. One by one, those present began to reminisce, to call forth the deep and abiding love held in the hearts of all those there for the work, people, and ideals of AHP. The room was incandescent. In a large circle in Rollo's living room, people sang their love songs to a community that for over a quarter century had fed and fanned the flames of their deeper passions. We were sharply mindful of the dreadful economic realities facing the organization, but we did not have the collective will to end the game.

Out of the conversation, largely through the organizational wisdom of then President Will McWhinney and of Ruben Nelson, we began to visualize a new kind of organizational form for AHP. It was one that could embrace the wide (and wild) diversity of its members. It seemed to us that much of the creativity-robbing tension in the community, which had become such a draining, demoralizing, and undermining experience, came from trying to find ways to reconcile the needs and demands of its very different constituents. The skeptics and secularists like me held back so as not to have to deal with the psychics and channelers. Those whose interests were more spiritual or even just playful found our pointy-headed secular intellectualism arrogant and snobbish. Long before the right-wing backlash had described the paralyzing effects on academic life of a surplus of "political correctness," AHP members had become embedded in our own intellectual molasses, trying to peaceably coexist in a community where one person's truth was another's superstition.

As we came to the startling awareness that the organization was experiencing in microcosm what was going on in the culture as a whole, we suddenly saw a new role for AHP. Our conversation became animated. What had begun as something of a wake took on the feel and tone of a birth or a baptism. One by one, shoulders lifted, we began to breathe more freely, the humor returned, and people who a few hours before had thought they were participating in AHP's last gasp found new energy and new enthusiasm. They were willing to make new commitments. We decided to go forward, not to save AHP but to reinvent it.

Those of us present at that meeting decided we would try to transform AHP into a postmodern or postindustrial organization. Our plan was to try to invent an organizational form in which the "energetic economy" would be changed from an industrial-age model to a meaning-driven, sustainable community. People would not be members to "get something"; rather, we would become an enabling context, a cultural container that could support members whose work was compatible with the ideals of humanistic psychology. Our mission would become the work of our members. It had been an association in which members sent dues to a central Board that would do interesting and meaningful things in the world on their behalf—a child-parent relationship. We would turn it into one in which the whole community would be geared toward self-initiated participation in the world, defined by and fueled by the energies of the people themselves—a situation of adult-adult mutual involvement.

I was later to describe this as a move from shallow to deep democracy. I was quite pleased with myself for this concept, but before I had time to enjoy it for long, I began to see a vastly trivialized version of such an idea popping up. So I am looking for new words.

The meeting marked another turning point in my own sense of mission and vocation. My apprenticeship with Carl and the Person-Centered Approach team, the psychological reconstruction I had done after the Laing-Rogers meeting, and the intense learning in the study group finally came together. I felt ready to assume an adult leadership role in the world, or at least in a tiny piece of it. I was seeing the world and my place in it very differently. I had finally figured out that the experts, all the "theys" I had spent my life looking to for guidance or to blame, were simply folks. What an exhilarating time that was—and still is. I have no idea if everyone crosses this particular existential threshold, but each day I wonder at the sharp contrast between the "before" and "after" sense of myself.

For over forty years, I had gone about my business feeling that the person I referred to as "I" was somehow in here, inside my skin, sealed off from the "out there" by some semipermeable membrane that marked the boundaries of selfhood. I had always felt that this "I" was somehow pitted in some existential combat against a nameless "they" who made decisions, created structures, and exercised their leadership thanks to some mysterious authority that they achieved (or had been granted) by some unnamed legitimization process to which I would never have access. I had been content, even proud, to do my work at the margins of power.

In my work as therapist, feminist activist, and emancipatory educator, I had some intellectual understanding of the experience of "otherness," that inchoate yet heartfelt sense that somehow one is relegated to live out life as a recipient of cultural movements—even as protestor or critic, but never as one of the authors. For over a decade, thanks primarily to my contacts with Paulo Freire and his work, I had been aware of the psychological consequences of marginalization; but, perhaps protected by a healthy case of denial, I had never fully realized the extent to which it applied to me. One day, driving on the road to Mount Rainier in Washington, the mountain radiant in the pink glow of early morning, this changed.

I was tuned to a broadcast on National Public Radio. There was some crisis afoot, I think in the Soviet Union, and as usual, as the story unfolded, the anchors were interviewing a parade of experts. Each expert, establishment males one and all, freely pontificated about what was going on. In the proverbial flash, I suddenly realized that these guys were making it up as they went along! They were smart, well read, and even thoughtful, but what not one of them acknowledged was that the events of the day were utterly without precedent, unexpected, and no one possessed either blueprint or map for what would happen next. The Princeton chap was sure one action would be taken, the Yalie another, and the Kennedy School pundit, with equal poise and self-confidence, suggested something completely different. I realized they were not, as they professed, commenting upon reality, but were in fact busily constructing it. As their opinions became theories, their theories became "reports," and their reports became the public opinions of the day, these men were constructing the culture we were all to live. In that moment, I realized that the difference between these fellows and myself was that they clearly felt no hesitation about passing off their speculations and opinions as valid, useful, and worth listening to. Every clearly articulated sentence exuded a sense of entitlement and authority that I had never known. Another watershed moment.

The force of this insight was two-fold. On the one hand, I understood the extent to which cultures are made up as we go along. Each of us and all of us, at the macro level and at the micro, are continuously trying to understand, explain, account for, and cope with the ever unfolding existential realities of our lives. When that process is going on inside the head, we call it reflection. When we put it out, we call it communication. When we make it public, we call it leadership.

On the other hand, I realized that what separated me from the cultural leaders had a great deal more to do with the psychology of entitlement than with anything real. I knew I was knowledgeable enough, experienced enough, and articulate enough to participate constructively in the culture-making process. What I lacked was my conviction that I was entitled to a leadership role in the public cultural conversation. This changed on my ride to the glacier.

The following February at the AHP board meeting, I accepted the nomination for president of the association. Even in that process, I had to take on the self-doubt demon. When another board member, a man with a national reputation, said he would like to be nominated, I almost ceded to him. Old habits take a long time to croak. But I didn't cede, and was nominated and elected. I ran with a particular agenda for AHP and for myself.

Perhaps the most moving aspect of the learnings, growings, and changings going on in me during these years was a deeply felt understanding of the psychological effects on me of growing up as a woman and as a member of the English working class. What had once been largely theory was now my own lived truth, and I began to realize that if my voice had been silenced in this way, then so had millions of others. What a wicked squander of human resources, what dangerous neglect of people-power, what immoral abuse of generations of people, what a foolish over-reliance on the wisdom of some and under-utilization of the knowledge and experience of many.

It was clear to me that if our culture and the planet were to survive, we had to find ways to pool our resources as a species. We had to get at the knowledge kept hidden in the silenced members of our kind and to bring everyone's wisdom to the service of our communities. This was to become my personal agenda and I wanted to try to convince AHP to make it its.

For many reasons it seemed important to focus my efforts on the further emancipation of women and girls. Working with a small group of generous and exceptionally talented women in San Diego, I helped found the organization Women for Change, whose agenda is to effect cultural change on behalf of women and girls. Since 1989 we have held two national-scale conferences as well as several smaller events, and we are gearing up to create written and video-taped materials that carry our vision into the world. My path has taken another turn.

I have not found the harmonious, coherent, self-actualized self I thought I was looking for. I have been unable to trim and organize my resumé, separating main stream from tributaries. In fact, the fluvial metaphor, which ever since my encounter with the mighty Amazon had held such potent meanings, has lost its power to illuminate my process of becoming. Instead, my understanding has changed about what brings a sense of coherence to life—at least to mine.

I am no longer interested in finding some unchanging core abstraction such as a "true self." As my life moves into new cultures, as I engage in untried activities, make new investments, and experience fresh delights, I no longer seem to place the value I once did on ideals of consistency, identity, and individuation. Boundaries become fuzzy, contextual, and ever-changing and I place higher value on what used to be criticized as "other-directedness"—cherishing my connectedness with other people, closeness, and flexibility. I have set down the search for transcendent realities and see my lifework more like gardening than purification. Each season something new is planted; it flowers, fruits, is harvested, and then falls dormant, only to be forked over and reset with new seeds at the season's turn.

A better metaphor for the self and its becoming seems to be the patchwork quilt. Each experience gets cobbled onto the others with soluble stitches, held in place more by contexts and commitments than by constitution. When times or needs demand it, that little piece of "Brazilian Maureen" can slide over next to the social activist patch from Oberlin. Later it can be rearranged and slide over to the spiritual Maureen and help her through the labyrinth of some new mystical teaching she is experiencing. All that I have been can be used and reused in endless kaleidoscopic transformations from context to context.

The guiding principle is, as Spike Lee said, to "do the right thing." What the right thing is, of course, is not as clear as it was in my earlier objectivist times, but it is not some utterly subjective nihilism, either. The right thing is usually determined concretely by the situation, by the complex flickerings of webs of commitments, obligations, wisdoms, and human aspirations. If we talk about them, think about them, maybe even pray or meditate about them, it is rather surprising (and reassuring) how often our actions are life-enhancing rather than life-negating, and how, no matter how diverse our histories might be, the right thing to one person is often a good deal like the right thing to another. I'll settle for that for now, trying not to forget how easy it is to fall into paradox and foolishness and muddiness. One thing is clear, however. There are rich learning fields aplenty yet to be explored. Here goes!

❖

My studies with Clark Moustakas, beginning in 1955, gave me the chance to be privy to the works of leaders in the field of humanistic psychology: Clark, Carl Rogers, Abraham Maslow, Art Combs, and Ross Mooney shared unpublished writings with me, without expecting comment or critique. This is how I first encountered Art's work in education, psychology, and values clarification.

Art had been one of Carl's first students at Ohio State University. Art's writings acknowledge the influence of Carl Rogers, Donald Snygg, Earl Kelley, and Prescott Lecky (whom many regard as the first descriptor of humanistic psychology). Earl had chaired my doctoral committee at Wayne State University, and this was one of many significant connections I felt toward Art.

I later met Art at his beautiful home in Greeley, Colorado. In life as well as in theory, this warm and gentle man is the epitome of a person who embraced the Rogerian triad: acceptance, empathy, and congruence. I felt I was in the presence of another mentor, and I have been able to keep up with him since then through Clark and another dear friend, Bob Blume (who was a co-teacher with me in Michigan, and who later became Art's associate at the University of Florida).

The innovative paths he followed in humanistic education and psychology are humbly documented in his autobiography.

❖

3

A Search for Personal Meaning

by Arthur W. Combs

I first met Carl Rogers in 1938 when I was a graduate student at Ohio State University. The experience was destined to change my life.

When I graduated from high school I probably would have been described by my teachers as intelligent, well read, desperately eager to please, slow maturing, and often a free thinker. A humanistically oriented psychologist would have diagnosed a young man characterized by deep feelings of rejection, low self-concept, uncertain of acceptance by his peers, a loner, sometimes stubborn or rebellious. The quotation under my graduation yearbook picture read, "There is more faith in honest doubt, believe me, than in half the creeds." My feelings of rejection came about, in part, as a consequence of being first born. They were exacerbated by a mother who herself suffered from severe feelings of inadequacy and a sense of not belonging. These made her unpredictable to her children. We did not know how to deal with her rapid shifts in mood, from loving and caring to angry and rejecting. In addition, I was physically slow to mature. That left me constantly behind my peers in physical and social growth, a discrepancy made wider by being skipped a grade in school.

After high school, I wanted to delay going off to college because I did not know what I wanted to do. But my parents were afraid that if I did not go then, perhaps I never would. My father urged me, "Scientific agriculture, son. It's the field of the future." So I enrolled at Cornell University to pursue a career in plant pathology. The

Great Depression was on and I worked long hours to pay my way. In the middle of my third year, additional factors—falling in love and increasing doubts about my choice of occupation—combined to result in rapidly falling grades. I decided to leave the university just one step ahead of the registrar and went home to Fostoria, Ohio. During the next year and a half, I worked at a variety of jobs. I also volunteered to teach a gymnastics class at the local YMCA. That experience proved so satisfying that I decided to become a teacher. Accordingly, I hitchhiked back to Cornell, married my girlfriend and, two days later, entered the College of Education at Ohio State University.

Rogers at Ohio State

The College of Education at OSU was an exciting place. Many on the faculty and in the Laboratory School were deeply involved in the "progressive education" movement. Among them was the pioneering educational psychologist Sidney Pressey. Pressey hired me as his research assistant and I planned to go on for graduate work with him on graduation in 1935. Unhappily, my wife and I were so poor that it became imperative to find a job. Accordingly, I accepted a teaching position in the high school at Alliance, Ohio.

I enjoyed the experience immensely and students responded well to me. Many came to me for aid with their in- or out-of-school problems. Feeling inadequate to cope with many of the problems they presented, I decided after several years to return to OSU for graduate training in counseling. Thus it was that I came under the influence of Carl Rogers in the summers of 1938 and '40 while working on a master's degree. On its completion in 1941, I accepted a graduate assistantship to begin work on a doctorate with Carl.

He was just then shaking up traditional psychology with his introduction of nondirective therapy. The nondirective technique was the direct antithesis of most practice and became the subject of widespread debate. Carl's innovativeness went much further. Until that time, what went on in the counseling hour was a mystery known only to therapist or client. It was rarely open to external scrutiny. Rogers had the courage to record and publish the protocols of therapy so that all could see and critique what went on in the interactions of counselor and client. This opened the whole field of therapy to research exploration. In a series of studies, Carl and his students led the way to examine the intimate dynamics of the therapeutic process.

The early forties were a marvelous time to be a graduate student with Carl. We became so nondirective that, if you had asked me in those days, "What time is it?" I probably would have replied, "You're wondering what time it is."

We had no tape recorders. Instead, we recorded sessions on dictaphones or phonograph records and played these back in our seminars. We would listen to what the client said, then lift the needle to ask, "What would you say?" Following that, we would drop the needle to hear what the counselor actually said, followed by further debate. Just being part of this stimulating group of graduate students under Rogers' mentorship was a great high. We had the feeling we were on to something big, at the cutting edge of an idea and a process destined to change the field of therapy.

Soon after I arrived to join this group, I asked Carl to take me on in therapy. He did and I had a priceless opportunity to experience counseling from the point of view of the client. I used the time to explore my relationships with my family of origin and began to relinquish my deep-seated needs for their love and affirmation. That set me free to seek personal fulfillment elsewhere in the world. The experience in therapy also provided valuable insights about the therapeutic process and a warm, caring relationship with a truly remarkable man. I was flattered when he hired me to compile the index for *Counseling and Psychotherapy*, the book that introduced the nondirective approach to the world.

As a student I had another more painful but amusing experience with Carl. One evening he invited all of us to his home for a backyard barbecue. As the evening wore on, we lounged about, talking and enjoying the camaraderie. For a long time, I lay on the grass in front of Carl, listening to the conversation as various students plied him with questions. Next day, I fled to the hospital with what the doctor said was "the worst case of chiggers I've ever seen!" I was covered from head to toe with chigger lesions. It took two weeks to clear them from my body. I have never prostrated myself at the feet of any master since!

Preconditions for a Humanistic Psychology

During the forties, Carl was primarily concerned with defining and researching the nondirective method. Two of his students, however, were intrigued with the underlying theory and its implications beyond the counseling relationship. Victor Raimy, for example, wanted to include a theory of the self concept in his dissertation on "The Self Concept as a Factor in Counseling and Personality Organization" (1943). Rogers, however, urged Vic to downplay the theoretical formulation and concentrate the dissertation on his research findings. Fortunately, Vic ignored this advice. His theoretical contribution was destined to become one of the earliest definitive statements on the nature and function of the self concept. In later years, his dissertation was in such demand that the Ohio State Library published it as a significant historical document.

I, too, was fascinated by the broader implications of nondirective therapy. The importance of empathy in the counseling process and the discipline of careful listening required by nondirective counseling laid the foundation for a phenomenological approach to psychology a few years later. I was also intrigued with the implications of nondirective thinking for the processes of education. My 1945 doctoral dissertation was a comparison of the Thematic Apperception Test with autobiography. To explore that problem, it was necessary to design a scoring method applicable to both instruments. Out of my experience with clients in nondirective counseling, I invented a phenomenological scoring system. It called for making inferences about: the subject's purposes or goals, his or her perception of the blocks to their achievement, and the means chosen to surmount the obstacle. I was starting to approach psychology from the point of view of the person.

My Syracuse Days

On completion of my qualifying exams, I accepted a position in the College of Education at Syracuse University. Shortly after, Carl transferred to the University of Chicago and offered me the opportunity to head the counseling center he planned to establish there. I was flattered by this gesture and considered it very carefully. I decided, however, that accepting his offer would mark me forever as Carl Rogers' protege. I did not want to be known as a Rogerian.

Instead, I wanted to be my own man, free to explore what I might become in my own right. Accordingly, I completed my dissertation with Horace English, took my final orals on VJ Day, and turned to building a clinical psychology program at Syracuse.

With colleagues in the areas of reading and special eduction, I established a psycho-educational clinic open to students and the community. Simultaneously, I began to build the graduate program by introducing courses in clinical psychology. When the courses showed sufficient enrollment, I petitioned the administration for additional staff. In this fashion, by 1950 I had established fifteen such courses requiring four additional professors—enough to comprise a full-fledged program in clinical psychology, complete with clinical practice facilities and internships in five mental hospitals.

An Intellectual Conversion

In 1946 I met a second person who vitally affected my life, even more than Carl. Donald Snygg, a professor of psychology at Oswego State University, taught an occasional course at Syracuse. On one of these occasions he left one of his reprints with me. It was entitled, "The Need for a Phenomenological System of Psychology." For some months it lay on my desk among things I intended to read. When I was invited to make my first major address to a national conference at the American Orthopsychiatric Association meetings in New York, I took Don's paper along, expecting to read it sometime on the trip.

I had been asked to speak about nondirective therapy. On arrival at the conference, I discovered to my consternation that I was scheduled to share the platform with Rogers, inventor of nondirective therapy, on one side of me and Peter Blos, its most virulent critic, on the other. I managed, somehow, to get through the speech. Carl complimented me on it, but I remember little else until I woke up hours later sprawled across the bed in my hotel room.

Next evening, on the train home to Syracuse, I began to read Don's article. The impact was astounding, a veritable intellectual conversion. Dozens of problems in psychological theory with which I had been wrestling suddenly fell into place with clarity and congruence. In great excitement, when the train arrived at Syracuse, I called Don for an appointment the next day.

When I walked into his office, I said, "Don, this is the most terrific thing I have ever read. Do you know what you've done?"

To which he replied, "What the hell are you talking about?"

I began to tell him some of the implications I saw in his ideas, and soon we were both eagerly involved in pursuing the ideas in every direction. That afternoon we outlined the perceptual theory that culminated in our book, *Individual Behavior: A New Frame of Reference for Psychology.* In the two years that followed, we became great friends, meeting weekly to write and critique the manuscript. Though we embellished the original ideas, we never changed the basic outline we set down that first day.

In the summer of 1948 Don and I spent an afternoon with Carl Rogers at his summer home on Seneca Lake. Carl was intrigued with our ideas, kept the manuscript for three or four months, and agreed to write a short statement for the jacket. At the next American Psychological Association conference, I presented a paper entitled, "A Phenomenological Approach to Adjustment Theory." Carl was in the audience and told me he was speaking on the same topic the next day. Sure enough, his presidential address contained many similar ideas. Don and I were flattered at his several references to our work. Carl's address was published immediately by APA. My paper, however, had to run the usual gauntlet of peer review and did not appear in print until a year later. This was a cause of occasional embarrassment in later years when some people assumed I had taken my ideas from Carl without acknowledging the source.

Applying the Perceptual-Experiential View

I have spoken of the development of perceptual-experiential psychology with Don Snygg as an intellectual conversion experience. It has been just that. Everything I have done professionally since has been deeply influenced by that frame of reference. Perceptual theory has provided the fundamental assumptions for my work as writer, teacher, counselor, trainer of practitioners in the helping professions, and administrator or consultant in psychology, counseling, psychotherapy, and education. It has also permeated my personal life, providing trustworthy guidelines for thinking, behaving, and becoming in every aspect of my existence. A source of deep satisfaction to me is that so many others have found it a useful approach to psychology.

I feel I am both a product of the humanist movement and a significant contributor to its advancement in psychology.

In 1950 I was just completing my year as president of the New
York State Psychological Association (NYSPA). Psychologists in
the state were beginning to seek licensure for the profession. They
called upon me to head the Joint Council of New York State
Psychologists, formed to achieve that end. The problem was huge: to
bring together the twenty-three widely diverse psychological organizations in the state, to write a bill on which they could agree, then
to lobby it through the legislature—all this in nine months. I accepted
the assignment as a challenge to see whether the perceptual approach
I believed in would stand the test when applied to a tough practical
problem. It did. We expanded the NYSPA to encompass members
from all walks of the profession. Following that, we designed one of
the first licensing bills in the country and saw it passed unanimously
in the state legislature—only to have it vetoed by Governor Dewey.
It was not until two years later, after I left the state, that our bill
became law.

Encountering Hostility and Rejection

Later that year I experienced the most traumatic event of my career.
Returning to the university from a Christmas vacation trip, I was
called to the Dean's office and informed that letters were in the mail
firing three of our four clinical psychology professors. The university was desperately seeking to solve its budget problems by releasing all untenured faculty. No amount of argument or pleading could
reverse the decision. In a state of shock, I turned to the dreadful task
of informing my colleagues and our forty-five doctoral students as
they returned from the holidays that our program was being terminated. What a nightmare! Faculty and students were devastated. I
began the heart-rending task of finding new places for our staff at
other universities, helping beginning students transfer to other colleges, and helping older ones to speed up completion of their programs. By June, the staff had found new positions and half of the
students left for greener pastures. With one other faculty member, I
was left to carry the remaining students through to completion of their
degrees. During this period, I came closer to landing in a mental hospital than at any time in my life.

At this point the chancellor of the university, besieged by abandoned students and their outraged parents, tried to help matters by transferring the clinical program from the College of Education to the Psychology Department in the College of Liberal Arts. This plunged the program into the midst of a rock-ribbed, behavioristically oriented department whose members regarded clinical psychology as unscientific and perceptual psychology as alarmingly subversive. For the next two years, I struggled to shepherd our remaining students to completion of their degrees in a totally hostile environment.

At the same time, I had to defend myself personally against repeated attacks on my credibility and scholarship. I was ignored in faculty meetings. My requests or proposals were rejected out of hand. I was twice passed over for promotion. When I appealed the latter action, the investigating committee reported that I was an extremely popular and successful teacher, had more doctoral students and publications to my credit than anyone in the department, was president of NYSPA, and so on. Nevertheless, they took no action because, they told me, as scholars outside the discipline of psychology, they were loath to reverse the professional judgment of my peers. In these two years, I learned how devastating daily attacks on one's self-concept can be. It was only the caring support of some very good friends and numerous expressions of approval from sources outside the department that carried me through.

New Beginnings in Florida

In 1953 I received an invitation from the College of Education at the University of Florida to join the faculty there to "do whatever you like." I accepted at once. My new colleagues there did not find perceptual-experiential psychology weird, unscientific, or unacceptable. Quite the contrary. I discovered that, as educators everywhere, they generally met it with an attitude of "of course." It made sense to them, fitted their experience, and provided useful guidelines for understanding and coping with the problems of practice. I reveled in this reception, turned my back on clinical psychology, and spent the next twenty-three years at the University of Florida exploring and implementing the implications of perceptual theory for counseling and education. During my stay at UF, I wrote nine books or monographs and more than a hundred articles addressing the problems of education, therapy, administration, and supervision from a perceptual-experiential frame of reference.

In 1959 I published a revision of *Individual Behavior,* this time without Don Snygg as coauthor. With Don Avila and William Purkey, I also wrote *Helping Relationships: Basic Concepts for the Helping Professions* (1971). Both books were highly successful, requiring two revisions since first publication. In 1960 I was asked to head the Association for Supervision and Curriculum Development's yearbook committee, comprised of educators from across the country and representing all walks of the profession. Together we produced *Perceiving, Behaving, Becoming: A New Focus for Education,* the 1962 ASCD yearbook. The volume began with four papers on the nature of the truly healthy person, contributed by Abraham Maslow, Carl Rogers, Early Kelley, and me. The remainder of the book was devoted to the implications of those ideas for educational thought and practice, as perceived by the yearbook committee. The book has had an enormous impact on the profession and continues to be a best-selling yearbook twenty-five years later. I prize it especially as a demonstration of changing practice by building from new assumptions.

A Role in Humanistic Education

Many of education's professional associations are preoccupied with housekeeping matters of standards, ethics, the welfare of practitioners, or with the wielding of political influence. During the fifties and sixties, however, ASCD was primarily concerned with people and ideas. Its membership responded warmly to my message. They elected me president in 1967; I was the first psychologist ever to hold that office. The Association's president served for three years, first as president-elect, then president, and finally as vice-president. I spent much of those years speaking and consulting or meeting with educators in schools and colleges throughout the country. I became a vital spokesman for the cause of humanistic education, the expression in education of concurrent humanist movements in psychology, sociology, anthropology, political science, theology, and medicine. I felt very much that I was part of something much bigger than myself. At the same time I felt privileged to contribute to advancement of the movement.

My years at UF were the most intensely productive of my career. In addition to consulting, teaching, and writing, I began to apply perceptual thinking to the practice of teaching and counseling. At first this took the form of experimenting with the application of counseling theory and techniques in my graduate classes. It occurred to me that since counseling and teaching are each learning processes, they should be governed by the same fundamental principles. This was not a fashionable idea at the time. Counselors often regarded their profession as distinctly different from and superior to teaching. As a consequence, they often tended to treat teachers with overt or covert disdain. I took a different tack. I began to think of counseling and teaching as helping professions, each seeking to aid its clients or students to perceive new and better ways of seeing themselves and the worlds they had to confront. The goals of counseling and teaching are the same. Both are learning processes. They vary only in the subject matter addressed and some of the techniques they use to achieve their goals.

I became keenly aware of the importance of assumptions in human thought and the havoc created for learning and reform when they are ignored. There is nothing more dangerous for human progress than half-right ideas. Partly right ideas provide partly right solutions. That encourages everyone to keep on trying in the same inadequate directions in the vain hope that trying harder, more often, or with different techniques will solve the problems. The invention of perceptual-experiential psychology and its application to the problems of psychology, counseling, teaching, and administering were object lessons for me in what can happen when long-held basic assumptions are replaced by better or more appropriate ones.

Research on the Helping Professions

Such thoughts led to the organization of a seminar designed to explore the nature of the helping professions from a perceptual orientation. Examining teaching and counseling through the eyes of the helper, we arrived at a series of hypotheses, stated as dichotomies, about the perceptual organization of good and poor helpers. Here are a few. Good helpers see themselves in essentially positive ways; poor ones do not. Good helpers believe that people are able; poor ones have great doubts about that. Good ones tune in to the perceptual experience of their subjects and coworkers; poor helpers are preoccupied with how things look to themselves.

Daniel Soper and I tested a series of fifteen such hypotheses on graduate students in counseling. We were astounded to find that fourteen of our fifteen hypotheses clearly discriminated between the good and poor practitioners (1963). The findings have since been corroborated repeatedly with research on teachers, Episcopalian ministers, administrators, and a variety of counselors and public officials (see references). The key to understanding human relationships lies in the perceptual organization of the participants. Good practice in the helping professions, it appears, is not the product of knowledge or methods but the belief system of the helper. To understand the dynamics of helping, we need to know what the helper is trying to do and what the helpee thinks is happening.

A Personal Approach to Teacher Preparation

Sometime in the early sixties, I tried my hand at writing a theory of teacher education, drawing on the implications of our good-poor helper findings and perceptual psychology. The paper soon grew too long for an article but too short for a book, so I set it aside. It lay in my desk drawer for several years. Then one day, in the course of a conversation, I mentioned it to J. B. White, dean of the College of Education. He asked to read it, then urged me to get it published. Accordingly, I went back to work on it and produced *The Professional Education of Teachers: A Perceptual View of Teacher Preparation.* When the book appeared in 1965, I had many requests for "students trained in that way" or "where can we see a program like that?" Alas, there were no such programs or students who had been through anything like it.

Five years later, a group of colleagues from the Elementary Education Department asked if the ideas could be put into operation at UF. I was delighted. Twelve of us spent six months designing a program to implement the theory I had proposed. We then placed it in operation side by side with the existing program, where it ran successfully for the next five years. Working with this faculty and these students was one of the most stimulating and fulfilling experiences of my professional life, a practical affirmation of perceptual-experiential thinking. Despite producing some of the most innovative, truly professional teachers I have ever known, the program began to disintegrate as a contracting economy forced retrenchment in the university. Key faculty were lost, and the program came under fire from those who felt it departed too sharply from the status quo.

Burnout and Renewal

After thirty workaholic years, I was nearing retirement age and beginning to suffer from professional burnout. Feeling a need to reorder my life, in 1972 I engaged in therapy for three months and then took off alone in a camper to tour the West. For three more months, I immersed myself in the solitary pleasures of camping, fishing, and hiking the trails of our national forests and parks. Then, one night in Glacier National Park, I was overcome with loneliness and despair. I remember screaming and beating the walls of my camper. After a while, I fell asleep. When I woke in the morning to the sound of birds, I had an indescribable sense of peace and certainty about what I had to do. I needed to return to Gainesville, dissolve my marriage, divest myself of my administrative duties, and begin to live a new style of life.

Looking back on these events, they seem like a second conversion experience, this time a personal rather than an intellectual or professional one. I came to place great value on personal authenticity: to be who I am, what I am, wherever I am. I began to seek a better balance between my professional and personal lifestyles. After years of devotion to serving others, being a good human being became more important than being a good psychologist or educator. Not that I rejected my educational and psychological roles; I continued to value and honor them, but they no longer dominated my life. I also made a remarkable discovery: when I did what was best for me, it was better for others as well.

After several years of living alone, I met and later married Susan Kannel. She is much younger than I but committed to the same need for genuineness and personal authenticity. For the next twenty years, this relationship became the most beautiful and fulfilling experience of my life. In 1976 I resigned from the University of Florida and we moved to Greeley, Colorado. I divided my time between our home and family—made even more delightful by the births of two beautiful daughters—on one hand, while making a living as writer, consultant, and in the private practice of counseling, on the other. For a five-year period I also served as Distinguished Professor at the University of Northern Colorado. I consider these years the happiest and most fulfilling of my life, sadly terminated by a divorce in 1992.

During this period I wrote or edited several publications reporting on our teacher education experiments at the University of Florida. I have continued to interpret perceptual-experiential psychology and its relationship to the humanist movement in some thirty publications since coming to Greeley. Among these: the third edition of *Perceptual Psychology* with Fred and Anne Richards, an article entitled, "Why the Humanist Movement Needs a Perceptual Psychology," a monograph on *Humanistic Education: Objectives and Assessment,* a third revision of *Helping Relationships,* and three new books: *Myths in Education, A Personal Approach to Teaching,* and *A Theory of Therapy.* Most recently, I have been deeply involved in the problems of educational reform, speaking, consulting, and writing about the need to tackle reform questions from new and more current basic assumptions (see *The Schools We Need: New Assumptions for Educational Reform*). I also get deep satisfaction from my work as a psychotherapist. It is a marvelous advantage to have an occupation one can engage in long after retirement from institutional involvement.

Tribute to a Mentor

In closing, I am deeply grateful to Carl Rogers on two counts: professionally, for introducing me to the field of psychotherapy, and personally, for my experience in therapy with him. The first laid the ground work for my own contributions to psychological theory and its implications for practice in psychotherapy and education. The second helped set me free of the emotional baggage from my childhood and opened the way to healthier being and becoming. I had very little contact with him after he left Ohio State, beyond the afternoon Don Snygg and I spent with him at his Seneca Lake retreat in 1948. On two occasions in later years, our paths crossed briefly at psychological conferences. Two anecdotes from these encounters remain with me and shed light on the kind of man Carl was.

I recall a conversation sometime in the fifties. We were idly talking between conference sessions about our experiences as therapists. Carl voiced his frustration at being unable to help one of his clients. "I've been seeing her on and off for three years. Recently, I told her, 'Look, why don't we call it quits. I don't think I am being very helpful to you.' Do you know what she said? She said, 'Dr. Rogers, you are a famous therapist and you have had many successful clients in your career. But—I'm the most important client you have ever had!' You know what? She's right—and I'm still seeing her!" I value this incident as an indication of his fundamental humility, authenticity, and openness to experience—key factors in Carl's own descriptions of the truly healthy human being.

The second incident occurred during the sessions honoring his seventy-fifth birthday, at the American Psychological Association meetings that year. I was invited to present one of a series of papers on Carl's contributions to education. Half-way through my talk, I saw him rise and leave the hall. I was a little hurt at this seeming snub. Later in the day we met again, and he apologized for his behavior. "I left, Art, because there was a presentation I particularly wanted to hear about a new approach to————. You know, I really can't get excited hearing about my past. It's where I can go from here that really turns me on!" Ever the rebel and pioneer. My hurt disappeared in the joy of encountering a kindred spirit.

My last encounter with Carl came through correspondence. Just before he died in 1988, I wrote a review of his book, *Freedom to Learn for the '80s.* I sent him a copy of the manuscript along with a letter telling him about our teacher education program at Florida, an innovation much like those he reported in his book. I also took the opportunity to tell him some of the things I had been involved with since I last saw him and to express my regret that we had seen so little of each other during the previous thirty-five years. He wrote back, "I appreciate knowing more about your life and work. I, too, have felt it very strange that our paths have crossed so seldom when our hearts and minds were running in such similar tracks—Let's try to change the past and keep in closer touch with each other—I'm delighted to have renewed our contact and I send you my warmest love and greetings." I was deeply touched by his letter but, before I could reply, his death cut short any possibility of renewing our relationship.

I am glad I have known this man. I love him dearly and treasure his influence on me as well as on the profession.

As for my own contributions: by all odds, I believe the invention, with Donald Snygg, of perceptual-experiential psychology is most significant. I believe that American psychology is slowly but inevitably moving across a position spectrum from an external system of observation, represented by stimulus-response and behavior modification, to a system seeking understanding of persons through perception and experience. Today's psychologists can be found at various points of transition across that spectrum as they move, little by little, toward a more humanistic psychology. What Snygg and I proposed in 1949 is an outline for such a systematic psychology, beginning from a more adequate set of assumptions for understanding the dynamics of behavior and personality. I have spent my entire career exploring its ramifications for psychological theory and for the practice of therapy and education. As I wrote in "Why the Humanistic Movement Needs a Perceptual Psychology," I believe the shift to a perceptual view is essential for the profession. I am not so naive, however, as to believe the position I have advocated is final. All scientific theory is sooner or later superseded by something better or more inclusive, and perceptual-experiential psychology is no exception. As Don and I wrote in the introduction to *Individual Behavior* in 1949, "As an outline of a theory we expect that, like everything else in science, this frame of reference we propose may undergo shifts and changes as it is subjected to wider consideration. As fallible human beings we can only hope that this is, 'If not the truth, then very like the truth.'" My search continues.

References

Combs, A. W. "The Validity and Reliability of Interpretations from Autobiography and the Thematic Apperception Test," *Journal of Clinical Psychology* 2 (1946) 240–47.

———. *The Professional Education of Teachers: A Perceptual View of Teacher Preparation.* Boston: Allyn and Bacon, 1965.

———. *Myths in Education: Beliefs that Hinder Progress and Their Alternatives.* Boston: Allyn and Bacon, 1979.

———. *A Personal Approach to Teaching: Beliefs that Make a Difference.* Boston: Allyn and Bacon, 1982.

———. *A Theory of Therapy: Guidelines for Counseling Practice.* Newbury Park, CA: Sage Publications, 1989.

———. "What Makes a Good Helper?" (review of a series of researches, 1958-89). *Person-Centered Review* 1 (1989) 51–61.

———. *The Schools We Need: New Assumptions for Educational Reform.* Lanham, MD: University Press of America, 1991.

———, Ed. *Perceiving, Behaving, Becoming: A New Focus for Education* (yearbook). Washington, DC: Association for Supervision and Curriculum Development, 1962.

—————. *The Professional Education of Teachers: A Humanistic Approach to Teacher Education.* Boston: Allyn and Bacon, 1974.

—————. *Humanistic Education: Objectives and Assessment.* Washington, DC: Association for Supervision and Curriculum Development.

Combs, A. W.; Avila, D. L. *Helping Relationships: Basic Concepts for the Helping Professions* (rev.) Boston: Allyn and Bacon, 1985.

—————; Purkey, W. W. *Helping Relationships: Basic Concepts for the Helping Professions* . Boston: Allyn and Bacon, 1971.

Combs, A. W.; Richards, A. C.; Richards, F. *Perceptual Psychology: A Humanistic Approach to the Study of Persons.* Landham, MD: University Press of America, 1988.

Combs, A. W.; Soper, D. S. "Perceptual Organization of Effective Counselors," *Journal of Counseling Psychology* 10 (1963) 222–26.

Raimy, V. C. "The Self Concept as a Factor in Counseling and Personality Organization" (doctoral dissertation). Columbus, OH: Ohio State University, 1943.

Rogers, C. R. *Counseling and Psychotherapy.* Boston: Houghton Mifflin, 1947.

—————. *Freedom To Learn for the '80s.* Columbus, OH: Merrill Publishers, 1983

Snygg, D.; Combs, A. W. *Individual Behavior: A New Frame of Reference for Psychology.* New York: Harper & Row, 1959.

✣

In my thirty-year effort to raise my feminine consciousness and to study my behavior as a male from the dominant white culture, a number of books affected me. When I read Natalie Rogers' *Emerging Woman* in 1983, it had a particularly significant impact: many of the people she touches in the book were persons with whom I interacted personally.

In fact, I came close to meeting Natalie years earlier, in 1966. She had been a psychotherapist at Dearborn School for emotionally disturbed children (attached to Lesley College) just before I took over as headmaster. Now, after reading her book, I was determined to meet her. At an annual conference of the Association for Humanistic Psychology, I sought her out and introduced myself. Since then I have been a devotee, a learner, a friend, a brother, and a board member of her organization, the Person-Centered Expressive Therapy Institute.

Natalie has contributed significantly to humanistic psychology and education, as well as to creative consciousness. Her work in the field of expressive therapy influenced Carl greatly during his later years. As well as training expressive arts therapists, Natalie has taught courses in Europe, the Soviet Union, Japan, Latin America, Germany, Argentina, and Russia. Her latest book, *The Creative Connection,* was part of her doctoral dissertation at Summit University of Louisiana.

Natalie and her brother David extend the concept of family bioanthology in a very direct way. They are the second generation of what I believe to be a three-generation family story. The third generation is making an impact that will also deserve special attention.

✣

4

The Creative Journey

by Natalie Rogers

> *Creativity is like freedom:*
> *once you taste it you cannot live without it.*
> *It is a transformative and healing process.*
> —Natalie Rogers, *The Creative Connection:*
> *Expressive Arts as Healing*

The symphony of my life seems to have three major themes: creativity, self-empowerment, and social justice. Each theme has had its development, crescendo, and denouement. Expressing my own creativity and establishing creative environments for others are major motifs in every part of my adult life: as a mother, as a psychologist, and as an artist and writer. Today that theme continues as I teach and facilitate person-centered expressive arts therapy, an expansion of my father's work. Expressive arts therapy interweaves the various arts—movement, art, music, writing, sound, and improvisation—in a supportive setting to facilitate self-expression, growth, and healing. It is a process of discovering vital parts of ourselves through any art form that comes from an emotional depth.

The Overture

During my childhood the melody of creativity played gently through my rather protected life, nurtured by my artist mother. The drumbeat of the second theme—the struggle to feel equal as a girl-child—was beginning to roll. My involvement in social issues started at age thirteen as I went to an Ethical Culture Society work camp near a mining town in West Virginia. It continued in my adult life as I involved myself in various ways: working full-time for world government, joining the Peace Corps, speaking out for women's equality, leading groups on male–female relationships, boarding the *Pacific Peacemaker* (a sailing vessel demonstrating against nuclear testing), and facilitating cross-cultural workshops in Latin America, Europe, Japan, and the (then) Soviet Union. If the melody of my childhood was flowing and gentle, my involvement with social issues has been *allegro*, filled with fast pace, intense feeling, and a constant yearning for social justice and world peace.

Being born female, I have struggled for self-empowerment throughout my life. However, I did not become conscious of the devastating effects of sex-role expectations until I was forty. Slowly, my eyes were opened to their subtle (and not so subtle) influences on my life. Since then I have looked back on my upbringing to understand the family and societal values that held me captive. My reactions to my second-class citizenship were strong. I winced at every sexist TV commercial. I counted the number of men versus the number of women on every liberal organization's board of directors. I agonized about the male-dominated university system, the male-dominated Senate and Congress, the male-dominated everything! For a ten-year period, I raged at every unequal and unjust situation that came across my path, including the men who took part in them: my father, my brother, my husband, my lovers, and the male-dominated organizations in which I was a member. My own blaring brass horns pounded in my ears. My pain, tears, and outrage—though justified—exhausted me. I could see that much of my effort was alienating only me. I had to find ways to nourish myself as well as find other methods to change society. I returned to my passion: creativity.

Writing my first book, *Emerging Woman: A Decade of Midlife Transitions,* was a creative way to sort out my thoughts and feelings regarding twenty years of marriage, a divorce, and my new beginnings. It was therapeutic for me and provided a document of courage for other women. During this time I was discovering my professional strength. Inspired to combine my psychological training in the person-centered approach with my love for art, movement, music, and writing, I have developed an approach that I call the Creative Connection.® This form of psychotherapy has been healing for me as well as for my clients and groups. Later, as I created the Person-Centered Expressive Therapy Institute, I found my niche, my home, my community, and a useful way to be in the world.

As my expressive arts work has matured, I find the themes of my life coming into a harmonious blend. Facilitating expressive arts groups focused on issues of local or global concern is meeting my need to have an effect on the social and political world. For example, when the Persian Gulf War began, the participants in our training program threw away the schedule to delve into immediate feelings and thoughts. Among us was a holocaust survivor, an Hispanic, a German, a Latin American, and a Vietnam veteran. We found the arts to be profound media for expression. Some of the art and writing turned into political action. Also, during the week of the Los Angeles riots of 1992, people in my multiethnic class uncovered their despair and rage through movement, writing, and art. We agreed it was crucial to talk honestly to each other and find constructive channels for our feelings. At an Earth and Spirit conference, I led a group that explored our personal connections to nature and all beings. As we built trust between us, we explored our connection to and caring for animals and plants as well as humankind. Thus, my need for social relevance and expressive art are woven together.

Where does my father, Carl Rogers, fit into this picture? People often ask me to speak about my father, but it is important to me to give fair (if not equal) time to my mother. My mother, Helen, played a more important role in my creative development. Her tender, loving care and outgoing qualities fostered these same qualities in my brother and me. Also, I feel certain that it was Helen's emotional support and extreme faith in her husband's ability that gave Carl the courage to stick his neck out professionally. Her inner wisdom guided them through many crucial decisions.

Father–daughter relationships are complex, but frankly, I never saw Carl as a hero. Several people have told me I was one of the most important persons in his life, and he certainly was one of the most important in mine. However, I am embarrassed to say that I often thought of him as naive and frequently dense when it came to understanding interpersonal relationships. Hindsight can be illuminating.

I now understand that he was not dense, only uncommunicative. He was a master of listening and letting you know you were understood. However, in my relationship with him, he often lacked the willingness or ability to say what he was thinking and feeling at the moment.

Carl developed a special quality of listening, not only as a counselor, but as a father and a friend. There were times in my teenage and adult life when he listened to me in his nonjudgmental, empathic way, which enabled me to make important decisions. Long before I studied his work, I absorbed much of his philosophy and style as I grew up. I also absorbed his rebel spirit. I don't remember his telling me to stand up for my own beliefs, but I got the message anyway. I learned to use my own discriminating powers in deciding right from wrong. I highly value my ability to be empathic, to listen at a deep level, and to question any authority figure—and all this, I believe, was passed on to me through Carl.

In his later years we worked together and frequently confided in each other. We had a lot of love for each other. Although I have always vacillated from appreciating him to being really annoyed at him, I am grateful that I grew up with a gentle, caring, scholarly father who devoted his life to understanding the helping relationship and its implications for a troubled world. He left this world a better place. Being with him at the time of his death (and with my mother at hers) had a profound impact on my life. It was a great comfort to be with each of my parents as they slipped gently away. In the end, I felt I had given them all that I could in return for their love and support. With my mother, I seemed to see her spirit leave her body as I held her hand. With my father, although he had been in a coma for three days, it seemed evident that as we spoke to him and meditated around him holding his hands, his breathing eased considerably. These experiences enabled me to open my mind and heart about the process of death and dying.

This overture gives you a sense of my life. The following pages develop the various movements: my childhood years, my adult years as a wife and mother in Boston, and my California years, including working with my father and developing my own professional program. I end with my efforts to build cross-cultural bridges as one path to peace. The themes of creativity, self-empowerment, and social justice develop along the way.

Childhood Years

When I stop to examine the blossoming of my work, I realize that per-son-centered expressive therapy fulfills a lifetime interest and involve-ment in the creative process. To share with you the evolution of my present work is to tell you my personal journey—the story of being the daughter of Helen and Carl Rogers, of traveling through a par-ticular educational system, and of discovering myself through the expressive arts. In looking at how I came to facilitate creativity in oth-ers, I turned back the pages of my life to see where my own creative juices had been nourished or blocked. I asked myself, "What in my family and school environment encouraged me to dance, paint, draw, and to be imaginative and spontaneous? When did I stumble and with-draw? Where did I get the strength to rebel and push on?"

Rochester, New York

I know from experience that spontaneity and self-expression are nurtured in a loving, nonjudgmental, and stimulating environment. At Harley School in Rochester, New York, I was given such an edu-cational opportunity. Although my parents were struggling through the Depression years (I was born in 1928), their top priority was to send my brother, David, and me to a private, "progressive" school. The classes were small, with only fifteen or twenty pupils per class, and fostered a sense of joy in learning. Our curiosity and freedom of spirit were rewarded. Both our school and home environments gave the message that to be a conformist was a deadly path. We were encouraged to think for ourselves, to be our own authorities.

Miss Danforth comes to mind as a teacher who inspired cre-ativity. As our third-grade music teacher (if I remember correctly), she played long passages of Wagner's *Siegfried and Brunhilde.* Colored scarves, tambourines, woodblocks, and cymbals were on the floor, as well as crayons and paper. We were encouraged to dance, to create spontaneous dramas, and to draw to the music. It was heaven to me. The scarves billowed as I expressed the power of that music through movement. I banged the cymbals as the music swelled to its crescendo. I melted when the gentle tones were played. We danced to the music of "Hansel and Gretel" and created the drama. I chose to be the witch wearing a tall black hat, a flowing cape, and a large putty nose. I loved acting out the ugly, mean crone. Where else could a good little girl snarl and make ugly faces at her classmates and get approval for it? Tchaikovsky's "Pathetique," Wagner's "Das Reingold," and other romantic pieces were the backdrop for expression through movement and art. (Today, I create similar environments for adult professionals. I wonder if the Miss Danforths of the world know the impact they have when they create supportive situations for children to express themselves freely.)

During these years at Harley School—grades one through six—art was a frequent happening. The art studio room was large, bright, airy, and equipped with a potter's wheel, painting easels, and abundant materials. We could draw, sculpt, paint, and make woodblocks or collages. Freedom reigned. I particularly remember being inspired by the apple tree bursting forth in fluffy pink and white blossoms outside the studio window. I set up the easel and enthusiastically tried to capture the scene. When I couldn't get the effect I wanted, I asked the teacher for help. She never said I was doing it wrong. She suggested ways of experimenting with mixing colors and methods that might get the desired results. First came spontaneity and my own creative burst. The technical help followed when I needed and asked for it. "Learn by doing" was the philosophy.

When I came home from school and told my neighborhood friends about my project, I was saddened by what they told me about their art classes in the public school. They sat at desks, were handed small pieces of paper, and were told what to draw and how to draw it. There seemed to be no joy in the process of making art, only the questions, "Did I do it right?" or "What will my grade be?"

Not all my creative endeavors were painless. My mother wanted to expose me to the joys of music through piano lessons. At the renowned Eastman School of Music I had a friendly young woman graduate student as a teacher. I diligently practiced scales and simplified pieces of Bach. I loved music and had the desire to play well, but the system at the school destroyed this desire within a few years. Although I was seven or eight years old and extremely shy about performing, I was told that every few months there would be a recital in front of the student teachers and college faculty. I was required to sit at a huge grand piano in a large classroom and perform for teachers who were watching with pen and tablet in hand, grading every move. If I performed well, I was given the "privilege" of playing in another recital with the other top contestants. Thus, the sloppy players were eliminated and the best went on to bigger recitals.

Although I was in a state of terror and anxiety before each performance, I managed to sit on the cold black piano bench and play like a robot. My fingers knew what to do even if my mind and heart were paralyzed. So, after each recital I was applauded and advanced to the next level of performance. I would cry (to my mother) and beg not to go through that process again. The finale was on stage in the Eastman Theater auditorium. Dressed in my black patent shoes and frilly dress, I choked back the last tears as my mother promised me I'd never have to be in a recital again. I did it. I suppose I did it well. All I remember is the cold fear. I never learned to enjoy playing the piano and quit for good.

This painful experience taught me that if we emphasize performance, grades, and perfection, we are likely to kill the true enjoyment of making music or any other creative act. Those who wish to pursue an art form to perfect their skills can always do so. But most of us just want the pleasure of creating for ourselves and for our friends. I work with people daily who believe they have no ability or talent for dance or music or art because they were put to such severe tests as children and are now afraid to try.

Columbus, Ohio

When my father accepted a full professorship at Ohio State University in Columbus, my brother and I went to University School, the teacher training school on that campus. Many young, motivated student teachers were practicing their newly developed skills. Again I was in an educational setting where freedom of choice and responsibility for our own education was emphasized. The core curriculum course demanded that students choose their own area of study, make a plan to pursue it, do the necessary research as a project, and give a report to the class. We were trained to think and be self-starters, using our ingenuity and creativity at each step.

My most memorable project (one that shows my early interest in the educational process) was some research I designed and carried out in the ninth grade. I compared the philosophies and methods of several elementary schools. The introduction to my thirty-five-page report (which I still have) posed these questions: What are the differences in the philosophies of education? What are the methods of teaching and the philosophy of traditional schools compared with the progressive schools? My intention was to get data to show which was the better method.

I visited three elementary schools that provided a sample of both traditional and progressive methods. I wrote detailed observation notes on the environment (desks that were nailed down compared to movable furniture), the behavior of the teachers (laying down strict rules and asking for conformity as compared to respecting the child by first listening and then suggesting a way). While observing the traditional school, I wrote, "It is like having puppets at the desks instead of human beings." My comments about the fourth grade in the more progressive school included: "In the afternoon the children take the responsibility of planning their own studies with the aid of the teacher. I think this is very helpful for them since it helps them to think about the world around them and its problems. *If the teachers planned all their work for them I don't think they would get as interested in it as they seemed to be. Half the fun and work is to plan out how you're going to find out the things you want.*"

In a handwritten note to the principal of my school, my teacher wrote: "Natalie has put her youthful finger [I was thirteen years old] on some things which many adults—even students of education—frequently overlook. . . . I think this is a good case in point of the unlimited opportunity inherent in the emphasis upon self-directive learning."

In this paper I referred many times to the difference between the educational process in the German dictatorship and that of a democratic society, a clue to the fact that I was already deeply troubled about the rumblings in Europe. My political consciousness was budding at the time the Third Reich was emerging.

The philosophy and values of the educational system in which I was raised fostered creativity. In turn, I have used these values to develop similar environments for others. This philosophy includes: encouraging curiosity and experimentation, valuing individual freedom and responsibility, giving support and constructive criticism instead of judgment and grades, valuing the creative process more than the product, choosing to pursue one's own interest and goals rather than predetermined goals of the teacher, and having respect for the inner truth of each individual.

My awakening into the social and political realities of the world came at age fourteen. I spent the next two summers at the Chestnut Ridge work camp in the mountains outside Morgantown, West Virginia. Cosponsored by the Ethical Culture Society in New York City and the Quakers, this project asked teenagers to build cabins that would help create a summer camp for coal miners' children. Those summers dramatically influenced my life. For the first time I saw abject poverty. It was heart-wrenching when we took the campers back to their shanty homes, where many siblings went barefoot and were crowded into one room to sleep. Their skinny arms and legs also made it obvious that there was not enough food. I never forgot those scenes.

I learned another lesson when some of the campers asked me why I was hanging out with Jewish kids. I didn't know what "Jewish" meant, and I wasn't aware that the group I enjoyed was a special religious group. Bewildered that my fellow work-campers were discriminating against my best friends, I was challenged to think about my values. Strong social views emerged. As a female, I felt empowered since I was an equal member on the construction crew rather than a go-fer, as had usually been the case when I worked with my father and brother. I developed leadership abilities despite being the youngest work-camper. Being tall and physically mature, I passed myself off as sixteen or seventeen years old and discovered I was attractive to boys who were eighteen and nineteen. Rather than being intimidated by the revelation that I was attracted to Jews, I found the relationships stimulating and warm.

My junior year in high school seemed dull after that. Since my brother, David, had been accelerated in order to join the Navy V-12 program (a college program paid for by the government), I got permission to be accelerated as well. I doubled up on courses to get out of high school a year early; I longed to move on to a more liberating life in college. I graduated at age fifteen, then turned sixteen the month after I entered Stephens College.

Helen: The Aesthetic, Artistic, Nurturing Mother

It was my mother, Helen, who created the environment of physical warmth, aesthetic surroundings, and artistic stimulation. Having studied at the Chicago Art Institute she was employed as a fashion artist before her marriage. She had a keen aesthetic sense which was handed on to us. I remember the art books on the living room coffee table: Thomas Benton, Winslow Homer, and Edward Hopper—all contemporary American artists full of color and emotional impact.

Mother gave us the encouragement to create. Being somewhat critical by nature, her methods of teaching tended to be "this is how you do it" rather than "enjoy the process." Nevertheless, my appetite was whetted and the creative act was encouraged and appreciated. She frequently brought out her paints and paper for us to use at the kitchen table and encouraged us to enjoy color, drawing, and composition. She took us to art museums and occasionally treated us to children's art classes. I particularly loved the children's books she selected that had delightful illustrations. Mother's sense of composition and color was noticeable in our home, in our clothes (she made most of mine), as well as in the pictures she painted. I cherish this sense of aesthetics that she passed on, and I have used my creativity to keep me mentally and physically healthy. My father always gave credit to mother for our attractive and nurturing environment. She even taught Carl how to paint when they were in Mexico for several months on sabbatical. Although he seemed to approach the venture methodically, he eventually became more spontaneous, playful, and creative with his images and colors. It is my understanding that Mother eventually discouraged Carl from painting because it was the one area in which she flourished, separate from him. He understood her need to have her own area of expertise.

Mother's love, warmth, and genuine caring for us was good medicine for self-esteem, which is one of the foundation blocks for creativity. To take risks, experiment, make mistakes, try again, ask "dumb" questions, and not be worried about what others think, one must have a sizeable amount of self-esteem.

She had years when she would paint and years when she didn't. Taking care of her home, her children, her husband, and her friends always came first. Art was considered a luxury she did after everything else was completed. Unfortunately, I adopted this attitude and have found it very difficult to shake. It is particularly difficult because our culture does not reward the artist. Our Western culture prefers to reward computer programmers, baseball players, and movie stars.

She did love the process of painting. She frequently gave the pictures away to special friends. She never thought of taking slides of her work or exhibiting or selling them. It is difficult for me to understand why Carl didn't document her work, since he photographed and documented most things in *his* life. In her declining years when I suggested we organize a retrospective exhibit, she was horrified. "I'd never ask people to go to the trouble of packing up their paintings to ship them. Don't be silly!" was her reply.

Although Mom encouraged the visual arts and music, I was the only one in the family who loved to dance. As a ten-year-old, I would come into the living room where my parents were reading or chatting, put on a classical record, and start to move. It felt good to experience the emotional quality of the music and allow it to flow through my body for expression. Although I asked my parents not to watch me, it was important to me that they were present. It encouraged me to focus intently on expressing myself fully. In retrospect, I understand the importance of having a silent, nonjudgmental witness.

By the time I was fourteen, I was five feet, eleven inches tall and felt too big to dance. (If only Judy Jamison had been around as a role model!) Nevertheless, I enjoyed the grace and flexibility of my body and loved swimming, tennis, basketball, and field hockey. I've always known the importance of staying in tune with my body. It is shocking to look back and realize that at age sixteen I was so influenced by the media hype that I thought my body wasn't perfect and took to wearing girdles! Fortunately, I had experienced a potent sense of my self through expressive movement and, even though I stopped that form of dance, I returned to it at age forty-four with an intuitive knowledge that it was one path to regaining my selfhood.

Sibling Rivalry

Creativity was the major theme in my young life. The biggest problem was the sibling rivalry between my brother and me. The minor theme being played out was: girls are meant to be pretty and sweet, boys do the important and responsible things in life. Although my brother and I loved each other a lot, our sparring, teasing, and mutual torture kept the whole family on emotional edge at times. David was two and a half years older than I and was given responsibility and advantages at an early age. Being the youngest, and a girl, I was frequently protected and favored. I envied his strength, intellect, and status as a boy. I imagine he envied the tender, loving attention that was showered on me, the pretty little girl. Dave, being bigger and stronger, could pin me down and playfully torture me. (I never really got hurt.) In return I teased him mercilessly until he was prompted to attack. He then got blamed by Mother for instigating the fight.

My brother often told me I was fortunate to be a dumb girl. The incredible part is that at some level I *believed* him. I idolized him. He was tall, handsome, and admired in school. His classmates seemed much more attractive than mine, and I wanted to be included in his group but they usually saw me as a pest. When I was sixteen and in college, I visited Dave at Cornell Medical School in New York City. I finally gained some of his respect when his college roommate and I fell in love.

I have come to realize that my self-concept as a female—a person who was not expected to accomplish much or make a difference in the world—came as a result of my relationship to my brother as well as how my father viewed my mother and me. The feeling of being "one down" or "less than" was supported by the society in which I grew up. The media—movies, advertisements, billboards, radio, and eventually TV—all reinforced that I was meant to be a "body beautiful" woman with a polished kitchen floor.

Carl: The Shy, Scholarly Father

People often ask me what it was like to have a famous psychologist for a father. What kind of father was he? How did he influence my professional work?

My father was always the first to say, "I wasn't a very good parent when you kids were little." Involved in his work at the Child Guidance Center in Rochester during the working day and committed to his writing in the evening, he abdicated much of his father role. He was shy and nondemonstrative. I have very little recollection of his cuddling or playing with us. At that stage of his life, he was a very serious intellectual, trying to gain respect by taking responsibility for the direction of his profession. I remember him as a fairly stern disciplinarian, although he was gentle and kind. Sometimes he told us bedtime stories. These were true stories about his childhood as a farm boy in Illinois with his dog, Shep, or about his adventures in China as a twenty-year-old.

My feelings toward my father were ones of admiration, respect, and a longing for more closeness. I know I tried to please him, but I never idolized him. He was there, like a rock. I knew he adored and approved of me from a distance. The only punishments I remember were the rare occasions when he sent me to bed without supper or dished out a not-too-hard spanking. He loved us a lot—there was no doubt about that. His ability to show it was limited, however.

Most people assume that I grew up in a client-centered household, that is, with parents who were experts at being empathic, congruent, and good listeners. Not so. My childhood was from 1928 to 1943, from birth to age fifteen. Carl's first book on the client-centered process was published in 1942[1] when I was fourteen. So it was during my years in high school that he developed his notions of empathic listening (during his years as a professor at Ohio State University). Although Carl had rebelled against his very strict Congregational upbringing, some of that cloak still hung over his dealings with us.

Parents were definitely the authority. Rules were rules, and "No" meant *no*. We were to "Do as you are told, with no monkey business!"

He respected us and encouraged us to do well in school, to be leaders, and to be ethical. Both at home and at school, freedom of thought was nourished in an environment that taught self-discipline along with a sense of responsibility for oneself and others. My parents abandoned their religious indoctrinations and seemed to replace those with the edict that one must be productive and have a positive influence on the world. This is so ingrained in our family that it seems to have been handed down with the genes. My three daughters complain that this pressure on them is as great as it was on me.

I learned very early in life that the way to be close to my father was to work with him, side by side. As a family we spent our summer vacations at Seneca Lake in New York, where Dad, with the help of friends, had built a long cabin in the woods overlooking the lake. As a little girl I was happiest when he asked me to help him with a project such as building some steps to the beach or creating a new footbridge over the glen. At those times I would fetch the hammer and nails, hold the boards in place, or try my hand with the saw. The camaraderie of working together was warm. He was shy, so words or physical demonstrativeness were not the bond. The bond was in creating something together.

I never felt close to my father until I was about thirteen. My mother, on the other hand, was always there for me as a little girl. She would hug me and bandage my scraped knee, or take me with her to the market. We baked cookies and cakes, sewed doll clothes, and played games. As I entered adulthood, I found it more difficult to be close to her. She was at a loss to understand me as I became rebellious and independent. At that time, my father became my confidant.

In high school and college I became aware of my father's work in client-centered therapy. He seldom talked about his work as a professor or therapist at home, so I was amazed when I read his book *Counseling and Psychotherapy*. It was a "wow" kind of experience. He was saying all of the things I already believed. Obviously, without his talking about it very much, I had incorporated and internalized his way of being, his philosophy, and his respect for each person's ability for self-direction. It came as a surprise to me that he was espousing these values in the classroom and in books.

The Father–Daughter Professional
Relationship Begins

In my college psychology class I discovered that my father was becoming well known. The young teacher at Stephens College in Columbia, Missouri (at that time, a progressive school) was awed to have the daughter of one of her favorite psychologists in class. It was my first such experience. I started to read his writings along with those of Abraham Maslow, Clark Moustakas, and others. Each man was validating my own sensibilities, and as I read, I would nod my head, saying, "Yes, of course, that's the way I experience it."

As I pursued intellectual interests in college, I felt closer to my father. My parents had moved to the University of Chicago where Carl was founder and director of the Counseling Center. When I went home on school vacations, I frequently became involved in his work. I watched his counseling sessions through a one-way mirror and sat in on Center discussions. Research methods were being developed that allowed scrutiny of the counseling process. The main question was, "What really helps a client change in growthful ways? What hinders the process?" I helped in some of this research, coded transcripts of counseling sessions, and wrote up my conclusions for my college term paper.[2] Later this was published in the Counseling Center's journal.[3] It was exciting to see my first article of twenty-five pages in print.

I was learning a great deal through these discussions and associations with my father and his graduate students. I was experiencing the real meaning of the "non-directive approach," as it was called in the beginning. I was seen as a natural therapist by his students who were five to ten years older than I. The empathic, honest, and caring qualities were not difficult for me since I had learned them by osmosis at home.

Virginia Axline was also at the Counseling Center at that time and was developing client-centered play therapy. Observing her at work with young children in the Counseling Center play room was fascinating. I read her book *Play Therapy*,[4] which I think is still one of the best in the field. Seeing her enter into the world of the child, respecting the inner being, allowing a tremendous range of feelings and play acting, yet setting very firm limits, greatly influenced me. I wanted to do that work some day. In fact, twelve years later, after marriage and three children, my first internship as a psychology student was working with disturbed children. I used many of those same play therapy methods. In some sense I am using much of her philosophy with adults today.

To summarize, I would say that my home and school life endowed me with values and a philosophy of learning. My parents used their own creativity in drawing, painting, writing, and building. It was a disciplined but loving home life. Productivity was paramount to godliness. My early educational settings were ones in which my curiosity and creativity were encouraged. I experienced learning environments that insisted I take responsibility for my own education, and I felt the excitement of intellectual discussions and research and the closeness of working with my father. The most negative influence, which wrought havoc in my life and put limits on my creative abilities, was the societal judgment regarding the worth of girls and women. This was also acted out, unknowingly, in our home environment. Perhaps it was the always present (unconscious) feeling that I was less than my male counterparts that fueled my passion for justice.

Working for Peace

I chose Stephens College in Columbia, Missouri, after seeing the dating situation on the Ohio State University campus. It was 1945 and most boys (as they were called then) had been drafted into military service. You can see my highest priority: I wanted to go to a college where I would find a man to marry. This girls' college (as they were called then) was a second-best choice, as far as I was concerned, but turned out to be a fortuitous decision. Without the dating scene, I put all my efforts into learning. I had no need to hold my intellectual abilities in check. The young professors were friendly and eager to teach. I was an excited student. I soaked up studies in the humanities, the arts, and international relations; and I discovered that girls were great friends.

Stephens was a two-year college, so I transferred to DePauw University in Greencastle, Indiana. It was the only school I ever detested. It felt confining, uninspiring, and dull. The only shred of evidence remaining from my DePauw days is a poem, which I wrote during my literature class in 1947. World War II was finally over, and I used Walt Whitman's style to vent my despair about our use of the atom bomb.

Misplaced in the conservative, restrictive setting of DePauw University, I searched for an outlet that would free my spirit. I went to a convention in St. Louis put on by the United World Federalists. This convention changed my life. Having felt helpless, anxious, and depressed about the world situation during the war, I now saw a beam of hope as the United Nations came into being. At the convention, brilliant political minds joined forces to urge the strengthening of the United Nations into a federal world government. They wanted to give it the power to enforce peace.

After the regular convention was over, the student section of UWF held its separate meetings, starting at 10 p.m. Never before had I met young men and women like this. They had political savvy and were geared for action. I was inspired! One night at about 1 a.m., after listening to student organizers Harris Wofford and Helen Ball, I found myself with arm raised high, volunteering to take a semester out of college to do full-time volunteer work for the UWF. Fifteen of us from ten states offered to give our time on a bare-expense basis. We would go to New York City to be trained and then spread out in our home states to bring this vision of a strengthened United Nations to high school and college campuses.

When I phoned my parents and told them I was going to postpone the last semester of my senior year in college, they were shocked. Although they approved of my motives, they tried to persuade me to finish college first. I was not persuaded. I had found a group that shared my values and knew how to speak out in ways that I was eager to learn.

Those three years, 1948 through 1950, were far more educational than anything I learned in college. Although terrified at the thought of speaking in public, I was now motivated to learn. Never having paid much attention to political theory, I now read authors Clarence Streit, Cord Meyer, Jr., and Emery Reeves' *Anatomy of Peace*. Harris Wofford's book, *It's Up to Us,* was a call to every young person to stand up in favor of a world government. (Harris is now the U.S. Senator from Pennsylvania.) Along with fourteen other volunteers, I arrived in New York City for some rigorous intellectual and practical training.

After the training, I spent six months on the south side of Chicago using my parents' apartment on Stoney Island Avenue as my home base as I toured Illinois and Indiana organizing chapters for UWF. Many adults patted me on the head and called me naive. I experienced them as lacking in vision and courage. I organized dozens of high school and college chapters dedicated to educating themselves and speaking out for a better world.

After returning to DePauw to finish my last semester, I was invited back to New York to work in the Student Division of the UWF with a group of outstanding but yet unknown men and women:

Alan Cranston, Norman Cousins, and John Holt, to name a few. So by age twenty I was employed by a dynamic group of people working on the twelfth floor of a building on West 12th Street. I walked to work each morning from my apartment on East 12th Street in Greenwich Village. Who could ask for more? It was challenging—and taxing. We worked six days a week, had late-night meetings, traveled frequently, and expended tremendous amounts of energy getting out publicity.

The twelfth-floor gossip was that Natalie Rogers and Larry Fuchs were having a romance as they worked and played together. They were right. In 1950 we married and moved to Cambridge, where Larry went to Harvard graduate school and I took up my role as wife.

Adult Years, Boston

Our life was good. We had a cute apartment in Cambridge within walking distance of Harvard Yard; we were young, in love, optimistic, and enthusiastic. However, what I did to myself and how my husband colluded with me in the state of matrimony is incredible. I withdrew from being an activist, a thinker, and a doer. The fact that I was at least as good as he was in many areas—in human relations, in intellectual ability, and in life experience of being independent and responsible for myself—was somehow forgotten as I took on the role of wife. I applied to Harvard myself and was told I wouldn't be accepted unless I was a full-time student. Although we had no children at the time, I thought it would take at least half-time to take care of my husband, so I withdrew my student application.

The concept that we might share equally in educational opportunities and taking care of each other never occurred to either of us. Instead I edited, typed, and helped organize his papers or do his research. Why should a man question what this role does to a woman? His ego and his work benefit greatly from this system. Amazingly, I was quite content with this role for many years. I don't remember wondering why I wasn't going to classes and writing papers for myself. No one else asked why either.

Although fifteen of our twenty years together were warm, loving, and exciting, with picnics, hikes, faculty parties, and loving our children, my identity disappeared as a thinking person, capable of sifting information and coming to conclusions. By a subtle process many women will recognize, I began to lose my identity in the marriage. His friends and colleagues became my friends. His career became my motivation. I protected and promoted his time and space to work, but who protected any time for me?

There are also many joyous memories. Becoming a mother was the highest priority in my life. Pregnancy was a wondrous nine months, and I searched for a doctor who believed in natural childbirth. The complete ecstasy of holding my first daughter in my arms just seconds after delivery was never to be forgotten. The totally nonverbal communion between mother and infant is experiencing love at the most profound level. This was true for me for each of my three birthings.

Being with our daughters was of real interest to me as a full-time job for many years. I loved pushing Janet in the stroller in Harvard Yard and playing with her in the park. By 1957 Frances and Naomi were welcomed into our family, and I had three kids under five years old. (It was our plan and typical for those times.) As the girls got older, we did art projects and sewing projects, and went to the library, the zoo, and local concerts. As a family, we lived in Hawaii for two separate years and went to the Peace Corps for two years. Packing up and leaving our suburban Boston home each time was a huge but rewarding effort. Having three children with us as we shifted cultures made the adventure challenging. Probably my own enthusiasm for exploring a new culture rubbed off on them, somewhat. Their curiosity and response to new lifestyles also enriched our views. Involving myself in their various schools—as an active cooperative nursery school mom and in various PTA groups—was a big part of my life. Being there when they came home from school to listen, feed, and attend to their needs nourished me as well as them. Parenthood always has its trying weeks and months, but I never longed to be free of that responsibility. During the frightening moments (emergency trips to the hospital, times of emotional distance or anger, concern for their health or well-being), it was the deep love for and devotion to these remarkable beings that kept me going.

Frequently I got the entire family involved in "creative Sundays," following the pattern my mother had established for me. I set up art materials on the dining room table—it looked like an enticing buffet. We painted and made collages and clay pieces just for the fun of it. I also created incentive for my daughters to dance and play music. I was consciously trying to provide for my children the accepting, nonjudgmental, playful environment for art and creativity my parents and teachers had offered me. However, I had lost much of my own spontaneity and had become an inhibited, "proper" and sedate mother.

My husband was an associate professor at Brandeis University, where Abraham Maslow was chairman of the psychology department. When I met Maslow at a social occasion, he suggested that I enter the graduate psychology department. This ignited a fire in me, and in 1956 I was the first faculty wife to enter graduate school. (Brandeis University was very young then.) As I went back to school, one course at a time, getting babysitters for the few hours I was away, I thought of myself as furthering my education to make me a more interesting wife—not that I would ever become a recognized professional person. I continue to reiterate this theme because in my work now, I find women looking at me with some awe. They don't seem to understand that I, too, have had to deal with a sense of inferiority or second-class citizenship. It has been a long, slow process to realize that I actually have something to offer the world community.

With Abe Maslow as my mentor and thesis advisor, my interest in combining my experience in client-centered therapy and creativity got the green light. Abe was particularly interested in the creative, self-actualizing person. He encouraged me to design a research project that would be fun and creative. He understood the importance of phenomenological research. Observing and analyzing experiential data was valid thesis material. I hate to think what would have happened to me if I had had an advisor who insisted on statistical analysis of the creative process.

I wrote my master's thesis, "The Play Therapist's Approach to the Creative Art Experience,"[5] using information and examples I gleaned during an outdoor class I set up for children, including my own, in our own back yard. We were living in Hawaii that year because my husband was doing research there. It was an ideal place to have an outdoor art class. I encouraged the children to use their feelings and dreams as sources for their creative self-expression. Using my father's philosophy and the work of Virginia Axline set the scene for creative art expression. I think I have always known that creativity is a seed within each of us. It needs only to be watered, fertilized, and given some sunshine in which to develop.

Art in the Peace Corps,
Philippine Islands

When Jack Kennedy was elected president, my husband and I were drawn to the service of the Peace Corps. My thirst for adventure encouraged him to accept an appointment in 1962 as director of the Philippines project. We rented our house, packed up our three daughters, and went to the Philippines for two very rewarding years. The warm-hearted Filipinos were eager for American philosophy and skills.

Our children attended a Filipino teacher-training school. Noticing that their art classes taught tracing and coloring methods, I offered to show the teachers some other possibilities. At a national conference of teachers, I lectured on "Self-Expression Through Creative Art"[6] and offered an afternoon of hands-on experience using clay, paint, and collage. Five hundred people were in the audience (a first for me), and about fifty teachers chose my afternoon workshop in expressive art. They seemed stimulated by their freedom of expression in the art room. The atmosphere was animated. Whether their educational system allowed them to incorporate self-expression through art in their classrooms is another question. Nonetheless, they published the lecture in their art education journal, and I had the opportunity to put my theories into the public arena. It motivated me to explore other avenues of teaching.

I was very aware that as an American I was put on a pedestal. I was offered an opportunity to speak, write, and teach—something that my credential-oriented Boston environment would not have offered me. Both flattered and humbled by people's interest in expressive arts, I accepted invitations to present myself in public and in the classroom. Doing so was also an opportunity to gain self-esteem.

Psychological Work in Boston

When we returned to Boston I continued my psychological training. My internship and licensing involved supervised work in a state mental hospital and at the Cambridge Guidance Center, a community clinic focusing on individual and family therapy. Later, as a therapist for emotionally disturbed children at the Lesley College Schools for Children and with the encouragement of the director, Stan Plattor, I developed parent support groups. Stan also asked me to be a consultant to the teachers, who were nourished by my ability to listen to their frustrations as they worked with hyperactive, disturbed children.

Developing myself professionally threatened my husband and our marriage system. In turn, Larry became more controlling and intimidating. The end of our marriage occurred when I found my anger at his trying to keep me in the one-down position. For two years previous to acknowledging my anger, I had been seriously depressed. Psychotherapy helped me identify my suicidal feelings, which then turned to anger. The anger gave me the energy—a life-saving force— to pull out of the relationship. Our divorce, in my opinion, was a product of our inability or unwillingness to work ourselves out of an unequal situation.

I learned a lesson about a woman's place in the professional world when Stan, the director, left the Lesley College Schools. He was replaced by a man who was insecure in his job. My popularity and effectiveness with the teachers and students seemed to threaten him, so he limited the scope of my work in a dictatorial fashion. He called me into his office, *ordered* me not to work with the parents or the teachers, and told me to cancel some of my therapeutic work with the children. I couldn't believe it! I sat up straight in my chair across from his desk and said, in my feisty way, "You mean you want me to do *less* than I am capable of?" He stared straight at me but gave no response. I got up and walked out.

But I did not obey his orders. I continued to confer with parents. One day, at the request of teachers, I came to a teachers' meeting at which this man presided. His face turned scarlet with anger—anger that I should flout his authority. The next day he fired me. I was told, "Get out, immediately!" I pleaded that I should have a month to terminate therapy with the children. He said, "No! Get out tomorrow. If you come back in this building, I will call the police to drag you out!" I still tremble thinking of that scene. Today, I wonder if I had any legal rights. I had just battled for a year and a half for an equitable divorce settlement, and I didn't entertain any thoughts of standing up for myself again.

In my various work settings—the psychiatric hospital, a children's hospital, a community clinic, the school for disturbed children, and my private practice—I was integrating movement and art into my psychotherapeutic practice. Person-centered expressive therapy was born out of my personal integration of the arts and the philosophy I had inherited. Because I was unsure, at first, about introducing these methods to clients, I suggested they try something—drawing or moving, for instance—and then asked them for feedback. They said it was helpful. Their self-understanding rapidly increased and the communication between us improved immensely. The same was true as I introduced movement, sound, and free writing (uncensored, nonstop words or sentences) for self-expression. Clients and group participants reported a sense of "new beginnings" and freedom to be.

I introduced these methods to my supervisors and employers as well as my clients. There were very few, if any, courses on the therapeutic aspects of expressive arts, although the dance/movement therapy and the art therapy associations had been established.

At the College Mental Health Center, a private psychiatric unit for college students, I introduced movement and art to my individual clients and therapy groups. An unpublished paper describes the expressive arts methods I used.[7] My work emphasized understanding the world of the psychotic student by his or her communications through art. I was not interpreting the art but creating a trusting environment in which people would feel free to express any emotions on paper or through movement. My paper points out the need to invite the psychiatric and nursing staff to some informal expressive art sessions to enable them to discover for themselves the legitimacy of the experience. I invited the young psychiatric director, the psychologists, and the nurses to my home for a Saturday of expressive arts. In the process, we looked at some of the difficulties in our staff communications and appreciated the power of this method for interpersonal work. Through their own expressive arts experience, this lively staff also learned what I was doing with in-patients.

Carl's research into the psychotherapeutic process revealed that when a client felt accepted and understood, healing occurred. It is a rare experience to feel accepted and understood when you are feeling fear, rage, grief, or jealousy. Yet it is this very acceptance and understanding that heals. As friends and therapists, we frequently think we must have an answer or give advice. However, this overlooks a basic truth. By genuinely hearing the depth of the individual's ability to find her own answer, we are giving her the greatest gift. Empathy and acceptance give the individual the opportunity to empower herself and discover her unique potential. It is this accepting, understanding, and permission-giving environment in which the expressive arts are offered.

California: Taking Big Risks for Learning

In 1974 I moved to San Francisco to start a new life as a single woman. At age forty-two I would have my first experience of living alone. In my journal I wrote:

> I am about to make another major shift in my life. I have chosen to pull up my taproot, to leave my East Coast home of twenty years, knowing that my children have left the nest, and that I will create a place for them wherever I am. I am about to leave my support group: people who have nourished me and to whom I have given much. I will move 3,000 miles and start a new life— design my own work, make new friends and shed some of the material possessions I have acquired over the years. It feels like a tremendous leap into the unknown.

I established myself professionally by offering two training pro- grams: one in client-centered therapy, and another in "Training of Woman Counselors of Women." Each program drew on my skills in yoga and art. At the same time, I was rediscovering my own enjoy- ment of self-expression through art. I was also adding to my skills as a counselor by taking workshops in art therapy with Janie Rhyne, author of *Gestalt Art Experience.* Janie welcomed me to her home/ studio with warmth and, as we shared life stories, I was inspired by her experience of living in an intentional community and developing her own form of art therapy.

The most daring event in my life at that time, however, was to enroll in Anna Halprin's intensive Dancer Workshop training pro- gram. Walking into that dance studio placed me in a situation that con- trasted outrageously with my former life. I was used to my grassy neighborhood, my efficient homemaking, my carefully ordered day, and a generally buttoned-up existence. I had spent years thinking I was either too big to dance or too sedate as a wife and mother. Now I wanted to feel physically self-confident and return to my childhood sense of freedom of letting my body "dance itself." Always one of the oldest students in this intensive training program, I had Anna as a model that said aging and dance go hand in hand, beautifully.

Movement is life, life is movement. If you don't believe it, just try holding completely still for a minute. Impossible. Breath is movement. Our bodies express our internal state all the time. We know intuitively if someone is sad or angry. How? We are picking up the person's body language and movement. I took my art journal with me each day to Dancer's Workshop and spent the lunch hour putting my feelings on paper with color. As I reviewed my art work, later, I realized that the movement had greatly affected my art. There was a new vitality and directness to my pictures. I also found that I was writing poetry for the first time in my life. It started me thinking that I had always like art, dance, and writing but had never understood that one art form stimulated and nurtured the other. It was in this experience that my concept came into being of the *creative connection*— a connection between one art form (dance) and other art forms (visual art and writing). Other people were developing notions of *intermodal therapy* at the same time, but at that point I was not aware of it. I had never heard the term *expressive arts therapy*. Many of us were making the same discovery at the same time. This intermodal way of using the arts—the enhancing interplay among movement, art, writing, and sound—opens us to profound feelings which we can then express in color, line, or form. When we write immediately after the movement and art, a free flow of words—sometime poetry—emerges. The Creative Connection process describes a sequence in which one art form deepens another. It is like the unfolding petals of a lotus blossom on a summer day. In the warm, accepting environment, the petals begin to open to reveal the flower's inner essence. As our feelings are tapped, they become a resource for further self-understanding and creativity. We gently allow ourselves to awaken to new possibilities. Each opening may deepen our experience. When we reach our inner core, we find our connection to all beings. We create to connect to our inner source and to reach out to the world and the universe.

The Person-Centered Approach Workshops

Although I had studied with and done research for my father, I had never been his colleague. In 1974 I was visiting my parents in La Jolla and asked Dad, "Would you like to work together?"

"Sure, I would," he replied. "What should we do?"

I sat down at the typewriter and drafted a proposal for a ten-day residential workshop. We invited a staff of five people, then took my initial draft and co-designed an intensive residential summer program called "The Person-Centered Approach." For six summers we worked together in various parts of the world, from San Diego to Nottingham, England, with from sixty to one hundred and fifty participants in each program.[8] These PCA workshops were tremendous learning experiences for all of us, staff and participants alike.

Our work as a staff group at these workshops had a very special quality. Each of us felt the support and freedom to try out new aspects of ourselves. Maria Bowen, John K. Wood, Maureen O'Hara, Jared Kass, Alan Nelson, Joann Justin, Dad, and I were the core group of faculty. Others were added, occasionally. We spent three or four days together prior to each workshop, planning and creating ingenious ways to give participants as much freedom of choice as possible.

More importantly, we spent time working out our individual frictions and differences. Each of us had time to talk about our lives and our problems with relationships or jobs, and to be listened to with genuine concern. Although we shared some humanistic values, we were very different individuals with a wide variety of interests. We laughed and cried together. We got angry at each other and found ways to appreciate and use our anger constructively. We played and laughed and did rather foolish things together. We shared our dreams as well as our visions of the future. We were all learners, and we made collective decisions. Carl took part in all of this, enjoying the sense of community and camaraderie. In our team, he did not have any more authority than the rest of us. Although we all respected him, none of us put him on a pedestal. Even if he had wanted to control the group (which would not have occurred to him), these particular people would never have let him get away with it. The trust that evolved in our staff encounters was the foundation for facilitating the large community that was coming together.

For me, the most important aspect of our staff experience was the sense of being a good human being even though at times I made mistakes or looked foolish. This meant I could try out new behavior in the large community—take the risk of being fully myself, totally honest and open in front of a hundred people—and come back to the staff group and feel accepted. Not right or wrong, but accepted. As a staff we worked hard to keep our communication process open and honest, and it paid off. Such home-group acceptance has a remarkable ability to help individuals empower themselves. It is a lesson I learned at the deepest level.[9]

This staff also had to deal with the special problems of having a father and daughter working together on a team. Although I had respect for him, Carl's passivity on the team continually angered me.

His inability to be aware of his own anger (which he admitted) and deal with it in our team frustrated many of us. Also, establishing my own identity while working next to him was not easy. We all had to figure out how to handle the reaction of many participants who saw Carl as the leader, or even the guru (which he hated), when actually we were a very strong team. The other staff members had to cope with those participants who saw this as Carl and Natalie's workshop (which it wasn't). And I had to deal with participants who projected a lot onto me as Carl's daughter. Many people who saw Carl as their father-figure automatically saw me as their sister, whether I knew them or not. Some sisters are loved, some hated, and I received large doses of both without knowing why. It took several summers to figure this out, but with the help of some honest participants I realized that some people were projecting their family difficulties onto me because they saw Carl as their "good father" and me as the daughter who received the attention they had always wanted. Many people, particularly women, envied me my position as daughter of this beloved person. In my experience, such envy always covers hidden anger.

Being on the facilitation team of more than ten large residential programs (I also teamed up with Carl and others in France, Mexico, and Italy) provided me very intensive learning in group dynamics and group facilitation. It was also a time when I differentiated my work from my father's. Traditionally, psychotherapy is a verbal form of therapy, and the verbal process will always be important. However, I find I can rapidly understand the world of the client when she expresses herself through images. Color, form, and symbols are languages that speak from the unconscious and have particular meanings for each individual. As I listen to a client's explanation of her imagery, I poignantly see the world as she views it. Or she may use movement and gesture to show how she feels. If she uses movement for self-expression, I can understand her world through empathizing kinesthetically. When she adds sound to her movement or art, it deepens the experience for each of us. And if she then writes about the whole experience, she uses yet another language.

Working closely with Carl made me realize how very different we were in terms of our personalities, and yet how very similar were our thought processes. As mentioned above, I needed to express my anger at the injustices of the world and at those who perpetrated them. Carl was more passive. I needed to express myself kinesthetically and through color and form. Carl was satisfied using verbal expression. And sometimes I needed to challenge his subtle forms of authority. The faculty seldom called an end to a session, waiting for participants to take that responsibility. But when Carl put his shoes on, we all knew the meeting was over. Such was the subtle form of leadership.

My greatest peeve was that I could not get my father's verbal recognition of my professional work. A prime example of this occurred when we were working together at a Person-Centered workshop in Japan. We had shared the platform, each giving a good talk, his on theory, mine a personal/political view of women and power. In our after-hours rehash I said, "I thought your talk was really good." He nodded his head in acceptance. Then I said, "I would like your reaction to my speech."

His answer: "I'm not very good at that." That was the end of our conversation. Thud.

It was difficult for me to be in his shadow. People usually directed their attention and their questions to him even though we were sharing the same platform. True, he was the world-renowned psychologist and I was a newcomer. But I frequently spoke on controversial subjects such as "Women and Power," and to have audiences respond mainly to him reinforced my sense of second-class citizenship. If he had been sensitive to the situation, he could have contributed to its solution while on the platform. He added to my frustration and my anger at the male-dominated world by not giving me any verbal support during or after the event.

Sometimes his actions spoke even though he had no words. When I started my Person-Centered Expressive Therapy Institute, he accepted my invitation to be a faculty member full-time for the first summer, and part-time for the next two summers (those were the last three years of his life). As one of our team, he started to learn about the significance of expressive arts work. In one of his counseling demonstrations, the client asked to talk about the art she had created earlier in the day. His interest and fascination are evident on the videotape of this session. In his person-centered way, he got the client to explore the meaning of her art.[10]

Birthing the Concept of Person-Centered Expressive Arts

Over the six summers of doing PCA workshops, my own interest in the creative process blossomed. In the residential settings, the whole group would spend many hours sitting and talking, sharing profound emotional feelings, telling their personal stories, communicating, arguing, and making decisions. It was all very fruitful, but my body was pleading with me, "Move, dance, draw, paint, play, make music! Find ways to express yourself nonverbally. Use your intuitive and creative power." So, within those ten-day PCA experiences, my colleague Jared Kass and I offered what we called "Studio Time" or "Movement Group." We invited participants to talk about the troubling issues in their lives; then we created an improvisation (which usually included movement, art, and sound) that would help them explore those issues. Many of the exploratory methods were cocreated by the group members. We discovered who we were by the art we created.

Expressive art refers to using the emotional, intuitive aspect of ourselves in various media. We express inner feelings by creating outer forms. To use art expressively, for instance, means to go into our inner realm to discover feelings to be expressed through visual art, movement, sound, writing, or drama. It is true, of course, that talking about our feelings is also an important way to express and discover ourselves, meaningfully. But in the therapeutic world based on humanistic principles, the words *expressive therapy* have been reserved for nonverbal and/or metaphoric expression. Humanistic expressive arts therapy differs from the analytic or medical model of art therapy, in which art is used to diagnose and treat people.

Expressive art is a process. It is the process as well as the product that heals, informs, and creates avenues for insight and development. Through the expressive arts we have the opportunity to express ourselves dramatically, poignantly, and colorfully, thereby gaining insights as to who we are. We can release our feelings, expressing them nonverbally, and gain insight into our deeper selves. Through the intense process of focusing during the creative act, we actually transform the repressed feelings into constructive ones. We also heal ourselves by integrating our inner polarities or opposites, coming into fuller balance and alignment. We can use the arts to explore these conflicting elements and discover ways to become whole. An intellectual understanding of any emerging symbolic images also provides for psychological growth. Recognizing the healing qualities of the creative process and the symbolic image or movement opens the door to acknowledging the mystical and transcendent quality of expressive art.

My daughter Frances Fuchs, a psychotherapist skilled in the use of art and hypnotherapy, says, "Art has the capability of being both the midwife and child of our inner selves."[11] Being keenly aware of our inner self helps us connect our inner reality to the outer world, bringing us closer to nature, other humans, and a global perspective.

Expressive arts therapists are aware that involving the mind, the body, and the emotions brings forth the client's intuitive, imaginative abilities as well as logical, linear thought. Since emotional states are seldom logical, using imagery and nonverbal modes allows the client an alternative path for self-exploration and communication. This process is a powerful integrative force.

Our bodies and movement also reflect our physical health and well-being. Do we have a sense of balance and of being grounded? Or are our heads in the clouds? Are we flexible or stiff, fast or slow, angular or flowing? As we begin to be aware of our way of moving in life, we also become conscious of how our emotional and physical well-being are connected. Movement can affect how we feel, and how we feel can affect our way of moving. A reciprocal relationship exists between movement and emotions. In movement we get in touch with our sensuality and sexuality, and we are able to integrate these with our spirit. Certain movements allow us to release—to release anger, frustration, blockage—with explosive, angular, stamping, fist-fighting energy and motion. Dancing or moving is a healthy, creative, instructive way to be aware of ourselves and to release those energies constructively. Holding in all of those feelings builds up a head of steam, making our bodies into pressure cookers.

In Nottingham, England, the PCA program was housed at the university, a campus of ivy-covered grey stone buildings built around a quadrangle. While most of the group was meeting in a hall on the ground floor, verbalizing their thoughts and emotions, Jared and I were offering our movement group upstairs. We had been through three very English-style drizzly days. On the fourth day, when the sun came out, Jared was suddenly inspired to get the whole gang outside. During one of the movement games we were playing, he said in a dramatic voice, "Follow me down the stairs to the land of make-believe!" We all realized his intent and gladly danced down the winding stairs of this ancient university and onto the green grass of the quad. A silver-haired woman from Holland asked to be queen and, before we realized what was happening, we had raised her on our hands and were carrying her around. We had a parade! People were pretending to play trumpets, marching in step. The procession was grand. The queen held court, a pope was throned (and dethroned), robbers and beggars appeared, and we had a tar-and-feathering, a wedding, and a death. An upright piano appeared on the lawn, was stolen and recaptured.

All of this with very few words. It just kept going; it was two hours of the most concentrated "play" any of us had ever experienced.

The only directions given were "Follow me to the land of make believe" and, after the parade, a suggestion to "Go quickly to your rooms and bring back any props that would add to the play." Hats, umbrellas, scarves, a broom, a bathrobe, a raincoat, and assorted items were tossed in a pile on the sidewalk. People helped themselves, then discarded props as their roles changed.

While I've never fully understood this and other such events, I do know that we were creating on the metaphoric and mythological levels. Psychodramatists might say we were engaging in archetypal psychotherapy. We were acting out our subpersonalities, whether they be devil or saint, queen or thief, bandit or angel. Trying on these roles in a playful atmosphere seemed to help us rediscover parts of ourselves and give us a fresh perspective. I know that anyone in that event has never forgotten it. Most important, it was fun.

At first Carl was somewhat mystified by the art work and sounds coming from our group. Later, as he saw the outcome, heard the feedback, and participated in some of the sessions in our upstairs room, he realized that we were expanding his theory of creativity. I was coming to the realization that we are all capable of being profoundly, beautifully creative whether we use that creativity to relate to family or to paint a picture. Much of our creativity grows out of our unconscious, our feelings, and our intuition. The unconscious is our deep well, and most of us have put a lid over it. But we can relearn how to channel our feelings constructively into creative ventures: into dance, music, art, or writing. When our feelings are joyful, the art form is uplifting. When our feelings are violent or wrathful, we can transform them into powerful art rather than venting them on the world. Such art helps us accept that aspect of ourselves.

Self-acceptance is paramount to compassion for others, and Carl understood this. He even joined in the dancing with real pleasure and several times found that the Creative Connection process opened him to his own poetry.

As my work progressed, I stated the principles it embodied:

All people have an innate ability to be creative.

The creative process is healing. The expressive product supplies important messages to the individual. However, it is the process of creation that is profoundly transformative.

Personal growth and higher states of consciousness are achieved through self-awareness, self-understanding, and insight.

We achieve self-awareness, understanding, and insight by delving into our emotions. The feelings of grief, anger, pain, fear, joy, and ecstasy are the tunnel through which we must pass to reach self-awareness, understanding, and wholeness.

Our feelings and emotions are an energy source. We can channel that energy into the expressive arts to be released and transformed.

The expressive arts—movement art, writing, sounding, music, meditation, and imagery—lead us into the unconscious. This often allows us to express previously unknown facets of ourselves, thus bringing to light new information and awareness.

Art modes interrelate in what I call the Creative Connection. When we move, it affects how we write or paint. When we write or paint, it affects how we feel and think. The creative connection is a process that brings us to an inner core or essence which is our life energy.

A connection exists between our life force—our inner core, or soul—and the essence of all beings.

Therefore, as we journey inward to discover our essence or wholeness, we discover our relatedness to the outer world. The inner and outer become one.

As I learned about group dynamics in the PCA workshops and though my own expressive arts groups, I put forth my theory:

Personal growth takes place in a safe, supportive environment.

A safe, supportive environment is created by having facilitators (teachers, therapists, group leaders, parents, colleagues) who are genuine, warm, empathic, open, honest, congruent, and caring.

These qualities can be learned best by first being experienced.

Relationships such as a client–therapist, teacher–student, parent–child, wife–husband, or between intimate partners can be places to experience these qualities.

Personal integration of the intellectual, emotional, physical, and spiritual occurs by taking time to reflect, critique, and evaluate these experiences.

These principles both reflected and added to what I had learned through my father's work. One letter that came to me after Carl's death put it this way: "Natalie, I see now how vital a role you played in his life at that time. The PCA workshops were not only an opportunity for you to work with him, but a gift to him that opened up new worlds of creative applications of his ideas and stretched his dreams even more. Your own work with the body gently pulled him into new ease of expression with his own body and to begin to appreciate new dimensions to a person-centered approach that could include the body and fantasy and playfulness as alternative ways of creating a safe environment where people could begin to risk new ways of thinking and acting."[12]

As I worked within the PCA workshops, the threads of my pursuits—psychotherapy, art, movement, music, and writing—were becoming more clearly defined. I was beginning to identify an area of work that was bringing together all my life interests into my work. Since many people at the PCA workshops were excited by our experimentation, we all had an opportunity to learn together without worrying about what we should call this process. Depending on the immediate needs and wishes of the participants, Jared and I invented art projects, improvisations, guided visualizations, and music. The groups cocreated many sessions to heal the painful histories of the people participating. After finding ways to enact the rage or grief, or to paint its sorrow, we would also evolve celebrations.

Here, in the permissive, accepting environment of the PCA workshops, came an offshoot. Steeped in the philosophy, values, and concepts of client-centered therapy, we were evolving a holistic, integrative process that elaborated Carl's theory of creativity. At that time we felt as though we were rebelling against something: against sitting and *talking* about our life experiences. Now we realized we were *extending and expanding* the person-centered process to include the whole body and expression through the arts.

Expressive arts are potent media in which to discover, experience, and accept the unknown aspects of self. Verbal therapy focuses on emotional disturbances and inappropriate behavior. Expressive arts move the client into the world of emotions and adds a further dimension. By incorporating the arts in psychotherapy, we offer the client a pathway for using the free-spirited parts of herself. Therapy may include joyful, lively learning on many levels: the sensory, kinesthetic, conceptual, emotional, and mythic. Clients report that the expressive arts have helped them go beyond their problems to envisioning themselves as constructively taking action in the world.

We could sit and talk about being frustrated, blocked, or angry for hours and hours and the energy might not shift. But if we use our bodies to express our emotions through movement (in a safe and accepting environment), we can deeply experience, accept, release, and transform them. We let the monster out of the cage, look at it, and ultimately accept it as part of ourselves. The raging beast eventually becomes our ally for strength, determination, and a will to move on.

People's biggest fear, of course, is that their raging beast will strike out and do damage: that their rage will turn into real violence. Indeed, the rage *will* turn into real violence if we bottle it up continually. On the other hand, a safe environment offers a chance to put our anger into dance—to express it freely without hurting others or ourselves. This, in turn, transforms the anger into strength and self-empowerment, thus shifting this potentially destructive energy into constructive form. Healing has occurred.

As I began to write about our discoveries (1979–80), I found that we were not alone. Indeed, psychology departments of some universities were offering expressive arts programs. Lesley College in Cambridge, Massachusetts, where Jared was a faculty member, was offering a whole program in the expressive arts, headed up by Shaun McNiff and Paolo Knill. Sonoma State University in California had an expressive arts department that was based on Carl's philosophy of self-directed learning. Hobart Thomas and Mac McCreary, whom I later came to know and admire, had developed a unique and highly creative arts program.

Not only were art therapy and movement therapy coming into their own, but many of us were finding the connection *between* the arts significant. On a deeper level, this connection is ancient. Early cultures didn't compartmentalize their self-expression and spirituality. A rain dance involved music, art, movement, chanting, a sense of community, and an understanding that collective energy could transform individuals and possibly nature itself. We were rediscovering a process that heals and transforms.

The person-centered approach to expressive arts therapy evolved further as a Norwegian colleague, Columbus Salveson, and I teamed up to facilitate an intensive training for professionals in Norway. We invited two other staff which enriched our learnings. For two years

(1982–84) I went to Norway for three weeks each summer and again in January. Since the same group of twenty-six participants attended each session, I saw the long-term results of the expressive arts process. It was clear, from the feedback of those participants, that the expressive arts had helped them reach into their unconscious and enabled them to express themselves and gain helpful insights. I could see the changes in these folks, and understand the tremendous depth and power of the expressive arts. People's lives actually changed for the better as they engaged in this process. Their intellectual input and constructive feedback made me realize that I needed and wanted a long-term program in the United States. Such a program would allow participants to write and do research projects to expand the conceptual foundations of the work.

Person-Centered Expressive Therapy Comes into Form

My wish for ongoing studies of both the experiential and cognitive aspects of the expressive arts motivated me to create an institute—to develop a training that explores the dynamics of the person-centered approach to expressive arts. The person-centered approach emphasizes the therapist's role as being empathic, open, honest, congruent, and caring as she listens in depth and facilitates the growth of the individual or group. Incorporated in this process is the belief that each individual has worth, dignity, and the capacity for self-direction. This reflects trust in every individual's inherent impulse toward growth. My very deep faith in the innate capacity of each person to reach toward his or her full potential is the foundation for my approach to expressive arts therapy.

In my work over the years, it became apparent that the Creative Connection process fostered integration. It is clearly stated by one client who said, "I discovered in exploring my feelings that I could break through inner barriers/structures that I set for myself, by moving and dancing the emotions. To draw that feeling after the movement continued the process of unfolding."

The accompanying figure is a visual presentation of the principles and process of the Creative Connection using expressive arts therapy. It shows how all art forms affect and influence each other. Our visual art is changed by our movement and body rhythm. It is also influenced when we meditate and become receptive, allowing intuition to be active. Likewise, our movement can be influenced by

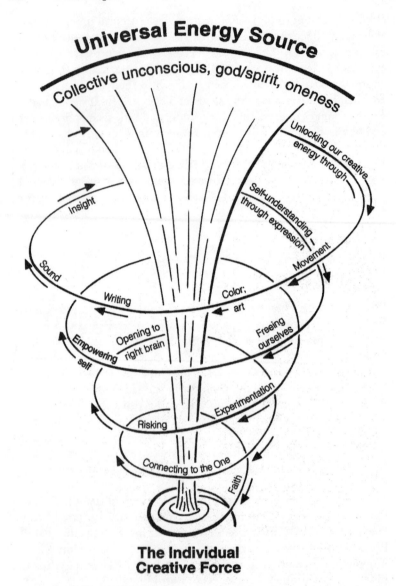

**The Individual
Creative Force**

The Creative Connection Process: By moving from art form to art form, we release layers of inhibitions, bringing us to our center—our individual creative force. This center opens us to the universal energy source, bringing us vitality and a sense of oneness.

Reprinted from *The Creative Connection: Expressive Arts as Healing* by Natalie Rogers (Science and Behavior Books, 1993).

our visual art and writing, and so forth. All of the creative processes help us find our inner essence or source. And when we find that inner source, we tap into the universal energy source, or the collective unconscious, or the transcendental experience.

In 1984 when I was looking for a colleague to cocreate the program, it was my good fortune that my artist-therapist daughter, Frances Fuchs, had the time, the knowledge, and the ability to do this. She invested a year working with me as an administrative partner to create a nonprofit organization and design its program. We called it the Person-Centered Expressive Therapy Institute (PCETI). For four years, Frances also joined the faculty and the board of directors. I invested $10,000 (half my savings at that time) and gathered colleagues for an advisory board and a working board. Wanting to replicate the excitement of the collaborative PCA faculty, Frances and I invited Carl, Red Thomas (of Sonoma State University), and Nancy Bloom (a friend and movement person) to be on our faculty for the first summer. Exciting as this teamwork was, at the end of the program I realized that paying five faculty, even minimally, had put us back to square one financially. I had to look at other ways to make the program feasible. I decided to teach the program with only one other colleague at each session, bringing in a guest for two or three days. Initially this guest was Carl.

I had felt proud to invite my father to be part of the facilitation faculty. To be able to introduce him to the fullness of the work I was doing turned the tables in an interesting way. With Frances on the faculty, we took advantage of the three-generational aspect to have a family panel discussing our respective creative development and how these interconnected. (This was not entirely new. Several times Frances, Carl, and I had appeared at public events, small and large, to discuss world and psychological issues.[13]) At this informal gathering in our summer program, participants told us they were just as fascinated by our family dynamics (not all of them smooth, by any means) as by what we discussed. It was my impression during that particular panel that Frances and I were talking to each other—that is, having a dialogue—and that Carl was talking to the audience. This annoyed me, and I felt we were demonstrating the scenario of my life. He did not want to engage in dialogue and interaction but was willing to be on stage with his ideas. The videotape taken by one of the participants supports some of my impressions.

For the most part, however, it was a real pleasure to have Carl work with us. One day he held a demonstration counseling session with another participant, Mary.[14] She had created three pictures in the expressive art work in the morning and had discovered some aspects of herself that needed further exploration. Carl was an exquisite empathic companion as Mary uncovered the fear of actually using the personal power she saw coming forth in her drawings. Carl also cofacilitated a small demonstration group with Frances, having the participants create and explore their expressive art projects. During his few days at our training program, he enjoyed getting into the dance or movement aspect of the work since this was one area that had been forbidden to him as a child. It was a real pleasure to watch him move freely around the floor with the other participants as the drums and music played.

What happens when we allow our bodies to tell us how to move? Rather than starting with a feeling, we can wait for a body impulse. The first step is to close your eyes and go inward, and actually wait for an impulse in your body that moves you. You may think this is impossible—that it is our thoughts that move us. If, however, you wait long enough and let go of your thought process, your body will have an impulse to move. It may be a tiny gesture or a sweeping movement, but it will happen. Dance therapist Mary Whitehouse explains the process as one of being moved and moving at the same time. Movement therapist Janet Adler calls it authentic movement. Or as one man in my workshop put it:

> I have to say, I didn't dance. *IT danced me!* I'm just a businessman. I've never seen a ghost or a spirit, but it danced. It did something important for me. It gave me tremendous pleasure.

At such times people are no longer thinking about their bodies. They *are* their bodies. It is an astonishing event.

In November 1986, Carl, Frances, and I made our last joint appearance in a project sponsored by our Institute in Santa Rosa, California. It was titled, "Fostering Creativity: A Three-Generational View." Father/grandfather, mother/daughter, and daughter/grand-daughter talked about our current interests and discussed the creative process with each other. Carl had just returned from Moscow and related fascinating stories of his encounter groups and lectures there. He was turning eighty-five and still going strong. I have since been told many times by Russians that my father's trip to the USSR changed the face of psychology there. As Moscow University professor Julia Gippenreiter expressed it, "Before Carl Rogers came, psychology as a field drew little interest because we focused on things like measuring eye movement, or some other such irrelevant research. When we heard that Carl Rogers was coming, we couldn't actually *believe* it. When he did arrive we fought to get into his workshops and swarmed to his lectures. Having experienced the Person-Centered Approach from this genuine and rather humble man changed my focus in psychology, as it did many others. I am now teaching teachers how to relate to their pupils and am using the principles of facilitation in my University classes."

When Carl returned from this trip, he told me he had no idea Soviets had read his writings since none of his books had been translated into Russian. He was incredulous that people knew something about his work.

In January 1987 I was preparing to leave to lead a workshop in Mexico City. The night before I left, I had a vivid dream: I was searching for Carl and kept saying, "But I can't find the body! I can't find the body!" The next morning I called Dad to make sure my dream had not come true. He assured me that he was feeling peppy and said his friend Ruth Sanford was visiting him. But that dream had an unusual strength and power to it. I knew it was different. So I wrote a letter to Carl's assistant, Valerie Henderson, and reminded her that we had a pact: she was to call me if something happened to Carl, wherever I was in the world. I gave her my phone numbers in Mexico.

I was glad I had heeded my dream. Three days later a call came. Carl had slipped and fallen in the middle of the night, breaking his hip. Although he did well after the surgery the following day, he then had a cardiac arrest and went into a coma. David flew to La Jolla from the East, and I came from Mexico. Carl's closest friends from the Center for Studies of the Person were with him.

The next three days were a time of feeling unusually close to my brother. Also, my daughters Naomi and Frances arrived to support me and to be with their grandfather. We discovered that his labored breathing was greatly eased if the three of us held hands and held his hands, creating a meditation circle. His being in a coma for a few days gave many people time to say their goodbyes. On February 4, 1987, he died peacefully in the hospital. At the time, Naomi, Frances, and I were holding his hands.[15]

I particularly like the way friend and Assemblyman John Vasconcellos talked about Carl at the memorial service: "In a physical sense, Carl Rogers has left us. That is the sad news. The joyous—and hopeful—news is that Carl Rogers has left many of us more intact, having 'become persons' more whole and healthy, more faithful and trusting, more able to lead our lives affectively and effectively. We are living examples of his vision: that we human beings are innately inclined toward becoming constructive, affirming, responsible, and trustworthy."[16]

New Horizons

The months after my father's death were an emotional roller coaster for me. The loss felt huge (and unexpected), yet there was also a sense that I had been released. My inner sense was that his passing had opened a psychic door for me as well as having brought great sorrow.

Expressive art served me well during that time of mourning. Two artist-therapist friends invited me to spend time working with them. Connie Smith Siegel invited me to spend a week at a cottage on Bolinas Bay. I painted one black picture after another. Every time I became bored with such dark images, I would start another painting. It, too, became moody and bleak. Although Connie is primarily an artist, her therapeutic training and ability to accept my emotional state gave me permission to be authentic.

Also, I went to a weekend workshop taught by Coeleen Kiebert and spent more time sculpting and painting. This time the theme was tidal waves—and again, black pictures. One clay piece portrays a head peeking out of the underside of a huge wave. My sense of being overwhelmed by the details of emptying my parents' home, making decisions about my father's belongings, and responding to the hundreds of people who loved him was taking its toll. Once again, my art work gave free reign to my feelings and so yielded a sense of relief. Coeleen's encouragement to use the art experience to release and understand my inner process was another big step. I thought I *should* be over my grief in a month, but these two women gave me permission to continue expressing my river of sadness. That year my expressive art showed my continued sense of loss as well as an opening to new horizons.

As is often true when there is deep suffering, there is also an opening to spiritual realms. Three months after my father's death, I flew to Switzerland to cofacilitate a training group with the artist-therapist Paolo Knill. It was a time when I had a heightened sense of connectedness to people, nature, and my dreams. Amazing events took place in my inner being. I experienced synchronicities, special messages, and remarkable images. One night I found myself awakened by what seemed to be the beating of many large wings in my room. The next morning I drew the experience as best I could.

One afternoon I led our group in a movement activity called Melting and Growing. The group divided into pairs, and each partner took turns observing the other dancing the process, "melting," and then "growing." Paolo and I participated in this activity together. He was witnessing me as I slowly melted from being very tall to collapsing completely on the floor. Later I wrote in my journal: "I loved the opportunity to melt, to let go completely. When I melted into the floor I felt myself totally relax. I surrendered! Instantaneously I experienced being *struck* by incredible light. Although my eyes were closed, all was radiant. Astonished, I lay quietly for a moment, then slowly started to 'grow' bringing myself to full height."

Reflecting on these experiences, it seems that my heart had cracked open. This left me both vulnerable and with great inner strength and light. A few days later another wave picture emerged. This time bright blue/green water was illumined with pink/gold sky.

The roller coaster continued upon my return from Europe. I was still trying to be the chief administrator, fund raiser, and faculty person at The Person-Centered Expressive Therapy Institute. As my sixtieth birthday neared (one more life transition), I fell apart. After weeks of feeling confused, disoriented, unable to make decisions, weepy, angry, and exhausted, I did give up. I awoke in the middle of the night feeling extremely anxious. I asked myself, "If you were your own therapist, what would you do?"

My reply: "Let it out! Say what's really going on inside!"

Still in bed, I threw off the covers and began kicking (a good Reichian therapy method). The words that came blasting out were, "I don't want to do this any more! I don't want to do this any more! I don't want to do this any more!" A flood of tears burst forth and barely stopped for three or four days. It was frightening. "This is what it means to be out of control," I thought. I had visions of being carted off in a straightjacket. As my daughters and friends came to assure me I'd be all right, and as I received good medical advice from my brother and others, my mind cleared and I began to have some restful sleep once more.

In creating the Institute, I felt I had created a monster. Although it was serving the public well, it was devouring me. In retrospect I can see that this crisis had to happen for me to let go—let go of pushing, promoting, and driving myself and other people. At that point faithful colleagues, family, and board members stepped in to hire an executive director, Joseph McIntyre. He took on the organizational decision-making, budgeting, and planning, which released me to teach, speak, travel, and write. That quick action by Mel Suhd, Shellee Davis, Gail Laird, Claire Fitzgerald, and others was a wonderful gift. Shellee, having been through the expressive arts program at Sonoma State as well as our PCETI program, was beautifully equipped to come on board as codirector and faculty member. She and I became a collaborative team.

Having shed the administrative responsibilities brought me back full circle to being able to fully enjoy and appreciate the workshop participants and students who were contributing to the expressive arts field. Being a part of their growth process and having them write papers about their development has always inspired me. It also brings new data to the field.

The person-centered expressive therapy training program is a fertile field of experimentation and cross-fertilization of all the arts. We are integrating the philosophy and values of Carl's work with the process of self-expression through creative art. Although using expressive arts is very different from Carl's mode, we find it crucial to create a safe, person-centered environment for our work. As a facilitator of creativity and as an expressive arts therapist, I provide an atmosphere where we can reexperience the direct communication with color, line, form, music, and movement that we knew as children. There is no way to be that child again. We know too much. But we can recapture the healing aspects of spontaneous self-expression through the arts.

Whereas most therapies focus on problems, pain, suffering, grief, and anger, our approach via the expressive arts includes that work but also encourages the individual to go beyond, discovering ways to express joy, laughter, hope, and universal connectedness.

Latest Movement: *The Themes Harmonize*

As my life symphony continues, the latest movement brings the themes into harmony. As I have learned to empower myself, I try to bring the person-centered approach and the expressive arts into the world arena to foster creativity in other cultures and to build cross-cultural bridges.

I often wonder, "How am I contributing to the world so that it may become a safe and healthy place for my grandchildren? How can

I help prevent war? How can I contribute to international understanding and help heal the earth? I want to be part of the solution!"

Although I live an active life as a teacher, international group facilitator, psychotherapist, writer, and artist, I am like many people involved in the humanistic world of personal growth and creativity: I wonder if my life and work actually make a difference. I know that I long for a world where cooperation and collaboration are the accepted values. I long for a world where women and minorities truly have equal opportunity, and where greed is replaced by a larger vision—one in which self fulfillment is accomplished by being a creative, caring person, rather than accumulating things.

I would like to believe that teaching the person-centered approach to expressive arts is part of this evolutionary process of change. My experience tells me that those of us who are midwives to the creative process play a crucial role in today's chaotic world.

Effecting Change

To effect change in the world takes the effort of highly conscious, integrated, creative people who are responsive and willing to act on their beliefs. The philosophy, values, and process of person-centered expressive therapy is one avenue of fostering the development of such individuals. Experience shows that when a critical mass of people have changed their perspective on world events, have spoken out, and have taken action, it can change the course of history. Such was the case in the anti–Vietnam War movement. People who empower themselves—through expressive arts or otherwise—also begin to change their perspective and find strength to act on their beliefs.

Here is a personal example. It bewildered me that I experienced the Persian Gulf War as though my own family were maimed. While many Americans were cheering as the bombs dropped, I experienced tremendous guilt. While other people were out celebrating a "victory," I was wracked with pain that we had killed 150,000 people, many of them women and children. I wondered, "How is it that I cannot hold up any personal wall to ward off the suffering that is going on thousands of miles away?" But I also realized that having the capacity to suffer with innocent victims brings with it the capacity to fully enjoy the celebration when the Berlin Wall came crumbling down, or feel the exhilaration in my body when courageous Russians stood steadfastly in front of their White House to stave off a military coup.

Through movement, I became aware of my anguish. My feeling translated itself into a poem. Writing it was like opening the steam vent in a pressure cooker. I wept as I wrote it, and wept as I read it to my authentic movement group the next day. They were my support network and encouraged me to use the poem to take the next step: to send it to radio stations and to political leaders, to use it as a potent tool for antiwar action. I needed the validation that the poem was well written and had impact. After receiving that support, I went home and sent it to a radio station. They called me in to read it in person. I also mailed it to over thirty-five political leaders, with the following statement:

> This poem burst forth out of my despair about the
> Persian Gulf war. I hope it will awaken and activate
> people to insist on bringing the troops home before a full
> scale ground war begins, and to insist that we steadfastly
> pursue diplomatic negotiations and a peace conference to
> solve the Middle East problems.

I felt a tremendous sense of relief as I took some action.

Although you may or may not agree with my politics, I think you could agree that my transformation through the arts to action is a model for anyone.

I know I am not alone as a person who, at crucial moments in history, feels emotionally, kinesthetically, and spiritually connected to others. Many religions embrace the notion that we are all One. Yet opening to the actual experience of that kind of connectedness is rare. It can be cultivated by becoming *aware,* by tapping your *creative energy,* by finding your *personal core* or center, and by opening to the *universal energy force.*

The sense of interconnectedness and compassion on the global level is the spirit that will eventually lead us to methods of peace-keeping.

Creativity Is Revolutionary

It is also true that creativity is revolutionary. Dictators do not tolerate creativity because they know that such self-expression brings forth independent thinking, spontaneity, and self-empowerment, and invokes higher powers. Thus creativity is subversive to those who demand conformity to a political system. Over the years as I have been enriched by my work in other countries, I have gained a sense that I am helping to build a world network based on equality and human dignity. I have taught expressive arts in most countries in Europe and Japan as well as in countries that have been under the rule of dictators. I wish to point out, theoretically and with personal examples, that person-centered expressive therapy is of particular value to nations emerging from despotic despair. The expressive arts involve people in their imagination, metaphoric imagery, dance, and sound, which brings vitality and life back to their deadened spirits. Rather than focusing solely on the grief and despair, they also find the opportunity to reexperience the creative, childlike, playful, and hopeful aspects of self. *Where death and tragedy loom large, there is a need to dream, envision, and regain faith in the possible.*

Building Cross-Cultural Bridges

Building cross-cultural bridges brings learning in both directions. It is second nature for me to create a trusting atmosphere in which people can communicate with each other, verbally and through art images. As I listen to them—to the "music" as well as the words— they start to truly hear each other. My genuine acceptance gives them permission to speak their fear and grief and allows them to comfort and support each other. They desperately need such support. My visit brings them together in new ways. They will continue meeting and giving each other courage.

My recent trips to the Soviet Union (1989 and 1991) have also been a two-way bridge for cross cultural understanding. Our Russian friends tell us that the direction of psychology has dramatically changed with the input of humanistic psychologists—Carl Rogers being among the first to visit, in 1986. Many Russians say his talks opened the door to new ways of teaching and applying psychology. It is heartwarming to know that a few individuals can make a significant difference in the personal lives and political direction of a country—a country rich in cultural heritage of music, art, and literature but one that had been sealed off from information about psychology and humanistic values. Psychotherapy had been outlawed for seventy years. Clinical training and supervision were not available. Mental hospitals were institutions in which to jail political prisoners. The situation is best described by the Russians themselves. A statement put out by Garmonia, a new nonprofit counseling and training center in St. Petersburg (formerly Leningrad), reads:

Ugly ideology which existed in our country for seventy years harmed our people. It spoiled their minds, erasing true human values and rejecting the sacred uniqueness of every human being. Reorienting people's minds toward humanistic ideals is the major goal of the reconstruction taking place now. . . .

Not all changes in Soviet life have been positive. Political instability, national conflicts, and economical hardships have all increased human suffering, intensifying fears and feelings of hopelessness, igniting aggression and self destructiveness. . . .

To help people live through critical periods, to provide them not only with physical support but, even more important under present dramatic circumstances, to encourage their personal growth in the face of sudden devastating hardship. . . . Thus psychotherapy and psychological help acquire major importance. In the present circumstances they are hopelessly inadequate. Leningrad, for example, a city of five-million people, has only a few dozen professional therapists, smaller cities have fewer, and most towns are likely to have none.

It should be kept in mind that psychotherapy has been officially regarded as a kind of ideological tool mainly used to enforce the adjustment of a personality to the ugly way of life. Professional training conditioned psychologists and therapists to match psychology to Marxist philosophy. Even now, psychological education is far from satisfactory.

I have also been told that because of Carl's visit, and visits from other humanistic psychologists, psychology has now become a very popular and important field of study in Russia. It is certainly a much needed program since they have had no hotlines, no methods for crisis intervention, and very little clinical training. In Communist days, people didn't have emotional problems—or so the government dictated.

After my father's death in 1987, Dr. Alexey Matushkin invited me to continue on with his work. I explained that I would want to teach my own work, which was quite different from my father's.

I handed him literature to acquaint him with person-centered expressive arts therapy. After studying it, he sent me an enthusiastic invitation.

I was asked to give intensive training in Person-Centered Expressive Therapy for psychologists, educators, social workers, doctors, hotline workers, and researchers. In 1989 I invited colleagues Claire Fitzgerald and Fran Macy to work with me as a team. In 1991 Fran and I followed up this work. We offered expressive arts experiences to facilitate individuals and groups in self-awareness, nonverbal communication skills, and higher states of consciousness. These experiences were integrated with clinical training in person-centered counseling.

These two trips to the Soviet Union left me a wiser human being. My efforts to understand something of the politics, the economics, and most of all the human condition of those who have experienced life under seventy years of a repressive, brutal regime have touched me so deeply as to change my own outlook on life. When people ask me what I learned, I reply, "courage and patience." Every time I walk into my huge neighborhood supermarket filled to overflowing with produce, meats, and every imaginable food, I recall my visits to the state-owned markets in Moscow where people wait to get a few pounds of sausage and a slice of butter.

Creative Vision

We can never expect that the peoples of the world will be of one mind—there will always be conflict and controversy—but we can expect that people will be able to respond creatively to find mutually beneficial solutions. It is imperative that our educational systems, our corporations, and our political leaders stimulate, foster, and use the creative process to promote personal well-being and bring about imaginative, enlightened collaboration for peaceful solutions to this troubled planet. The Creative Connection process—the person-centered philosophy and the expressive arts process—is one means of awakening creativity and allowing people to become authentic and empowered. It takes us out of our linear, logical mode and stimulates our intuitive, holistic way of knowing. Although we don't want to abandon our logical ways, we need to balance our problem-solving methods with the more encompassing, creative ways of thinking.

If we are resolved, as a world community, to settle our disagreements peacefully, it can happen. We have all the technological resources and the brain power to solve our global crises. The clash seems to be those who want to have control over others and those who want cooperation and collaboration. The hierarchical system has not worked. *To survive, our image must change from ladders and pyramids to circles!* We need a willingness and determination to look at the potential solutions creatively, cooperatively, and without greed. Nothing is really holding us back from solutions to our world dilemmas except the lid we have put on our creativity. As we change our consciousness, so will we change the world. The Creative Connection process fosters a change in consciousness that helps individuals experience a transpersonal state of awareness—an understanding of the interconnection and interdependence of all life forms. This broadening of consciousness happens as we become deeply aware of our inner essence. By going inward to what is deeply personal, we feel connected to the universal.

Opening ourselves to the creative force within will give us the ability to envision the possible. Envisioning the possible excites our will and determination to create it. Holding the vision is an important step in the creative process. We can be pioneers who light the candle.

Epilogue: Where, Now?

As I turn sixty-five, I have birthed a new book, called *The Creative Connection,* which pulls together the theory, the methods, and my personal development through person-centered expressive art.[17] Mel Suhd has been my mentor as I pushed through self-doubt and discouragement to find that by writing, I learned what it is I have been teaching. (I also acquired my doctorate.) I am delighted and somewhat astounded that "the creative connection" is no longer just a concept, it is a way of being and doing. In creating an institute, I have created a community that nourishes me and those that are deeply involved in it. I am delighted that others are now teaching/facilitating this process in their own ways.

And I feel there is something new, for me, just around the corner. I long to spend more time doing my own art work, but banishing the inner critic who says, "You are a dilettante when it comes to art" is difficult.

I ask myself, "Where am I going now?" Recently I had a dream that gives me clues. First scene: *I am at a group meeting or conference and go to the large swimming pool early in the morning. No one seems*

to be around, so I take off my nightgown and swim nude. Next
scene: *I am in a tree about a half mile high, looking down at a
Caribbean shoreline with azure blue waters. It is gorgeous below. I'm
hanging on (nude again) and saying to myself that I want to let go.
My question to myself: "Is the water below deep enough?" I do let go,
and I start falling. But instead of plummeting, I am floating down
slowly, as though a parachute were on my back. It takes a long time
to float down. I begin to dance and move in the sky. It's fun! I stretch
and reach and see a cloud go by. Something else, like a jellyfish, is floating down, too. I look below and see the water gradually coming
closer.* I wake up. The words "free fall" come to mind immediately.

The mystery of the dream remains, but the sense of letting go and
floating through the rest of life appeals to me. This ending is just
another beginning.

References

1 Carl Rogers, *Counseling and Psychotherapy: New Concepts in Practice.*
Boston: Houghton Mifflin, 1942.

2 Natalie Rogers, "Changes in Self-Concept in the Case of Mrs. Ett"
(unpublished term paper). DePauw University, 1947.

3 Natalie Rogers, "The Case of Mrs. Ett," *Counseling Center Journal,*
1948.

4 Virginia Axline, *Play Therapy.* Boston: Houghton Mifflin, 1947.

5 Natalie Rogers Fuchs, "A Play Therapist's Approach to the Creative Art
Experience" (master's thesis). Brandeis University, Department of
Psychology, 1960.

6 Natalie Rogers Fuchs, "Self-Expression Through Creative Arts," *PSEA
Journal* (Public Schools Art Education Association) I:2. Republic of the
Philippines Department of Education, 1963.

7 Natalie Rogers Fuchs, "The Use of Encounter Techniques in Group
Therapy with Hospitalized College Students" (unpublished paper), 1972.

8 The Person-Centered Approach workshops took place at: University of
California, San Diego, in La Jolla, 1974; and the University of California,
Santa Cruz, 1974; Mills College, Oakland, CA, 1975; Southern Oregon
State College, Ashland, 1976; Camp Uncas, Sagamore, NY, 1977;

Nottingham University, Nottingham, England, 1978; and Princeton University, Princeton, NJ, 1979.

[9] For a full description of these Person Centered Approach workshops see chapter 8 in Carl Roger's book: *Carl Rogers on Personal Power.* New York: Delacorte, 1977.

[10] PCETI video: Carl Rogers counsels Tess Sturrock at the Person-Centered Expressive Therapy Institute training program, August 1986.

[11] Frances Fuchs, "Exploring Women's Creative Process" (master's thesis). Sonoma State University, CA, 1982; p. 18.

[12] Andre Auw in a letter to Natalie Rogers, March 9, 1991.

[13] See "New World/New Person: A Three-Generational View" with Carl Rogers, Natalie Rogers, and Frances Fuchs, held February 28, 1981 at the Marin Civic Center, San Rafael, CA. Also, "Fostering Creativity: A Three-Generational View" held November 1986, at the Luther Burbank Center, Santa Rosa, CA.

[14] PCETI video: Carl Rogers in a demonstration counseling session with Mary McClary at the Person-Centered Expressive Therapy Institute training program, August 1986.

[15] For a collection of memorial articles about Carl Rogers written by family and friends, see the Association of Humanistic Psychology newsletter, "Perspectives," May 1987, and the *Person Centered Review* 2:3 (August 1987).

[16] John Vasconcellos, "Eulogy," Person Centered Review 2:3 (August 1987), p. 353.

[17] Natalie Rogers, *The Creative Connection: Expressive Arts as Healing.* Palo Alto, CA: Science and Behavior Books, 1993.

For PCETI information or tapes, contact the Person-Centered Expressive Therapy Institute/P.O. Box 6518/Santa Rosa, CA 95406/707-526-4006.

✛

One of my dreams is to visit Haruko Tsuge, the quiet but inspiring matriarch who took humanistic psychology to Japan. She was single-handedly responsible for having some of Carl Rogers' works translated into Japanese and integrated into the Japanese emergence from a political monarchy into a system that recognizes democratic individuation.

Thanks to Suzanne Spector, I have been able to maintain communication with Haruko and her coauthor Akira Takeuchi, and *Positive Regard* has this beautiful story to inspire its readers.

Haru's story, and the brilliant way that Akira wove in her biography, carry this book to dimensions I had not expected in the original design. Opening ourselves to another culture through their writing, we have an opportunity to perceive a new way of understanding person-centered living and self-empowerment. We also witness a vivid extension of Carl's extended family. Haru is the primary inspiration for many of the contributors to this chapter, who also became inspired by Akira, Natalie Rogers, Carl, and others. In turn, they may be considered notables whose stories deserve to appear in succeeding collections. I hope someone in Japan gathers such a collection with Haru as the "kernel" or the "bud."

✛

5

A Unique Inner World

by Haruko Tsuge and
Akira Takeuchi

The title of this book, *Positive Regard: Carl Rogers and Notables He Inspired*, focuses on aspects coined by Carl Rogers as "the experiencing process." When I think about the words *positive regard* and *inspired*, I am reminded of how the experiencing process—the flow of life that has no name—came to be a special quality in the lives of both Carl and another rare individual, Mrs. Haruko Tsuge (nicknamed Haru).

Haru met Carl by taking his class at the University of Chicago at the end of her studies there. On her return to Japan, she became the first counselor at Japan Women's University. She kept in touch with Carl through his writings, which she read over and over again. In 1971, in the La Jolla Program, she had a chance to show Carl what she had learned. Later, during their long period of communication and feedback, Carl encouraged Haru's unique way of being as well as her ideas and opinions. Today, in 1992, she still reads Carl's writings. In this way, she continues to receive positive regard from him.

In time, people wanting to emulate Haru and the way she lived began to gather around her. They gathered because she created an atmosphere of acceptance, which allowed everyone to share of themselves and to experience others in a mutually respectful way.

It has been practically impossible to express what really happened between Haru and those around her. No established way exists for conveying in writing what occurs at an experiential level. The exchange and communication of experiences occurs both horizontally, on a person-to-person level, and vertically, as in a teacher-student relationship. The exchange occurs continuously (through positive regard) and intermittently (through inspiration).

Yet people can be touched at the deepest experiential level through reading about others' lives. Even through the book's title, I experienced positive regard for myself, and this has given me the confidence to write this biography. At the end of the chapter, I express my thanks to the people who made the writing of this project possible, as it has been an extremely meaningful experience for me.

After collecting data directly from Haru as well as from other significant people, I had much information; but it was important that this chapter be more than a mere stringing together of stories. Haru did not want to be merely described, or to have the book read as something separate from the reader. She hoped readers would open up to a relationship on an experiential level: to be both subjective and objective while reading.

The pattern of her life is uniquely her own, and I wanted to set the stage on which she could be seen most naturally. Her life does not fit into the typical success-story biography. She did not set for herself a specific objective in life; rather, through the various problems she faced, she created a distinct way of being.

By being truly her own person, Haru has moved forward in life by listening to her inner self for guidance. She has maintained an active relationship between her personal experiencing process and external reality. By being honest with herself, she chooses the path that is most comfortable and natural to her. She lives up to her own expectations instead of others' expectations of her. She is able to accept what is happening around her as well as her own inner reality.

What you are going to read next is a section written by Haru herself. As stated, this will not be a mere stringing together of things that happened in Haru's life. To get more out of your reading, I hope you keep in mind the following questions: "What events made Haru the unique woman she is?" and "What brought her to Carl Rogers?"

My Way of Being Personally and Professionally

by Haruko Tsuge

I was born on November 7, 1908, in Otsu, a city near Kyoto and facing Lake Biwa, the largest lake in Japan. *Biwa* is also an old Japanese musical instrument, and the lake was named after it because of its similar shape. Otsu was my mother's home town and so, according to our old custom regarding a first child, I was born at her parental home.

My father's parental home was in Nada, near Kobe, a town famous for Japanese sake. My father was an electrical engineer, a graduate of Purdue University in Indiana. He died on November 6, 1909 in Nada, after a serious injury caused by a fall at work. Soon after I was born, my mother returned to Nada, leaving me in her parents' care. Her father was an obstetrician and gynecologist.

My name is pronounced Haru in Japanese, although a Chinese ideogram is used for writing it. The character consists of the sun and the moon, and it means "bright and light." Usually Chinese characters have at least two different pronunciations, called *on* and *kun*. The former is akin to Chinese pronunciation, and the latter is genuine Japanese. Japanese pronunciation of this Chinese character, in the case of a girl's name, is Aki, which means "autumn."

I was named by my grandfather on my father's side, who was well versed in Chinese and Buddhistic literature. In Japanese, the word *haru* means spring, so he probably preferred spring to autumn, both in sound and meaning, and also for intuitive reasons. It was rather an unusual way of pronouncing the ideogram in Japan.

I myself appreciate his choice a great deal, because part of the character refers to the sun and the moon. As I grew older, I came to like it more. The combination of the sun and the moon—the contrast of light and shadow, day and night, active and passive, and life and death—appeals to me. Often, early in the morning or late at night when I gaze at twinkling stars or see the full or crescent-shaped moon, I cannot help feeling something holy, as if I am in resonance with the spirit of the cosmos.

From birth I was reared by my mother's parents, whom I called Father and Mother, and by "Mamma," who was in Mejiro in Tokyo. She was staying at her alma mater, the school that became Japan Women's University (founded in 1901 by Jinzo Naruse, a pioneer in the field of higher education for women). Once or twice a year, she came home. I remember her telling me stories, sewing my doll's

clothes by hand, creating a miniature garden in the yard, and making me a small book of simple pictures, which she drew with single strokes of a writing brush.

As Father was a practitioner, our household included a pharmacist, one or two midwives-to-be, and a maid. I was the only child among them. In my very early years, my cradle was a square hamper about thirty inches long, twenty inches wide, and sixteen inches deep, commonly used as a luggage box. In those days, its separate lid of the same shape was used for sending clothes. It was Mother's invention, I suppose, to put me in this willow basket, on a cushion with a blanket underneath. It was portable, and I have a vague feeling that it was a snug, cozy nook for me.

Mother used to place it just in front of a scroll or calligraphy or a framed scroll in an alcove of a guest room. Father would change these scrolls according to the four seasons, or for each month. Mother told me later that I would be in good humor looking at the scroll for a long time before falling asleep. Now and then, someone came to take a glance at me. I have a recollection, like a dream, that I enjoyed looking at the funny shapes and figures, sometimes as if they were alive in the calligraphy.

My elementary school days started on April 1, 1915, but I don't remember anything special except my report card. It was handed to me by my teacher, a young man, just before the first summer vacation. It was very good, and for the first time I knew that my way of being in school was okay. I was a gentle, quiet child, always listening and observing, perhaps because of my inward awkwardness in real-life experiences as an only child among grown-ups. In those days a monthly magazine for children, *Kodomo* ("child"), was my favorite companion, a source of information by pictures. It had Japanese letters of two kinds and some simple Chinese ideograms. In school, I soon got accustomed to very big classes, usually with sixty or seventy boys and girls in Otsu Central Public Elementary School. In the open and free atmosphere there, I began to enjoy my acculturation process in a very natural way.

In April 1923, at the age of fifteen, I went to Tokyo to live with Mamma as a member of her family by her second marriage. My grandfather had died the previous year in Otsu. In 1915 or 1916, Mamma had married an electrical engineer, a widower with three children. I was transferred to Girls' High School, attached to Japan Women's University, and attended the same school with my stepsister. She was in the second grade, I was in the third. One of the most impressive and meaningful experiences in my fifth grade was that I was told, "You are analytical" by my class teacher.

In April 1926, I became a college student of English and American literature. This was quite contrary to some of my teachers' and friends' expectations, because during my high school days, I had gotten the highest grades in physics and mathematics. But I knew it was only a phenomenon. By using a correct formula in relation to the questions of examinations, I could excel without a true understanding of the underlying reality.

On the other hand, owing to my experience of learning English for five years in my Girls' High School days and, especially, together with my encounter with an unusual lady, English became like a trusted companion in the inner search for truth in my life. Mrs. Eleanor Dixson Takagi had just moved to Tokyo from Oakland, California; and for three years, every Saturday afternoon, my sister and I were nourished by Eleanor's atmosphere of democracy and her pioneering spirit. These sessions helped form a new set of values.

In the autumn of 1929, there was a World Engineering Congress in Tokyo. As my stepfather was a graduate of Cornell University, my sister and I accompanied our parents to Cornell parties held in the Imperial Hotel. (The building had been built by Frank Lloyd Wright; remarkably, it had survived one of the biggest earthquakes in Tokyo in 1923.) At these parties, I got acquainted with an elderly engineer with two ladies—his daughter and niece—from Syracuse, New York. I also met another engineer, Maximilian Goldberg, the founder of National Cash Register Company in Dayton, Ohio. Later, to my wonder and joy, I found myself writing letters in English to these two elegant, thoughtful ladies, Marjorie and Frances—both of whom were Friends, or Quakers. I also wrote to Maximilian Goldberg. For a long time, all through my school days, the hardest task was writing a composition under a title given by a teacher; but writing these letters was a joy. What a difference! However, correspondence was cut short by the sudden outbreak of war.

In 1949, soon after World War II, I started teaching English in a junior high school in nearby Fujisawa. After the war, according to a new school system, English became a required subject in compulsory education. I was able to accept this invitation to teach in public education because my husband's eldest sister, who had been an elementary school teacher for more than twenty-five years in Nara, was living with us after her mother's death. She was a helpful member in our family. I was already married and had three sons; the eldest had entered college, and the youngest was at preschool age.

I was very happy with teaching English, but at the same time I became aware of many problems and responsibilities as a public school teacher. It seems that privilege and responsibility go together, hand in hand. One of the challenges I faced was, "How can I experience the spirit of democracy, and become a trustworthy person open to the world, as well, in relationship with young learners?" I also wondered about testing: for instance, "Is an intelligence test truly valid and reliable in testing intelligence? What kind of value has the testing?"

After six years' experience of teaching English with boys and girls, my long-cherished desire to get in real touch with the spirit of democracy was heard by Max Goldberg and his friend Dr. Frank Shultz, an expert in the field of counseling. They invited me to become a graduate student in the Department of Education at the University of Chicago, for a year of study, and offered to arrange everything for me. The more I reflected on this invitation, the more awe-inspiring it seemed. I could not help asking myself, "How could I be worthy of their miraculous gift?"

I kept thinking about it in the train traversing the continent from Seattle to Chicago on Christmas Eve, 1954. I gazed at the vast, snow-covered plains and cottages whose windows were filled with lovely Christmas decorations. I remember sitting in the dining car at a table covered with a snow-white cloth for a special Christmas dinner. There were few passengers on that special occasion, yet it was an experience I still cherish every Christmas Eve.

The next day, when I arrived at the University of Chicago, I moved into International House on the campus. Sitting on a bed alone in my room on the fifth floor and realizing my special situation of being a student again, free from a teacher's responsibility, I was happy for a time. But soon afterward, deep in my heart I felt some anxiety emerging about my worthiness and my ability to meet the unknown future requirements.

Everything was new and exciting and full of new learning. For instance, I wanted to feel refreshed and decided to take a bath. Sure enough, my first meaningful lesson was in the notice on the wall of the bathroom. It was as follows, as I remember it:

> The optimist washes the tub after taking a bath,
> The pessimist washes the tub before taking a bath,
> The lady washes the tub before and after taking a bath.

The message was full of wonder for me. I interpreted it to mean that everyone is equally qualified to be a lady, free to choose feeling and acting in optimistic or pessimistic ways, as well as the third way of acting in a most human way as a person in daily living. The thought was so charming and wonderful that I could not help hugging it to myself, retaining it, even unconsciously.

This third way of acting, or the middle way, is a concept well known in Oriental cultures. Discovering this in Chicago enabled me to feel happy that I had found a small bridge between the East and the West.

One day in autumn 1955, Professor Allison Davis, a cultural anthropologist, kindly advised me to get my master's degree before going home. It was shortly before I was preparing to return. I told him of my financial problem. Encouraging me, he arranged for a university scholarship and my living expenses under a PEO Sisterhood scholarship. It was really a miracle for me. Owing to Dr. Davis' understanding and thoughtful help, I could finish my master's in the autumn of 1956 and stay on till March 1957.

An ending means another starting: my turning point, as it were. I had a vague feeling that I was still in the process of searching for something like the essence of life education. One day, I recollected that my dear Korean friend Oksoon Kim had mentioned something about Dr. Carl Rogers' client-centered Counseling Center on the campus. In the university schedule for the autumn quarter of 1956, I found his course, "Practicum I." Though I did not have the required qualifications except for my M.A., I was anxious to get in touch with his client-centered atmosphere. So I handed in my written application, which was one of the requirements. It was miraculously accepted. This was to be his last class in the University of Chicago, though I was unaware of that during the quarter.

In this weekly class, I felt curiously free, yet also uneasy in the atmosphere of the client-centered student-centered class. I experienced it first in the group as I watched and listened, then afterward in the library reading his books *Counseling and Psychotherapy* and *Client-Centered Therapy* (especially the author's preface). Gradually, I began to gain some understanding of the meaning and value of this approach. I am very grateful for the generosity of this student-centered teaching, which allowed me the freedom to be in the classroom and to experience in my own way and at my own pace without speaking up a word myself. To tell the truth, at the beginning those words—counseling and psychotherapy—were new and not in my vocabulary. I am sure, however, there must have been some uneasiness concerning my strange way of being in the class, which was quite contrary to usual class discussion.

In the spring of 1957, I came home. The next spring, I started teaching in my alma mater, Japan Women's University, at the Mejiro campus in Tokyo, in the Department of Education. In summer 1961, Dr. Carl Rogers came to Japan with Helen for lectures and a series of workshops. I visited with them in the hotel after four years' silence; and while they were in the Kanto area, I was blessed to be with Helen. In parting, Carl and Helen gave me *On Becoming a Person,* just published. Since then the book has been my living and guiding partner in my life process toward "On Becoming That Self Which One Truly Is."

At this point I should like to share with you my living process toward "on becoming a person." Starting in 1958, my work in Japan Women's University brought me great enjoyment. I found this in every reciprocal relationship with students in class as well as in the counseling center. The center at first was just a counseling room, and I was the first counselor.

In 1966 I was fortunate to be joined by an unusually gifted colleague. Mr. Akira Takeuchi was not only a clinical psychologist but also a remarkable poet. He remained at the counseling center until my retirement in March 1977, when he moved to the Kansai area. Now I am blessed to have him as my biographer.

Even in those early days on campus, my daily interactions with people made me realize that all of us are teachers as well as students, moving back and forth between these roles as the situation demands. Gradually, another insight began to emerge and grew stronger as I interacted with students and clients. The awareness can be best expressed in these words: "You are full of wonder, and so am I." This seemed to me like the crystallized essence of our experience together. It was the emergence of a relationship in which both persons felt mutually prized. These learnings were exciting and growthful experiences for me. They were developments from my first learnings in Dr. Carl Rogers' last class in Chicago and were matched by studying his two books there, and later reading *On Becoming a Person* at home. The insights gained became my main resources for daily living.

This period when I was a new teacher and counselor was a marvelous time for me. The campus provided me excitement and problems, anxiety and satisfaction, as I was setting goals and struggling with processes. It was, in fact, a special kind of wonderland for me.

Japan Women's University

Let me explain some background concerning this special place. At the beginning of the twentieth century, JWU was established as a liberal arts college. The aim was to foster a deep consciousness in each student of her responsibility as a person, as a woman, and as a member of the nation. The founder and first president of the college, Jinzo Naruse, was born in 1858. He studied abroad at Andover Theological Seminary and at Clark University in Worcester, Massachusetts. One of the great educators of our Meiji era, he had many friends among the foremost philosopher-educators of the world. John Dewey was a close friend, and when Dewey and his wife came to Japan on their way to China, they visited with Naruse on February 17, 1919. Unfortunately, Naruse was suffering from terminal cancer and was confined to bed in his simple house on the campus. However, he was very happy that he could enjoy exchanging pleasant conversation with his old friend, even though the visit was brief. Again, on February 20, Dewey and his wife visited the Homei (laboratory) Kindergarten and the elementary school, offering an encouraging contribution toward Naruse's future project at the university. Naruse died on March 4.

As mentioned, I joined the JWU faculty as a member of the Department of Education, reestablished after World War II. This department placed special emphasis on the founder's philosophy of education as a "Revival of Learning." How I enjoyed reading in English *Experience and Education* by John Dewey, *The Prophet* by Khalil Gibran, and *Gateway to the Great Books* by Robert Hutchins. I used these in my seminars with students as well as with student-centered learning in my counseling classes every week.

During these times, I was searching for ways to understand the heart of education. "How can liberal arts promote a genuine liberal education?" was a question that I constantly asked myself. Since my early school days, I have been learning that a truly liberal education results in meaningful autonomy, independence, and freedom of thought.

As the years passed, I came to realize, mostly by intuition, my very real need for further growth along the lines that had begun in Chicago with Carl Rogers. I felt my need for the special kind of energy, something like a magnetic field, that seemed to surround Dr. Rogers. Finally, in April 1971, I discovered the Center for Studies of the Person and realized that this was the magnet to which I was drawn.

The Inspiration of Carl Rogers:
My Way, My Life

One day in April 1971, soon after my arrival in La Jolla for a six-month stay, I happened to come across Hunter's bookstore. Having enjoyed a poster in the shop window that had a sketch and the words "I love mankind, but it's people I can't stand," I entered. Naturally, I stopped in front of the section on philosophy and psychology. I picked up a book with a fascinating picture on the cover. To my surprise, I found that it was by Carl Rogers and Barry Stevens: *Person to Person: The Problem of Being Human.*

The following Wednesday after the staff meeting, I told Carl of my joy at encountering his enchanting book. I told him that the book was so full of life, and it was one I would like to share with my friends and students. He was listening to me, nodding with a smile. Then he said, "How about translating it into Japanese? I will arrange to introduce you to Barry when she next comes to La Jolla."

This was another surprise. How far-reaching his reaction was! Carl often asked others, "What is your reaction?" I was hesitant to answer because it seemed that his question was so drastic and meaningful that it would take some time for me to understand his profound meaning. Gradually, I came to realize that my natural reaction was correct, and I learned. Each time my natural reaction will lead me to a new, meaningful experience.

Later, in August, I received a call from Carl, giving me Barry's telephone number in La Jolla. I called her, envisaging her portrait on the cover of her book *Don't Push the River.* The next day we met in Scripps Park. She was an elderly, large, tall woman in a long printed cotton robe-dress with a long silver necklace. I was wearing my Japanese clothes, a *yukata.* In an instant, I sensed her warmth and wondered if we had kindred spirits, as in a fairy tale. Barry and I enjoyed talking person to person, sitting on the grass, changing places occasionally for the cool of the shade. The following day, we were again together in Scripps when two hippies happened to come up to us. I was scared. Afterward I asked Barry if she could discern real hippies. She answered definitely, "Yes, by looking at their eyes." It was a very impressive answer. She also said that it is important to let yourself flow naturally and go with your initial feelings. "When you are ready, you will know what to do," she added.

These ideas had been so natural to her way of being that probably her presence alone inspired me to follow the natural flow of events and sense when I was ready for our project. Thus, in 1974, *Person To Person: The Problem of Being Human* was completed in Japanese by Akira Takeuchi and myself and published by Meiji Tosho Publishing Company.

The conclusion of the book is a kind of summary of its essence. It reads:

> The End: a commencement. If this is truly "The End" of this book, then nothing has happened. If the reader carries it farther, adding to the experience of these pages, then something is happening . . . .. For some, this will be vertical—individuals going "farther" than any of us in this book have done—more deeply into themselves. The horizontal "farther" is many of us, individually, moving ever closer to being ourselves and letting others be themselves. This helps to release some persons to the vertical. Without the horizontal "farther," the vertical comes to nothing anyway.

Here I was reminded of John Dewey's "continuity" and "interaction" in his book *Experience and Education.* I feel such gratitude for both books since they crystallize the true spirit of education. They show the need for continuity while valuing the ever-changing, fluid nature of education. In these two aspects lies the wisdom of education. And it is this same blending of values that enables people to become real persons and to help others achieve the same goal. It seems paradoxical, but in life—which is full of wonders—it works.

During my participation in the La Jolla Program, from June 22 to July 12, 1971, my first experience in an encounter group was very moving. Afterward I felt like saying, "I love mankind, because the people help me stand." Later, back in my apartment in La Jolla, I was absorbed for a few days in writing down my impressions. My experiences were so strong that I overcame my dislike of writing. I desired to have it read first by Helen Rogers. I wanted her to give me her approval of my writing because she was like a "holy mother" to me. Later, Carl wrote an introduction for it. It began as follows:

I first knew Haruko Tsuge in 1955 or 1956 when she came to the University of Chicago for a year of study. In her last term she asked me if I would include her in my Practicum. Her facility in English was not sufficient that she could counsel clients as the other students were doing, but I permitted her to enter the Practicum for what she might learn. To the best of my recollection she never said a word and I thought that the experience had been a total failure and just another example of my soft-heartedness toward sincere foreign students.

Then, in the last paragraph, he wrote:

When I was in Japan in 1961 I came to the conclusion that I would never really understand the Japanese. Their culture and their way of thinking is so foreign that it is almost impossible for an American to grasp. The account as follows is a sensitive, perceptive attempt of a true oriental to describe and express her reactions to a peculiarly American experience, the encounter group. To me it illustrates how, though we may view the world through differently tinted glasses, we are at bottom all experiencing, feeling, thinking human beings. I only hope the reader will enjoy it half as much as I have.

The above two shocking and thrilling paragraphs reflected my real situation, both in and out of myself, as if with a magical mirror. Gradually I began to realize that his introduction was his sincere awakening and inspiring message for the reader. What is my personal goal in life? How can I approach it? These are the internal questions that all humans have. I have a feeling that Carl's penetrating message appealed to everyone who has experienced the meaning and effect of the encounter group in a real situation in relation to these questions. His message was based not only on his scientific research but on his confidence in the human organism. That has been for many years the spirit of his significant learning in therapy and education.

As I reflected on his deep understanding of human nature, I could see that this kind of understanding—genuinely experienced, yet difficult to describe—is able to open up enriching and growthful experiences for me and others. Inspiration for me would be an ethereal, living spiritual being, which exists and works upon us in real human relationships toward our internal revolution. Inspiration is unseen. It exists, and works, and is never ending.

One beautiful day in July 1980, I was invited by Carl for lunch with Dr. Andre Auw, a dear friend to both of us. At Carl's the two of them put on aprons and started working in the kitchen. I waited in the sitting room. While I was sitting in a lounge chair, I started looking for Helen's spiritual presence. She had passed away the previous year. I missed her a great deal.

As I was sitting and thinking about Helen, Carl came out of the kitchen, plucked a lemon from a tree outside, and disappeared, leaving a smile. He saved me from my moment of depression.

After lunch, Carl brought a book to the table, and in the frontispiece he wrote: "For Haru Tsuge—an emerging woman herself— with much affection, Carl Rogers, July 1980." The book was *Emerging Woman* by his daughter, Natalie Rogers. Carl's inscription reminded me that I was a woman as well as being a person. It was a helpful reminder. Later, inwardly I thought I heard Carl's inspiring voice say, "What is your reaction?"

I believed that the book appealed to both middle-aged and younger generations' minds and hearts. Natalie named this group of people the "emerging group." Her message, like Carl's, echoes that of a famous piece by Bach, "Sleepers Wake, a Voice Is Calling." It is a call to the newness of life—to becoming.

Later, under what seemed like spiritual guardianship by Helen, I was able to be of help in creating a Japanese edition of Natalie's *Emerging Woman*. Sogensha published this translation in August 1988.

In the evening of January 1980, our house in Fujisawa became engulfed in flames. As the outside of it was stucco and the windows were rather small, in the old-fashioned western style, firemen had great difficulty in pouring water into the house. Everything inside was burnt, though the outside was left standing.

A few days later, just before the wreckage was to be torn down, my second son, Kenji, who also lived on the same property, went into the house for a last look. He had told me the previous day that there was nothing left. Now he came back with a picture in his hand, which he had found on the top of a heap of wet rubble and burnt ashes. It was Carl and Helen's picture, which Helen had given me on Christmas 1973. It looked fresh and neat. The image of a phoenix flashed through my mind. I understood the image must have been

Helen's inspiring message, encouraging me to look for the good side of the fire, instead of concentrating on the negative aspects. She had told me in April 1971 that I should differentiate between the important messages and meanings in life and discard "junk." The image of the phoenix was a "blessing in disguise."

Carl and Helen were free and independent in thought, individualistic as well as relativistic in their way of doing and being. To me, Carl is the Einstein of behavioral science. His sense of balance was marvelous. He was able to sense phenomena naturally. He realistically combined the best qualities of synthesis and analysis: positive and negative, active and reactive, conditional and unconditional, professional and lay. His message "The way to do is to be" is the essence of his way of being: congruence: transparency and genuineness.

As you can see, in my recent years, I have come to realize that every experience in my life was an essential part of my way of being as I moved toward integration. In a wonderful and mysterious way, these separate and fragmented parts joined to become a single, lovely, symmetrical circle.

Thank you!

Appreciating the full moon,
April 17, 1992
Haru

From Akira Takeuchi

To return to the question of what made Haru the unique person she is, I review some of the aspects she has described about her life. Her childhood includes parts of the answer. People usually feel that being adopted by two different families is not a good way to be brought up. Haru herself mentions, "I didn't have a place I could call home, someplace where I belonged"; she also adds, "however, I tried to make wherever I was at the moment my home. And I had to develop that ability because of my circumstances."

Out of her own experiences, Haru gives us words of wisdom, such as "Every problem has a positive side as well as a negative side." This too may be connected to her experience of having been adopted twice. But how was she able to tune into the positive side of things and bring it to life? One of the episodes she describes indicates that Haru's mother and the other adults around her were aware that Haru already realized she was uniquely herself even at a very early age. They allowed little Haru to slip into a trancelike state as she sat in a comfortable willow hamper "in good humor looking at the scroll for a long time before falling asleep."

The little child was actively trying to relate to each part of the scroll through her sense of perception. Although the object was static, she had the impression it was moving. She was fascinated. The calligraphy stirred her curiosity. It also symbolized something that was ever changing, in that it brought up endless associations for her. By looking at it, as with a mirror, she got in touch with this fully functioning part of herself.

Is it dangerous to assume this much about Haru from one story? I don't think so. This experience stayed with her through her early school years, and one night toward the end of 1991, she was telling me about her early days when this episode suddenly came back to her. The sudden memory touched her so deeply that it motivated her to write her autobiography. Remembering this story was like the start of a new beginning. She felt enabled to write about her life experiences with the necessary patience, and she felt good about it as well.

The story also ties in with her experiences in Chicago. Even though she didn't speak, she was inwardly functioning very fully. As she later wrote in one article, "When I became interested in what was happening within me, I opened up inwardly to myself. I enjoyed looking at my feelings for long periods of time."

When Carl wrote about his experiences with Haru, he couldn't see any connection between the Haru in his class in 1957, who did not speak a word, and the Haru in 1971, who told him that she had devoted herself to student-centered counseling. The mystery lies in Haru's unique way of working by herself on her inner process.

Even if Haru had spoken English fluently when she took Carl's class, it still would have taken a long time to have been herself in class. "I appreciated that Carl and the students let me be as I was," she later mentioned. I can see Haru operating this way when she is with people and in workshops.

In 1977, to commemorate Haru's retirement, Carl expressed his feelings in "A Tribute to Professor Haruko Tsuge." He sent it to the research magazine of the education department at Japan Women's University. In it, he discusses what was going on in the group (in La Jolla) as well as what was going on within Haru. She would tune into herself, matching how she felt with what she wanted to express. Only after this would she speak. The entire group would then be pulled to her. The process is summed up well by Carl:

Haru's influence on these large meetings was noteworthy. There were many articulate persons present, and many of them spoke up forcefully. Haru was very quiet, and spoke rarely, in a very soft and sometimes hesitant way. Yet whenever she began to speak, the whole group fell silent and listened intently.

As she focuses on her inner experiences and listens to her inner voice, Haru moves toward even greater integration. The words that come out of this kind of concentration are deep, and they can lead people to an expansion of consciousness. In another passage, Carl describes Haru's unconditional positive regard:

> She showed a delicate sensitivity to the process which was going on, and to the persons involved in that process. She displayed a profound personal wisdom as she told us what she discerned in the events in the group life, and the meaning these experiences had for her. I believe that for the group she came to symbolize "the wisdom of the East."

What Carl wrote clarifies that how Haru managed to inspire so many people around her reflects something deep within her: a specialness that goes to the core of her being.

> She is strong, yet flexible and resilient. She has been able to provide a way for people to move from old attitudes to new ones, from rigid ways of behaving to flexible ones, without a sense of threat. This is no small feat!
>
> . . .
>
> In a very real sense she was our teacher, since she was more open and transparent in the expression of her true feelings than many of us are able to be. In my terms she has walked very softly through life, but by being sensitively and transparently herself, she has initiated a quiet revolution in the lives of many persons, not least in her own being.

If Haru had not studied with Carl, this biography would not exist. In addition, if the positive regard and inspiration from Haru did not exist, many people's lives would also be different. My first experience with her is an example. In the summer of 1965, I was in an open meeting at a counseling workshop. One participant said he would like to have some support for being a beginner. One of the facilitators asked him what he meant by "beginner." Both of them did not hear what the other was saying and only repeated what they said over and over. The group got stuck and became stagnant.

Then I heard a voice that didn't seem to belong in the place. It came from a woman who seemed to be very content. She simply said, "I am willing to talk about my experience as a beginner." By her simple statement, she showed us something very important, which had been lacking in the interaction to that point. I think it was how to be alive and fully functioning. I could feel everyone starting to breathe again.

This was Haru, whom I hadn't met before. Her cheeks were rosy as a child's, and she had beautiful gray hair. She spoke without any hesitation, and I was struck by her clarity. I agreed with her without reservation. When she finished and sat back down, I sensed a slight bow. She seemed a bit shy.

My experience with her was quite new and unlike any other experiences I had had in counseling. I was drawn to that clarity and this something that I couldn't name, so I attended a group facilitated by her. One day she called on a woman, who suddenly started talking very expressively. It was somehow as if this person had been waiting all along for her turn to come. Now that it was here, she wanted to take full advantage of it. That happened several times with several people. I knew that Haru had not planned these events for the group. These people had not appeared to be eager to talk, nor did Haru possess any inside information. So how did she know to call on each person at exactly the right time?

During lunch after the last group meeting, I managed to get a seat directly across from Haru. I realized I had better talk to her now; it might be my last chance. Anxious that my words were different from what I really felt, I tried to share what I had experienced in the group. "What I feel from you is some kind of presence that helps me get in touch with my own inner freedom. I am curious about what it is. What is this thing that makes me feel this freedom? It is so mysterious."

She looked at me and said, "There is a very unique inner world within you."

At first I was puzzled by what she said. I couldn't believe that this had any connection to what I had just been talking about. Furthermore, what she said didn't feel at all like support to me. Her Japanese sounded somewhat broken, too. At the same time I felt she was showing me respect when she said this, instead of, "You own that inner world." There was respect from that part of me that knows I cannot be the owner of this vast and mysterious inner world.

To my surprise, at the next moment I found myself saying, "You're quite right." I nodded vigorously (which in Japan is rude to do when someone compliments you). I couldn't help myself, there was this strong force coming up from inside me to nod. My nodding meant, "What you say is right. The reason I feel such awe for you is because you help me become aware that there is this distinct world within me, too—right?' I was aware that a relationship between Haru and I had started to grow.

This vignette depicts the essential qualities of Haru's counseling then. She studied counseling through Carl's writings at that time, and the style she had already developed by 1965 did not change much after she attended the La Jolla program in 1971. Rather, her move toward a more person-centered approach became very obvious. In a paper for the counseling center at her university, Haru wrote the following when she returned to Japan. "The purpose behind counseling and education is to actualize each person's inherent goodness." At every opportunity, Haru urged people to share and talk about their experiences and relationships. For her, counseling and education were both endeavors that helped people realize the goodness within.

Haru had written many articles to help people understand the connection between counseling and liberal education. The counseling center she ran was highly regarded. Nevertheless, her ideas did not become the subject of serious discussion, neither among the university faculty nor outside. Instead, it was the students who were excited by her philosophy.

Students who had trouble adapting to school life as well as students who were actively searching for something came to her counseling center. The stigma about going to counseling disappeared and students started paying attention to what they wanted to learn. They began talking to each other about what academic studies meant to them, which led to seeing that counseling and liberal arts were not separate things.

This idea strengthened and was facilitated in 1974 when Haru translated *Person to Person* by her old friend Barry Stevens. Barry's book was a rich treasure of her life experiences. Haru later started to write more about her students' lives and their experiential process. A good example is the article "The Discovery of Mysterious You and Mysterious Me: The Meaning of Encounter Education, Based on My

Experiences."[1] In one section Haru talks about real education as taking place in encounters between people.

> In my case as I become more able to listen to others, my awareness of this "sensitive and mysterious you" increases and I come into deeper contact with this "mysterious me." My contact within myself is quickened because there is this "mysterious you."

> . . . While I listen, I experience a sense of wonder at the mysterious world of the other. When I express my wonder to that person he or she responds and it goes back and forth. Thus, the mutual experience is developed and deepened.

> . . . Encounters with others generate emotion, awareness and wisdom, which in turn propel us toward experiencing Truth, Goodness, and Beauty.

Haru was able to go to this point, to reach this realization, because of her encounter with Carl Rogers and his counseling in Chicago, feedback in her counseling classes and her individual sessions with students, and also because of her experiences in encounter groups. She feels, "My experiences in encounter continued to live in me, growing, developing, and making me thrive. I do not repeat the same experience at the same level, but rather it is like a new me is born at an even higher consciousness." By contrast, she dislikes discussions in which people compare and debate the value of one thing, idea, or issue over another.

Encounter groups had been a major part of Haru's 1971 stay in La Jolla. During that time, she also became intimate with a foreign culture, which led to exploring what culture meant to her. When she told her best friend about this, the friend replied, "The great good we can do for others is not just to share our riches with them, [but also] to reveal theirs to themselves."

As it happened, someone in La Jolla had done just that for Haru. The day before the program ended, a group participant named Keith wrote a sonnet for her.

Haru

The jasmine to the rose is not compared
By being red, nor does the nightingale.
The wrens in melody alone prevail:
In every hue and tone is love declared.
    And thus, for me to say "Just this by far
    of you delight, and pleasures me" accents
    Too crudely single precious elements
    Refining out the wealth of all you are.
For you are one and many, beauty bright
And beauty moving like the rising sun
Seen shining in multi-colored run
Across the heavens: warm, alive, and light.
    And like the flower, the ore, the sun: you bring
    Faith, hope, and love to everything.

Haru couldn't stop crying as she read it, she ran off to her room to be by herself. Later she wrote, "Truly I couldn't read out loud the second stanza. How could he get in touch so deeply with my inner world, which even I myself was almost unaware of?" She had never thought about what she was actually doing, even though this introspective process had been going on for a long time—in fact, ever since she was that little girl in the willow hamper.

Keith must have felt Haru's presence, how she inspired others and radiated warm positive regard in her encounter group. He was able to grasp and reveal deep and essential qualities in Haru. Even though neither are originally from Japan, "jasmine" and "nightingale" easily remind me of Haru as she strives to listen to her own voice. And the fourth line, "In every hue and tone is love declared," could have come from Haru herself (although she is very careful about using the word "love" in Japan) to express her way of seeing things.

Haru's poetic feedback to Keith expressed her feelings about him as well as the poem:

The third stanza with two special additional
concluding lines was just too beautiful to me at first.
Then I came to see that "warm, alive, and light. And like
the flower, the ore, the sun, you bring Faith, hope and
love to" me, Keith—you are the very one who possesses
this wonderful quality in yourself, feeling it so deeply

and expressing it so beautifully and thoughtfully with your own words. Without the beauty in yourself, how can you feel it?

Keith thus became the "mysterious you" to Haru. His own beauty allowed him to see so deeply into Haru and show her qualities that she was not even aware of having. Both recognized the "mysterious you" within each other.

Until I read Keith's poem, Haru had seemed a godlike person who always saw everything in a positive way. After reading the poem and then two articles by Haru about her experiences in encounter groups, I saw she is unconditionally open to meeting the "mysterious you" in all of us. Furthermore, she actively seeks this kind of encounter.

People close to her attest to this in the sections that follow.[2] Students who have given Haru feedback regarding their relationship with her are significant people in her life. Through their responses and comments, Haru is better able to know herself and see more of herself. These individuals, who have received positive regard and inspiration from her, have written about the quality of their experiences and how they have been influenced by her.

The writing by these significant people cannot be categorized as having a specific identity. It is rare in Japan to have this kind of collection: a group in which each individual has retained his or her individuality. Thus, these articles all carry distinct views of Haru.

From Tomoko Ogawa

When I get together with Haru, I am able to talk very comfortably about my experiences and don't have to think about what to say. I feel like I get back in touch with my own inner resources.

It is like I experience an expansion in consciousness. I feel like I am surrounded by the abundance of the universe. Right before I felt that way, I would be totally absorbed in what was happening between us. That's why I find myself always going back to Haru.

From Michiko Ohno

Mrs. Tsuge may know a lot about me, but I know little about her personal life. She never told me that what I said was wrong. She never scolded me, though there may have been times that I should have been scolded. Anyway, I think she knows that I would not have been able to change myself if she had scolded me.

Mrs. Tsuge never repressed her feelings and thoughts—what was going on within—even if they were inconsistent. When I compared myself to my teacher, I realized that I didn't accept myself like she does, and I realized I was the one who needed to modify my behavior. If I had not compared myself to her and seen what I do, I would be stuck in my ways. If I had ignored her way of being, it would have been like stopping being myself, like throwing myself away.

I don't feel this way except when I am with Mrs. Tsuge, as I cannot help but believe that she is the one example of someone who has an inner world, does not throw away parts of herself. She herself seems to recognize that she can be herself. It seems so natural to her. She is the epitome of someone who values all of herself. If she were God, I would be unable to reach her. But she is the closest example of an enlightened being. She is both a woman and a mother with whom I can connect.

Even if I don't see her for many years, I can communicate with that part of her within me. Haru's presence is consistent, and I am able to live on my own. When I was a university student, I didn't have the confidence to live like Mrs. Tsuge. But the day I met her, she made me realize that if she could be the way she was, then so could I. I knew that it was the only way I could live, but it also hurt too much to live like that. Had I not met Mrs. Tsuge, I would have given up being truly myself long ago.

The more I can be selfish, the more I can naturally move to a place of love. If I lived like most people do, worrying about what others think or what they are doing, if I had not been totally selfish, then I also would not have been able to love from the bottom of my heart. I also would not have been able to grow. If I cannot feel all the emotions of being alive, it is not a life worth living.

Mrs. Tsuge is not someone who goes to extremes like I do. She is calm; she doesn't get ruffled. But she accepts my recklessness. Others see me as reckless, but she doesn't. She understands why I have to live the way I do. In our relationship, I didn't do anything to make her accept me. She just did. I was passive in that sense. Other things do not matter to me. What is most important to me is being myself, and Mrs. Tsuge is a living example of a person who lives like this.

That's all I really know about Mrs. Tsuge. If you asked me for more, I wouldn't be able to tell you anything else. I am like an adolescent in love, I can't talk to the person whom I like the most. It is like when I am with Mrs. Tsuge, my mind goes blank. I don't know what to say. I am more able to stay centered when I write her a letter afterward.

I have never been let down by her. It is reassuring that she accepts me for who I am. I feel blessed that I was able to meet a person who would have been so hard to find, had I had to search on my own. God did not abandon me.

The reason I am alive today is because I met her when I was hurt and withdrawn. Before that, I had thought that wanting to be myself was wrong. She helped me realize that it was okay to be myself.

"You have your own character. As you have that, you can live your own way. It is okay to be who you are. Yes, that is the only way you can live"—she helped me find the way without telling me specifically what to do.

"It is not good for you to live that way," or "I could never be as stupid as you are"—I have heard these words from many people. But I think that people saying this sort of thing are more dangerous than the way I live. I cannot be like them.

Mrs. Tsuge's inner world is something that feels contagious once you have touched it. Everyone understands her world in their way, and then they pass that on to someone else. Since each person's experience is so different, if you don't get a variety of views about her, it would be difficult to get the whole picture of her. Her world can be seen in many different ways.

If you have never been directly involved in her world, then you cannot transfer it to others. If what you pass on to others is not grounded in your own personal experience, it is not worth much. Each person sees a different "kernel" of Mrs. Tsuge's world; each passes on something different.

That which is growing in each of us after having met Mrs. Tsuge is different. It is like a miracle that each of us is so different and that what we have received is just as different.

From Hiroko Sakata

I am standing at a new starting point. I have experienced many difficulties in my life. Whenever I have been in a difficult situation, Haruko Tsuge has helped me, through her own unique way. Although I did not want these problems, she would say, "It is natural to have problems. Carl Rogers says that recognizing that there is a problem is the first step. True learning can occur from that point." Hearing Haru say that she appreciates her problems helped me feel secure, encouraged, and emotionally settled.

I understand now that consciously facing a problem is not negative at all. On the contrary, there are many positive aspects. My difficult private problems have guided me, my husband, and my daughter to the true, deep sharing I have had with Haru. It is amazing, yet wonderful, that every problem deepens our relationship. Moreover, our relationships keep growing year after year! I would never have imagined that we would have built such deep and meaningful relationships.

It was in 1965 when I first met Haru. I had failed all my entrance examinations except the one for the education department at Japan Women's University (JWU). I was very depressed back then, but in hindsight I can see that it was a very meaningful experience. I was very lucky to have attended and experienced Haru's class.

Her way of teaching was new—different from that of any other teacher. Instead of a one-way style, in which the student listened passively, Haru created an environment in which the student was encouraged to react to the ideas and topics of discussion. It is important to emphasize just how different her style was. She believed that learning in which everything went from teacher to student was bad for both sides. This was a great but radical method of teaching for us young Japanese. I was unaccustomed to this flexible approach, and I was very perplexed at first. Here I began my long journey to search for my true self.

In class, Haru utilized an enormous amount of energy to encourage students to discover what their own reactions were. When we were unable to talk about what we felt and thought, she told us to write her a letter instead. She encouraged us to have deep relationships among ourselves and with her in our search for the truth.

At the JWU counseling center, Haru tried not only to have a center for counseling but also to provide a place for students like me to discover who we were and to become comfortable being ourselves.

To Haru, our studies in liberal arts would help us in all areas of our lives. This gave me great support. The center was a place where we students could be ourselves and be free to open up through sharing with others.

Getting in touch with my inner self on a deep level and connecting with others was very attractive. There seemed to be an interweaving of human relations without the facade that prevented us from sharing our problems. Later, I was fortunate to get a job as a counselor for children, university students, and their parents.

Whenever I had a serious problem, I would go to Haru for help. She has been one person who truly shares. She has always been fully present as she listened to me. Her words and attitude have helped me see what was going on within me. Gradually I could look at what was happening more objectively. After I shared my pain and sorrow with her, I would get a sense that I was responsible for what I had experienced; I could feel my inner power beginning to emerge. She never pushed or forced me to see. It all seemed to happen so naturally.

> Being with Haru,
> The door of my heart opens spontaneously
> And that which was hidden comes out.
> Haru respects it and gives it meaning.
> Oh, what a response!
> Her life itself is moving: one of becoming, growing.
> She inspires me.

Her energy is like a spring that never dries up. Her gut-level understanding and her gentle, modest, and graceful approach to pursuing the truth have encouraged and stimulated me to live the way I do.

On the other hand, I have also been through a time of not feeling confident about relying solely on my intuition and feelings. To understand other schools of thought in human relationships, counseling, and psychotherapy in Japan, I participated in seminars and meetings. During this period of intellectual growth, my daughter was born. For the first time, I understood that I could never bring up a child using only the knowledge I had acquired. I had to rely more on my gut feelings and my intuition than this acquired knowledge. So this person-centered approach is the core and basis of life for me.

I was like a kite that flew high in the sky.
That kite wanted to know what else was in the sky.
The kite saw many things upon earth from far away
and enjoyed being free, as the kite had not known
whether it had the power to fly
and had had no chance to fly for a long time.
It was lucky and wonderful for the kite
that its long string was still connected to the earth
so that it couldn't float away.
The kite still knew its roots, the string,
as this was its starting point.

While the kite flew high in the sky,
the strong wind blew it sometimes and
the heavy rain and snow came down on it,
and sometimes it floated away, rested on a cloud.
It seemed that the kite was torn up into pieces,
and had no power to fly again.
But the kite was all right
Because of the support of the person holding the string,
who was looking at the kite with warm, ever-lasting
positive regard.

The kite can now come back to earth
because of the power, wisdom, and knowledge
that had been bestowed upon it.

I was inspired by Haru on another occasion during the Third International Forum, held at the University of California, San Diego, in 1987. I had attended the La Jolla Program in 1977, so on my 1987 trip I felt like I had come back home.

My most impressive experience at the forum occurred at the last community meeting. In our last chance to get together in one room, some 140 people from twenty-two countries convened. Anyone who had had a valuable experience, either positive or negative, could stand up and relate it to the others.

One of my friends stood up and told a fairy tale that she had written during the forum. It was about how a bird (herself) had felt lonely and isolated and went to its nest and befriended itself. The tale was moving and touching. Another friend went up and gently put her arms around the woman's shoulders. I also moved close and hugged them both. Tears were pouring down our faces.

The three of us were part of a team that had been struggling to translate Natalie Rogers' book *Emerging Woman* into Japanese. Both the translation process and forum were intense emotional experiences: I strongly identified with being an "emerging woman," and I experienced "diversity, commonality, integration" during our various times together.

While we were translating, we sometimes moved to the verge of splitting apart; but due to the warm regard and support from Haru, Akira Takeuchi, and the other fourteen women in the "Emerging Group" (Natalie called us this), we managed not to split up.

At the forum, about ten Japanese women who respect, admire, and are proud of Haru stood up one by one, gathered around her, and began to sing a famous Japanese song, "Soshunfu." One woman played the flute. This all happened spontaneously. I usually do not like Japanese group behavior, but this was completely different. From each woman, something new was emerging in her move to become a whole person. We were separate but not isolated, and we became something whole, singing in harmony.

Some years later, Haru told me about the meaning of the song "Soshunfu." I had understood it to mean "early spring has come." But I found out that it was the song itself that was waiting for and yearning for spring; it was still cold winter! I thought of Japanese women. Despite the fact that we are humans, we are expected to meet our husbands' and children's needs before our own. What a woman does for herself comes second. Gradually things have been changing and we are beginning to bloom.

The 1987 forum was the last that Carl Rogers was involved in planning. Haru talked about it to me. I felt I had received a deep message from Carl. On the way back to Japan, a colleague and I talked about the background music playing in the video of Carl Rogers. The piece was Bach's "Sleepers Wake, a Voice Is Calling." When I heard the title, it was as if Carl Rogers was saying to us, "Wake up, sleepers! Let your souls wake up!"

I am grateful that I have been able to maintain contact with Haru Tsuge and Akira Takeuchi for such a long time. Through Haru's influence, the words "too late" have disappeared from my vocabulary. Through my inner voice and through my connection with her, I have come to believe something new will always emerge. I may be led to something unknown, but that's okay, too. My inner power helps me wait until the light enters the darkness.

From Motoko Sekiguchi

Haruko Tsuge is eighty-two years old as I write this in May 1991. Although she has retired from Japan Women's University under the age clause, she still plays an active part in her field of expertise: education. With great energy, she conducts two or three workshops throughout each week. She has a large following of people who adore and respect her, and she accepts this with modesty, never allowing it to shade her vision of how to cooperate with these people.

It was more than ten years ago when I first met her. I have a vivid recollection of her then. She struck me immediately with her incredible energy. When I called on her the first time, her house had just recently burned down, and she was living next door in her son's house for a short while. She described the fire vividly and as though she were talking about a party she had had the day before. With a mischievous smile, she said, "As the fire didn't spread to the neighbors' homes, I was quite relieved. Even so, how easily my house burned down. It burned very well!"

She continued, "To my surprise, I found a picture that escaped the fire. And the picture was completely untouched! I think it was a miracle. Though I lost everything, I learned from this. I learned that I won't ever lose what I really value."

I was surprised. To anyone else, the loss of one's house would be a very serious or even devastating matter. But not to Haru.

She showed me the picture, in which Dr. Carl Rogers and his wife were with her. Haru continued to live up to his precepts after she came back to Japan, and she has shared them with people through her own years of teaching. But rather than completely assimilating his ideologies, she has maintained her own individuality and creativity in her teachings. Through her efforts, she has created her own special world which is harmonized by two rare matchless spirits: one is Dr. Rogers', the other is her own.

The day we met, I had a problem I wished to discuss with her. She immediately began to listen to me with a gentle ear. While talking with her, I felt that she was very close to me. I also felt as if all my words were soaking into her open heart, and that I was wrapped up in her deep understanding of me. Her reception moved me deeply, and I felt as though I were being brought back to life. I had never had such an experience. I felt as though I were being held tightly in someone's arms. The feelings from that experience have lived on till today.

Looking back, I can see that it was the beginning of my realization that nothing can take the place of myself.

Now when I feel confused and things seem to be too tough to solve by myself, I call Haru. She listens to me attentively and tells me the impressions that emerge from her mind at that moment. She does this very carefully so as not to disturb my own personal process. On the one hand, she sympathizes through our common beliefs and emotions. On the other hand, she never takes away from my individuality, because she greatly respects my character. She appreciates and regards both our resemblances and differences positively and equally.

On a few occasions, she has refused to talk about important problems. At such times, she often says things such as, "I'm sorry, but I'm too tired to listen to you today. So if you need me, will you call me again tomorrow morning?" or "I have to go out for a while. If I listen to your very important problem in a hurry, I am afraid that I might miss the point. So I think that I'm not able to share your problem right now." She thinks that if she forces herself to listen to me right at that moment, she might not be supportive of me. How honest and faithful she can be!

I have not always been a good student to her. Through my own arrogance, I sometimes miss her very significant messages. But she is never disappointed in me; she believes that all of this is necessary for my learning process. Her attitude helps me realize that, though I respect her very much, I have never had the feeling that I am less worthy than she. Therefore, her way of relating to individuals does not rely on an interdependence of each other, nor does it include a pecking order.

I believe she is a born inspirer, and I am always thankful for her guidance. I can usually anticipate her reply if I tell her that I appreciate her help. She might look at me with a warm, innocent smile on her face and say, "Oh, thank you, but I've taught you nothing. You've learned everything from within yourself. In fact, I sometimes feel as if our energies merge and I also learn from you."

Though she is a quiet and gentle lady, she is always shining. Her radiant light shines ahead of people and each of them follows the light, but they are still able to set and reach for their own creative destination. She gives each individual's personal process the highest value. I understand her to be a person who does not try to force her beliefs on others. She never wants to make clones of herself. She wishes that each of our untapped abilities will someday blossom to its full potential. She provides uncommon and strong support for this.

As her field of vision has a very wide range, she refrains from giving a person too many messages and too much information. She knows that too much giving, without recognition of what a person really needs at the very moment, may not be healthy support. Far from it, it may be only a disturbance. As she is relating with someone, she tries to observe how she responds to the person and what occurs in her mind, and she asks herself seriously, "What can I do for this person now?"

She never wants to exert a strong influence on anyone, but she does want to be encouraging to everyone. As far as I know, she has always been a source of encouragement to all who know her, not only through her affection but also through her remarkable objectivity. In this way, she creates many positive relationships. Through her own creativity, she shows me how I can be a creative person.

She has given me the gifts of her regard, her deep understanding of me, and her wisdom. I do not think I should continue simply drawing wisdom and insight from her. I want to try to understand her more deeply, and I wish to share her unique inner world. Then I am going to present to people my treasure, which I inherited from her and her predecessors. I will begin with my family. But I think I have unconsciously already begun this process. I feel certain that each of my children has connected with her through my mediation.

Perhaps I do not do it as well as she does. She may not particularly care whether I can preach to others the kind of wisdom she embodies, but she may delight in my trying. She has been love itself, and only love can repay love.

From Keiko Akiyama [3]

I consider dreams as being very important, and I also practice self-development through meditation. When I am confused and nervous and I want to calm down quickly, I practice my focusing method. I developed Eugene Gendlin's process by adding body work. To meet my own needs, I have changed parts of these methods. I felt this would lead my clients and myself to self-awareness on a deeper level—awareness not attainable in a conscious state. I believe it helps people to take off their many layers of veils (*persona*) spontaneously.

Previously, I thought that experiencing the process and feeling of release was the most important thing, rather than the meaning of images that arise in the process. Recently, however, I have had great interest in each of these images. So I wish to try to share some of my experiences with you, as I felt Natalie had done with me through her book. Haru understands the importance and meaning of Focusing even though she doesn't practice it herself. Furthermore, she does make a class on it available to as many people as possible. In one of her remarkable transcendental perspectives, she firmly believes and teaches that when someone experiences something at the organismic level of the body, this knowledge can be retrieved when it is needed, even if the person has not "understood" what has happened.

After I heard Carl had died on February 4, I became confused, neither being able to treat myself nor able to do anything for about a week. I felt depressed, and I was surprised at how his existence had such a great effect on me. That summer in the United States, the International PCA Forum's theme was planned to be "Diversity, Commonality and Integration." Simultaneously, I discovered the theme also had meaning for our process of translation of *Emerging Woman,* and I decided to go to the Forum. Until then I had not grasped the actual feeling of going and was unable to decide whether to attend. Now I was looking forward to talking with Carl about integration, which I was feeling was extremely difficult yet important for our translating process and our world.

But I would never be able to communicate with him from my deeper inner self. Without the satisfaction of having a personal relationship with him, I had read his papers and had seen him at two workshops in Japan (where my lack of participation had left me feeling let down). I regret I did not become actively involved or have some personal communication with him during his stay in Japan.

I believe in the hypothesis that a person who dies physically will appear to other people spiritually—in a dream or a vision—in times of need. At the time, I believed this occurred between people who had had personal relationships in this world. I had no convictions about nonpersonal relationships.

I noticed, "Though I had always said I should live each day as if it were my last, I now feel as if I did not live to my fullest." In this situation, I started to go into Focusing (with the help of a friend). I closed my eyes slightly and felt a frozen stiffness of sadness in my inner body. The image was a purple pouch. As I was so cold, I muttered, "This really can't be." The image changed to a sheaf of papers in a soft, moss-green leather sack. The essential quality was a five-centimeter cube, like a brilliant obsidian-black jelly.

Next, I found a feather in an orange-colored background. I gazed at the feather. The surroundings changed into a bright pink sky. Then the image changed to pure white bird tail feathers. These gradually began to take on the appearance of a big, beautiful bird with some green patterns at the tips of its feathers. Almost a divine, brilliant white bird, like a Chinese phoenix. I wanted to show it to my colleagues. I felt deep emotion, admiration, adoration. The sublime holy bird left me with veneration for him as he flew up, left, and out of my view, into the far distance. There was a small golden after-image.

The sky changed from yellow to orange. I was left with a stiffness of sadness, however. I felt that the holy bird went to the home of the transcendental and the greatest, or to the next world that was prepared for him.

"How does your body feel?" asked the person who was helping me.

I listened to my own body. I felt my right hand was dark. I focused on it. "Ah! I am in a whale's stomach." I did not feel as displeased as I thought I would. Through the whale's dimly lit stomach, similar to a poorly lit tunnel, I progressed forward to the exit, depending on a tiny bit of light that was reaching me. After a while, I reached light and a warm, comfortable place.

The scene shifted. A short-haired little girl wearing a red kimono and a yellow *obi* (sash) with a red pair of *hanao getas* (thonged wooden sandals) was walking forward from the left. "Oh!" I thought, "The girl is me!"

And when I put a hand-pouch on my left arm in order to pick some beautiful pink flowers that were over my head, I realized, "Ah, I am carrying something of importance with me." Looking at the pouch very carefully, I became aware of a drawing of a mandala on it.

"Whew," I let out a deep sigh. I felt surrounded by a warm, gentle, peaceful place with a brilliant light shining all around me. Within this brilliant light, another light appeared in the left side of the sky. I looked at it and wondered what it could be. I moved forward to begin my exploration of that light, even though it seemed very far away.

As I looked up at it, I thought, "Oh, my God!" The increasingly brilliant white-golden light was approaching me. Around me there was more glaring. The dazzling light moved back and forth toward me. I held firmly to what seemed important: it is possible for the light to come to me. I felt happiness and appreciation. "I am all right." I ended Focusing.

From that time on, the absence of Carl Rogers did not bother me, as if I had forgotten him.

Two weeks later I had the following dream. I was repeatedly saying to some companions, "I haven't any actual feelings about those things"—that is, about receiving payment for volunteer counseling or about going to the United States. Carl had been sitting on my left and was silently listening to our discussion.

"I think there is some important meaning, because they talk to you so eagerly. How about trying to do that?" he asked. He stared at the pupils of my eyes.

I was surprised and woke up. "Oh, Carl appeared in my dream! He said, 'How about ———?'" I felt free, for I could be myself; and he was free so he could be himself.

I decided to look for myself. And I was aware of the prepared white road in front of me. I felt I would be free to go ahead, back, or to either side.

After a while, I also dreamt the following. I was proceeding on tracks like the Arakawa line (a streetcar in Tokyo) or a mountain tram. A steam locomotive crossed in front of me. Big black locomotion! White steam!

When it has passed, my rails curve to the left, and I cannot see my destination. At the left side of this curve, Haru stands smiling, lifting her left palm, perhaps to show me a way. I feel secure and continue.

I woke up and thought, "She is always standing for me at the curve veering to the left, no matter to what degree the curve is angled."

Some years ago, I imagined Haru would light my way. Now I am convinced of that. When I explore unknown and unpredictable worlds, the light will help me gain much more energy and courage to continue forward. I don't imitate her way; rather, her light helps me define mine.

At one time I thought, "It is gloomy. There is no satisfaction in going to the Forum without Carl Rogers. Most of Carl's spirit was conveyed to Haru much more than to others. Learning from her is more than enough. As for our meeting with Natalie, it will be necessary for only one of us to see her."

However, my thoughts changed gradually as time passed. I felt Haru may have had a purpose for inviting me to the Forum. I also felt that Carl Rogers' planning of the Forum was his last gift to me.

When I did attend, I was able to meet Natalie, who seemed to have become a transparent humanistic beauty, more so than four years previously. I worked out the details of translating the book with her and experienced a little of her programs. It was pleasant that I did not flow against the current.

Through these experiences, I realized I had lived all my life with some type of support from people I know and even from those of whom I had no personal knowledge. Through the eternal intertwining of our ancestral lives, I felt what was meant by the saying "Blood is thicker than water." I am presently on an intersection of my ancestral blood line and Ki (spirit, soul, energy). As Haru has often said, "Gathering many wonders becomes wonderful."

From Makoto Matsumoto

The difference between Mrs. Tsuge's approach in counseling and that of other counselors becomes very clear in cases in which the clients are not particularly aware of themselves. It is difficult to understand the inner world of someone who is not yet in touch with him- or herself. It is most amazing to me that Haru is able easily to help clients find out what is happening within. When clients are with her, even if they are not very aware, Haru helps them feel safe enough to explore their inner worlds. This helps them develop a sense of self.

Mrs. Tsuge creates an atmosphere in which people can feel connected and at the same time be separate. I never met Carl Rogers, but I assume that he probably had the same ability to foster this sort of atmosphere. I learned psychoanalysis first, so I had not learned to develop a Rogerian style of relating with my clients.

The way Mrs. Tsuge listens is different from that which is called Rogerian. She tunes into the other person's inner world and helps create a space where the two of them can both share something together, sympathize with each other, and eventually help the client feel a sense of self.

Mrs. Tsuge's acceptance of her clients goes beyond the level of verbal acceptance. I think she has the ability to understand feelings even before they are named and to understand what feelings are being expressed even when they go back to a very early age for that person.

From Kuni Asada

When I participated in Mrs. Tsuge's encounter group in 1977, I had been asking myself many questions. Why can't a person's personality and its expression always be the same? The way others see me and the way I see myself are not the same. How can I decide which is the real me when there are all these variations of me? How can I feel more calm about all these changes? Can I make the way I see myself and the way others see me congruent? At the time, my answer was that human beings are constantly changing, depending on the situation. That's just how humans are.

It seemed to me that Mrs. Tsuge's inner and outer expressions of herself were in harmony with each other. My first impression was that she is a radiant and distinct individual. This came out in the quality of her voice when she introduced herself, "I am Mrs. Tsuge."

Later I saw another part of her: the way she was in an encounter with another person. Here she would transcend the separation between herself and others. In encounters or relationships, something happens between people. Whether or not any verbal exchange occurs, a certain bonding arises that is obscure and difficult to describe. It is a sort of fusion, in which each person's boundaries merge for a while. The two people have a sense of not knowing whose feelings or thoughts are whose.

When at least one of the people is deeply in touch with this organic merging process, and when the two are open to the relationship, they can have an authentic experience. That is, when one is open to this experience of merging with another, one can feel what is happening at the moment. Through mutual sharing and through each person being him- or herself, a special connection is made. Each can resonate with the other, and something new can emerge from this exchange. New self-awareness arrives, along with an awareness of what is happening in the other person.

In the next step, this new self-awareness is integrated into each person's previously existing awareness. Through the birth of this new awareness, the two people become separate individuals again. Self-awareness is no longer mixed up with the awareness of what is happening within the other person.

Verbalization of what has occurred can then take place. It is important that this process is not judged by labeling it prematurely. Talking about things at this later stage furthers each person's process of differentiation.

When Mrs. Tsuge is in touch with her own inner experience and values what is happening within, her openness influences every member in the group. She is an incredible human being, so these kinds of awakenings take place in her groups. She is insightful to what is happening with other group members, and she becomes like a catalyst. Each person is awakened to his or her own experience.

This awakening is more remarkable when one has had direct contact with Mrs. Tsuge, but it can also occur through reading about her experiences. Carl Rogers sums it up well: "That which is most original is most general." People need to be open to the possibility of awakenings within themselves, and not to think it can only happen with Mrs. Tsuge. When such an awakening is taking place in another person and you can feel it within yourself, then it is also happening within you. This is an experience that is mysterious and beautiful.

She brings another awareness with her. When people are themselves in relationships, they come in contact with new aspects of themselves; and these aspects can be brought out, shared with the other person, and influenced by the other in complex ways. This process occurs even before it is ever verbalized. Despite limitations to verbalizing, talking about what is happening can bring much clarity to the relationship. Two individuals share of each other and value their experience as being unique and meaningful.

Through my interactions and experiences with Mrs. Tsuge, I was able to come up with a four-part answer to my original questions. First, people change but they cannot become whole by themselves. Separating oneself from others is not the way to achieve individuation. Others are needed.

Second, a person can fuse with another person and at the same time differentiate. In a relationship, both parties have areas in which they are separated and areas in which they overlap. This is similar to the third point: that merging with another person and being separate are not mutually exclusive. Each person can merge with the other and at other times be separate. Fourth, as each person becomes more integrated—in other words, more true to him- or herself—both individuals' self-realization is accelerated. Self-realization starts with (rather than being hampered by) fusion between two people. The process of self-realization is not for only one of the parties.

Later in my relationship with her, I found out about the deep and special connection between Haru and Carl. When she talks about her experiences with him, I can see how Carl was open on an experiential level with others. Haru resonates with Carl, in a sense, in that she too is open to this level of mutual experience. Furthermore, she is continually moving forward, always discovering new things about herself, and ever open to her inner world.

Because this level of interaction is so deeply ingrained in her, everybody who works with her is able to get in touch with themselves at the same depth. I think this is partly due to her experiences with Carl.

Based on my experiences with Mrs. Tsuge, I believe that the three conditions for personality transformation, which Carl himself described, hold true not only for transitions in which the differentiation of each person is clear (as in the West) but also for transitions in which there is not such a clear differentiation between individuals (as in Japan). This duality—of being a separate individual and at the same time transcending one's boundaries—is not contradictory, but rather complementary.

From Kumiko Tamura (Uchida)

One day after coming back from an orientation seminar for freshmen elementary school teachers, I heard from a colleague that the children in my class had been behaving much better than usual. This was a shock to me because they had always been quite noisy.

I felt the students had rejected me, and I had to face their rejection. In the classroom, a few of them who had been good on the previous day gradually began to express their anger with me: "Other teachers often scold us because our class is noisy" and "It's better for me when you are gone."

I was at a loss. In a half-crying voice, I said to the class, "Many of you came to me to speak with me before class. If you are unhappy with me, why do you come?"

One girl said, "I have so many things to tell you."

The students realized that because they all had something to say, they were usually noisy. The atmosphere in the class became better. I realized they were no longer rejecting me.

For three years, I was their class teacher. Then I became a first-grade teacher. In the spring, for our Athletic Festival, the school planned that our folk dances should be creative; each class would have a different style of dancing. I wanted my class to dance freely to the music, but at our first practice, no one began to dance. Since my previous sixth-grade class had liked to dance as soon as the music started, I expected that these first-graders—who were young and full of life—would follow suit. It was failure. I had been too optimistic.

I began to dance by myself. I was groping for what to do. The children were gazing at my dancing as if to say, "Your dance is good," but they still didn't move.

In total bewilderment, I was suddenly reminded of one of Haru Tsuge's ideas. When we were lost, she had told us, we could visualize something natural, such as a tree or cloud. The answer would emerge.

I saw a tree dancing in the wind. I thought, "This is it." I took my class outside and said, "Look at the tree dancing." I sang them a song about a chicory tree. And I kept dancing.

Several children eventually joined me. The first was a boy from a special-education class in the second grade. The other students laughed at us, pointing and saying, "Look at the two fools dancing." We didn't care.

Other children gradually joined us, but not all. I didn't want to force them. Some of the watching children were moved by the sight. Eventually all the students danced. I later called Haru and we talked about it. She told me that it takes some time for some people to become ready to do things.

In these two cases, I felt that Haru helped me and my students. For five years of my elementary school teaching, my day often began by calling Haru around six in the morning. I talked to her about my situation at school. She often told me, "Kumiko-san, learn from the children. Listen to what they are saying. Everything you need will be provided for you in your inner world. Listen to your inner voice." Her profound wisdom and love has penetrated my inner world and encompasses me. The knowledge and wisdom I have acquired from Haru is also helping others, through me. I have discovered my calling in life. Haru told me I should do what I am most satisfied doing. I found out that I can easily enter into the children's world and help them grow and develop. This is the vocation that suits my way of being, best of all. I am now teaching Japanese language and literature in a senior high school.

I first met Haru at JWU, where I took her class and her two seminars. A junior when I met her, I immediately thought, "She is the person I need to learn from." Thank you very much, Haru Tsuge.

From Mari Yoshida

I always felt hurt when I was a child. Most people around me saw me not as an individual but as the daughter of my parents and as part of their troubled life. It bothered me a lot when others complained about my parents. Although I hated the situation, I remained there. I could find nowhere that I could be myself.

People always scolded me. I got used to it. It seemed normal for me to be constantly scolded. I did not know why they scolded me. I got angry at what people were saying to me, but I didn't know what to do, other than being patient. I did not know then what was right and correct for me. I could not imagine any other way to be.

Because I could not find my true self, I was very confused about how to value myself in relation to others. Sometimes I was a good girl, sometimes I was a bad girl. My value to myself increased or decreased according to how others felt about me. I tried to behave in a manner that fit my impression of people's expectations of me.

I first met Miss Uchida in elementary school when I was ten years old. Encountering her made me change very quickly. In the classroom, she would ask me, "What do you think?" and "How do you feel?" and "What is the meaning for you?" This meant I had to search my true self for the answers. I had never before had an opportunity to be heard in this way. I had never thought that if I could understand or question my feelings and opinions, I could become a true person.

The task she asked of the boys and girls in our class was to search our inner selves. By searching myself, I discovered that I had been rejected by my parents and others. People around me had rejected my negative thoughts and opinions, so I had suppressed those.

Gradually I came to recognize and accept both my negative and positive feelings. I soon began to establish my own point of view. Miss Uchida asked me to be myself. I understood that it was good for me, and I accepted that it was natural for me to be my true self.

Miss Uchida used *Person to Person: The Problem of Being Human* as our textbook. She wanted the students to have the freedom to learn what they were interested in. When I read parts of the book, I could finally understand various things I had experienced. One passage described a child whose father had been in jail and whose mother had been both psychotic and very affectionate. The child felt normal, and others felt this also. This story helped me a lot.

When I was a child, every emotion appeared in my face quickly. When my face changed, people scolded, "You are too sulky" or "You are not attractive." As I was afraid of being scolded, I told myself to listen to these adults. I thought I had to improve myself because I was wrong.

Unlike anyone else, Miss Uchida always accepted my opinions as being positive. Seeing my expressions—even the negative ones—she would say, "It's great that you express yourself so quickly." What I was usually scolded for was now what I was being praised for. Miss Uchida accepted me for what I was. She accepted my emotions, both good and bad, for what they were.

She always said that everything that occurred inside me had a meaning. Everything is meaningful because we exist here and now. I began to believe in myself and to feel better about myself. I had denied my true self when I believed that I should not do or feel anything negative. When Miss Uchida accepted all of me, I began to realize who the real me was.

After Miss Uchida came back from the United States, she put up some posters with the following phrases:

"There is only one me"
"I am not a child anymore"

I understood deeply that I was not anyone other than myself. My father was no one other than himself, and my mother was herself. It did not bother me anymore when people said negative things about my parents. It was because I was now comfortable with myself. As I write this essay, I am appreciating my father and mother, who gave me my life. I feel grateful that they each live in their own way.

I give many thanks to Miss Uchida, who appreciated my true self and so helped me discover my true self. If I had not encountered her, what would have happened to me? I believe it must have been fate that created my chance to meet her.

I wonder why she accepted me. I tell myself that it must be because there is someone who will truly recognize me. And I asked her, "Why did you treat me so positively, when many people treated me the opposite way? You are so unusual!"

She answered, "Because you opened yourself and showed me how you felt." I do not know whether I opened up first or Miss Uchida accepted me first. Either way, I am grateful that it happened.

I met Miss Uchida. Miss Uchida had encountered Mrs. Tsuge. Mrs. Tsuge had encountered Dr. Carl Rogers. It is mysterious.

Endings / from Akira Takeuchi

As individual as the foregoing accounts are, certain striking similarities are apparent. Each person describes Haru in terms of the relationship with her, rather than in terms of history or hearsay. What this means is that being in a relationship with Haru is an experience in which you are invited and allowed to be yourself. Haru's major goal in her relationships with her students has been to help them accept themselves for who they are. She may not be aware of all that she has given these individuals. But they show us the significance of the unconditional positive regard and inspiration they received.

Readers who know Carl Rogers can probably see how his positive regard and inspiration has flowed through Haru to these people and now permeates these essays. In conclusion, let me cite one more passage from Carl's "Tribute."

In her quiet way, by being openly herself, by working indefatigably to give a place to personal counseling in Japan, by inspiring younger students to become seekers after truth, she has exerted a very great influence. Softly and quietly, in her very gentle and wise way, Haru Tsuge has aimed her work toward the future. She says in a recent letter to me, "My major work has been to help students to become secure and sensitive enough to be aware of their own inner feelings, so that each one may realize her own unique potentialities in the real world, and in her relationships." I believe she has gone a long way in carrying out this major goal.[4]

Haru's work after her retirement has not changed very much. She went from helping students to helping individuals. The number of people she has inspired is increasing. The number of people who have listened to their inner voice and have found Haru has also been increasing. I reminded Haru of this, and she replied, "The present generation is more educated than I was at that age."

To me, Haru's words came from her trust in human beings and her trust that they do progress. She feels there is something mysterious in her trust, and she often says things such as "It is kind of mysterious how it works out, but I have always been able to meet the people I needed to meet whenever it was necessary," or "I have never planned my life; I went with the flow. Yet I have always been able to do what I needed to do, even if it was at the last minute." When she was young, before she got married, Haru didn't value herself very much: "I don't have anything within me that I can offer the world." She strove to find that which was real, something that would touch her soul at a very deep level.

Haru's mother, Harue, ended up living a life of service to others despite her desire for self-realization. Her grandmother Toku, who was Haru's foster mother, did what she wanted and refused to fit into socially defined roles. These women undoubtedly influenced Haru very deeply, touching her on all sorts of levels.

Her experiences with them eventually led Haru to meet Carl and to find, for her, the real thing. They helped her discover in other people the "mysterious you," which in turn led her to tap into her own "mysterious me."

In the last two articles, we see how Kumiko Uchida was inspired to be herself by Haru, and Mari Yoshida was inspired to be herself by Kumiko. This is in line with a proverb often cited by the founder of Japan Women's University, Jinzo Naruse. He would say, "The results of education should be evaluated after a hundred years." Coming from the same generation as Haru's grandparents, he was a rare kind of Japanese: he was open to discussion and respected its place in solving problems, but he was also aware of the importance of waiting. It was Carl Rogers who guided Haru to be aware of the chain of thought she received from her alma mater. That is the whole idea of life, human beings, education, and the order of the cosmos according to Jinzo Naruse.

Haru gets up very early in the morning. She calls this time her golden hours. On such a morning just before Easter of 1992, Haru had just finished writing her autobiography. She could still see the full moon and stars from her window. There were now no more demands or pressures, no more struggles to answer the questions she had asked herself in the process of writing.

Something spontaneously came up from the depths of her being. She remembers that the writing she had just finished looked like the calligraphy scroll, and it sounded like a monologue. As she looked at the finished project, it suddenly became like a poem that illuminated her entire being.

She wanted to share this with her readers. If we see writing as a meeting place, then Haru, Carl Rogers, Helen Rogers, Barry Stevens, and you can participate in the meeting of each other. Through reading, we can all tap into the flow of life that is the experiencing process.

Usually the following kind of passage appears near the beginning of a chapter. However, Haru said, "This piece came up after I had finished writing. Therefore, I want the readers to read it after they have read everything else."

Theme
by Haruko Tsuge

Carl Rogers: Guiding Star for Those of Us
In Search of Truth in this Complex
And Wonderful World in the Cosmos
————Toward "On Becoming a Person" by Way of
Our Moving Experience whch Has Both Elements of
"Diversity – Uniqueness" and "Commonality"
In Natural "Integration," in Mutual Relationship with
Inner Self and Others whose Living Forces Are
Deeply Rooted in the Universe

This is Haru's way of being personally and professionally.

Acknowledgments

In the process of writing this chapter, Haru and I were given a lot of unexpected support from many people. Like a miracle, their support appeared at the right times and in just the right ways. Haru said this occurred because we have been influenced by the way Carl Rogers lived: deeply and widely. Haru and I would especially like to acknowledge the following people.

Dr. Andre Auw edited Haru's English draft with love and understanding and helped us learn the Western way of logic and thinking. A famous psychotherapist living in Hawaii, he deeply understands Japanese culture and has had a long and close friendship with Haru. His spirit expresses itself in the simple and poetic sentences of his latest book, *Gentle Roads to Survival,* a tribute to Carl Rogers. Inscribing a copy of his book to Haru, Dr. Auw wrote that the word *Gentle* in the title came from Haru's gentle way of living.

Dave Ilyn helped with the rewriting and proofreading of the English manuscript. A resident of Japan, he was introduced to us by Motoko Sekiguchi.

Mrs. Hiroko Sakata, who also wrote a section of this chapter, helped us do the background research for this project. Moreover, through her participation in our frequent meetings and discussions, she helped clarify our ideas and often introduced new points of view. Haru once quoted a Japanese proverb: "Where three people gather together, deep wisdom will emerge." Mrs. Sakata studied under Haru and now works as a counselor at Mukogawa Women's University.

Wanda Cook and Kyoko Ono accepted our urgent plea for help with translating the various contributors' sections, and Haru and I do not know how to express our gratitude to them. Kyoko Ono studied under Haru, has a masters degree in psychology from Sonoma University in California, and is a graduate of the Person-Centered Expressive Therapy Institute training course by Natalie Rogers. Wanda Cook presently resides in Japan and is a volunteer at a telephone crisis counseling center that uses Carl Rogers' approach to helping others. These two women also manage and offer classes at the Tokyo Gestalt Institute.

Without the support of these people, this chapter would not have emerged.

References

1 In *The Education of the University and Counseling, 3* (June 30, 1972): 2–7; Mejiro, Tokyo, Japan.

2 Due to time limits, we were not able to get articles from all the significant people in Haru's life. Those who did not have time to write were interviewed by telephone. Some of them have known Haru longer that I, and they have included things about how they have seen her grow and change.

3 Excerpted from Natalie Rogers, *Emerging Woman,* translated under the supervision of Haruko Tsuge by Keiko Akiyama, Natsumi Shimamura, Hiromi Mitani, and Hiroko Sakata. Osaka, Japan: Sogensha, 1988.

4 Carl Rogers, op. cit.

❖

In my quest to have him write this chapter, my meetings and correspondences with David Rogers spanned a two-year period. He avoids people's efforts to honor him, yet his life work has made such declinations difficult. (David, I thank you lovingly. With all the good reasons you had for demurring—most especially your desire to remain "a part of" your father's story rather than being on your own platform—you still heard my rationale about the importance of telling your story.)

David's committed involvement and his various prestigious positions (mentioned later) have afforded him opportunities to pursue his keen interest in researching and writing about world health issues. His autobiography radiates a real sense of his interest in political and social issues, and we learn that he decided against private practice so that he could remain, in some ways, a public servant.

❖

6

A Ripple in the Pond

by David Rogers

Almost two years ago, Mel Suhd described an idea that he hoped to build into a book. It was his theme, as I understood it, that those whose lives had been touched by certain charismatic individuals were shaped in ways that in turn led them to behave differently than they might have otherwise throughout the rest of their lives. It was, if you will, the pebble in the pond effect. The ripples would extend outward in ever-expanding circles during the lives of those other individuals, and they in turn would touch yet others.

Mel thought it would be interesting to take a group of people who had been associated with one person—in this instance, my father, Carl Rogers—and ask them to write personal autobiographies. These were not to be simply recitations of where Carl Rogers had changed or influenced the individual—that was to be left to the reader, who could perhaps see some common themes emerging. Because of my more-than-obvious association with Carl Rogers, Mel asked me if I might write a chapter. For many reasons—not all clear to me right now, but including an innate reticence about looking inward or backward, the pressures of a rather busy schedule, etc.— I demurred.

But Mel was both sneaky and persistent. About a year later, he asked if I would permit him to adapt an interview with me, previously published in my medical school's alumni journal, so that I could be included in the book. This I agreed to do; it required absolutely no effort on my part.

Recently this was sent to me. Rain Blockley had done a fine job of adapting that piece. However, as I read it over, I felt that while it was a perfectly good account of my professional journey through life, it told very little of me as a person, or about my relationship with my father, or my wife, or my children, or my other interests. I sounded selfish and single-tracked.

Thus, this preamble. Rather than re-editing that interview, I thought it might be easier to put some words in front of it that might give the reader a somewhat more three-dimensional view of David Rogers.

I was born in New York City during my father's graduate student days at Columbia Teacher's College. I have no recollection of New York City, but remember from a rather early age our life in Rochester, New York, where we moved when I was two. This, I believe, was a most formative period. We had a nice home surrounded by lots of vacant lots and a large dump to explore, in which there were snakes, centipedes, turtles, and the cocoons of the great moths. I remember this as a happy and secure time. My mother was cheerful, adventurous, and artistic. She spent large amounts of time with us. My sister (two years younger) and I seemed to have all kinds of exciting adventures.

My father seemed less in the picture, except as a good, pragmatic carpenter and bestower of tools upon me. Most of my memories are of watching him build things, or helping him build them—our cabin at Seneca Lake, or a boat in our garage. Thus, it is "doing things" with him, rather than conversations, that I recall. We would wash the dishes together, mow the lawn, and the like. I remember him as being shy, outdoorsy, gentle, but not around very often. I don't really remember many conversations with him.

I do, however, remember how much he taught me about carpentry. He built a little bench for me in the basement and on every birthday or Christmas, I would be given very grown-up tools. He also taught me about the great moths, and I remember avidly collecting their cocoons, letting them hatch, and putting out a female cecropia in a shoe box covered with gauze to attract the male moths at night. (It worked—Dad woke me to watch four or five beautiful males fluttering about. We caught one, let them mate, and proceeded through the whole process again.) I guess I would say that Dad and I were comfortable comrades.

There is one feeling I had about Dad that I remember, in retrospect, with shame. I went to a fancy college preparatory school, I believe on scholarship. My classmates came from much wealthier families and I remember often being embarrassed by my rather shy father in the presence of hearty, hail-fellow-well-met fathers who were better dressed, were possessed of small talk, ran large businesses, and seemed "in charge." They always seemed to have much more to say and be much more at ease with youngsters. In retrospect, how very wrong I was!

During my junior year in high school—a time of great importance to me—we moved to Columbus, Ohio, as Dad became a professor at Ohio State. I vividly recall that I made that move absolutely miserable. I cried, I indicated that my life had been destroyed and would never be the same, and in general, I made my parents' lives thoroughly unpleasant. This is of particular interest to me in that, after about three or four months in Columbus in a new, much more liberal and permissive school, I discovered the enormous excitement of learning and began to get better acquainted with my father in his professional world. I remember that our house frequently had graduate students moving in and out of it, and some of the conversations between my dad and those students—I was always permitted to sit in on them—began to give me a sense of his philosophy and his own professional concerns. It was here I began to realize that my father was a highly congruent man with a splendid value system. The kind of positive, unconditional regard he gave to others clearly extended to me and my sister. I don't believe I'm romanticizing this. I always felt that I could do or be whatever I wished to without losing his interest or affection. It was a precious gift he bestowed upon me.

In many ways, I was a typical teenager. I think I was intellectually more involved with study than most, but football, swimming, tennis, and the pursuit of young women dominated my life. At this time I grew very interested in a young woman from a very conservative doctor-father family. Her name was Cora Jane Baxter. She was bright, hard driving, much more radical than I, and passionate about causes of the times. We were in different schools—she in a girls' preparatory school, I in the Ohio State University High School—but we had long, intense discussions about everything in the world. After I had completed a rather swift period at Ohio State, I went to medical school, she went to Wellesley College, and we continued our courtship long distance. We were married during my junior year in medical school, while she was still at Wellesley, and began having a family while I was a house officer at Hopkins. During the period from 1950 to 1959, we

were in Baltimore, New York, and Berkeley, California. During that time we had three children who were and are of enormous importance to me—a daughter, Anne; a son, Gregory, born two years later; and Julia, born yet two years after that.

I remember our lives in Pelham, New York—where we settled after a period in the Navy, as I became a young faculty member—with great affection. The kids were attractive and energetic, and I loved teaching them everything about the outdoors, about carpentry, about carving, about sports. Cork was an intense mother who in turn taught them reading skills, history, writing, and the use of their minds. She read to them with great regularity.

It's my bet that my children felt (as I now do) that I was too busy professionally to give them enough attention, although I always spent weekends and vacations with them. Their mother was highly intellectual, personally tormented, and (from what I have heard in recent years) often terrifying for the children. To my profound sorrow, I was genuinely not aware that they were having a tough time with her—which clearly proves my too-frequent absence. It's fair to say our marital relationship, while idyllic initially, was not a good one. I got most of my satisfactions from interactions with my colleagues and my children.

In 1959, we moved to Nashville, where I assumed the role as chair of a Department of Medicine. There Cork plunged into a world of being a chairman's wife, entertaining our house staff and students, and interacting with the faculty. There was, again, a wonderful and rich outdoor life; but overall it was an intense, hard-drinking, hard-living, hard-working life. While the children were clearly very successful as students and developed skills as athletes and outdoorsmen, the strained relationship between Cork and me was clearly not lost on them. As our marriage deteriorated, Corky had periods of rather serious psychiatric illness, which required hospitalization.

In 1968 I made what, in retrospect, was probably a foolish decision. In part feeling that a change of scenery might do well for Cork, I accepted the deanship at Hopkins. I made the move with her encouragement. At the same time, I had an episode of illness that I believed to be a heart attack. The torment of our marriage and my conviction that I might die did nothing to start me off on the proper foot in my demanding new role in Baltimore. I think that Hopkins period was perhaps the hardest on my children and on me of any period in our lives. Anne, my oldest daughter, felt deserted; she went off to college largely on her own and then off to medical school. Greg stayed in Nashville to complete his senior year in high school, never to really fully return to the family. Julia, fortunately in a wonderful Friends' school in Baltimore, developed many friendships and other pursuits but was often left with a tormented, abusive mother, while I plodded through my work in the deanship without real joy. Cork and my subsequent separation and divorce (made at the suggestion of the children) led to yet more serious psychologic deterioration for her. She died some two years later. Life was pretty bad for all of us at that time, and I spent less time with the children than they and I needed.

A whole new chapter in my life opened not long thereafter. Since my days as a young faculty member at Cornell, a young woman named Barbara Lehan had worked with me—first in New York, then in the chairman's office at Vanderbilt, then in the dean's office at Hopkins. It was always the most chaste and proper of relationships, but we liked each other, understood each other well, and shared artistic and outdoor interests. This began to develop into an enormously rich love that culminated in our marriage in 1972.

So, the last twenty-one years have been some of the richest and happiest of my life. In part thanks to Bobbie, I have been reunited with my kids, in whom I have enormous pride. Anne is a splendid, tough, caring doctor working on the West Coast. Greg is a thoughtful, fun-loving athlete, teacher, and businessman married to a lovely woman who is also a teacher. Julia, an artist in her own right, is teaching fine arts at a boys' school in Philadelphia. They are all bright, thoughtful, attractive friends. I like being with them.

What characteristics do I have that have been shaped by Carl Rogers? Perhaps first is a similar value system. I prize people, I care about them as individuals, and I like to see them grow. I enjoy interacting with people of all ages, and I seem to turn many of them on. Perhaps the greatest pride from my professional career is the number of young people I seem to have helped grow professionally and personally as students or house officers. I believe that continues to be my most important interest in my present role. Nowadays I seem to feel more comfort with myself, to have more time to listen and encourage young people, and to indulge in some other activities that have long been important to me.

I realize that over the last twenty-five or thirty years, I've become an increasingly good wood sculptor. It is rare that I do not have something under way, and the beauties of wood and the creation of pleasing shapes—some nonobjective, some literal—are intensely satisfying to me. My relationship with my wife—we take very good care of each other, listen carefully to one another, and prize our marriage above all else—has given me room to be more loving and caring about a great many others.

I work with AIDS and all its tragedies, but doing that work has greatly expanded my friendships to include many extraordinarily dedicated people. Many are gay and lesbian, and I simply would not have otherwise gotten to know and admire them.

In either group or individual settings, I am open, quite comfortable with myself, caring of others, and able to bring them out. I am unashamedly passionate about causes, and others seem to respect and admire me for that trait. The precious gifts that my father bestowed were comfort and confidence in being myself, and the security of knowing I would be loved and respected by him no matter what I did, which gave me great freedom. He also taught me to admire and prize genuine scholarship and achievement. I think about him often.

My Professional Life

I graduated with my medical degree from Cornell University Medical College in 1948 and began my career with a focus on infectious disease. After fifteen years as president of the Robert Wood Johnson Foundation, the largest foundation in the world devoted to health care, I returned to Cornell in 1986 to teach.

My return brought back many memories. Some of the places around here haven't changed very much, and sometimes I'll walk into a particular room and think, "My God, this is where I used to do such and such as a frightened, awkward Midwest kid getting ready to go to anatomy class." And I'm back in the same place, and it looks exactly as it did then.

I had entered medical school at age eighteen, and it was a joy. I had gone to Ohio State for a year. My father was a professor there, and the high school I attended was called the Ohio State University School. It was a mixed bag. There were faculty kids, but there were also kids who had gotten in trouble in the public schools. Something of the tenor of the school can be gleaned from the title of a book that was written about it: I think it was *We Were Guinea Pigs.*

Actually, I had started out at the Harley School, in Rochester, New York, where my family lived before moving to Columbus. It was a very classy, conservative college-preparatory school, where classes ran from 8:30 to 4 or 5 and where you were examined on everything.

And all I did was cut up. My father would get upset with this, but I'd say, "Look at my grades."

Then we moved to Columbus, and here was this very permissive experimental school, with no requirements about attending class and virtually no exams. The first three months, I didn't go to class—I found out all about girls and just how permissive the place was. I was annoyed, too, because nobody seemed interested in giving us tests, and I had nothing to show that I was smarter than anybody else.

Then, at some point, I seemed to catch on to what this school—and learning itself, for that matter—was all about. I was reading something—I don't even remember what it was—and suddenly I thought, "This is really fun. This is exciting." From then on, I worked my butt off, not for good marks, but for me. The school permitted you to go as fast and as far as you wanted, and the whole experience has had a profound effect on my approach to education ever since.

During our junior year, we had a career week, during which the students could do whatever interested them. The father of a young lady I was seeing was a pediatrician, and I tagged around with him for a week. It was so exciting that I not only determined to go to medical school but ultimately married his daughter, Cora Jane Baxter, as well.

Thinking I'd be going into the service soon, I decided to give up my senior year in high school to move over to the university campus. I took an odd sort of double schedule and, the following spring, went back and graduated from high school. Then I entered medical school at Cornell the following September.

When I started, it was with the idea of going into psychiatry—well, either surgery or psychiatry. Surgery because of the love I've always had for doing things with my hands, psychiatry because of the powerful influence of my father. He lived as he wrote: he was very humanistic, very supportive, very prizing of people. He was exactly that way with his kids.

Strange though this may sound, what drew me to Cornell was the architectural beauty of the medical center. I was accepted at Harvard and Cornell and had no idea which to choose. It never occurred to me to ask anyone's advice about this, so I sent away for the catalogs, and since the curricula were similarly incomprehensible to me, I looked at the pictures.

Around this time, I'd gotten quite intrigued with city planning and architecture and Lewis Mumford, and right on the front of the Cornell catalog was an elegant picture of the New York Hospital. Harvard just didn't have anything like it, and I thought, "That's beautiful. That's where I want to go."

College had been a blur, but medical school was precious. It was a great joy. The faculty seemed to care a great deal about us. Faculty life was less frantic than it is today, and there were more epaulets for teaching. You didn't have to earn all your salary through a busy practice. Dr. Robert Petersdorf has used the very apt term "threadbare gentility" to describe academic life as it existed then.

One very important commodity academia could offer was time, contemplative time. It was not unusual for students to go over and spend a half hour with one of their professors. There was more social intercourse as well. If students had some kind of function in the evening, faculty would be well represented there.

In retrospect, I am amazed, too, at what the faculty would tolerate. For example, when someone proctored our first-year exam in anatomy, I got so incensed at the implication that future physicians couldn't be trusted that I decided to convey my outrage directly to Dr. Joseph Hinsey, our dean and professor of neuroanatomy. I walked into his office and told him how insulted I had been. How would he do this? I just gave him hell. Not only did he sit still through it all, my impression is that the proctoring stopped.

On another occasion, I was unhappy with a particular course and, when I finished the bluebook exam, I picked up another book and filled it with my thoughts on what a crappy course this was. It was an incredibly obnoxious thing to do. It's amazing they didn't throw me out of school for it.

Given that I had had only one year of college, I may have missed some of the liberal arts experiences. But I was able to pick up some of them later. One of my professors, Walsh McDermott, was very helpful in this regard, partly because he had little patience with my complaints. I remember, during my fellowship with him, bemoaning my lack of scholarship in the humanities and the fact that I couldn't read German, as he could. He just stopped me cold and said, "That's the damnedest bit of nonsense I've ever heard from you. How do you think I learned these things—because I had a course in college? You know how to learn. You know where the library is. If you want to know all those things, why don't you go learn them?"

He was a wonderful, joyous, flamboyant teacher. His style was summed up very well by a cartoon that appeared in *Samaritan*, the school paper. It shows a caped figure suspended upside-down in midair in front of the class, waving his arms wildly. One student is saying to another: "Walsh isn't his usual hyperbolic self today."

I got to know him much better when I returned to Cornell Medical Center as a fellow after two years of house-staff training at

Johns Hopkins. David Barr, Cornell's chairman of medicine, suggested I talk to Walsh, who was then head of the division of infectious diseases. As I recall, I went to see him with something of a chip on my shoulder and informed him that, while intrigued with infectious disease, I was equally intrigued by renal disease, heart disease, and so on.

His refreshing attitude was, "You know, I'd worry if you said anything different. How could you possibly know if you've never tried it?" Specialism never had much appeal for him. He used to say that he could start tomorrow to study a subject that he thoroughly disliked, and within three months he would be absolutely fascinated by it.

Bob Pitts was another man who had a particular influence on me. The chairman of physiology, he not only gave superbly crafted lectures but did his students the honor of taking them seriously. When I got interested in some aspect of brain physiology, he let me use his lab at night for some rather tricky surgery with cats. His own work with the kidney was nothing less than elegant. He was a stern, rather taciturn man—even bitter toward the end of his life—whom I admired enormously.

David Barr was also a powerful influence. I mentioned earlier the high level of interest the faculty had in student activities, and no one exemplified this better than Dr. Barr. When my classmate Mort Bogdonoff and I thought it would be nice to have a symposium on liver disease, he took an immediate interest, making calls and opening doors that enabled us to get top people such as Charlie Hoagland from Rockefeller and Frank Hanger and Arthur Patek from Columbia. After three months of working our butts off, we filled Uris Auditorium. To this day, I know a huge amount about liver disease. It seems remarkable, in retrospect, that this patrician professor would deign to devote so much attention to a project of a couple of second-year kids.

Equally impressive—unnerving, in fact—was the profound trust he was willing to place in the judgment of young people. For example, when I was chief resident, he called me in one day to ask my opinion about a fairly important patient-care issue. I told him what I thought, more or less off the cuff. The next thing I knew, he was marching me down to the hospital board room, where he made an impassioned argument before the medical board, stating as fact precisely what I had told him. He never asked me if I was sure about my data and, as I said, I hadn't given the issue much thought. I could easily have given him some bull. So his trust really scared the hell out of me.

Right there and then, I vowed to myself that I would never tell this man anything that I hadn't thought through. I saw this same trait on a number of occasions—this willingness to trust the judgment of young people. He made me grow up fast, and I tried to emulate this excellent teaching tool in my own career.

Another wonderful teacher was Tom Almy, the head of the division of gastroenterology, a very self-effacing man who was a splendid clinician and gave beautiful lectures. He later headed the Cornell division at Bellevue Hospital, where he did a superb job. He then became an absolutely beloved professor at Dartmouth, where he remains today.

I married during medical school, which was very unusual for that time, particularly since my wife was still a student at Wellesley College. Her parents weren't overly enthusiastic about our marrying at age twenty, and we had to promise that she would finish Wellesley. She would come down to New York for one weekend, and I would go up to Wellesley for the next. It went on that way for the better part of two years.

After a year's fellowship in infectious disease, I was chief resident in the Department of Medicine and then spent two years in the navy. In 1954, I returned to Cornell as an assistant professor and, concurrently, was a visiting investigator with Dr. Rene Dubos at the Rockefeller Institute. Working with him was thrilling. He was a wonderful man, very French, with a magnificent intellect and a very broad view of science and mankind. He was very involved with the tubercle bacillus, and I was working with the staphylococcus (staphylococcal infection was then the scourge of our hospitals, and I was working on why this might be and what might be done). I just loved to spend an hour talking with Rene about science or research.

He also taught me a lot about writing, as Walsh did. I once remarked to him that I envied the ease with which he wrote, and he looked at me as if I'd taken leave of my senses. He said that the way to write is to avoid giving yourself excuses for not writing. He said he had a place in his apartment that was devoted exclusively to writing and that he would not allow himself distractions. He might sit there for an hour, he said, and write no more than one or two sentences, before his thoughts would begin to flow. In his view, anyone who claimed to be waiting for inspiration to write was just kidding himself.

In 1955 I succeeded Walsh as head of the division of infectious diseases; he became chairman of public health. Ed Kilbourne and Micky LeMaistre were on the scene, and I had a terrific series of fellows—

Roger DuPrez, Glenn Koenig, Don Louria. Infectious disease was still very much a challenge, even in the wake of the spectacular advances of the 1930s and 1940s. Rene Dubos had defined the challenge when he said that, whatever the nature of our success in dealing with microbes, there would be others coming along to take their place.

Taking my cue from this insight, I once did a study in which I looked at a hundred consecutive deaths on the medical service before we had antimicrobials and compared them with a hundred consecutive deaths after that date. The study, which appeared in *The New England Journal of Medicine,* showed that almost as high a proportion of patients had died of infections but that the nature of these infections had changed. Of course, it is hard to imagine a better illustration of Dubos' insight than the coming of HIV, the human immunodeficiency virus, in the past decade.

Meanwhile, Hugh Luckey had suggested I consider the chairmanship of the medical department at Vanderbilt University, which was his medical alma mater. When I went down to take a look, I was intrigued. Here was a school that had a long way to go but that also had known what real excellence was. At Cornell, I was one of a crowd. At Vanderbilt, if I succeeded, I'd know why, and if I fell on my face, I'd know why.

So in 1959, at age 33, I went to Vanderbilt University as chairman of the Department of Medicine. Since I had started medical school at 18, it was not a new experience for me to be among the youngest in a group. As chief resident in medicine at New York Hospital, I had been the youngest person on the service. What I learned was that people may be a little startled at first but, if you are competent, you are very quickly accepted. Although several of the Vanderbilt faculty in medicine had been my teachers, it did not prove to be a problem.

Vanderbilt was smaller than Cornell. There were only fifty students per class at that time, and the hospital had four hundred beds, not eleven hundred. But we also had the Veterans Administration hospital and Nashville's hospital, and I made rounds in those.

I could still be productive in research as well. Mornings I would spend at least two or three hours in the lab. My ground rules were that any resident or student could interrupt me, but the dean and the president and senior faculty could not.

I was a respected bench researcher, with techniques that would be viewed as utterly trivial today. Even before I left Cornell in 1959, I would tell young people in my lab that while I could give them direction, they would have to get a lot in the way of technologies and techniques from others.

It was a well-funded time for research, and we were building explosively. When I went to Vanderbilt, there were twelve full-time faculty; then there were fifty, and then seventy. At the outset, I think, the entire budget in the department was something like $250,000. In eight years, it was almost $3 million. But we had absolutely no idea of how to set priorities. If there were three directions in which we could go, we went in all three. We could go just as fast as our talents could carry us.

The appeal of Vanderbilt's challenge overrode any doubts I had about racial and civil-rights questions in Nashville. I had thought, "How are you, as a liberal New Yorker, going to survive?" I had a very Southern house staff and faculty, so we viewed some situations quite differently. The most serious incident, though, had nothing specifically to do with the medical school and, in fact, threatened to tear apart the whole university. The crisis was precipitated by a black student in the divinity school who was arrested for taking part in a sit-in. The university trustees happened to be meeting at this time and, when the chancellor made the mistake of taking the issue to the trustees, they compounded the error by expelling the student.

The divinity school, of course, rose in righteous wrath. The board dug in its heels and was ready to wipe the deck with the whole divinity faculty. But some of us joined with the divinity school, which meant that the board would have to wipe the deck with part of their medical school, too. This they were not quite willing to do.

Both David Barr and Walsh called me. I told Dr. Barr that I'd threatened to resign, and he said, "In my experience, you shouldn't use that tool unless you really mean it."

I must say it hurt me when he said that. I told him that for me, this was not a game. I didn't want to be part of a university that would do this. I didn't have the faintest idea what would happen to my career.

My family was threatened. Crosses were burned on our lawn; we had to have guards around the house. My three children then ranged from six to ten years old. It was a frightening experience.

And, clear though the moral issue seemed to be, the human issues were not all that simple. It was a kind of classic tragedy. The chancellor was a fine man—much more likable than the young divinity student who had been expelled. I remember calling my dad and telling him this. He said, "Big issues often arise around difficult, small people."

Boy, did I feel it. Here I was, about to wreck my career over this student, but when the university reinstated him, he wouldn't even come back. It made me madder than hell.

In 1960, about a year after all this happened, the Chamber of Commerce gave me a distinguished service award. My mother used to insist that this was due to my stance on civil rights, which was absolutely not the case. It was for my performance as a professor. I used to tell her, "Believe it or not, I do something else around here other than stand for civil rights."

Perhaps the award did, in part, indicate backing for the stand I'd taken. That was some of the agony and schizophrenia of the South of that time. It was a community trying to deal practically and sensitively with something deeply embedded within it. And, when I recognized that, it allowed me to be much more effective in civil rights, because I wasn't so righteous. Instead of berating people, I tried to help them work through this problem that I knew they were going to resolve. And ultimately they did. When I go to the South now, my sense is that they've done much better than we have in race relationships in the North.

Meanwhile, back at Vanderbilt, I was trying to be the best doctor-scholar I could. As a way of showing the importance I attached to clinical medicine, I said I'd take the clinicopathological conference (CPC) every week for the whole first year. Before, the CPCs had been sleepy little sessions. Overnight, they became standing room only, with everyone showing up to watch the pathologist make an idiot out of the new professor of medicine. I worked very hard on those CPCs, in part because I hated being wrong and showed it. In fact, I got very good at the CPCs, and it sent a message.

I also said to my chief resident, "If you don't call me after 2 a.m. at least four times during the first month, you are going to be in trouble. It's going to be rare that I'll actually help you, but if you have a tough case, I want to be there in the middle of the night."

The tradition of being chief clinician by virtue of being chairman of medicine has changed. Some chairmen may still do it, but in many instances the managerial aspect of the job has overwhelmed the clinical role. Hugh Luckey and David Barr, in particular, were chief clinicians at Cornell. As Dr. Barr's chief resident, I had been told to call him if a difficult problem came up at night, and he'd come in. I did it sparingly, because he had to travel an hour from his house to the hospital, whereas it Vanderbilt I was only ten minutes away.

The wonderful thing about a house staff is that they always forget the times you didn't help them at all, while remembering the one time you did. One evening, when nobody knew what was wrong with a seriously ill patient, I told them to do the basic blocking and tackling to keep her alive while I ran over to the library. Somehow I lucked out and came up with the diagnosis, so we were able to save her. They remembered that. What was more important, they remembered that I was the guy who cared enough to show up in the middle of the night and struggle alongside them. I've just come back from a visit there, and I was glad to see that this attitude—going all out for the patient, whatever the difficulty—is still very much alive.

One other change I made, which in retrospect seems to have made sense, was to make a complete turnabout in faculty clinic assignments. When I arrived, the full-time faculty had a lock on the specialty clinics, while the part-time faculty were assigned to the general medical clinic. The part-timers did a lot of griping about this arrangement. "You make me turn the key to my very efficient office," they'd tell me, "to come over to your lousy general medical clinic, where all I see is the same stuff I get in my office all the time. And that's blackmail, because that's what I have to do to keep my privileges."

I agreed, and within the first month, I changed the ground rules so that every full-time faculty person had to spend at least half a day per week in the general medical clinic. They could still have their specialty clinics, but those would be add-ons, not a replacement for time in the general clinic. Meanwhile, I told the part-time group that they were exempt from the general medical clinic and were free to go to the specialty clinics, where they could truly enhance their clinical skills.

Naturally, I heard a lot of wails and groans from the full-time faculty, and the younger ones were just watching to see how long it would be before exceptions for senior people would start turning up. But I didn't let up, and of course, I had to do my turn too, every week.

After about three years, I thought I could stop, because my life was getting so busy. But then one day I was going by the door of an examining room, and one of my senior professors was being berated by the junior person who ran the clinic. The junior person was saying, "Damn it, if the chief can do it, you can do it, too." I sadly realized there was no way I could stop taking my turn.

Not surprisingly, the new system resulted in a big improvement in the general medical clinic. Once the faculty realized they couldn't get out of it, they had the muscle to make it good—for example, by making sure there were charts and enough nurses. When we had our weekly faculty meetings, there would be very lively discussions of patients they'd seen in common. In sum, the general medical clinic became a central point of reference for faculty, house staff, and students. It was wonderful, although a chairman couldn't do anything like that nowadays. A chairman today who required that his full professors work in the general medical clinic would have a mutiny on his hands.

My activities as chairman were very different from what a chairman does today. I think the change has seriously weakened internal medicine. It shows up in the decline in graduates choosing this field, both here at Cornell and nationwide. If they do choose it, they often don't get as much support as they should from their faculty and are likely to find a lack of role models in generalist patient care.

Because of superspecialization, the faculty tends to be not only narrowly oriented but quite unused to the unpredictable nature of illness: the superconsultant in endocrinology is not used to dealing with middle-of-the-night emergencies.

The approach a physician adopts to patient care derives in large part, I think, from the kind of training and mentors he has. As a student and house officer, I was fortunate to have some very powerful mentors—people like David Barr and Walsh McDermott—whom I wanted to emulate. Today, I see little of that for the house staff. I once asked my older daughter, a general internist with Kaiser Permanente, if she'd had any particular mentors during her training. She looked at me as if I were crazy.

The situation is somewhat better, I think, in surgery. In general, it's much more hierarchical. But I think the intern is more likely to know where his responsibilities stop and those of the resident start. The young professor of surgery is usually a better surgeon than the resident, whereas in internal medicine, I would guess, the resident tends to be a better generalist than most of the full-time faculty.

The opposite side of the coin, of course, is that when I was starting out, I could talk glibly of the wonders of being a generalist. I do not know if I would today, given all there is to learn. I also feel fortunate to have embarked on a career at a time when I could be involved in everything: patient care, research, and teaching. People couldn't possibly do them all nowadays. I never was involved in private practice. It was always an option, but I never considered it seriously. I love taking care of patients, but it was never income-producing for me.

In 1968 I moved back to Johns Hopkins as dean. I didn't give up clinical medicine. I would trade off with Mac Harvey and try to take his rounds whenever possible. But I wasn't in it enough, and I missed it profoundly. The is the one period of my career I've had second thoughts about. My wife was ill, and it seemed possible that a change of scenery would help matters. Maybe I left Nashville for the wrong reasons.

On the other hand, I had been at Vanderbilt for nine years, which was a good long time. As a chairman, I couldn't help thinking about broader issues in the delivery of care, and now Hopkins had an interesting opportunity to build a whole health-care system for the city of Columbia. Columbia was a planned community of 250,000 people, which was then in the process of being developed.

Bob Heyssel, a visionary doctor, came along with me from Vanderbilt and, of course, his success at Hopkins has been monumental. We designed this program for Columbia, as well as a system for the inner-city area of east Baltimore. The latter came about because the Hopkins faculty was offended by the notion of planning a suburban project when the need for better care was so acute right outside our door.

Another achievement ensued that might not have happened at Vanderbilt. When I arrived at Hopkins, there had been only one black graduate since its opening. In my first year there, we admitted thirteen black men and women to the first-year class.

But the position of dean in medical schools is limited. I had no troops. I had no money, because it was all in the departments. All I had was the power of persuasion. It helped that I was also the medical director of the hospital. Russ Nelson, president of the hospital, was splendidly supportive. Because of the feeling that the deanship was not everything it should be, he gave me a major role in the hospital. It was helpful mainly because it prevented my chairmen from whipsawing the two of us.

The fact that Hopkins still required its faculty to be on a full-time, salaried basis also gave me considerably more clout than I might have had in other places. Every chairman received pretty nearly the same salary, whether he was in the basic sciences or a clinical department. This great tradition of Hopkins is illustrated by a conversation I had with a young surgeon who came in and pounded my desk: "Damn it, I can make ten times as much money by practicing surgery on the outside."

I could say, without anger, "Be my guest. It's a perfectly appropriate goal, but not here. I've got four young people who would give their right arm for your position. Blessings on you."

In other words, I couldn't be blackmailed, which I think happens to deans all the time today: "You pay me well, or I'll take my practice elsewhere." And the schools have gotten so dependent on this income that we permit these awful, embarrassing inequities in salaries to arise. I'm ashamed at the income some of us make, particularly when I recall that academic medicine used to be a kind of priesthood, in which one gave up income for other precious things: contemplative time, the chance to do research, to spend time with students, to teach, to be curious. Unfortunately, those have been taken away, and now everybody has to be busy as hell practicing medicine to make their salary. That was not the case when I was a chairman of medicine, but it was rapidly becoming so when I became a dean.

Academic medical centers are stressed institutions in the United States, even more so now than when I wrote about it in 1978 with Robert Blendon for *The New England Journal.* The basic problem is that the cost of these centers is growing much faster than their ability to meet some of society's most critical health-care needs. A glaring example: in projections of national need, the great preponderance of opinion is that we should be graduating 80 percent generalists and 20 percent specialists. Instead, we're producing just the opposite: 80 percent specialists and 20 percent generalists. That's very expensive and very careless. Meanwhile, governments at all levels are determined to constrain health-care costs; business is desperate to constrain costs; public esteem for the medical profession has diminished. The portents are not good.

The evidence appears to be that the public has a split view of the profession. If you ask them questions about the health-care system as a whole or the medical profession as a whole, their views tend to be rather negative. But if you ask them about their own doctors, they generally have good things to say.

What often seems to bother people is a paucity of personal contact with the doctor, the sense that too much of their care involves inordinately expensive technology. To some extent, such feelings are misguided—but they are quite real, and as a profession, we're going to have to deal with them. That won't be easy, and we've got a long way to go.

Going to the Robert Wood Johnson Foundation in 1972 was almost an accident. When the trustees of the foundation found out that they had a $1.2 billion enterprise on their hands, they decided to go the professional staffing route. They talked to a number of people across the country, including me. Initially, I must admit, I didn't take this very seriously. I thought becoming a foundation executive was something you did when you absolutely ran out of gas. Still, I called Alec Heard, who was then chancellor of Vanderbilt and chairman of the Ford Foundation, and his advice was to think seriously about it. He said, "You've always been interested in changing the health-care system. You've always been an impatient young man, and it's about time you tried something big and learned some patience."

So when they offered, I accepted. To put together my team, I talked with some giants like Alan Pifer, president of the Carnegie Corporation; and John Gardner, formerly secretary of Health, Education and Welfare and president of Common Cause. Their advice turned out to be quite similar. They said, "Don't take people who look just like you. You've worked almost exclusively with doctors; pick people from other fields. Pick people of different ages and ethnic and racial backgrounds, and make sure both sexes are well represented."

Essentially, that's what I did, trying to pick the best of what would purposely be a varied group. and, wow, did I do well. I picked Margaret Mahoney, who was with the Carnegie, and who knew an awful lot about both health care and the foundation business. From the Commonwealth Fund came Terrance Keenan, their wonderfully capable general factotum. From Washington came this absolutely brilliant young man named Bob Blendon, who had been with Elliot Richardson at HEW and who had worked with Bob Heyssel and me on the Hopkins projects in Columbia and east Baltimore. He wrote me a three-page letter spelling out what he could do for me, which in essence said, "I can make you about ten times as smart as you really are."

Shortly thereafter, I selected Linda Aiken, a brilliant nurse-sociologist; and Ruby Hearn, a very knowledgeable young black biophysicist from Yale who had been instrumental in setting up Sesame Street at the Children's Television Workshop.

My own background in health policy was nothing much beyond what I'd learned in connection with the Columbia and east Baltimore projects. I had the traditional liberal concerns about health care for the poor and considered myself a fairly emancipated medical thinker, but this group was constantly proving me wrong. I would say something that would have seemed perfectly self-evident to the executive faculty council at Hopkins, and Bob Blendon or Linda Aiken would simply take me apart.

I had a very conservative board, and this was really a very liberal staff. So playing this piano with any semblance of harmony sometimes took enormous energy and care. But the creative tension was productive.

Walsh McDermott joined us not long after he retired as chairman of public health at Cornell, in 1972. He was just superb. Not only was his wisdom and historical perspective on health policy a terrific resource for all, but he also prevented us from becoming stale intellectually. Early on, he proposed that once a month we all leave the foundation headquarters and go over to the Nassau Inn to discuss some issue or other with a guest expert. The idea was appealing, but with a million things on my mind, the last thing I thought I needed was an intellectual colloquy at the Nassau Inn once a month. Well, it was the making of us. It opened our minds and pushed us to think about issues we might never have tackled.

This foundation had come into an enormous windfall, and the major question was what direction we would take. We came to that through the genius of Bob Blendon and Walsh McDermott. One of Walsh's suggestions was to invite groups of the brightest people in the country, from a whole variety of fields and disciplines, and in effect pose the question to them: if you had $50 million a year to spend on health care, how would you spend it?

We did this two or three times, and the experience was both stimulating and discouraging. I came to realize how difficult it is for even the brightest people—and maybe it's all the more difficult for the brightest people—to think about outcome instead of process. Very few of the people we invited stepped back and asked: "How do you get to the post office from here?" Instead it was, "I'm very good at what I do, and I can do it better if you give me more to work with."

While we did distill some good ideas from these sessions, maybe the most valuable realization for me was that I ought to stop being so scared to death of plunging in. Nobody else knew how to do this either. With the help of that staff, I trained myself to be a futurologist, to step back from my academic orientation, look at the facts, and decide as best I could on the route.

We could have taken our cues from academe or from the hospitals or perhaps from the American Medical Association and other professional groups. Instead, thanks to Bob, we decided to take our cue from John Q. Public: what was he concerned about when it came to health? We began to be poll watchers and even commissioned a few of our own.

Since the public's major worry seemed to be the difficulty in finding a doctor, we decided to turn our principal attention to the problems of access. I think the country made a lot of progress on that until the late 1970s. We reduced the problem to where it was affecting less than 10 percent of the population. In a democracy, that seems to be the point below which interest in an issue collapses—particularly when it's going to cost more than a bit to make further headway.

Part of this success had to do with the fact that the country was producing more doctors. But we were also vigorously implementing Medicare and Medicaid, and private health insurance was expanding. Before we started slipping back, about 92 percent of our citizens had coverage.

Being a futurologist is both unsettling and soft. We worked enormously hard at researching issues, bringing in groups to help us do it, setting national programs in motion, putting in place evaluations. As you can imagine, the road took some unexpected turns. For example, in 1972 it made sense to initiate service-delivery models in anticipation of national health insurance, which seemed to be just around the corner. Then, all of a sudden, the prospect of national health insurance just disappeared, and we had to do some scrambling. (In fact, the progress made in improving access to health care was one of the reasons national health insurance faded from the scene.)

In many instances, though, we did put programs in place that proved to be trailblazers. We launched a major effort in emergency-medical services that, within two years, got picked up throughout the country. We had a lot to do, I think, with the great expansion of rural health programs that occurred in the 1970s. And we gave a boost to generalist careers.

Then medical care in the United States lost ground in the 1980s. Whether or not you blame the Reagan administration, it seems fairly clear that as a society we began to downgrade our concern over health care for the have-nots. If there has been any net progress in the last twenty years, the direction has been wrong for the past decade. We have not stemmed the escalating cost of health care at all, except for a period in the Nixon administration when prices were frozen. The cost of health care has increased relentlessly at about double the rate of inflation. It has been unchecked by all efforts to contain it.

Medicine is very labor-intensive, so we can't expect to see an actual reduction of costs. But it certainly ought to be possible to keep increases in line with the general rate of inflation. Donald Berwick has argued very persuasively that doctors can do a lot more than they're doing to contain the cost of medicine. There's considerable evidence that economical medicine is not only fully compatible with good practice but is an essential feature of it. Yet, too often, we train our residents as if the best medicine entails using the most tests and technology.

Hopefully, things are now starting to turn around. It is widely known that we have 30 to 37 million people who are uninsured or left out—figures, incidentally, that come from the Robert Wood Johnson Foundation—so at least the problem is getting some attention. Another good sign was that in the early 1990s Congress acted to expand coverage of children and pregnant women, which was where some of the worst slippage had occurred. We do scandalously little for our youngsters.

I find the Canadian system appealing. In their dealings with the federal government, U.S. physicians have always given top priority in maintaining their income through the fee-for-service system. As a result, we doctors got richer, but the government piled regulation after regulation on us. Canadian physicians, in contrast, have insisted on their professional autonomy rather than their economic autonomy, which to me is a more sensible choice, for both doctors and society as a whole. Whether such a system can be transplanted is another matter.

Tools for measuring the quality of care, on the other hand, have improved considerably. Organized medicine is much more accepting of such tools today, and there has been some real progress in developing these tools. This is not to say that we don't have some way to go in both respects.

Another area of progress is represented by the greater influx of women into medicine. Women generally find it more acceptable than men to talk about social or psychological or family issues. On the other hand, hospitals have become increasingly impersonal and technology-oriented, and that's where we educate our doctors. Overall, my impression is that we talk more about caring and compassion but probably give less of them than we once did.

On a broader scale, one question I've never been able to understand is why, given the power of our profession, we don't do more to champion the needs of the nation's have-nots. We're in a unique position to be advocates for the health of these people, and yet we continually fail to take on this role.

The failure, I think, has less to do with morality than with the fact that our training is almost exclusively in one-on-one medicine. I see so many doctors who simply cannot fathom why society is critical of our profession. They will say that they work eighty hours a week, take good care of anyone who walks into their offices, do the best they can—and it's all true. What never occurs to them is that society might also hold them responsible for those in need who never find their way to their offices. We need to be more aware of those people.

Taking care of the poor was once academic medicine's major role, but this is less the case today. Even if academic centers can't afford to provide care for the poor, they are in a unique position to articulate the dimensions of the need. Care for the poor should be a rallying point for these institutions, but there is little evidence of an inclination to make it so.

The current AIDS disaster will give impetus to better coordination of care. At the designated AIDS center at New York Hospital–Cornell, for example, patients are cared for in a highly coordinated way by a whole range of professionals: internists, psychiatrists, nutritionists, nurses, occupational therapists, lawyers, social workers. The entire approach is democratic—nothing about the doctor being the only captain of the team. The captain is whoever is best able to help the patient on a given day, whether it is a nurse looking after ulcers on his leg, or a lawyer advising him on his job rights, or a psychiatrist dealing with his suicidal feelings. We need to apply this degree of coordination to other chronic conditions and to extend it to a whole variety of settings, from the intensive care unit to the intermediate-care facility to home.

After I left the Johnson Foundation in 1986 to return to Cornell, I began helping shape public policy on a range of issues related to AIDS. The first job I took on was the chairmanship of New York Governor Mario Cuomo's advisory council for the AIDS Institute, which is the funding and coordinating body for all state activities relating to AIDS. I chaired a task force for New York Mayor Ed Koch that was concerned with the availability of hospital beds and residential facilities for AIDS patients—a sobering experience of the tangle that is the city's bureaucracy. Also, I am involved in the AIDS center at Cornell (where I have direct contact with patients and caregivers).

As vice-chairman of the National Commission on AIDS, I have been rather critical of the federal effort against this disease. We need more funding for care and education and perhaps for research as well. I think we have consistently denied the extent of the danger this disease poses to our society. It's worth every buck we put into it now, because we'll only have to pay a hundredfold later. Even if we grant the possibility that the United States and other advanced countries will escape the fate of Africa, at this stage we can hardly be confident of that.

My own view—and most informed medical opinion, I believe— is that AIDS is moving slowly but relentlessly into the heterosexual population. Already we are seeing this in certain rural areas and in some of the most impoverished parts of our cities. Again, it may be that those patterns will not be duplicated elsewhere, but I think it would be reckless beyond belief to proceed on that assumption.

Our society has to do whatever it can, then, to protect itself. Our young people in particular have to understand what this disease is about and appreciate the urgency of protecting themselves against it. And, in view of the urgency and lethality, it seems utterly absurd that we have bogged down in futile arguments that have to do more with lifestyle than with true morality. It is outrageous that we are exhausting ourselves in arguments about condoms or sex education, when the danger posed by this virus and the way to avoid it are so clear. Education may not be a total answer, but it's certainly the best— indeed, the only—answer we have at this time. I think it's sheer folly not to invest as heavily in this as we possibly can.

At one point, I said I thought we were funding research quite generously, but some of the research community took me to task and insisted that a lot of programs weren't being funded. Certainly the ultimate answer will come from research. In my present role, I am personally more conscious of dreadful shortages of funding in patient care and education. The fact that this disease has primarily affected two groups that society is inclined to shun—gays and drug users—has permitted a more reluctant response than we would see otherwise.

As for the response of the medical profession, in terms of people avoiding or discriminating against infected patients, I would point out that only in the past three decades have doctors functioned in a relatively hazard-free environment. When I went to med school, the risks came primarily from tuberculosis and polio. In virtually every class, somebody dropped out with tuberculosis. When I was chief resident here during New York's last major polio epidemic, one of our residents died. Sometimes, when I was dead tired, I used to wonder if I would take it home to my three little kids. To someone from my generation, then, it's a little surprising to encounter reluctance to treat potentially dangerous patients.

On the other hand, there is no denying that caring for these patients poses risks. I think we have to give health professionals much better training in on-the-job safety as well as find ways to reduce job hazards. It's also absolutely crucial that we provide full-compensation insurance on a no-fault basis for physicians and health workers who do become infected. No questions about their sex lives or risk factors—full compensation on the basis of what their income would be over the course of their lives. Any other policy sends a terrible message: namely, you take the risks, but if anything happens, you're on your own. We must protect, support, and indemnify health workers.

Added to the risks, of course, is the disapproval many doctors feel about AIDS patients. Anyone who has ever had to care for an IV drug user knows how frustrating it can be. They misbehave, they're ungrateful, they screw up your entire ward and raise hell all over the place. And no group is likely to have less sympathy for such behavior than doctors, who probably have a more visceral hatred of failure—and less personal experience of it—than any other group. You will never find a more dedicated group of achievers, and here they're being asked to take care of some of society's biggest losers. Perhaps it is this fact that has led the profession to do so little to champion the have-nots.

Roger DuPrez, a New York Hospital graduate who is now a wonderful professor at Vanderbilt, used to have an answer when house staff griped about having to take care of alcoholics or other unpleasant patients. He said, "One very important thing about being a physician is to learn to take good care of people you don't like."

Physicians are very self-critical, and over time, I think, we'll do the right thing. What we're asking for is not saints but true doctors.

✚

    I first met Tom Gordon when I was president of the University Without Walls and he was tutoring graduate students. He attracted those who were interested in leadership and parenting, as his Effectiveness Training Institute is known throughout the world for its work with parents, teachers, leaders, men, women, and couples.

    Tom Gordon's life and work are a very important part of this book. When Carl arrived at Ohio State in 1940, Tom was one of the first people to study with him. Later, in the 1950s, Tom accepted Carl's invitation to write a chapter on group-centered leadership for *Client-Centered Therapy*.

    Ultimately, Tom successfully adapted his knowledge and understanding of humanistic psychology and created the idea of effectiveness training for the aforementioned populations and professions in various parts of the world.

✚

7

Teaching People To Create Therapeutic Environments

by Thomas Gordon

During my life with Carl Rogers, he was another father, a close friend, a mentor, a model of a warm and giving person, a superb teacher, my therapist, my client, and in his later years a critic.

His arrival at Ohio State in 1940 to begin his academic career kept me from dropping psychology to go into medicine. His courses there brought humanism into my conception of psychology, which had been impersonally theoretical and experimental. He helped me find a master's thesis research study.

The Rogers family became for me a model of the way families should be and the way marriage should be. Carl's wife, Helen, was a lovely and giving woman. And David and Natalie, their children, were the kind of kids every parent would like to have.

During the Chicago years, Martha Ann and I were fortunate to be accepted by Carl and Helen as frequent companions and close friends. This friendship continued throughout my graduate school years and on into the five years at the University of Chicago as one of Carl's faculty colleagues. During those years we vacationed with them at Seneca Lake, played a lot of bridge, painted together, barbecued on the shores of Lake Michigan, fished in Northern Wisconsin, dined together a lot, learned from them how to make mobiles, and saw them at the frequent psychology department parties. Clearly Carl and Helen were important people in our lives.

When I became intrigued with the field of group leadership in the 1950s, Carl asked me to write a chapter on group-centered leadership for his *Client-Centered Therapy* book.[1] I felt privileged, needless to say, to have my ideas in one of his books—his most important one, at that.

Later, I was one of the Counseling Center staff members carrying out the large psychotherapy research program under a grant from the Rockefeller Foundation. Two of my papers ended up published in Rogers and Dymond's *Psychotherapy and Personality Change.*[2]

I spent five years on the Counseling Center Staff: teaching the counseling practicum; developing a course in group therapy; and creating the student-centered teaching model with Carl, E. H. Porter, and Arthur Shedlin as we planned a counseling training program for Veterans Administration counselors. It was at the Center that all of us tried to learn how to function in a democratic or group-centered organization. Working with Carl almost daily taught me a lot about democratic leadership. I also observed how organized and productive he was, both as an administrator and as a faculty member. At our faculty meetings Carl was never afraid to champion the Counseling Center's work or argue for giving students more freedom, yet his contributions were never hostile or blaming. I tried, with only moderate success, to model his tact.

Carl left Chicago to take a joint appointment in the psychology and psychiatry departments at the University of Wisconsin. Soon after, I moved to Pasadena, California. For a period of five or so years, we saw each other infrequently, mostly at American Psychological Association meetings, where we always had dinner together. Even after he joined the La Jolla–based Western Behavioral Science Institute in California, we seldom spent time together.

Criticism—the first—came from Carl shortly after Parent Effectiveness Training (PET) gained national recognition from my guest appearances on many radio and TV talk shows, including prominent ones such as "Phil Donahue," "Mike Douglas," "Today," and Johnny Carson's "Tonight Show." Friends reported Carl's criticisms, and Carl himself wrote me a long letter. His criticisms were: PET was too "commercial"; because PET was skill training, it could not be effective; I had failed to give Carl credit in my PET book; and I had prevented my publisher from selling the paperback rights so I could get more royalties from books supplied to PET course participants.

I responded by letter only to the last two accusations. My publisher and I had agreed we should have no references in the book; and as to the last accusation, I receive no royalties at all from books supplied to PET instructors. Carl never acknowledged my letter. Needless to say, I was deeply hurt. I simply could not reconcile these actions with my totally positive perception of Carl as a person.

Later I read his *Freedom to Learn for the 80s* book, in which he clearly stated his reservations about interpersonal communication training and his preference for his encounter group approach. This was very puzzling to me, because on the same page he lauded David Aspy and Flora Roebucks' research on the positive effects of their skill training approach as one of "two studies that are landmarks in the field of education."[3] Carl devoted twenty pages to the remarkably positive result of those studies on both students and teachers, and yet he apparently had a need to criticize skill training.

Some years later Carl and Helen attended a symposium at which their son, Dave—by then a nationally prominent physician—and I gave presentations on the need for more prevention in the field of mental health. After that, our paths did not cross.

However, when Carl lay dying at Scripps Clinic, I rushed there, held his hand, thanked him quietly for being such a significant and inspiring person in my life, and told him how much I had loved him. Sadly, he was unconscious and could not hear my words, but I was certain he had always known my feelings anyway. He died a few hours later, but he continues to live in my heart and often in my thoughts.

Early Years

I was born March 11, 1918, in Paris, Illinois, a small town where my father was a minister in the Disciples of Christ denomination. Before I had reached my first birthday, my father reluctantly resigned from that position as a result of what he later described as a "factional dispute in the congregation." Never again would he assume the position of minister, although I later learned he fully expected to.

My mother was trained as a public school teacher, but she never took a teaching job after marrying my father and becoming an instant mother to his four-year-old son, whose own mother had died in childbirth. My brother, John, was to have a rather profound effect on me throughout my childhood.

When I was not yet two, we moved to Danville, Illinois. My father accepted a position as Executive Secretary of the Chamber of Commerce there, a position he was to hold for ten years. What few memories I have of my early years in Danville are very pleasant ones. I experienced almost unconditional love from my father, who never punished and who played a lot with both John and me. In years to come, long after his death, I would often bring to mind a visual picture of my father's gentle hands—hands that never inflicted the pain of punishment.

My father loved to joke. He kidded with us as well as with friends, waitresses, barbers, shopkeepers, and the like. While sometimes it was embarrassing to me, it would become a very prominent trait of mine, beginning with high school and continuing throughout my life. Kidding, playing practical jokes, and making puns became assets as well as liabilities and brought me both enjoyment and censure.

My mother's influence on me was distinctly different from my father's. While she occasionally showed a sharp sense of humor herself, my mother was rather serious minded, intellectually curious, and sensitively aware of social injustices. My relationship with my mother was closer and her influence greater than my father's. What infrequent punitive discipline I received, my mother was the one who administered it—with her ivory hairbrush or a small switch from one of our two cherry trees. A memory that never fades is of her struggle to tear off a stubborn cherry tree branch to use as a whip while John and I watched through the sun room window, laughing out loud at her obvious frustration. So her switching our legs a few times was more humorous than aversive to my brother and me.

There are a few other vivid memories of these early preschool years. Endless hours were spent in the small public park not more than 500 feet from our house. I played on the swings and slides, picked wildflowers for my mother, and often built dams in the narrow stream that snaked through the park. In retrospect, our nearby park and the adjacent forest gave me and my friends an unusually large "area of freedom." We would often wander as far away as two miles from home, through thick woods and on down to Stoney Creek to skinny dip or catch crawdads (freshwater crayfish).

My parents enrolled me in Danville's most highly rated kindergarten shortly after I turned four. I had already learned to read a little, and I remember reading the billboards when the family went for our usual Sunday afternoon drive. Kindergarten provided my first experience with a warm and effective teacher. I loved Mrs. Snyder and recall how rewarding it was to learn and to excel.

Because I would be only five and a half years old in September, I was not allowed to enroll in first grade of public school. So I remained in kindergarten for another year and started public school in second grade. I remember being able to read and do simple arithmetic better than some of my classmates. Unfortunately, I was skipped again—this time into a fourth-grade class with a teacher whom I would place at the far other end of the scale from Mrs. Snyder. However, in the fifth grade I had my second excellent teacher, and I continued to excel.

My first awareness of how wide the differences in intelligence between people could be came while seeing my brother do so poorly in school. He was four years older than I. My parents did everything they could think of to help John with his studies: they hired tutors, held him back a grade, sent him to a military school, and later spent more than they should have sending him to Lake Forest Academy in a suburb north of Chicago.

I recall vividly how sad I felt each time we visited John when he was away at these schools. I frequently cried on the way back, urging my parents to bring him home. Somehow I was certain it was a tragic mistake for John to be away during the years he most needed the love and acceptance of his family. Perhaps this was my first inkling of what I would understand more fully much later—that what kids need the most is the therapeutic environment of parental acceptance, affection, and love.

My brother was a very good athlete, and I often tagged along when he participated in neighborhood games of football and baseball. Often he had to use his influence to persuade friends to let his little brother play with them. It was not long before I was accepted into their games by these older boys, because to their surprise (and mine) I proved to be a quick learner and a fast runner.

John also introduced me to tennis, but it was not long before I could beat him, as well as everyone else in our neighborhood. These early experiences convinced me that I had an aptitude for sports. For the rest of my life, participating in athletics has been a source of self-esteem, a strong spirit of competitiveness, and a desire to excel.

In my eleventh year my father took a new job as a lobbyist for the Illinois Manufacturers Association, and we moved from Danville to Springfield. Even now, I have a visual picture of our family driving out of the driveway, leaving our home and starting our trip to a new town. I was in the back seat, crying my eyes out as I yelled my last goodbye through the open window to Jack Shane, my best friend. Jack lived only a block away, and we had spent the last nine years being together most of the time: playing games, having lunch or dinner either at his house or mine, and very frequently sleeping over at one of our homes.

It was with Jack that I experienced my first deep male friendship, one with many dimensions: mutual acceptance, common interest, humor, loyalty, trust, and mutual self-disclosure. And it was with Jack's parents that I first learned to relate easily to adults other than my own parents. Jack was a gentle, kind, and empathic, nonmacho person. I'm certain this friendship built expectations that all future male friendships would be much like mine with Jack. (That was not to be, as it turned out later when we moved to Springfield.) Of interest to me now is that Jack and I spent much of our time together pretending we ran a business. Jack's father, a successful businessman, continually brought Jack a lot of old business forms: unused checks, invoices, receipts, ledgers, and so on. I remember that I really enjoyed playing at being a businessman. Later this was reinforced working (or playing) in my father's office in Springfield. Perhaps it is not coincidence that I would eventually have a business of my own.

I continued to miss Jack a lot, because I had difficulty at first finding close friendships in Springfield. In fact, for at least a year, during which I was in the eighth grade, I experienced many rejections from other boys. Worst of all in my new school, I had my first exposure to bullies. They scared me to death with their penchant for fighting and using violence on kids smaller than they. Unfortunately, I was by far the smallest and the youngest boy in that class. I lived that year in a constant state of fear of physical harm. I also was exposed to my first authoritarian principal. It was during that miserable year at Lawrence Elementary School that I developed frequent migraine headaches so severe that I would miss two or three days of school. Over the next dozen years, I heard from many physicians that my migraines were caused by "psychological factors." This was my introduction to the mysterious field of psychology.

Understandably, I was greatly relieved to leave the violence and fear I experienced in school and enroll in Springfield High. Thirteen years of age and still the smallest kid in my class, I had learned the hard way that all boys were not like Jack Shane. Kids could be mean and violent and could make others "sick." I couldn't wait to get to high school.

The High School Years

My father had been a fair tennis player, and he had frequently played with me on the clay singles court in Danville. However, I remember the disappointment I felt when, after I beat him for the first time, he announced he was putting away his racket for good. Nevertheless, at the Springfield courts I found other players, one of whom became my best friend. Bob Good was a handsome young man almost three years older than I and a close neighbor. We became fierce but friendly competitors in singles, and we were also doubles partners. In no time we won the Springfield Junior Doubles Tournament, and I beat Bob to win the Junior Singles Title several years in a row.

I was much too short and lightweight to make the basketball or football teams in high school, and the same would be true in college. I didn't reach my maximum height of six feet until sometime during my senior year in college. Because being on the football and basketball teams brought a lot of prestige in high school, my inability to be one of the "big kids" was a source of deep disappointment. Tennis was little valued by both students and the high school itself, where there had never been a tennis team. Nevertheless, when I later won the Central Illinois Junior Singles and Doubles titles, my self-esteem reached new heights.

Finding a close relationship in high school with a very popular girl also increased my confidence. "Going steady" with Ruth, being seen as a couple, and making friends with new couples opened the door to a rewarding social life: parties, double-dating, school dances, and going to Priddy's, the local hangout for dancing. Ruth taught me how to dance, and we became one of the school's best dance teams. And because "cutting in" at dances was at that time the accepted custom, my dancing ability gave me the confidence to dance with girls I had previously been too shy to approach.

One of the other coping mechanisms I employed to gain attention and be "somebody" in high school was not as effective. I rebelled strongly and overtly against the school's authoritarian administrators and those teachers who relied heavily on control and punitive discipline. While my reactive antics were usually reinforced by my classmates' laughter and their admiration for my "guts," they got me kicked out of my classes very frequently. I was never certain of the exact number, but I was ejected from class between twenty-three and twenty-six times (a school record, I believe), and I was suspended from school twice.

The assistant principal and school disciplinarian, Lyman K. Davis, once warned me that I would end up an inmate in Joliet Prison, like the delinquent student he knew in the not-too-distant past. In retrospect, I can understand the prediction, yet I knew that prison would never be my destiny. Although I was a trouble-making discipline problem, I was nearly a straight-A student, which I think was a puzzling contradiction to my teachers.

During the same period, I clearly recollect a rewarding three-year experience in a Sunday-school class taught by a woman in her early twenties. To my knowledge, Grace Cox had no formal education in human relations (although ten years later we would run into each other at a convention to discover that both of us had become psychologists). In her role as a Sunday-school teacher for a small class of twenty or so teenagers (later it grew to fifty or more), Grace came across as some brand new species of teacher. She somehow knew how to create a special climate that made us feel good about ourselves. I was well aware of the quality of her leadership, by which the responsibility for managing and governing the class was transferred gradually from the leader to the kids. We elected our own officers, formed task committees, and made all the decisions about topics we wanted to discuss or projects we wanted to tackle. Some of us took turns each Sunday being the discussion leader or facilitator. There was nothing we felt could not be discussed openly and honestly. For the first time in my life, I felt fully respected, valued, and accepted by a teacher. I experienced the positive effects of being a member of a self-governing group in which I had a strong voice. This remarkable woman somehow had acquired a deep understanding of participative management, student-centered teaching, and democratic leadership, and she became a role model for me. Her leadership style later became my own.

College Years

After graduating from high school in mid-year, I was still undecided about what occupation I would work toward. I did know it would be a profession, either medicine or the ministry. I received a full-tuition, four-year scholarship to DePauw University in Greencastle, Indiana. I managed to lose three-fourths of that scholarship by ending my freshman year with a below-C grade point average—the first significant "failure" in my life. Foolishly, I had taken a lot of weekend trips home to be with Ruth. Also, pressures from my fraternity to participate in many time-consuming activities left too little time for studying. Also, I was amazed at the unexpected competition from the many exceptionally intelligent students in my classes. Half the male students entering DePauw each year had been either valedictorians or salutatorians of their high school graduating classes. Fortunately, I woke up to the realities of college and earned half A's, half B's in my sophomore year. I maintained that average or better until graduation.

I had chosen to follow a pre-med program in college, but during my first year I became convinced the chemistry and biology, with their long afternoon labs, did not appeal to me. My chemistry labs took up so much of my time that I had to drop freshman basketball practices even though I had made the team. I wish now I had made the other choice but I stuck with the pre-med program, hoping I might get turned on by the required courses ahead: physiology, embryology, physics, quantitative analysis (chemistry), and anatomy. However, in my four years of college I was intellectually stimulated by only two courses: abnormal psychology and the synoptic study of the Bible. The latter course completely closed the door on my becoming a minister, and the former opened the door to my becoming a psychologist.

During that same abnormal psychology course, my mother had to be hospitalized for a year with "involutional melancholy," as it was called then. I was puzzled with the changes I saw her experience. Now I was certain I wanted to go to graduate school to study psychology. I was supported in this decision by my fraternity brother and friend, Don Grummon, who had already made the same decision.

However, one of my psychology professors was of the opinion that I wouldn't make it through to the Ph.D. degree. He based this pessimistic prediction on my work in his class plus the score I had made on the DePauw entrance exam. (I had not been informed of that score until that conference with him). Needless to say, my "somewhat above average" score (sixty-fourth percentile) was belied by my subsequent three years of half A's and half B's. Nevertheless, this test score and this man's evaluation of my level of "intelligence" stuck with me for several years, until I unexpectedly received strongly conflicting data later in graduate school. Meanwhile, ignoring my professors' advice, I applied and was admitted to the graduate school at Ohio State University. At that time the psychology department there was ranked among the very best in the country.

Looking back on my four years of college, I realize it was a special period of personal growth and social development, even though it was a very disappointing educational experience. I made some deep and lasting friendships with a few fraternity brothers, psychologically healthy men who did not engage in high-risk behaviors or rebel against authority figures as I had in high school. They studied hard, they had delightful senses of humor, they were achievers, they were campus leaders, they were fair and kind with others, they were bright, they were not macho. I would develop other such relationships throughout my life, but these men set the standard. They were my early male role models.

I also was fortunate enough to develop a close four-year relationship with a young woman a year and half older and a class ahead of me. Jane was very bright, with broad interests and high social skills. And she became a kind and understanding friend who brought out the best in me and helped me drop some of the worst. Had it not been for my insistence that I complete a long period of graduate training, we undoubtedly would have married. This close relationship terminated soon after my first year in graduate school.

The extensive DePauw intramural program nevertheless drew me into a lot of different sports—speedball (soccer), basketball, baseball, table tennis, volleyball, and bowling—in each of which I became competent. I became my fraternity's Intramural Manager, and each year we ranked very highly among the university's dozen or more fraternities. I was also on the DePauw tennis team for three years, although tennis was not a "prestige" sport.

I was urged to become the fraternity song leader (director). Although I knew nothing about music, I had a good voice, an ear for harmony, and the leadership skills to motivate the guys to attend practice, strive for excellence, and find enjoyment in group singing. From a history of very low rankings, our fraternity rose to earning third place in the yearly song contest.

All these experiences increased my self-esteem and my self-confidence, as well as revealing a new aptitude for leadership. On the other hand, I realize now that college did not challenge my self-concept of being a jack of all trades and master of none. This component of my self-concept remained firmly fixed for more than half my life. For twenty-five years after graduating from college, I would be searching for some activity (intellectual or athletic) in which I might achieve excellence (become one of the "big boys"). I couldn't deny my versatility, yet I had not shaken the reality that I failed to earn a Phi Beta Kappa key, be the very best in any sport, dance like Fred

Astaire, or sing like Bing Crosby. And the final "failure" was not being elected president of the fraternity, despite the fact that it was clear to me and everyone else that no member had contributed more than I. All the more evidence I couldn't make it to the top. I was elected vice-president—second best to a varsity football and basketball star.

The Ohio State Years

I knew no students at Ohio State nor any faculty. Somehow, I was soon introduced into an in-group of second- and third-year psychology graduate students (more "big boys") who lunched together at a table reserved every day by the restaurant manager. Interestingly enough, all these men had majored in psychology in college, whereas I had taken only two psych classes. Whenever their lunch discussions turned to psychological subjects, I felt like a neophyte. Burned into my memory was an embarrassing incident at lunch when I asked, "Who is this psychologist, 'Gestalt,' I'm hearing so much about in my theory class?" One of the "big boys" sensitively and quietly informed me that Gestalt was not a person but a German word for configuration or form, which had become the name of a then prominent theory. That sensitive person was Nick Hobbs, with whom I would develop another one of those deep and caring male relationships. Nick, who would later become president of the American Psychological Association and provost of George Peabody University in Nashville, was a strong role model for me. He modeled how much one had to study in graduate school; he was a gentle and giving person. Quietly self-confident, he was also very bright.

Much to my surprise, I received A's in most of my graduate courses. I recall being amazed at how much easier graduate school seemed. I felt none of the obligations of fraternity life, so I could spend most of my time studying. However, I quickly became dissatisfied with the type of psychology I was learning in my classes. It was all history of psychology, experimental psychology, and statistics—almost nothing about people, normal or abnormal. I began to think I had made a bad choice and should have gone to medical school. Then there occurred an event that affected me profoundly for the rest of my life. A new professor joined the department, and word quickly got around that he was a young clinical psychologist with a lot of experience treating maladjusted children and youth. In fact, Carl Rogers' newly published book, *The Clinical Treatment of the Problem*

Child, was one of the first books of its kind written by a psychologist. At that time, "treatment" of either children or adult problems was the exclusive arena of psychiatrists.

His first course at Ohio State attracted nearly every psychology graduate student plus many students from other departments. Even most of my upper-level graduate friends enrolled. Carl Rogers was seen as a pioneer in bringing counseling and treatment into clinical psychology, which had previously focused mainly on testing and diagnosis. Like a breath of fresh air to me, that class quickly dispelled any thoughts of my leaving psychology and entering medical school.

In Rogers' class I was truly an overachiever. I recognized that I had found a mentor, although I certainly did not know then that this bright young professor would also become a close personal friend and long-term colleague. Rogers' class brought me another big surprise. Even with the competition of all the "big boys" in the department, I ended up getting one of the top two or three scores on the final examination.

Now, school became intellectually stimulating—for the first time. Carl Rogers offered seminars that were truly group-centered, with each participant choosing his or her own unique project and presenting the findings to the group. He was the group facilitator and consultant. In addition, he was a student, too, learning from other members of the group. Throughout high school and college, I had never experienced such an effective and motivating learning climate. Those graduate seminars made all my previous lecture classes at DePauw seem ridiculously archaic. Within these exciting weekly seminars, the seeds of "nondirective" or client-centered counseling were planted by the participants.

Even experimentally oriented graduate students who had flocked to Rogers' course and seminars began to design studies to evaluate the process and outcomes of counseling. The complex process of counseling both youngsters and adults with personal problems could now be studied and evaluated. For the first time ever, thanks to a few research-oriented graduate students, our counseling interviews were tape-recorded and then transcribed word for word. Graduate students could thus study objectively what went on between counselor and client that either promoted constructive change or inhibited it.

As a first-year graduate student, I was a long way away from starting a doctoral dissertation, but with Rogers as my advisor, I completed a small study that became my master's thesis. Using a large collection of themes written by high school students in their English classes, I set out to determine if the subject matter and/or the writing style of these themes gave clues to the students' psychological and emotional health. I found a number of elements in these themes that clearly differentiated the healthy from the unhealthy students.[4]

Carl and his lovable wife Helen frequently invited certain graduate students to their home for Sunday suppers. On these occasions our conversations were not always about psychological issues. Instead, these were times for students and their hosts to get to know one another. Carl and Helen shared themselves openly, and their two young children, David and Natalie, were always included in the group. I grew to love each member of that family, and as I later learned, I became a very special person to them. For me, Carl and Helen Rogers fulfilled the role of a second set of caring parents, as well as providing a model of what a marital relationship and parenting should be. My friendship with them would continue and even grow deeper in years to come.

In my second year of graduate school, I earned my first salary ($1,500 a year) teaching undergraduates Psychology 101. In addition, I became a Research Assistant collecting data for Dr. Harold Edgerton, who was working to objectify the way the Civil Aeronautics Authority (CAA) pilot training program was evaluating the flying proficiency of civilian pilots. To qualify for this job, I was required to go through the CAA flight training and obtain a private pilot's license.

In my second year of graduate work at Ohio State, I met and fell in love with Martha Ann, a beautiful young woman who would later become my wife. She, too, was an excellent dance partner—a critical requirement for my dates since high school. All in all, graduate school at Ohio State was one of the most enjoyable periods in my life, for it provided intellectual stimulation and a new confidence in my ability to achieve academically. I also made many new male friendships, kept up my tennis, and did a lot of dancing.

One incident stands out more strongly than any other because it completely shattered my previous perception of myself as having only "above average intelligence." Once, I shared this belief with one of the advanced graduate students. He laughed and told me I must be mistaken. Revealing that he had access to the files in the statistics department, he promised to look up my score on the intelligence test given to all students entering graduate school. With disbelief, I learned that I had scored in the ninety-ninth percentile of graduate students throughout the country. Only then did I recall that while taking the entrance test at DePauw, I had left the room for fifteen minutes because I had developed a migraine headache that made me vomit. No wonder I had scored in the sixty-fourth percentile.

The War Years

The draft gave me a very low number, so, having already earned my civilian pilot's license, I applied and was accepted for Army Air Corps training only a few months after Pearl Harbor. In the second of three stages of the training, I was surprised that I began to enjoy flying. Upon completing the third stage of training and earning my wings, I was selected to take further training to become a twin-engine aircraft instructor. This was indeed good news to a young man who was to be married the next day, because it meant Martha Ann and I could be together as long as my assignments continued to be as an instructor in the United States.

My luck prevailed soon after arriving at instructor training head-quarters in Montgomery, Alabama. Instructor training required attending a class called "The Psychology of Instructing," taught by a flight surgeon with no formal training in psychology. During the class I offered so many gratuitous "additions and refinements" based on what I had learned in graduate school, the instructor asked if I would be willing to design and teach the course myself. He disclosed that he had always felt quite inadequate to teach it. This unusual switch was approved by Chuck Warton, the commanding officer of the instructor training school. He later became a close friend.

Looking back, this assignment marked the beginning of my life-long professional work: designing and teaching training pro-grams. I continued teaching this course after transferring to Randolph Field, Texas. There I trained other instructors to teach the course I had designed. Our main purpose was to influence flight instructors to drop the conventional authoritarian "tough guy" role that usually instilled so much fear and tension that students didn't perform well. We wanted to avoid unnecessarily high rates of washouts.

In this job, I had a leadership position for the first time. Heading a group of six fellow officers, I fell into the trap of "taking charge." I set the main goals myself—after all, I thought I was more expert—assigned the tasks, and assumed sole responsibility for evaluating progress. Certainly, I did little to dispel the notion that I was the boss and the group members were my subordinates. To my surprise and puzzlement, within a few months morale was bad, resistance was high, production was low, creativity was nil, and open and honest communication ceased between the group members and me.

I had failed to apply what I had learned from Grace Cox! I created a climate in which my group members didn't feel anything like the students in Grace's Sunday-school class. Fortunately, thanks to the honesty of one of the officers, who was also a close friend, I was able to see the destructive effects of my authoritarian leadership soon enough to make a complete turnaround. I began to invite full participation of group members, listen to their ideas and feelings, and transfer ownership of the project and responsibility for group governance to the group itself. This changed leadership style had startling and enduring effects: creativity flourished, communication opened up, tension decreased, and the work became enjoyable and satisfying to all of us. A sick group became a healthy one, and the project became fun.

My next assignment was to the Office of Flying Safety in Winston-Salem, North Carolina. My job was to find out why so many of the new B-29 bombers were involved in accidents. The accident reports gave the answer: many B-29 pilots seriously lacked technical knowledge about the airplane and its various systems. To help remedy this, I designed an extensive paper-and-pencil objective test which all B-29 pilots and copilots were subsequently required to pass.

During the course of these projects, I became acquainted with many well-known psychologists who were working in the Aviation Psychology Program headed up by Dr. John Flanagan. Later John would offer me my first full-time job—Director of Aviation Research in the American Institute for Research, which he founded soon after the war.

Looking back on those four years in the military, I can see both positive and negative effects on my development as a person and as a psychologist. I again developed new skills, further reinforcing my self-concept of jack of all trades, master of none. I learned to fly complicated military aircraft. My closest friend, Norm Cross, taught me the game of squash; and I became competent enough to become the Randolph Field squash champion. I took up golf and, with help of some instruction from a pro (and *one* memorable lesson from the famous Ben Hogan), I became quite proficient as a golfer. But still no mastery, no excellence!

Martha Ann and I developed many close friendships, some of which endured long after the war. We both had our first experience of becoming friends with people who were *really* wealthy. This was in Winston-Salem, a city that claimed more millionaires per capita than any other U.S. city. Most of them had been early investors in the Reynolds Tobacco Company. Our close friends, however, were Gordon Hanes and his wife, Copey. Gordon was the heir apparent to the Hanes Hosiery Company. He and Copey demonstrated that rich people can be gracious, unpresumptious, and down to earth.

My resolve to go back to graduate school and get my doctorate was seriously tested by two job opportunities: one with Hanes Hosiery, the other in the personnel department of a small and relatively new company known as IBM. I declined in both cases. I was determined to get my doctorate.

Back to Graduate School

I left the service as a captain, feeling more self-confident, more mature, and much less inclined to rebel against authority with self-destructive behaviors. Also I felt thankful that I had not been killed, as I feared I would. This generated a feeling that my life may have been saved for some purpose, perhaps some significant purpose, but one I couldn't yet identify. I would experience this same feeling later in my life.

Because Carl Rogers had just accepted an appointment in the psychology department of the University of Chicago, it was not a difficult decision for me to apply for graduate status there. Carl suggested I consider doing my graduate work in a new interdisciplinary department, the Committee on Human Development, headed by Robert Havighurst.

The interdisciplinary Human Development curriculum consisted of courses in psychology, genetics, physiology, sociology, and anthropology. It opened up areas of knowledge I never would have been exposed to had I chosen the psychology department. I took courses from some very distinguished scholars: Allison Davis and Lloyd Warner in sociology, Robert Redfield in anthropology, Robert Havighurst in child development, and Nathaniel Kleitman, a physiologist noted for his pioneering sleep research.

Chicago gave me my first experience in a cooperative learning group. Four of us graduate students in Human Development decided to help each other learn. We got lists of required reading for various courses and divided them up amongst us. Each reader would take notes and give a copy to the other three. We met two or three times a week for discussion. Sometimes one of us would agree to attend a full course, pass on notes, and/or coach the rest of the group. All this was possible because the University of Chicago did not require graduate students to attend courses. We could demonstrate our knowledge by taking comprehensive examinations, which were called Prelims. If we passed this critical exam, we could go on to write our dissertations.

Later, a faculty member told me the Prelim scores of our cooperative learning group were bunched quite close together, at the top, far above the rest of the scores at that time. Obviously, our foursome felt validated by our decision to work together. This experience, I know now, was the beginning of my strong belief in the superiority of cooperative learning versus the traditional climate of individual competitive learning in our schools.

Soon after the Prelims were behind me, John Flanagan, head of the Aviation Psychology Program in the Air Force, offered me a job as director of aviation research in a new research organization he founded in Pittsburgh. Thinking that doing aviation research with John might turn out to be my road to preeminence, I took the job. Although I was thoroughly enjoying my work at the Counseling Center, counseling at that time had not yet achieved the status of a profession. Very few psychologists had gone into private practice. This reality helped push me in another direction, toward a possible career in aviation psychology.

Things went well for awhile, but it gradually became clear that doing research was not my cup of tea. From John Flanagan, I learned how much I didn't know about research. Meanwhile, the project I directed required numerous trips to Washington, DC for meetings with the Civil Aeronautics Authority and the Aviation Psychology Section of the National Research Council, which had funded the project. At these meetings I made friends with "big boys" renowned in the field of research: Neal Miller, J. P. Guilford, Dick Youtz, Phil Rulon, Neil Warren, Donald Lindsey, Paul Fitts, Morris Viteles. The psychologists in this group were not only "big boys," they were giants in my eyes. Some were already distinguished, others would later receive various APA awards.

Another member of this outstanding group of research-oriented psychologists was Dr. James Miller, whom I admired for completing his Ph.D. and M.D. concurrently at Harvard. A few months later, when he became chairman of the psychology department at the University of Chicago, he surprised me by offering me an assistant professorship.

James Miler had one condition for my joining his department: I would complete my graduate work and earn my doctorate. It was not easy to select a topic, but as luck would have it, John Flanagan convinced me that the research project I had already completed would be acceptable to a doctoral committee. It took no time for me to write the proposal and fly back to Chicago to select members of my committee. They accepted my proposed project, and within a few weeks my research had been typed and submitted to my committee. There it was, a completed dissertation. What luck! Its title was: "The Development of an Objective Method for Evaluating the Flying Proficiency of Airline Pilots." Now to pass the final oral examination by my committee members.

Most of the faculty present saw my dissertation as arcane and intriguing. Their questions were more for the purpose of satisfying their curiosity than for evaluating my research competency. Knowing how tough most oral exams can be, I again felt Lady Luck was with me. Because my report already had been carefully scrutinized and refined by super-researcher John Flanagan before I submitted it to the funding agency, the committee members discovered no flaws.

Shortly afterward, I passed my German language exam and was awarded the Ph.D. degree in 1949. I resigned from the American Institute for Research and returned to the University of Chicago as an assistant professor in the Department of Psychology and a staff member at the Counseling Center. I had eliminated aviation research as the answer to my continuing search for excellence. Would I find it as a faculty member at a prestigious university? I was hopeful.

My Years in Academia

Soon after returning to Chicago, I was invited to the summer program of the National Training Laboratories (NTL) at Bethel, Maine as a research assistant to Dr. Herbert Thelen. Those few weeks that summer were very stimulating. I sat in on what NTL called T-groups, and later conducted interviews with the members of one group. These interviews revealed that the members made some very positive changes, not unlike changes people make in individual therapy, such as losing their shyness, increasing their self-esteem, becoming less hostile toward others, and trusting others more. Although I was critical of the style of leadership I saw at Bethel, I was impressed with the therapeutic potential of these egalitarian learning groups. I decided to organize a leadership training workshop the next summer in Chicago.

That workshop experience motivated me to write my first book, *Group-Centered Leadership: A Way of Releasing the Creative Potential of Groups.*[5] In that book I attempted to construct a model of group leadership quite different from the NTL style. My model was more democratic, more group-centered. I identified the attitudes as well as the specific skills needed by a democratic leader to create a participative, self-directing, self-governing, problem-solving, decision-making group. I also presented some research evidence supporting the amazing therapeutic effects that this democratic style of leadership engenders in individual group members. I was becoming dimly aware of a notion that by now has become a clear conviction: democracy *is* therapy. Put in somewhat different words, the experience of living or working in a democratic relationship with others makes people healthy, while autocratic environments make people unhealthy.

My book sold so few copies the publisher did not do a second printing. Worse yet, the department chair Jim Miller did not think much of it either, and that contributed to his not recommending me for advancement to be an associate professor with lifetime tenure.

Although disappointed, I had come to accept that the academic life was not for me. My five years on the faculty were spent teaching graduate students about individual and group psychotherapy, doing a lot of counseling, and participating heavily in an extensive research study of nondirective counseling, which the Rockefeller Foundation funded. I also had a part-time appointment at the Industrial Relations Center; and I learned how to do play therapy from Virginia Axline, who was writing *Play Therapy,* the book that became a classic in the field.

Although I felt I was a good teacher, I did not find it very rewarding. I was productive as a member of the research team studying the process and outcome of client-centered therapy, but I again faced my limitations as a researcher. Reluctantly, I accepted that teaching and research would not be my life's work—it would not be the end of my search for excellence.

I had a very light teaching load because I was very active working at the Counseling Center, teaching courses on psychotherapy, and conducting the practicum for students wanting to learn client-centered psychotherapy. I also organized a seminar in collaboration with S. I. Hayakawa. I think we named it something like: "Applications of Client-Centered Theory Outside the Clinic." Each participant picked an area where the theory might apply, e.g., teaching, management, legislatures, or law. As a result of the seminar, the group also developed a document with proposals that might help resolve the Cold War with the USSR.

As to my personal life, my marriage with Martha Ann was mutually satisfying. We made a lot of close friends, mostly married couples in the psychology department. What enriched our marriage the most was adopting a ten-day-old baby, whom we named Judy. I had always loved other people's children; now we had a daughter of our own. From her first day in our home, I felt a love for Judy that was deeper than I had ever experienced.

Under Illinois law, we had to wait six months before filing for adoption. A week before the end of the waiting period, our attorney called to say the natural mother had changed her mind. She wanted her baby back. We couldn't believe it. Judy wasn't her baby—she was ours! We were crushed, angry, and scared.

Martha Ann and I agreed we would fight to keep her. We asked our attorney to do anything he could to persuade the mother to change her mind. Fortunately, he was able to find various ways to prolong our custody of Judy, but we always feared the day might come when we would be hauled to court and forced to give her up.

Meanwhile, summer vacations while in Chicago were spent on fishing trips with our close friends, Don and Mary Grummon. I played a lot of tennis with other faculty members and for three straight years won the Faculty Club singles trophy. One of my opponents was Enrico Fermi, who supervised the first splitting of the atom on a squash court at the University of Chicago. During those five busy years, Martha Ann and I also had a very special friendship with Carl and Helen Rogers—dining together, playing bridge, painting, and picnicking. One summer we spent a week with them at their summer home on Seneca Lake in New York.

During my last year on the staff of the Industrial Relations Center, a young industrial manager came to see me. James Richard was searching for someone at the Counseling Center to become a consultant to his company in Davenport, Iowa. I accepted the job and commuted by train once a week to spend a full day consulting. Shortly after I started, Jim was advanced to plant superintendent. In that job he saw an opportunity to democratize the entire plant using my group-centered leadership model. He learned empathic listening and how to conduct productive staff meetings; he fostered heavy employee involvement in decisions. Cooperation increased, morale shot up, and the foremen were happier, worked harder, and were more creative. Productivity increased. I asked Jim to write a chapter for my book *Group-Centered Leadership*, describing exactly how he had democratized his plant. My confidence in my democratic model of leadership had become stronger than ever, and I decided to devote myself full-time to consulting.

As luck would have it, Carl Rogers returned to Chicago from the University of California, where he had been a visiting professor. He had met Dr. Edward Glaser, founder of a successful consulting firm in Pasadena, California. Glaser had asked Carl if he knew of a young man who might be interested in joining his firm, and Carl had given him my name.

Within a few weeks, I was on a plane to Los Angeles to be interviewed by Glaser and four of his associates. They offered me the job and I accepted, greatly elated that I would be doing consulting and living in California, too.

Soon after I returned from that trip, Martha Ann and I were told by our attorney that we now might be required to give Judy back to her natural mother. In a few days, he said, we might get a court order requiring us to deliver the child.

We responded by making a crucial and grave decision, supported by our attorney. We would pack up quickly, get out of town, and drive to California—with Judy, of course. We phoned Ed Glaser, told him we were coming, and asked if I could start the job three months earlier than planned. That was acceptable to him. With our car packed as full as possible, we left at dawn the next day, hoping we would never be contacted by the mother or her attorney. As it turned out, we never were.

My Years in a Consulting Firm

For the next three years, I was a psychological consultant to various organizations. Edward Glaser and Associates (EGA) used a particular formula for starting a relationship with a new client organization, namely, doing psychological evaluations of key executives, beginning with the chief executive. The consultant did an in-depth interview and administered a brief intelligence test and a sentence-completion test. The consultant then wrote an evaluation, usually two or three pages long. The executive received this written evaluation at a feedback conference, during which a counseling relationship was supposed to develop.

It was not long before I began to hate these evaluations. The intelligence test had not been validated, the sentence-completion test was very difficult for me to interpret, and the evaluation report was hard for me to write. I hated feeding back to executives an evaluation that often provoked resistance and defensiveness. I was certain this was not a good way to start a counseling relationship.

Glaser did not allow me to use a different way to start a helping relationship, so I was stuck doing those evaluations. In addition, my democratic model of leadership was an anathema to Glaser. Not only was it not his leadership style; he demanded that I insert in the preface of my book the following: "It should not be inferred that all the ideas presented here are shared by other members of this firm." It became a foregone conclusion that I would leave EGA and start my own consulting practice. What I wanted was the freedom to help managers learn a new leadership model that allowed greater employee involvement.

Despite almost universal resistance to the idea of democratic leadership, I found a few organizational leaders who were willing to give it a try. Today, of course, many business leaders recognize from their experience as subordinates that coercive power, in the long run, is aversive and counterproductive. At that time, however, democratic leadership was a new and untested idea. Thirty years later I would see a growing acceptance of group-centered leadership and widespread recognition that employee participation brings tangible and concrete results, such as decreased costs, improved production methods, better decisions, higher morale, better product quality, and so on.

After three years, I happily left EGA and moved into my new offices only several blocks away. I was greatly relieved. Now I could teach what I believed in.

My Years as a Consultant and Therapist

Concerned about being able to earn enough money just from consulting with organizations, I decided to offer my services as a psychotherapist. I designed my offices to include a play therapy room so that I could also work with very young children.

I soon got numerous referrals for counseling from several physicians, one of whom was Dr. Walter Rogers, Carl's younger brother. I also designed a leadership training course for supervisors and managers, which I taught in the Extension Program of the University of California in Los Angeles. And psychologists on the staff of the UCLA Industrial Relations Center invited me to be one of the trainers at week-long conferences held at Lake Arrowhead. I was surprised, however, to meet some strong opposition to my democratic leadership model from the UCLA group. They stopped inviting me as a trainer, and I assumed it was for that reason.

It became clear that to do leadership training, I would have to set up my own seminars. Together with Dr. Richard Farson, in a partnership called Gordon and Farson Associates, I put on two successful week-long seminars at the beautiful Ojai Valley Inn. We invited Carl Rogers as a presenter at the first seminar. For the second one, we invited the scientist Hans Selye, world renowned for his research on stress. Dick Farson and I did the actual hands-on leadership training, each with his own subgroup.

The outcome of the Ojai Valley seminars brought me pain. My partner formed a friendship with a wealthy participant in the seminar and, without my knowledge, they formed a research institute. This other man donated a large sum of money to get the institute started. I wasn't invited to join. It was the first time I felt betrayed by a friend. (Although I didn't know it then, it turned out to be a blessing in disguise. I would not have been happy in such a research-oriented institute.)

For the next six years (1957 to 1962), I was happy wearing two professional hats: as a psychotherapist in private practice and as a consultant to organizations—businesses, churches, hospitals, and various government agencies. Those years also brought some anguish and sorrow. Both my mother and father died, and Martha Ann and I separated. The breakup of our marriage was traumatic. I felt like a failure. Here I was teaching others how to build satisfying and lasting relationships, yet I couldn't keep my own marriage intact. My strongest feeling was guilt for depriving my daughter Judy of having her father home every night, even though I rarely missed a weekend being with her.

Soon after the separation, I began a new relationship with a young woman, and within a year we were planning our marriage. However, Ann became a professional model, moved to New York, took up with another man, and broke off her relationship with me. Without a doubt, this was the worst loss and rejection I had ever experienced. It took me months before I recovered from this emotional blow. Eventually, I got back to normal after realizing that I had depended strongly on this person's love for making me feel more worthwhile. I had needed her as a major source of my self-esteem.

After four years of living alone but dating a number of women, I married Elaine, a dynamic and outgoing professional woman who worked as an occupational therapist with Goodwill Industries. Soon afterward, we took custody of Judy, after neighbors informed me that Judy was being seriously neglected and emotionally abused in the home environment, and that Martha Ann had a serious drinking problem. Judy remained with Elaine and me during her years in high school, after which she completed four years of college at the University of California at Davis.

It was during the years of consulting and private practice that I became very active in both the American Psychological Association and the California Psychology Association. I served on various committees of both groups and was elected president of the state association. Winning that election was a big surprise. After my failure to be elected president of my fraternity, I had promised myself never again to run for any kind of office. Succumbing to considerable pressure, I accepted nomination for the state office but felt certain I would be defeated. It did not at all fit the self-concept I had then.

The Early PET Years

In the late 1950s, I had begun working with youngsters brought to me by their parents or referred by schools. Both parents and teachers labeled these children "emotionally disturbed," "neurotic," "maladjusted," or "predelinquent." As such, these kids were seen as needing counseling and psychotherapy—some form of "treatment" for their "sickness."

I was unprepared for my discovery that these youngsters seemed normal and healthy—not emotionally disturbed. In fact, most of them were certain it was their parents or teachers who had the problems and needed my counseling. These children talked openly about their family squabbles and conflicts, and they described incidents in which they felt unfairly treated. They complained that their parents and teachers seldom listened to them or understood them. They told about being unfairly punished. And they described incidents in which their parents or teachers had shown no respect for their needs. These children felt controlled by autocratic adults who demanded obedience. They felt they were treated like second-class citizens.

The youngsters also shared with me how they reacted with various behaviors to cope with parental authority. They made a long list: lying, negativism, tattling, aggression, cheating, disruptive behaviors at home and in school, truancy, disobedience, poor performance at school, sexual promiscuity, bullying other children, drinking, using drugs, excessive shyness, overconforming, compulsive eating, depression, illness, and even suicidal thoughts.

In my later conferences with the parents, they, too, did not see themselves as needing therapy or treatment. In fact, most of them appeared to be functioning quite effectively in their lives. There I was, trained to provide therapy to "neurotic" people, yet neither the children nor their parents wanted therapy or seemed to need it.

It was a sudden transformation in my thinking when I realized that these parent–child difficulties were *human relations* problems rather than problems of psychopathology. Clearly these families were simply having difficulty living with each other in harmony. Few had any of the essential human relations skills: ways to communicate openly and honestly, to listen, to resolve conflicts amicably, to establish rules and standards in the home, to show respect for each other's needs, or to make their relationships seem equitable and fair to both parent and child.

I will always remember the night I shared with Elaine my strong dissatisfaction with doing therapy. I knew I wasn't doing what I was "meant to do." After a lot of tears—and laughter, too—I came out of that discussion convinced I wanted to do something that would prevent these destructive and reactive behaviors of children.

Within a few weeks, I came up with an idea that would radically change my life. The idea seemed so "right" and promising that I decided to share it with no one except my wife. I was afraid someone else would beat me to it. The big idea was to design and market a leadership training program for *parents.* After all, the parent–child relationship, as I saw it, was almost identical to the boss–subordinate relationship. Drawing on my experience teaching and refining my leadership program, I had no trouble putting together a course for parents.

Quite deliberately, I designed the course to be completely different from the medical, or treatment, model with its own distinctive language (therapy, doctor, patient, treatment, fees). Instead, I wanted parents to see the program as an *educational* experience. I used the language of education (course, training, students, instructor, textbook, homework, tuition), and I carefully chose a name to fit this educational model: Parent Effectiveness Training.

It was important to me that the course also attract parents who as yet were not experiencing serious problems in their family relationships. I hoped PET would be seen as a preventive program. This is exactly what happened. Many parents enrolled in PET who had not yet experienced problems. Over time, PET dramatically changed my professional role from therapist to educator, from a treatment specialist to a prevention specialist.

PET immediately attracted media interest. The idea that "parents go to school" was very newsworthy. I had to turn away applicants because I had set a limit of thirty participants per class. Soon, other psychologists wanted me to train and authorize them to teach PET in their own communities in the greater Los Angeles area. I began conducting Instructor Training Workshops, and these instructors started classes in Los Angeles County, Orange County, and San Diego County. Then colleagues of mine in the San Francisco area also wanted to be trained to teach the course.

I put on a symposium at the annual convention of the American Psychological Association, which brought even more instructor candidates. Soon we were running ads in the professional journals of social workers, school psychologists, school counselors, nursery school directors, and pastors—ads that announced our Instructor Training Workshops in cities throughout the country. Many of our new instructors were asked to be interviewed by reporters for feature articles of newspapers in their own communities. Within a period of four years, PET was being taught throughout California and in key cities in Oregon, Minnesota, Arizona, Washington, Hawaii, and Ohio.

Early in 1969, a New York publisher phoned to ask if he could fly out to California to talk to me about writing a book. His wife had told him about PET. The outcome of that visit was a signed contract to produce a manuscript for publication by Peter H. Wyden, Inc. With no experience writing for a lay audience, I needed a lot of editing from Peter to lighten up my stiff academic prose. Nevertheless, I met the deadline, and the book was in bookstores early in 1970.[6] I received invitations to be on many well-known as well as local TV and radio talk shows. I was constantly asked to give lectures all over the United States.

Such wide publicity greatly increased the number of parents in our classes, as well as the number of applicants for our Instructor Training Workshops, which reached a peak of nearly fifty workshops a year. By 1975, there were PET instructors in every state. By this time I had incorporated as Effectiveness Training, Inc. (ETI) and had a staff of nine or ten employees. ETI sold certified instructors the Participant Packs that contained a workbook and the PET book. Instructors taught from a detailed Instructor Guide, which they were urged to follow fairly closely. Instructors were free to set their own tuition for their PET classes.

By 1974, the foreign rights to my book had been bought by publishers in Canada, Germany, France, Sweden, Norway, Finland, and Denmark. This brought requests to train PET instructors in these countries. Without exception, my visits to these countries were very rewarding in many ways. I made a lot of friendships, some of which have lasted for many years; and I was accorded a degree of professional recognition, approval, and renown that I had never dreamed possible. I no longer felt like a "second-class Pasadena psychologist," as I had once called myself.

As PET spread, I stopped my work as a therapist and most of my consulting with organizations. I did retain my twelve-year consulting relationship with Forest Lawn Memorial Park for practical and sentimental reasons. Its president, Fred Llewelyn, had become a close friend and a staunch supporter of my work. It was with this organization that I had tested and sharpened my model of democratic leadership, developed new procedures for fostering employee involvement, taught all managers the leadership skills, designed a radically new replacement for the conventional performance review procedure that is universally disliked by both managers and those they have to evaluate, and designed new methodologies for sales training. Most of these innovative procedures were inserted into a new course we called Leader Effectiveness Training (LET).

We began seriously marketing LET in the mid 1970s. Our list of organizations using LET has now reached several hundred and includes such well-known companies as Coca-Cola, Honeywell, General Dynamics, Chrysler, Blue Cross–Blue Shield, Mercke, Toyota, Subaru, IBM, and Jockey. We also teach LET in Australia, Germany, Switzerland, Canada, and Ireland.

Not long after the PET course was introduced in the San Francisco Bay Area, several school districts there wanted a similar training program for their teachers. As a result we designed Teacher Effectiveness Training (TET) and trained and authorized instructors to conduct it. In 1974 I asked Noel Burch, a PET instructor who had been a school principal, to collaborate with me in writing a textbook for the TET course.[7] It, too, was published by Peter Wyden, who by this time had become a close friend. That book earned Book-of-the-Month main selection. And like the *PET* book, *TET* was soon published in many foreign countries.

Although the early 1970s were a period of growth and many successes for ETI, my personal life went through very troublesome and tormenting times. My marriage to Elaine was deteriorating, and I began experiencing inadequate blood circulation in my legs. I underwent surgery to implant a dacron tube in my main leg artery.

After separating and returning to my marriage twice, I bit the bullet and asked for a divorce. Although Elaine and I had failed to make our marriage last, our subsequent relationship has been a friendly one. She moved to the Bay Area and became director of the Goodwill Industries of San Francisco.

The Solana Beach Years

For years I had wanted to move south to the San Diego area, and now that I had ended both my private practice and the consulting work, I was economically free to move away from the smog and congestion of the Los Angeles area. But how was I going to influence the ETI staff to move south with me? It took a year for us to make the decision and implement the move, and we only lost a few of our secretarial staff in the process.

It was far more difficult, meanwhile, to influence Linda Adams, my new girlfriend, with whom I had developed a close relationship. The eventual solution was that I'd buy a vacation home in the San Diego area for us to use on weekends, and we'd decide later if we liked the area. Fortunately, we found a house right on the bluffs above the ocean and spent most of our weekends there. Those delightful experiences helped influence Linda to accept the permanent move. We bought an old building in Solana Beach, converted it to offices, and in the spring of 1975 our company and staff moved south to start a new life in a new community.

And what an enjoyable new life it was for me. Linda's and my relationship matured and deepened. We grew more adept at problem-solving and no-lose conflict-resolution, and we found many mutually satisfying things to do together: playing bridge with friends, playing tennis, and traveling. I also found my second experience as a parent very gratifying. Over the years, Linda's daughter Michelle and I became the closest of friends, with a special kind of love for each other and a mutual appreciation of what is humorous in life. Without a doubt, the PET skills were of critical importance in enriching our relationship. Linda and I eventually decided to legally and publicly affirm our relationship as a family, ending our years of just living together. In 1976, we were married, enabling me to adopt Michelle.

Meanwhile, after Judy had graduated from the University of California at Davis, she married John Sands, a personnel director. Not long after we moved south, Judy and John took up residence nearby. When she gave birth to Erin, a daughter, I became a new grandfather as well as a new father.

Judy also went on to join ETI and coauthored *PET in Action*.[8] Linda, too, spent time there developing a course to help women take charge of their lives and learn how to get their needs met assertively without depriving others from meeting their needs. This course became Effectiveness Training for Women, and many of our PET instructors began offering it.

In the next few years, ETI reached a peak of thirty-five employees and 11,000 square feet of space. We designed a new course for young people, called Youth Effectiveness Training. We also hired Sidney Wool (our representative in St. Louis) to move to Solana Beach, where he could devote himself to marketing Leadership Effectiveness Training full-time. We developed a course for salespeople, called SalesTech, later revised and named Synergistic Selling. We also developed a course for the clergy and another for school administrators. I wrote a new book, *Leader Effectiveness Training*, which became the textbook for the LET course and was selected by four book clubs.[9]

The *PET* book by now was a runaway best seller, with hardback sales of 600,000. It eventually was published in all the Western European countries and in Iceland, Mexico, South Africa, Japan, South Korea, Taiwan, Indonesia, Hungary, Poland, Madagascar, New Zealand, Australia, India, Taiwan, Pakistan, Trinidad, and Canada. Total sales of the *PET* book by 1993 reached over three million copies.

The *TET* book, coauthored by Noel Burch, was adopted in many universities and was published in over a dozen countries. Ken Miller, who for several years was on the ETI staff in Solana Beach, moved to Florida and found a way to market this course directly to teachers, giving them graduate credit. After a few years, his organization earned the exclusive right to market TET in all of the states (except Illinois). Eventually TET was being offered in fourteen states.

My role at ETI gradually became more of a course developer and author. Linda took over the administrative functions and became the chief executive officer. Michelle graduated from Humboldt University and began working at ETI, although she ultimately found work in the TV and video industry.

Linda and I continue to be invited to foreign countries to promote our courses by giving speeches and making radio and TV appearances. This has given us the opportunity both to travel a great deal and to develop friendships with our foreign instructors and representatives. We will always remember our trips to Iceland, Bermuda, Ireland, the Netherlands, France, Germany, Sweden, Finland, Switzerland, Taiwan, Japan, and Australia. Most recently, we attended a conference in Hungary of all our European representatives. We now have trained 150 new instructors in Hungary. Other countries where we have most recently introduced our courses are Greece, Italy, South Korea, and Indonesia.

In 1989 my latest book was published. The hardback title was *Teaching Children Self-Discipline;*[10] the paperback title was *Discipline that Works: Promoting Self-Discipline in Children.*[11] I had decided to write it after reading a dozen or so books that had strongly advocated the use of discipline and punishment in child rearing. I call these the "dare to discipline" or "power to the parent" books.

The most difficult to write of all my books, this project took me four years. It involved reviewing all the research studies that had evaluated the effects of different parenting styles, i.e., authoritarian, permissive, and democratic. I also sought research evidence of the effects of rewards and punitive discipline.

The first half of my latest book evaluates the reward-and-punishment approach to discipline. Abundant research evidence confirms that punitive discipline not only is a poor deterrent, but has severe damaging effects on children. The second half of the book presents alternatives to punitive discipline: methods that foster self-discipline and promote the well-being of children. The book makes a strong argument that our society is employing the wrong strategies to reduce the self-destructive and socially unacceptable behaviors of young people. Hope for preventing alcohol and drug abuse, delinquency, dropping out of school, and gang violence lies in using a preventive strategy, as opposed to treating kids after they have been damaged.

Our Worldwide Training for Peaceful Conflict Resolution

ETI's most recent project was an attempt to make some kind of contribution to furthering world peace. Familiar with Carl Rogers' peace-making efforts in various hot spots throughout the world, I began to think seriously about what I, too, might do to hasten peace on our planet. All our courses had proven that our No-Lose Conflict Resolution method is both teachable and learnable. I decided to design a one-day conflict-resolution training and to offer it free of charge as our special contribution to world peace. I shared this idea with our instructors throughout the world, asking if they would volunteer to publicize and teach the training. We decided to pick one day when the training would be done all over the world.

On April 28, 1990 training started in Sydney, Australia at 8:30 a.m. One hour later into the next time zone, classes began in South Korea and in Japan, where instructors taught in 130 different communities. Singapore an hour later, then Madagascar, Estonia, Finland, Hungary, Switzerland, France, Belgium, the Netherlands, and Ireland. Nineteen classes started in South Africa. Across the Atlantic rolled our globe-circling wave of peacemaking, into Iceland, Bermuda, Canada, the West Indies, Mexico, and the United States. The wave ended its day-long journey at a class in Hawaii, twenty hours after it had begun in Sydney. Twenty-one countries and 15,000 participants, all in one twenty-four-hour period!

Who knows what ripples of peacemaking will emanate from this event? In Europe, the one-day training already has spawned an exciting project conceived by two of our foreign representatives. It is called "Youth for Peace." Every year this organization will offer a two-week camping and educational course for young people from any European country. Young people are taught the No-Lose Conflict-Resolution method, our communication skills, how to run a meeting democratically, and how to speak clearly in public. The first training, held in the summer of 1991, attracted youth from seven European countries.

Epilogue

Although in 1994 I became seventy-six years "old," I am very active here at Effectiveness Training, perhaps busier and more challenged than I have ever been. I am involved in a number of important projects. First, I have coauthored a book with the renowned surgeon Dr. W. Sterling Edwards, formerly chief of surgery at the University of New Mexico Medical School. The objective of our book is to teach health professionals (physicians, nurses, physical therapists, medical social workers, hospice workers and others) our proven system of interpersonal and conflict resolution skills to help them build better relationships with patients. Next will come a training program for health professionals. I have also coauthored a book with Carl Zaiss, a skillful instructor of ETI's Synergistic Selling and Synergistic Customer Relations courses. It became the textbook for both of these courses and will carry the title of *Sales Effectiveness Training*.[12]

A major portion of my time for over a year has been devoted to the development of a video PET self-instruction course, which will enable us to reach parents in communities where we do not have active instructors. I am also developing some activities that our foreign representatives and ETI might do in 1994, the year designated by the United Nations as The Year of the Family. Linda has designed a course for training high school students to be mediators of student–student conflicts.

I have no intentions of stopping my work, because I enjoy it too much. There is more that must be done to improve human relationships in the world, and I am grateful that I will be leaving a group of several thousand instructors who can carry on the work I've started and even find new ways to expand and improve on it. I always leaned toward wanting partners—now I have thousands of them!

I have been proud to hear from some of my professional colleagues that I was the "father of parent training in the United States." PET is now taught in thirty-seven foreign countries, in which a quarter of a million parents have been trained (thus adding to the million trained in the United States). Having experienced disappointment that my first book, *Group-Centered Leadership,* reached so few readers, it is hard for me to believe that three and one-half million *PET* books have been printed.

In the 1960s I experienced a lot of frustration trying to find organizations open to the idea of participative management and "democracy in the workplace." Today the director of our LET program can list several hundred well-known organizations in which we have taught our model of leadership. Active listening, I-messages, communication roadblocks, problem ownership, and no-lose conflict resolution are now taught in most other interpersonal skill training programs—for parents, teachers, managers, couples, mediators, physicians,nurses, and counselors. And throughout the world my books have sold over five million copies. Another source of personal satisfaction is that over sixty research studies have evaluated the outcomes of both PET and TET.

How did all this happen? Several factors contributed. PET and LET were the right courses for the right time—parents were afraid their kids would become hippies or drug users; U.S. industries were threatened by superior products from Japanese companies that had adopted a more democratic, participative style of leadership. Secondly, PET was a preventive program—"training before trouble"— that any parent could attend.

The third factor, I am now convinced, had the strongest effect. It was Carl who introduced a more participative and easier-to-learn kind of psychotherapy. This opened the door for psychologists to become psychotherapists and attracted the attention of a variety of professional groups: social workers, personnel counselors, school counselors, marriage and family therapists, nurses, and others.

While I fell into the group of psychologists who became therapists in private practice or in various agencies, I became more interested in *applying* the principles of client-centered therapy to other relationships. It's clear now that this interest added some new components to Carl's basic concepts.

I first converted Carl's rather abstract conditions for change (congruence, acceptance, and empathic understanding) into concrete and operational behavioral skills that were more easily teachable. Then I added another procedure because, unlike therapist–client relationships, ordinary person-to-person relationships almost always generate conflicts. So, I added a six-step procedure for resolving conflicts amicably, calling it the no-lose conflict resolution method.

Finally, because parents were getting "fired" by their teenagers for trying to coerce them to change their values, I devised a system for parents to be "effective consultants" when they collided with their children over values.

It was these teachable and effective skills and procedures that made our courses so helpful to parents, teachers, and managers. Converting the abstract concepts of client-centered therapy into specific skills and procedures contributed heavily to the effectiveness of our courses and ultimately to their rapid proliferation here and abroad. Also, I cannot help but hypothesize that Carl's unswerving conviction that people can learn how to build and maintain good relationships only through therapy or "basic encounter groups," as opposed to skill training, significantly limited the spread of the person-centered approach into the mainstream of human relations training.

Carl's momentous contribution, of course, was to identify the necessary conditions for the psychological health of persons and relationships. This is why I feel indebted to Carl and grateful for the opportunity to build on his work and disseminate it more widely.

Even more important to me, my relationship with this great man enabled me to discover what I had been looking for most of my life. I found a professional activity that brought me self-actualization, self-esteem, and a feeling of competence. And, not surprising, all those "big boys" don't seem so big anymore.

References

[1] "Group-centered Leadership and Administration," chapter 8 in C. R. Rogers, *Client-Centered Therapy: Its Practice, Implications and Theory.* Boston: Houghton-Mifflin, 1951.

[2] "The Effect of Psychotherapy upon Certain Attitudes Towards Others," (chapter 11) and "Developing a Program of Research in Psychotherapy," (chapter 2) in C. R. Rogers and R. F. Dymond, *Psychotherapy and Personality Change.* Chicago: University of Chicago Press, 1954.

[3] C. R. Rogers, *Freedom To Learn for the '80s.* Columbus, OH: Charles Merrill, 1983; p. 219.

[4] "A Psychological Study of Creative Writing." Ohio State University: unpublished master's thesis, 1940.

[5] *Group-Centered Leadership: A Way of Releasing the Creative Potential of Groups.* Boston: Houghton-Mifflin, 1955.

[6] *Parent Effectiveness Training.* New York: Peter H. Wyden, Inc., 1970.

[7] *Teacher Effectiveness Training.* New York: Peter H. Wyden, Inc., 1974.

[8] *PET in Action.* New York: Putnam, 1976.

[9] *Leader Effectiveness Training.* New York: Peter H. Wyden, Inc., 1978.

[10] *Teaching Children Self-Discipline.* New York: Times Books, 1989.

[11] *Discipline That Works: Promoting Self-Discipline in Children.* New York: Penguin Books, 1991.

[12] *Sales Effectiveness Training.* New York: Penguin Books, 1993.

❖

John Vasconcellos was one of the first contributors I thought of when I conceived of this book. His life and his work show how Carl Rogers' theories and work extend to realms other than psychotherapy. In John's case, the realm is politics.

Both John and the late Senator Wayne Morris of Oregon remind me that the phrase "I don't like politicians" does not fit for me. John is one of the persons who has inspired me, and in 1984, while serving as the president of the University Without Walls, I had the privilege of presenting him with an honorary doctorate.

He has a motto: "Toward a healthier state." His brainchild, the California Task Force to Promote Self-Esteem (which Diane Dreher describes in this chapter) is just one example of how John applies his own experiences and beliefs to committed political action. I have watched him at work in the California Assembly, sat in with him at legislative committee meetings, and spoken with other elected officials who have seen him as a model. John is a true warrior, fighting for causes that will improve the state of the union as well as the state of California.

❖

8

Toward a Person-Centered Politics: John Vasconcellos

by Diane Dreher

California Assemblyman John Vasconcellos called Carl Rogers "the pioneer of trust."[1] He considered Carl his mentor, friend, partner, almost a second father. John's life was changed dramatically by Carl's message of unconditional positive regard. He experienced Rogerian therapy in his early thirties and knew Carl personally for seventeen years.

An elegantly trained professional and a liberal politician of the classic New Deal variety, John found in Carl's ideas a way to link his personal journey to his deepest political values. Throughout his political career, John was to test the proposition that a serious progressive agenda—one attentive to the needs of those most in need—could be informed by a psychology, or a psychological orientation.

John discovered humanistic psychology at the beginning of his political career. Like two leitmotifs, psychology and politics have become joined in his philosophy of life, leading him to a new vision of himself, of what it means to be a person, and of government's moral responsibility to facilitate our fullest development as human beings.

In 1966, the year John became a candidate for the California State Assembly, he found himself and his identity "coming utterly apart" and sought help from a therapist who had been one of Carl's early students. Therapy helped John through a time of pain and confusion. He began to trust himself and others, setting off on a personal and political odyssey to demonstrate "that we human beings are innately inclined toward becoming constructive, life-affirming, responsible, and trustworthy."[2]

John met Carl in January 1970 at a "Freedom To Learn" workshop in Berkeley. Carl's influence has informed John's twenty-seven years of work on the Assembly Education and Higher Education Committees and led to his much-publicized Task Force to Promote Self-Esteem, and Personal and Social Responsibility. His approach to politics became grounded in the humanistic belief in our innate capacity to learn, grow, and take responsibility for our lives.

John has called Carl's approach "ultimately political in nature," providing "a totally new, faithful, and hopeful basis for public-policy decision-making." Carl's book *On Becoming a Person* became a means for John to assess his own personal and political growth; his Sonoma State graduation speech, "the Person of Tomorrow," sustained John's growing sense of self; and his paper "Growing Older . . . or Older and Still Growing" provided John with a "wonderful and hopeful sense of how I'd like to be for the rest of my life."[3]

Over the years, John and Carl became partners in a new affirmative politics of the human spirit. John was surprised, even shocked, when he first received a campaign contribution check from Carl. Never—before or since—had he felt so proud upon receiving a contribution.

John often visited Carl in La Jolla. Together they would discuss ideas and plan projects. They shared a deep personal commitment to progressive politics and world peace, as well as a friendship that enriched both their lives. Carl offered John personal support after his heart attack and bypass surgery in 1984, taking him to dinner at his favorite seafood restaurant in La Jolla, then inviting him back to his house. He listened empathetically to John's admission of loneliness and depression. At other times, John listened to Carl's concerns about continuing to contribute something meaningful to the world despite his advancing age and failing eyesight.

John and Carl met and talked frequently over the years. The story of their friendship unfolds in greater detail throughout this chapter. However, for these two pioneers in politics and psychology, one vital aspect of their partnership was acknowledging and encouraging one another. In 1985 John helped set up the Humanistic Psychology Archives at the University of California, Santa Barbara. Rollo May, Stanley Keleman, George Brown, Tom Greening, and John decided to do oral histories of the ten living pioneers in humanistic psychology, beginning with Carl. This led to several meetings with the university's oral historian, David Russell, for a ten-hour videotape series on Carl's life and work.

John still treasures a letter he received from Carl in 1986, which complimented him on "embodying and modeling in politics his person-centered vision of our human condition." In December 1986, at Carl's last public event, to honor his eighty-fifth birthday, John presented him with a plaque from the California State Assembly, commending him for a lifetime of peace work.

The day Carl died, a letter arrived at the Center for Studies of the Person nominating him for the 1987 Nobel Peace Prize. John had been instrumental in initiating that nomination for his friend, mentor, and colleague.

John's Early Years

John Vasconcellos was born on May 11, 1932 at O'Connor Hospital in San Jose, California, the first child of John and Teresa Jacobs Vasconcellos. His mother was the daughter of German immigrants. His father, whose family was Portuguese, had come to California at nineteen from Maui, Hawaii.

John's mother smothered her first son with attention. His next brother died at birth. Another brother, Jim, who became an engineer, was born five years later. Their sister Margaret, now a school administrator, is ten years younger than John.

The family lived in Irvington (now part of Fremont), California, then Hayward. They moved to Crockett in Contra Costa County when John was eight, and later to nearby Rodeo when he was twelve. John's father, whom he calls a "very dutiful, self-abnegating Catholic man,"[4] was a math teacher, school principal, and superintendent. John, always bright and inquisitive, became a model student. His traditional Catholic family gave him a strong ethic of helping others, of service to the community. His father, particularly, emphasized this lesson through various homilies as well in his own commitment to service.

John's political career began in the eighth grade when he ran for class president and lost by one vote—his own. "I was a good Catholic self-abnegating boy," he says.

His strong-willed mother was always very protective. John never had a bike or skates as a kid—she was afraid he'd hurt himself.

He was totally unathletic, "a good Catholic boy: no body, no feelings." Awkward and painfully self-conscious, he never bonded with boys his own age through the usual games or sports. He never learned to swim well because he internalized his mother's protectiveness. He couldn't bring himself to jump off the diving board. The fact that he was left-handed only increased his feelings of not fitting in. Instead, he concentrated on pleasing Teresa, "becoming her proof that she was a good mother." Now, after years of therapy and bodywork, John enjoys playing racquetball and beats people twenty or thirty years younger than himself.

But as a youngster, John buried himself in his books and spent lots of time alone. His math skills were phenomenal, and he invented ways to practice them: tallying up baseball box scores, keeping records of hit songs on the radio, playing with numbers and statistics. In his current job as chair of the Assembly Ways and Means Committee, he still does math in his head and amazes colleagues with his speed and accuracy.

John's father stressed formality and self-control. "We never get angry," he told his children. His mother told them "not to use the pronoun I. It's so egotistical." So John grew up "utterly contained," out of touch with his body, and unable to express his individuality or his anger.

High School and College

John's father shipped him off at fourteen to Bellarmine Preparatory, a Catholic boarding school, to break John's strong attachment to his mother. "It was like being expelled from home," says John, who resented his dad for years.

At Bellarmine, John did very well academically, always first or second on the honor roll. But he had no self-esteem at all, still looking to others for how he should be. He was so shy that when he ran for class office, he choked up in front of the other students and could only stutter, "V-v-o-o-t-e f-f-f-o-o-r m-m-e."

From Bellarmine, John went to Santa Clara University, another private Jesuit school. It was, he says, "a safe place." Friends and family had gone there. During his four years of college, he earned top grades but changed his major every six months or so ("I had no idea what I wanted to do"). He finally earned a degree in history.

Always questioning, searching, John spent lots of time in long talks with his closest friends discussing the nature of social commitment, the routes for Catholic action, and the ethics of that action. His strong sense of duty only increased his concern. He asked himself: what was he to do with the many talents he'd been given? How could he serve his community? What was his mission, his vocation in life?

John's external accomplishments masked the fact that he was still painfully shy. He became freshman class vice-president, sophomore class president, and then student body secretary. In his senior year, he became student body president, valedictorian, and Nobili medalist for the outstanding graduate—the only Santa Clara student ever to win all three positions.

Still, he admits, "I didn't know what it was to feel about myself." He still recalls his roommate telling him, "You don't know what it is to feel." John says he was "dutiful rather than responsible, intellectual rather than whole."

Political Beginnings

The year John graduated from Santa Clara, his dorm counselor Steve Early, a New York Jesuit, called him into his room to discuss John's future. "You should go into politics," he said. "You've been a very good student body president. Pat Brown should know about you." Relieved that Steve had not asked him to join the Jesuits, John simply shrugged his shoulders in disbelief.

Steve kept telling John that he was a "hot prospect" with a political future, and he used his collar to get him an appointment with California Governor Pat Brown, who had been raised Catholic. John's half-hour interview with Brown was uneventful. They talked about the fact that John had once dated Brown's daughter Cynthia, and Brown said he'd give him a job some day. After graduation, John spent two years in the Army to fulfill his ROTC duty, then returned to Santa Clara for law school. The same conversation with the governor happened three times. The last time, Brown called him "Jim," his brother's name, and John "didn't have the sense of self to correct him." Brown encouraged John to attend the 1960 Democratic convention in Los Angeles.

While John dutifully watched the convention, Brown decided to go to a nearby Catholic church, where, by utter coincidence, Steve

Early was saying mass. Afterward he asked Pat Brown, "When are you going to give John a job?"

By then John was practicing law in San Jose with former mayor Al Ruffo, whom John calls "a grand man" and another "second father." The Monday after the convention, Ruffo came into his office bittersweet, telling John, "The governor wants you to go to work for him, and I don't want to lose you." Torn between competing duties, John took a week to decide, then spent a year on Brown's staff. His work included helping on the John F. Kennedy presidential campaign. He returned to practice law for five more years, but by then everyone realized politics was John's destined career.

He and his buddy Rob Miller made a deal: to run each other's campaigns. Under John's campaign management, Rob became vice-mayor of San Jose. Soon after, longtime Democratic Assemblymember Al Alquist decided to run for the State Senate, leaving his district seat open. John thought about running. Then one Sunday morning he got a call from Rob Miller, who asked, "What are you doing today?"

"Going to the beach," answered John.

"I've got twenty of your friends here to plan your campaign. Get your ass over here," his friend insisted.

John went, as much from a sense of duty to his friends as anything else. He won the election in 1966 and has been in the Assembly ever since.

In the 1960s, when many people believed political dreams could make a difference, John and fifteen other young men formed the La Mancha Fund, named after the musical *Man of La Mancha.* Its goal was to promote positive change: to address the problems of hunger, poverty, farm workers' rights, and social injustice. In 1966 John and eight other La Mancha members joined Cesar Chavez on his historic Good Friday march from Delano to the state capitol. La Mancha was an early example of John's personal commitment to building a better world, to helping those most in need. The times have changed, but commitment to social justice remains an important part of John's political philosophy.

Personal Crisis and the Quest for Wholeness

In 1967 the Sacramento Press Corps voted John "the best freshman member of the Assembly." But beneath all the apparent success, John, like the nation around him, was coming apart at the seams. The old values and traditions did not make sense any more to a generation of young Americans who rebelled against the status quo and began the agonizing, exhilarating search for new alternatives.

"As I approached the end of my twenties and early thirties, I grew more aware of my alienation from the church, from myself, from life," John recalls. Finally, in 1966 he "hit rock bottom," and went to Tenny Wright, a priest he'd known at Santa Clara. Wright referred him to Leo Rock, a Jesuit trained in Rogerian therapy. John was determined to learn who he was beneath this hard-working, "high-achieving, people-pleasing robot."

With patience and understanding, Leo listened. He accepted John unconditionally, not for what he did but for who he was as a person, encouraging him to release the layers of fear and guilt that were holding him inside. Discarding the "self-abnegating Catholic boy" of the past, John discovered years of repressed feelings. To get more in touch with himself, he went to scores of psychological workshops and seminars. In 1969 John went to workshops with Dick Farson, Sidney Jourard, Abraham Maslow, Jim and Liz Bugenthal, Jim Fadiman, Rollo May, and John Heider, followed by a weekend with Carl Rogers in January 1970. "It was a stunning year," he recalls.

John's transformation amazed the Legislature. He had come to Sacramento with dark, conservative suits, narrow ties, a crew cut, and a tightly wound, controlled personality. Suddenly here was this person who refused to wear a coat and tie, wrote poetry about his feelings, stopped capitalizing letters, and raced off to bioenergetic sessions in Berkeley. His new energies exploded in outbursts of rage against political sellouts, and his hair burst forth in a mass of dark curls.

With his open shirts, long hair, and colorful personality, he didn't fit people's idea of what a politician should look like. John tells one story about a southern California judge who wrote him, wondering if his state car had been stolen because he had seen it driven on the San Bernardino Freeway by a "swarthy young man." John wrote the judge, thanking him for his concern, explaining that "I am a swarthy young man." Seeking to learn as much as he could about himself and his society, he spent a weekend in Watts with black Assemblyman Leon Ralph, volunteered as a teacher's aide in a high school remedial reading class, and filled his capitol office with books on humanistic psychology, politics, and philosophy until it resembled the home of a writer or graduate student.

Leo Rock says that "John is one of the most intelligent men I've ever met. [The change was] letting his heart into his life. He started to pay attention to his heart, to understand how much our feelings tell us about who we are."[5] Looking within helped this shy, brilliant, achievement-oriented young man turn his whole world around.

In an intense struggle to recreate himself, John battled his way out in 1966 and the years that followed. He emerged from the layers of repression much as Michelangelo's unfinished statues seem to fight their way out of the walls of stone that contain them. The walls that held John in were the traditional Christian definition of human nature as sinful, guilty, imperfect, and untrustworthy. In a recent poem, "The Dawning," he wrote:

> old ways of being
> which lock us inside
> leave us all crippled
> without inner guide.

Looking back at his childhood in a home where anger was not allowed, John came up with years of resentment and rage at his parents. For a time, he cut himself off from them to process it all. Then, attempting to begin a new, more personal relationship with his father, he started calling him by his first name, John, rejecting the title Dad. "He was very hurt by that," John recalls.

In an attempt to go deeper, John began doing bodywork in 1971 with Stanley Keleman, a bioenergeticist in Berkeley. Several years later, Keleman warned John that he had so much rage inside that if Keleman opened him up, John might lose control and destroy his political career. Although politics had become John's life, his answer was, "I have no choice. Let's go on." Today he says, "My pain was so great that I couldn't afford not to go after whatever it was."

And so he exploded in rage on the Assembly floor and was assigned two monitors to help him through it all. He became known as the "touchy-feely legislator"—an unusual reputation—and in 1972 invited a number of powerful colleagues (including Willie Brown, Bob Moretti, and Leona Egeland) to soak with him in a hot tub at Esalen.

In his quest to become a healthy human being, John sought out alternative parents to support him in his alternative vision of human nature. One of the most significant was Carl Rogers. According to John's friend Mitch Saunders, Carl "opened the prison of the old world view" and "evoked in John the recognition that human beings are inherently trustworthy and inclined to be positive and helpful."[6] It was a liberating release for him.

In the late 1960s, John's lived experience and progressive politics had been at odds with his old emotional baggage about human depravity and original sin. Carl held out a life-affirming vision of human nature which John terms *original grace*. "Neither money nor human nature is the root of all evil," John says in his book, *A Liberating Vision*. "The root of all evil is our belief that we're evil, and our resultant efforts which serve to make us so."[7] In his personal and political development, John has progressively emphasized our original grace as human beings, overcoming the old vision of sin and guilt with all of its concomitant cycles of fear, insecurity, and fragmentation that divide us from ourselves and one another.

By the time John met Carl in 1970, he had been through four years of Rogerian therapy, literature, and workshops. Once he met Carl, he went even further. According to Mitch, "he met a real human being who was embodying the very things he himself was attracted to embodying."

Leo Rock recalls his own first meeting with Carl, who introduced himself graciously and simply: "Hello, I'm Carl." Rogers listened attentively, his eyes warm and luminous. "John relates the same way," says Leo—surrounding the other person with the glow of unconditional positive regard. His battle to accept himself has enabled him to more readily accept others.

John sought out leaders in the human potential movement—Sidney Jourard, Carl Rogers, Abraham Maslow, Rollo May, Virginia Satir—and found in them kindred spirits who moved human beings beyond limited definitions of themselves into new, more positive directions. He read their books, attended their workshops, and engaged them in conversation. With these new friends John enjoyed what the Hindus call *satsang,* the communion of like minds. And this sharing enriched them all.

From Personal Growth to Political Effectiveness

John's quest for wholeness has made him a more effective political leader. Unlike the case of U.S. Senator Thomas Eagleton, John's therapy has never been a political liability, because he's always been very open about it. There has never been anything to expose simply because there has never been anything to hide.

Most critically, John has sought to confront conventional politics directly with lessons he took seriously from his explorations of personal growth and health. This developed over two different, yet related, dimensions in his legislative work: his relations with other political figures, and the substance of his approach to social issues. What is most striking is the courage of this effort while retaining—indeed, strengthening—his core commitments to those most in need in our society.

John learned to listen empathically to both liberals and conservatives. "I've lived both lives and have more appreciation for those who still live the old culture," he says. He has developed his intuition, insight, and skills of negotiation and mediation. His own inner work has given him "a deeper insight into the heart of myself and the heart of all of us."

In addition, his therapy has given him a more positive paradigm of problem solving. At the root of humanistic psychology is a belief in our ability to grow, to learn, and to heal ourselves and one another. When many people face a crisis, they blame others or ask, "Why me?" John looks beyond the problem to the solution, asking what he can do to help heal the situation. Indeed, the key to his political agenda has become a preventive view of the state's role in society.

For John, political and personal responsibility are inseparable. To be an effective leader, he knows he must attend to his own personal development. Beyond that, he sees "my every belief, act, and statement" as political. As he explains in his book, that holds true not only for John, a professional legislator, but for every one of us: "Our most important public policy is our personal policy, vision, belief, value system—regarding human beings and our own nature. It underlies *all* our other public policies. How we humans most healthily grow and develop is the central political issue of our times."[8]

"There is no politician in this country who has endeavored to translate his values into public policy as much as John," says Mitch Saunders. John works as an educator, helping us redefine ourselves and create healthier ways to become more fully human. His policies reflect this. In December 1974 he started a new political movement, "Self-Determination: A Personal/Political Network." In 1977 he helped set up the state Task Force on Positive Parenting.

In 1979 he established a Commission on Violence, to look into the causes of violent crime. The commission found that most violence was alcohol related, and most violent felons had been abused as children. Using the political arena to help us better understand ourselves and the roots of our social problems, John's commission demonstrated the close casual relationship between the personal and the political. With his approach, John has been years ahead of his time. In August 1993, the American Psychological Association announced the results of its research into the causes of violent crime, which echoed the findings of John's 1979 California Commission on Violence. The lesson is clear: Years of childhood neglect and abuse exact an inevitable, massive toll of suffering and anxiety as well as spiraling costs in our criminal justice system. How much healthier, saner, and safer our society would be if we could only learn to be better parents and better persons. More and more, John's policies have looked beyond a current crisis to emphasize prevention. Researching the root causes of a problem, he seeks to find a "vaccine" against it.

Transcending violence, apathy, and the slow poison of cynicism, John has worked to build a politics of trust. Through his own personal example, he calls on people to trust themselves and one another. Since I moved to Northern California to begin teaching English at Santa Clara University in 1974, I have been continually impressed by John's efforts to extend the lessons of humanistic psychology into the world of politics. Shadowing John in the capitol for a magazine article years ago, I witnessed an example of his openness. He got the kind of phone call that, in most offices, would have meant a private conversation behind closed doors. I got up to leave, but John motioned for me to stay, all the while expressing in strong language his heartfelt displeasure at one of his colleagues' decisions. Whatever his feelings, he had nothing to conceal from anyone.

John's gamble, in an environment in which the stakes are extremely high, is that complete honesty will create the capacity to reach compromise and actual results. During virtually any day in Sacramento, one or more of his colleagues will come to him with a thorny problem, a dilemma in which the contestants presume that it's dangerous to put all their cards on the table. His legendary skills as a negotiator are rooted in his willingness to put the stakes right out on the table.[9]

In June 1984, he received a letter from Carl Rogers acknowledging him for his unique approach to politics:

> I am greatly impressed by your ability to work within
> our institutional and establishment framework. I just
> don't have that kind of courage or perseverance or some-
> thing and so I admire it when I see it in others. The
> university setting is a reasonably favorable one but I even
> gave up on that. You operate in an arena which is much

rougher and dirtier and must be very difficult to bear at times, but you stick to it. You are a symbol of what can be accomplished in the world of politics as well as in education and other fields. You have the courage to fight for a human point of view.[10]

By his personal example, John creates his own ongoing revolution within state government, affirming a more human politics in his process as well as his policies.

Leo Rock says, "We invite people to be trustworthy in trusting them, and that's what John does." It's a powerful lesson. John's politics are based on intelligence and caring. According to Leo, "these are also the two essential elements in his personal growth." I would add to those two elements a third: courage. In its most radical meaning, *courage* comes from *coeur*, the French word for "heart." John has the courage to explore new dimensions, personally and politically, the courage to take risks, and to cite a familiar statement, "to boldly go where no one has gone before."

Leo says this goes beyond courage: "John has nothing to lose." To get to where he is, John has done the courageous inner work. His ego is not invested in his politics. He seeks something beyond that: the right for us all to become more fully human, more fully ourselves. San Jose businessman Robert Podesta, Jr. puts it this way: "Other politicians practice politics as it is. John sees politics as it should be."[11]

In 1980 the Assembly Democrats asked John to mediate between Leo McCarthy and Howard Berman, contenders for the Assembly speakership—arguably the second most powerful position in state government. His colleagues felt that if anyone had the skills to resolve this conflict, it had to be John. He did his best and thought at one point he'd gotten them together, but he could not bring about a peaceful resolution. Still, he won the respect and gratitude of his party; and the Speaker, Leo McCarthy, named him chair of the powerful Ways and Means Committee.

Many Assembly members were surprised. Could John handle it? The chair of Ways and Means handles the complex budget of the state of California, the sixth largest economy in the world. But John's acumen, phenomenal math skills, and hard work convinced them all in a fairly short time and changed his image in the capitol. He became known for his pragmatism as well as his progressive politics.

Busy as he is with his responsibilities in Ways and Means, John still practices his politics with a personal touch. He talks to his constituents when they recognize him—on the street, in restaurants, in grocery stores—and records their requests and suggestions, filling his pockets with notes scrawled on scraps of paper. He listens to people he meets at conferences and takes their lives, their successes, their challenges to heart. Later he sends them handwritten notes from his office. Thousands of us have been touched by such expressions of caring. By reaching out in ways that are highly personal, John recruits us as partners to advance a healthier vision of ourselves and our society.

Finally, John's is a politics of integrity. "John practices what he preaches. You can find out what John believes by simply observing him. It's written in the way he acts," says Leo Rock, adding that it's "a travesty in our country, how rarely is it actually the case that a politician is actually a public servant, even though they claim that. John truly wants to serve the public. That's primary. It's not ego or personal power but service that drives John." After all the negative campaigning in the last election, Leo says, "John is, in my experience, the one living person who prevents me from saying politicians are crooks and being swallowed up in that cynicism." With his integrity, John holds out a politics of hope.

The New Human Agenda

In the early 1980s John developed a "New Human Agenda" that articulated his vision of politics informed by faith in our human potential. In a newsletter sent out to his constituents, John set forth his definition of government's responsibility to the people and the people's responsibility to themselves and one another:

> Much of what government does we cannot effectively accomplish as individuals (e.g., funding for our schools, public hospitals, highways, sewage treatment plants, keeping our air and water clean and pure). Most of the rest of what government does is a substitute for our individual inaction (e.g., crime, battered wives, child abuse, litter). So we can best reduce the need for and expense of government services and taxes by our own responsible action as human beings, to prevent many of the social problems we are now experiencing. That's why I consider it essential that we recognize as extremely

critical the question, "How do we grow healthy human beings?" The question is better stated: "How do we provide environments (including human relationships) which enable persons to grow themselves into healthy human beings—persons who are:

- self-aware and self-esteeming,
- self-realizing and self-determining,
- free *and* responsible, competent *and* caring,
- faithful rather than cynical, open rather than closed,
- gentle rather than violent, ecologically responsible, motivated rather than apathetic,
- moral rather than immoral or amoral,
- political rather than apolitical?"

Insofar as we discover and operationalize answers to this question—we humans will become more self-sufficient, better able to take care of ourselves. We will also become better able to relate to our fellow human beings in ways that enable them to grow healthy in the first instance and/or, in the second instance, to recuperate from their unhealthiness. We'll hurt each other less, help each other more.[12]

Included in the newsletter was a list of recommended books by Carl Rogers, Sidney Jourard, Marilyn Ferguson, and others—books on personal development, futurism, humanistic psychology, and existential philosophy. This is the only time I've seen a list of recommended reading in a political newsletter, but then John is no ordinary political leader. He sees himself as an educator and a facilitator for others' personal and political growth as well as his own.

Also included in the newsletter was a list of resources—names, addresses, and phone numbers of humanistic programs in: birthing, parenting, marriage and family counseling, sexuality, hunger relief, education, energy, holistic health, mental health, violence prevention, community building, law enforcement, prison reform, management, aging, dying, and world peace. It reflected a vast political agenda incorporating all phases of human development from birth to death—a stunning example of John's holistic, humanistic approach to politics: supporting our essential human dignity and fullest personal development at every stage of life.

This newsletter argument—imagine, for a moment, 46,000 voters actually getting it in the mail—captures the essential political lesson John had gained through taking seriously the social implications of Carl's work. That is, the role of the state in a decent society is to do more than protect us from one another, or provide resources for the after-the-fact "expenses" of the social or economic environment. The state, or government, can serve a powerful role in facilitating the development of responsible citizens through investing in those "environments" that make us healthy.

The implications of this insight for the man whose professional responsibilities include drafting the annual budget of the state of California—over 57 billion dollars last year—have been enormous. For years now, John has asked his staff to include in their analyses of the state's budget allocations the degree to which programs increase or retard a preventive strategy to social issues. Preventive health programs, children's health and welfare, decent and effective education for our children—these have been the regular touchstones for John's politics.

It is difficult to overestimate the importance of John's commitment to these and other programs. Chair of Ways and Means during the terms of two conservative governors, John's capacity to defend and protect classically liberal programs on a new and unique grounding—an articulate argument about providing the social base for individual responsibility and self-esteem—has been one of his enduring legacies. While he points to the Task Force on Self-Esteem as the apex of his political work—because it speaks so directly to his view of the relationship between the heart and the healthy self—millions of Californians would point to programs he saved, lives he made more healthy, classes and clinics and counselors who have survived because he fought to save their budgets.

The Politics of Self-Esteem and Personal Responsibility

John challenges people to get involved, to take responsibility for improving their lives and their world. He often refers to his friend Dr. George Brown at the University of California, Santa Barbara, whose confluent education program blends the traditional 3 R's (Reading, 'Riting, and 'Rithmetic) with the 3 R's of "self-Respect, personal Responsibility, and human Relations." In the early 1980s, George told John that he'd gotten a call from the U.S. State Department because a Polish woman had wanted to participate in his confluent education program. During the intense early days of Poland's tradeworker union Solidarity, one of its members had discovered Brown's research while another had learned of gestalt psychology from a German theater troupe. Since then, humanistic psychology has empowered every leader of Solidarity, all of whom are committed to taking gestalt training and learning more about the humanistic approach.

John says that "there's no reason—except our own lack of sufficient faith—that each one of us cannot become another George Brown, envisioning ourselves and our world in much more hopeful and loving ways, attending to our own continuing personal growth, and acting publicly so as to help it all happen. It isn't enough for you and me to sit back and wait for someone else to fix our world. If we choose to take no personal responsibility for what is going wrong—and no part in improving it—then we forfeit our right to complain. If you and I instead choose to recognize our personal potential and responsibility, and involve ourselves—we have a whole new world to gain."[13]

Underlying any potential for responsible action is a necessary belief in ourselves. John's most important contribution as a leader, according to Leo Rock, is calling "public attention to the critical role that self-esteem plays in a democracy." Much of his vast legislative agenda over the years has been to promote personal responsibility and self-esteem. Sample projects include Californians Preventing Violence, the Senior Partners Project, Parents as Teachers, California Leadership, the California Human Corps, the Latino Advancement Project, and his much-publicized Task Force on Self-Esteem. He originally proposed the Self-Esteem Bill in 1984; it passed the Assembly but was voted down in the Senate.

John then suffered a heart attack and underwent seven-way coronary bypass surgery, followed by extensive work on his personal recovery. This included a new regimen of diet and exercise, therapy, autogenic hypnosis and visualization with Emmett Miller, followed by gestalt and bioenergetic work with Lou Pambianco. Meanwhile, the Self-Esteem Bill was passed in 1985 in both houses, only to be vetoed by Governor George Deukmejian. The following year, John met repeatedly with the governor, explaining how preventive work on self-esteem would save millions of dollars in our state criminal justice, welfare, and health-care systems. The bill was finally passed and signed on September 23, 1986, setting up a twenty-five-member task force charged with compiling all available data on the social implications of self-esteem and presenting a report in January 1990. The task force received an unprecedented 350 applications for the twenty-five positions.

The Self-Esteem Bill was a part of John's larger "Toward a Healthier State" program, initiated in 1986. It included proposals for reforms in public health, the economy, family counseling, child care, environmental protection, political campaigns, public education, public management, violence prevention, and world peace. It is a stunning and comprehensive list of programs—a "real agenda, not an election agenda," according to one lobbyist. And the program reflects John's own belief about the role of a leader, who should "educate and lead people to a healthier vision of themselves."

John and Carl as Political Partners

In the fall of 1986, during a radio interview in El Cajon, John was asked about his Task Force on Self-Esteem. "Was there anyone who inspired you to undertake this effort?"

"Yes," John answered immediately, "a friend of mine who lives nearby, over in La Jolla—Carl Rogers."[14]

As John was integrating the personal and the political, Carl was expanding his person-centered therapy into the realm of international politics. The 1980s became a time of powerful collaboration between the two men. In 1961 Carl had written in the preface to *On Becoming a Person* that we now have the means "to decrease the inter-racial, industrial, and international tensions which exist. I hope that it will be evident that these learnings, used preventatively, could aid in the development of mature, nondefensive, understanding persons who would deal constructively with future tensions."[15] Twenty years later, he made a personal commitment to applying his person-centered approach to conflict resolution on the global level.

On October 9, 1982, John made a surprise fly-in appearance at Carl's eightieth birthday party in San Diego. Carl and Ruth Sanford had just returned from a deeply moving trip to South Africa, recognizing the powerful potential of the person-centered approach in another troubled area of the world. Carl told John that he wanted to dedicate the remainder of his life to world peace; he wanted to "export facilitators instead of bombs."[16] John offered his wholehearted support. Mitch Saunders says that then "John had the opportunity to be a teacher to his mentor. Carl turned to John for guidance, and he became Carl's campaign strategist."

Carl and Gay Swenson, who became codirectors of the Carl Rogers Peace Project, had been working with colleagues for several years to expand the mission of the Center for Studies of the Person (CSP) in La Jolla to include international as well as interpersonal conflict resolution. During the winter and following summer, John met with Carl and Gay to share ideas and discuss future plans for international peacemaking. John was working on a "peace package" for the California legislature. Gay was working to build international collaboration by inviting Robert Muller, Assistant Secretary General of the United Nations, to meet with them and other colleagues while he was visiting California in August.

At that meeting, Muller referred them to Rodrigo Carazo, former president of Costa Rica and president of the United Nations University for Peace; contacting him led to further international cooperation. In September, while Carl was giving workshops in Europe, Gay drafted a design for an ongoing peace institute, and John helped put her in touch with some significant potential funding sources. In January 1984, the Carl Rogers Institute for Peace was officially established as a project of CSP.

John offered support and participated in brainstorming sessions as often as his schedule would permit. In January 1984, he organized and convened a weekend retreat at Dorothy Lyddon's Seven Springs Ranch in Cupertino (northern California). Twenty persons came together to discuss new patterns of politics and peacemaking. They included Carl Rogers and his friend Ora Brink; Gay Swenson and John Wood of CSP; Michael Murphy, founder of Esalen; Jim Hickman and Dulce Murphy of the Esalen/USSR Program; therapists George and Judith Brown from Santa Barbara; Willis Harmon, director of the Institute for Noetic Sciences; and Mitch Saunders, future director of California Leadership.

After much discussion, Judith Brown summed up their approach: "the very same rules apply in all human relationships—whether it's between spouses or lovers, or between the Americans and the Russians. The rules are universal: either we trust, accept, invite and include each other and become partners, or we distrust, reject, distance and exclude each other and become enemies."[17]

Early in September 1985, Carl broke his neck in a fall; yet three weeks later, he spoke to 300 people with John, Gay, Dennis Weaver, Robert Young, and others in a fund-raising event for the Peace Project. In November 1985, John joined Carl (who was still wearing a cervical collar) in Rust, Austria, for the Peace Project's first international person-centered workshop on "The Central American

Challenge," cosponsored with the United Nations University for Peace. Some sixty-five prominent political and lay leaders from seventeen countries met for four days, trying to transcend personal and political differences and to touch what was human in them all. On the final day, Carl was moved to tears when all but one participant signed a joint testimonial. The Rust experience inspired John to write this poem:

RUST ...

We arrived
amidst a heavy fog, which gradually
lifted to become
sunny by the conclusion of our workshop;
on Hallowe'en yielding to the day of all saints;
in a town whose steeples house the nests of storks,
we hopefully midwifed the birth of more faith and
hope for, and a process leading toward,
peace!

John described Carl's presence as "so gentle and comfortable and assuring—it was no less than 'saintly'—that everybody present could and did relax and come on forward to meet and engage each other. He was the atmosphere in which we could become persons, developing trust and even partnership in our mutual search for world peace."[18]

Meanwhile, John continued to combine the personal and political in his own work. He proposed his six-point Peace Package to the California Assembly in 1986, advocating arms control and a two-year educational exchange with the Soviet Union. The relationship between John and Carl had come full circle.

Continuing his work for peace, Carl, then 84, met John after a month in the Soviet Union where he, Ruth Sanford, and Francis Macy had introduced his method to 1,500 people. The Soviet Minister of Education had invited Carl to Russia to consult on individualizing instruction and fostering creativity.

"Isn't it somewhat dangerous to be doing that in a collectivist society?" asked John.

"Yes," answered Carl, "but not as dangerous as not doing it."[19]

In November 1986, Carl and Gay Swenson joined John at his "Toward a Healthier State" symposium, held at the University of

California, Irvine, to report on the Rust workshop and on Carl and Ruth Sanford's work in the Soviet Union and South Africa.

In February 1987, John was in Orange County for a political meeting on the Monday after Carl's hip surgery and subsequent heart attack in the hospital. As his friend lay dying at Scripps Hospital in La Jolla, John rushed to his bedside for a last farewell. Carl's daughter, Natalie, was there with his granddaughter, feminist therapist Frances Fuchs.

The women greeted John warmly. As Natalie embraced John, he burst into tears, and she consoled him, saying it was okay for him to cry. Carl was in a deep coma, and his family had just told him that he had contributed enough to life. They had released him, with love, to leave this life when he was ready. Yet when John entered the room, Carl stirred visibly, becoming very agitated in his breathing. Natalie interpreted this reaction as a sign of recognition, and the two women left the room, giving John some time alone with Carl.

John sat down beside Carl, stroking his arm, breathing as deeply as he knew how, trying to discover something deep within himself to call his friend back to life. He thanked Carl for all he had given him, and for providing his first therapist, Leo Rock, with the capacity to touch John's shattered life and lead him back to wholeness. He thanked Carl for helping him discover his own capacity for knowing himself, for growing healthy, and for leading his own life. And he thanked Carl for having (via the agency of Leo) brought into his life his dearest friend, Mitch Saunders.

Then he thanked Carl for being "the pioneer of trust." As he later stated at Carl's memorial service:

> That's who you have been, Carl. That's who you are, for
> me and for so many others. You trusted so fully, you
> invited us to "become persons." You called us to life. You
> gave us yourself and your vision, for all the world to
> truly live by. We love you and we miss you and we thank
> you. We will carry on your vision, in our lives and in
> your spirit.[20]

Carrying on the vision, later that year John became copresident of the Association of Humanistic Psychology, an organization Carl had founded. He is certainly the first politician ever to hold that office.

John's Political Legacy

In May 1989, while returning from a self-esteem talk in Orlando, Florida, John was reading Tom Owen-Towle's book, *New Men, Deeper Hungers,* and was struck by a passage about examining our lives, asking how we'd like to invest the time that remains to us, and what kind of legacy we'd like to leave behind. On May 11, his fifty-seventh birthday, John recorded his answers to those questions, looking back at what he'd done and ahead at what he still wanted to accomplish.

He had chaired the Assembly Ways and Means Committee for ten years, seeking to create "a balanced human budget" while educating California citizens about our fiscal situation. His work had become increasingly sophisticated and sure. Indeed, there is hardly anyone in the state who better understands California's sprawling budget. One day of sitting in Ways and Means will disabuse anyone who thinks that caring about self-esteem makes anyone soft and fuzzy.

As twice chair of the Joint Legislative Committee for Review of the Master Plan for Higher Education, John had followed through with his long-term commitment to education (especially higher, producing the major blueprint report); he also chaired an early version of this committee in 1971–74. The later committee generated the enactment of Assembly Bill 1725 on comprehensive community college reform in 1988. With his good friend the political philosopher Brian Murphy, he had just completed the report *California Faces... California's Future: Education for Citizenship in a Multicultural Democracy.* The report argued that higher education would have to play a critical role in ensuring that the democratic prospect was a reality for the "new majority" who would make California's future.

Among his many ongoing projects are the California Human Corps, through which every university student in California is strongly encouraged and expected to engage in ongoing community service as part of his or her education. The Campus Compact, a network of college presidents from public and private universities, supports this endeavor and plans to extend it to the national level. The Clinton administration's combination of public service with college funding appears to echo some of John's early work in this area.

As chair of the Assembly Select Committee on Ethics, John worked successfully to develop the nation's leading code of ethics, an ethics education program, and an ethical behavior sanctions process for the California State Legislature. Again, John combined his commitment to education and personal development to improve the political process.

Another one of his projects is the California Senior Partners Program, which encourages active seniors to volunteer services to assist less able retired people, creating a reciprocal community assistance network. Here is John in his characteristic way, bringing people together to help themselves, help one another, and build community in this fragmented modern society. With the changing demographics producing an unprecedented age wave in the twenty-first century, such a program may be vital not only to the health of senior citizens but to the future health and cohesion of our society.

In California Leadership, John works with his closest friend, Director of Programs Mitch Saunders, to build a new model of leadership to meet tomorrow's challenges with participation that is both inclusive (involving women and persons of color) and collaborative. California Leadership addresses current concerns in a proactive manner, setting up forums and ongoing programs that incorporate multiple perspectives and use the latest patterns of cooperative leadership.

In September 1988, Cal Leadership sponsored an intensive forty-four-hour educational experience on water use in California, involving twelve of the top water leaders, all white (ten males, two females), and eighteen emerging leaders: nine women, nine men; six Latino, three Black, two Asian, seven Anglo. Discussions and planning continued over three years. Cal Leadership also cosponsored a workshop at Asilomar with the California Economic Development Corporation involving seventy-six individuals (one-third women, one-third persons of color), which launched an eighteen-month process of discussion and decision making.

Since 1986, when he introduced AIDS Vaccine legislation in the State Assembly, John has been working to support research in this crucial area. In addition, he works with the AIDS Budget Task Force to determine each year how much money California needs to set aside to address the growing AIDS epidemic. Here again, John combines compassion with pragmatism to meet a grave problem in our society.

Carrying on with his commitment to world peace, John worked to establish in 1989 the first California Peace Day, to be celebrated on the third Sunday each May. Its stated purpose is to recognize people and practices that have helped us develop an atmosphere of peace in our lives and our world.

John has always supported programs for children and the family. He set up the Task Force on Positive Parenting and Celebrating Families in the 1970s and later the Alternative Birthing Committee. He also initiated legislation to require a course of study in human sexuality for all new California physicians, family therapists, psychologists, and psychiatric social workers. In 1987 he introduced more humanistic licensing for Marriage and Family Counselors. He cofounded CAL KIDS with Republican Senator Becky Morgan and State Superintendent of Schools Bill Honig to move children to the top of California's agenda. Through the Latino Advancement Project, he has sought to help educate and support the future success of Latino children. In 1989 he set up Parents as Teachers, a program to provide in-home parenting education for new parents, together with health screening and follow-up advice.

Calling people to assume greater political responsibility, he sought in 1990 to set up "Leading Californians: Demanding Leadership for a Change." This challenged people to voice their opinions and get involved in the 1990 gubernatorial and other statewide elections. Both this project and John's personal vision of leadership were drawn from the maxim: "When the people lead, the leaders will follow."

It is a staggering list of accomplishments, in a legislative body so often criticized for inaction. Indeed, oddly enough, John gives the lie to his own maxim, for he has often been way out in front of "the people" as well as their other representatives. But he must be onto something: the people in his district keep electing him (thirteen times now). His career proves a political truth that Carl Rogers would have loved: trust your own instincts, and trust others to be in your face if you are wrong. And *then* be flexible and open enough to craft a solution others can accept.

Leadership as Cooperation

Through John's twenty-seven years in the legislature, his work on himself has helped him develop a greater sense of both presence and mediation. He engages people on a personal level, transcending the usual partisan politics. He says in his book that when he first came to Sacramento, he avoided the conservatives in the Assembly, concerned that "they might contaminate me. As I grew personally, I came to recognize my avoidance as a symptom of my personal insecurity.

As I grew secure enough within myself to risk exposing myself to them, I found them to be humans, just like me."[21] Since then he has formed partnerships with Republicans and Democrats alike, inviting Republican State Senator Becky Morgan to serve on the board of California Leadership. Because John usually does not polarize issues, he does not blame others or make enemies. He may disagree passionately with people's ideas but he almost never attacks them personally. He goes for principle.

A recent example of the new leadership he inspires is the Assembly Democratic Economic Prosperity Team (ADEPT). When John and ten other Assembly Democrats first met in 1991 to deal with the economic crises in California, they concluded that they could overcome the state's economic problems only by healing the historical rifts between business and government, Democrats and business leaders. Applying Rogerian principles under John's leadership, they met face to face with over sixty business groups throughout the state: from fishing and tourist industries to insurance, aerospace, electronics, oil, and grocery businesses; from construction to fashion, banking to biotech. Instead of talking politics or holding press conferences, the group held focused, two-hour sessions to listen and to learn.

The ADEPT report, published in October 1992, reveals what they learned: "that traditional ways can no longer suffice in today's complex global economy. Neither the standard, stereotypical Republican *laissez-faire* model nor the standard, stereotypical Democratic command and control model works any more. We learned that only a third way—the way of trust, partnership, and collaboration—offers us any hope for our future."[22]

The challenge is new but the words ring a familiar cadence. Using active listening, building trust, partnership, and cooperation, ADEPT directly applies the strategies of the Carl Rogers Peace Project to California's economic problems. The context of humanistic psychology remains constant throughout John's innovative political ventures. Realizing that old, polarized "politics as usual" no longer works, he strives to facilitate new environments in which people can listen, learn, and work together to overcome the new challenges emerging in our complex world.

The ADEPT report was followed in the spring of 1993 by the ADEPT legislative package, created with bipartisan support. It proposed reforms in government agencies, a strategic plan for economic development, tax reform, business incentives, worker's compensation reform, economic conversion, improvement in the infrastructure, and further conferences on economic growth.

Advocating the familiar preventive, proactive approach to problem solving, the ADEPT report states that we must respond "to our changes and challenges before they grow into crises" and that "leadership in California must be explicitly inclusive, visionary, and inspiring."[23]

A Politics of Vision

The word *vision* characterizes John's approach to politics. From the title of his book, *A Liberating Vision,* to his latest programs and speeches, he looks beyond current crises to larger patterns and meets emerging needs with innovative programs designed to help us become healthier individually and collectively. This, he believes, is the predominant role and responsibility of government.

In his 1993 inaugural speech for Raymond Orbach, the new chancellor of the University of California, Riverside, John eloquently described his vision. In many ways, he explained, our society is like a dysfunctional family, experiencing a breakdown that may also be a healing crisis. He pointed to the four major revolutions that have shaken the foundations of our old world order: the computer revolution, the revolutions in race and gender, and the humanistic revolution in the way we see ourselves. He concluded, "in these times of chaos and breakdown which evoke so much of fear, it is our challenge as leaders to try to help have the vision, to help paint the pictures to enable other people and ourselves to see what is happening not in terms of negativity and fright, but instead to recognize these transitions as not so much breakdown and terrible but as breakout, break up, breakthrough towards some more hopefully whole, healthy, more diverse, and inclusive society." Describing the massive changes in the fabric of our society, John portrays them in a way that offers hope to many people who would otherwise retreat into defensiveness and anxiety in response to continuous revolution and rapid change in almost every level of life. It is reassuring in these times of change that John seeks to live what he believes, inspiring others by his words and example.

Mitch Saunders sees John's personal example as his greatest contribution as a leader. "I would guess that there are thousands of people who follow John, that he's the role model for," says Mitch. "There are people who look to him in the legislature, political advocates, lobbyists who look to him for inspiration—which is a bizarre thing to say about lobbyists. His policy influence and tomes on human politics pale in comparison to seeing him in action, where he is able to bring his intellect and full humanity to bear." It is his personal presence Mitch initially found so compelling that he asked John to be his mentor.

John's vision of leadership is one of inspiration and empowerment. He conveys this by trusting himself, trusting others, daring to trust in our human capacity to learn, to grow, to take charge of our personal and political lives. It is essential to our democracy to redefine leadership in terms of empowerment. For our country—any country—to be what Lincoln called a "government of the people, by the people, and for the people," the people must believe in themselves and their ability to make a difference. If we don't believe in ourselves, democracy cannot work.

John summed this up in his Riverside inaugural speech. After relating that his father had taught him that you can't give what you haven't got, John said: "Only the person who is willing to be living authentically and creatively, with integrity, with vision, with boldness and wholeheartedness and passion and risk taking, can lead a life willing to meet the challenge of our times."

John's Greatest Challenge

Throughout his life, John's greatest challenge has been "to reclaim myself, to accept myself." He recalls a dream he once had at Esalen where he saw a ferris wheel turning, bringing up more and more of himself.

His most turbulent interpersonal struggles are behind him. Over twenty-five years of therapy have helped him make peace with his parents and his past. After two or three years in the late 1960s when he didn't see them at all, John has worked to rebuild and redefine his relationship with his mother and father. Through the years, John would join his parents for the usual family visits and holiday meals. Since they lived halfway between his home in Santa Clara and the state capitol, John would stop by once a month or so for Sunday dinner and stay overnight on his way back to Sacramento.

His father, John Vasconcellos senior, died in 1983. His mother, Teresa, now 88, still comes to John's annual birthday party in the capitol each May. John says that she's "finally come to terms with my being myself" and they've "developed a real friendship over the years." His brother, Jim, an engineer with General Electric, lives in Pacifica. His sister, Margaret, who lives in Guerneville, is a teacher and director of programs for non-English-speaking students at Mission High School. John tries to stay in touch and they see each other at family functions.

But John's hectic life leaves him little time to spend with his family of origin, and with offices and households divided between Santa Clara and Sacramento as well as commitments spread all over the state, he has never married. Since his heart attack and bypass in 1984, he has lived more deliberately, striving to find a balance between his own life and the demands of his work. He takes more time to exercise and to stay in touch with friends. Yet the magnitude of his commitment remains with him. On his flights around the state, he often looks down to contemplate the land and his constituency. At such times he is reminded that "it's an awesome responsibility," to be a legislator. "There are only 120 of us and 32 million people in the state."

"Good friends, good therapists, and good staff" help John keep his balance. His staff, he says, are like family. They operate with openness and trust, share information, and represent him so well they enable him to "be a dozen places at once." He values his close friends—Mitch, Cindy, and Megan Saunders—who have become his primary family; and Brian Murphy, with whom he shares friendship, philosophy, and politics. To get perspective on his life, sometimes he just "hibernates with friends"; sometimes he takes off to relax and reflect in Hawaii before returning to the pressure-cooker existence in Sacramento. He does bodywork, plays racquetball, reads a lot, listens a lot, and learns more about his life every day. He is one of the most determined and self-actualizing persons I have ever met.

Epilogue

As I interviewed John one spring day in 1993, I noticed his living room was filled with symbols of what he so strongly believes in. The walls were graced by beautiful paintings by Maye Torres, a Native American/Mexican artist from New Mexico. These showed people dancing, their hearts open and glowing with color. On the coffee table were two newspapers. Looking at the top one, old and yellowed, I blinked at the date: January 21, 1961—the day of the Kennedy inaugural. Underneath was a paper from January 20, 1993—the day of the Clinton inaugural.

The papers reminded me of what must have been so many endings and beginnings in the life of this deeply committed and compassionate man of politics. The New Frontier of our youthful past somehow blends with the new frontier of our human potential, which John so eloquently calls us to by example: a new vision of leadership that will shape the twenty-first century. It is a vision of openness, honesty, and trust; of power shared and of policy cocreated through a harmony of many voices—voices of the marginalized and oppressed, the privileged and disadvantaged joined together in community to create our common future. We must learn to stand together, dream together, and work together, or we will surely fall apart. John's vision not only offers us new hope to become healthier individuals, it promises to breathe new life into the dream of our democracy.

New dreams, when drawn from essential human experience, often recall ancient truths. Twenty-five centuries ago, the Chinese sage Lao Tzu wrote about leadership in the *Tao Te Ching*, and Carl Rogers carried in his wallet this passage about leadership as empowerment:

> With the best of leaders,
> When the work is done,
> The task is accomplished,
> The people all say
> "We did it ourselves."[24]

This is a lesson lived by John Vasconcellos and Carl Rogers and echoed by all of us whose hearts have been touched by their example.

References

1 John Vasconcellos, "Carl Rogers Eulogy," February 21, 1987.

2 Ibid.

3 Both quotes in this paragraph are from the "Carl Rogers Eulogy" cited above.

4 My thanks to John Vasconcellos for interviews in Santa Clara, California on May 14 and July 23, 1993 as well as a phone interview on August 11. All quotes, unless otherwise noted, are from these interviews. I would also like to acknowledge his staff for providing information, correspondence, literature, and valuable assistance.

5 I am grateful to Leo Rock for an interview at Santa Clara University on June 2, 1993. All quotes from Leo Rock are from this interview.

6 I would like to thank Mitch Saunders for an interview in Santa Clara, California on June 4, 1993. All quotes from Mitch Saunders are from this interview.

7 John Vasconcellos, *A Liberating Vision* (San Luis Obispo, CA: Impact Publishers, 1979), pp. 132–33.

8 Ibid, p. 154.

9 For insights into John's politics here and elsewhere, I am grateful to Brian Murphy for sharing his advice and observations with me in July and August of 1993.

10 Letter from Carl Rogers to John Vasconcellos, June 16, 1984.

11 From a conversation with Robert Podesta, Jr. on June 12, 1993 in Santa Clara, California.

12 John Vasconcellos, *New Human Agenda* newsletter, March 1982.

13 Ibid.

14 Vasconcellos, "Carl Rogers Eulogy," February 21, 1987.

15 Carl Rogers, *On Becoming a Person* (Boston: Houghton Mifflin, 1961), p. ix.

16 For this and other information about the Carl Rogers Peace Project, I would like to thank the Director, Gay Swenson Barfield, for materials and conversations provided over the years, especially in June and July of 1993.

17 As quoted in Vasconcellos, "Carl Rogers Eulogy," February 21, 1987.

18 Ibid.

19 Ibid.

20 Ibid.

21 Vasconcellos, *A Liberating Vision,* p. 28.

[22] *Toward an ADEPT California: A Customer Satisfaction State.* A Preliminary Report of the Assembly Democratic Economic Prosperity Team (Sacramento, 1992), p. 9.

[23] Ibid, pp. 82, 31.

[24] Lao Tzu, *The Tao Te Ching,* chapter 17 (My own paraphrase of various translations). For more on Taoism and leadership, see John Heider, *The Tao of Leadership* (New York: Bantam, 1986) and Diane Dreher, *The Tao of Inner Peace* (New York: HarperCollins, 1991).

About the Author

Since 1974 when she moved to northern California to teach English after completing her doctorate at the University of California at Los Angeles, Diane Dreher has been inspired by John Vasconcellos's unique blend of politics and humanistic psychology. Using him as a role model, she has struggled to discover and affirm a healthier sense of self in her own life and work, continuously redefining what it means to be a teacher, writer, lifelong student, woman, and person in this world of challenge and change.

Diane has sought to apply the lessons of modern psychology in various ways. Beginning with her dissertation, her scholarly research has combined literature and developmental psychology. She has also published popular articles on peace, self-esteem, and personal growth. In 1977 she founded the Faculty Development Program at Santa Clara University, directing a series of interactive workshops on teaching and research structured by Carl Rogers' principles of group process. During the 1980s she supervised English department internships, placing many students in John Vasconcellos's district office. In 1988 she codirected a regional workshop on self-esteem for parents and educators in San Jose, with John as the keynote speaker.

In addition to humanistic psychology, Diane looks to Eastern philosophy as a means of breaking through the limits of the Western mindset. Having lived in the Far East in early childhood, she has been subtly influenced by Asian art, culture, and philosophy ever since. Her book *The Tao of Peace* (1980) records the personal blend of Eastern philosophy and humanistic psychology that guides her life.

Since 1987 Diane has been inspired by the work of the Carl Rogers Peace Project. She has met over the years with Gay Swenson Barfield at the Center for Studies of the Person in La Jolla, benefiting from Gay's friendship and expertise, then weaving these lessons into her own life and work. In the summer of 1990, Diane led a session on Taoism and conflict resolution at CSP's annual Living Now workshop.

Diane has also benefited from her friendship with Mitch Saunders, Director of Programs for California Leadership. She has known Mitch since the mid 1980s, when she met with him to research an article on conflict resolution. During the summer of 1987, they worked together to create a workshop for high school teachers, held at Santa Clara University. Diane has consulted periodically for California Leadership and drawn inspiration from Mitch's insight, empathy, brilliant demonstration of Rogerian listening, and ongoing work on new concepts of leadership.

At present Diane chairs the English department at Santa Clara University, where she teaches a continuing education class on Taoism and the Art of Leadership as well as regular classes in English literature. She also enjoys writing, training in aikido, tending her bonsai trees and small organic garden, spending time with close friends, and discovering more about her life each day in a new season of challenge, change, and celebration.

·:·

    I still have a picture of meeting Ruth Sanford at the door of her house in May 1991. Our delightful interview convinced me that her story needs to be shared with the humanistic community. Over the past fiftyc years, she has been a teacher, counselor, administrator, researcher, and therapist—a facilitator of learning for many, from grade-school children to doctoral candidates.

    From 1977 to 1987, she worked with Carl as cofacilitator and cofaculty in seminars and workshops abroad and in the United States. They also coauthored several papers and a textbook chapter. Ruth herself has authored (and continues publishing) professional papers on creativity in education, and the theory and applications of the person-centered approach.

    Bringing to life yet another perspective on Carl, this gracious woman's autobiography represents a fitting concluding chapter for this book.

·:·

9

On Becoming Who I Am . . .

by Ruth Sanford

The question has been asked, "What has been the effect of the life and work of Carl Rogers on your life and work?" I cannot reveal all of that because I do not know all of that. More and more, I become aware of ways in which those parts of Carl's life that I shared with him and those parts of my life that he shared with me are interwoven. Also I became aware that I cannot always see clearly what effect my knowing of him has had, on him or on me.

We had known each other and worked together in a variety of situations since the summer of 1975, but an evening in New York in 1980 was different. It was the annual gathering of the American Academy of Psychotherapists, of which Carl was one of the founders. Carl and I were guests with no responsibilities. We had heard addresses and discussions during the day, met many people long known to Carl, sat at a table with Fritjof Capra, danced, and were leaving the hotel.

After a silence which felt good after so busy a day, Carl said, "Ruth, you are all of a piece, *aren't* you?" It seemed no response was required, rather, that he had made a discovery which he had set to words. As I write this, I am not sure I know all that he meant, but the question has had a profound effect on my life.

When, in 1985, he invited me to be cofaculty with him at a conference in Phoenix on the evolution of the psychotherapies, I said, "Carl, what will I do there?"

His response was, "Just go there and be yourself." It was a new experience for me. I wasn't quite sure how I would be myself in a huge conference with so many leaders in the field of the psychotherapies, but that simple statement made it easier for me to work on what finally became the presentation (and later the paper) "Evolution of the Client-Centered Approach to Psychotherapy." That was the beginning of my researching some of the developments of Carl's theory and philosophy. What is more important, it stretched my belief, my concept, of what I was able to do.

Carl and I worked together to revise the chapter on "Client-Centered Psychotherapy" for the fourth edition of the *Comprehensive Textbook of Psychiatry*.[1] When he asked me to undertake the fifth revision by myself, I asked, "Why me? I don't feel I have experience in this kind of writing, and I'm sure there are many others who could do it very well."

His answer was, "Because you know and understand the heart of my work, and because you write well"—as simple and as clear a statement of his perception as one could have. I was encouraged to do it. Here again, he knew me and yet continually invited me to situations where I had to stretch my understanding or my skill or my confidence in myself.

I prepared two versions: one following the original closely, the other using more of my style and material. I gave both to Carl for his comment. He read the version based on his style and mostly his material, then he read mine. He said, "I like the new version. I like your version because it's fresh and it's accurate." So he not only expressed trust, but he followed up and affirmed it.

Carl opened doors for me; and I knew as soon as I stepped through one of those doors, I was on my own.

A door of another sort was my conversation with him about an important but very difficult relationship in which I was involved. Carl's response to me has made a difference in the way I see relationships and my part in them. He said, "I would hope that you would be able to accept and enjoy that relationship for exactly what it is."

As I translate his hope into my own experience with many kinds of relationships, many friends, I find more and more the value of being able to accept and appreciate or enjoy a relationship for exactly what it is. Let it grow as it will and as my nurturing makes it possible; if it doesn't grow in the direction I have expected, it can still be valuable and rich in its own way. I have found that when a close relationship is no longer a growing part of my life, I can choose to invest no more time and energy, and I can let it go without bitterness. These experiences demonstrated how it feels and how it works to apply in a relationship the conditions that Carl has described and demonstrated in his work.

Working with Carl day after day on some of our long visits to South Africa, the Soviet Union, and Mexico, I learned to value the fact that certain expressions—what I have since come to call *Carlisms*— genuinely grew out of his daily experience, his way of being with himself and others. One of those expressions was: "All of my professional life I have wanted to understand; and I have wanted to be understood, but I don't expect to." There can be great disappointment if one expects always to be understood, even when the other person has been listening to the words. As I struggled painfully at times with the feeling that I had been misunderstood or misjudged, I remembered what Carl had said. Increasingly, I needed less affirmation—a liberating experience. Only in my neediest moments did it become important to me that people recognize and approve a position, a thought, or a feeling that I had expressed.

Perhaps one of those Carlisms that has had a most profound impact on my life was one I heard him use often and which I have seen expressed in our work together. That is, "If I can be myself, transparently open in the moment, I am enough." In a kind of jocular way, I added a little piece of my own: "It has to be. It's all I've got." This has underlined for me the meaning of the self-actualizing tendency, the irreversible process of reaching toward full potential for the individual, including me. If I trust that tendency, which is at the base of the person-centered approach, then it is important that I learn to trust myself to be that person as wholly as possible in the moment. I have come to rely on that trust in my work with groups, in my work as a therapist, and in my personal relationships, including my family.

One of the most difficult parts of that practice is to know what is going on in me at any given moment, to become increasingly aware, as Carl put it, "of the feelings flowing within me from one instant to the next," and then to be willing and able to express that— as far as it's appropriate—to be known as having those feelings.

In South Africa in 1982, we faced a crisis. We were on a raised platform in an amphitheater with an audience of six or seven hundred persons for what had been announced as a weekend workshop in the person-centered approach. But because of his vision, Carl found himself unable to read a paper, as he often did when meeting with a large group. For the most part, those present knew little or nothing

about Carl's work. There was no opportunity for small groups. Without time for preparation or planning, we decided first to introduce ourselves and to tell why we had come to South Africa and what resources we had brought. Since we wanted to engage all of those present in as personal a way as possible, we decided to move quickly to their concerns and expectations by making microphones available and inviting participation. We noted questions and concerns, grouped them, and began responding alternately as our own interests led us.

In a short time, Carl and I were engaged in a lively dialogue. Soon after, the discussion drew in other participants. It was a productive morning. Carl and I were surprised at the ease with which we worked together spontaneously in so difficult a situation, and we enjoyed the way we complemented each other. It was a pattern that became effective in our work together in many other places in South Africa, Mexico, and the Soviet Union. We reached a new level of trust in ourselves, each other, and other persons.

Another thing I learned was the meaning of appropriateness. It may seem like a "should or should not" expression, but appropriateness involves not only knowing myself and being self-aware but also being aware of the other person or of the group and not being unnecessarily hurtful. It means that I express my own feelings as my own feelings without placing responsibility or blame on other persons.

I have found it difficult to address sharp differences or conflicts in any relationship that is of great depth and importance. Expressing my impatience or anger to Carl was especially difficult, but I experienced his willingness to hear what I had to say and to respond honestly, even when his response was not what I wanted to hear. At that point, each understood how the other felt. Should we not reach a resolution, we could agree that our perceptions were different, without destroying our friendship. I have come to accept such a resolution as an application of unconditional positive regard, one which can lead to the strengthening of a relationship.

From 1975 to 1987, my life took on a new kind of joy, a new sense of exhilaration and meaning in my work and my relationships. I felt most completely alive. And so, in answering the initial question about Carl's influence, I have also been answering my own question, "What does it mean to be all of a piece?" This brings me almost full circle in my attempt to write some brief indication of the kinds of change that have taken place in my life because I knew a man named Carl.

My Life

If life is, as I believe, a becoming, then every part of my past is a part of my present and is becoming a part of my future. How, from millions of remembered moments, shall I select those bits and pieces that represent my life? At best, it will be a mere fragment. But which fragment? How do I choose to be remembered by those who know me least or most?

I cannot begin at the beginning, for I was not there in that instant when two selves flowed together and made possible the beginning of my becoming. Those two selves I know well. She was twenty-two, full of dreams. He was thirty-three and full of dreams: dreams of building a home, a family. They still knew grief for a boy child born too soon who had never lived outside my mother's womb. At the time, they were living in a second-floor apartment in a small town in North Warren, Pennsylvania, beside the Conewango Creek.

My mother was to be the hostess for a large family Christmas dinner in 1906. She was awakened in the early hours of the morning in pain which she recognized as preliminary to my advent. I arrived in the early morning hours of December 26 and was from that time referred to as "the one who arrived too late for Christmas."

It is with indelible clarity, as if it were my own memory, that I recall my mother's description of the first summer of my life as idyllic. On any clear summer day when the early chores were done and my father was off to work with his lunch pail, she would settle me in my basket in the prow of her rowboat, along with a book and some sewing, and row to a favorite spot under a willow tree. There she would drop anchor and sit through summer hours watching me, talking with me, sewing—probably clothes for me or for herself—or reading a favorite book. Often she said she would take lunch and spend the day, the gentle rocking of the boat keeping me very happy and content. Those are the memories that come back to me so vividly that sometimes I even believe that I remember. It was, as she told it, the happiest summer of her life.

Who were these parents? Who is this person whose mother was a sensitive, disciplined child of a Methodist family with very strict ideas of what the good life is? It included hard work, avoidance of the evils of dancing (which my father loved), of cards, of movies, of alcohol. She described herself politically as Independent but always voted Republican.

Who is this person whose father was a staunch supporter of Eugene V. Debs through all of his campaigns? Whose father could have danced all night eight nights a week, as he told me sometimes? My father did not gain but in many ways was successful because he gave me the kind of love and support that made me feel I belonged in the world. He was a ventriloquist, a kind of Pied Piper, one who always took time to walk with me in the woods, to make jokes, to tease me out of a pout. I found myself taking care of my father because he often drank too much from the time I was eight or nine years old.

I grew up with these two loving people, who always let me know I was loved and cared for. In his actions and the way he was with me, my father let me know, "Anything you do is okay with me." My mother was a disciplinarian who always had time to sit and talk with me as I was growing up, should something trouble me. She also sat with me on a couch or in a chair and taught me poems, painting vivid images as she went over the lines until I learned from her, I believe, to love the imagery of poetry. She was willing to run out with us children and play in the mud after a heavy rain. This was a rare combination.

My little sister died of diphtheria when I was two or three years old. I was called an only child, yet our household was never or very rarely without other children living there as part of the family. These included young relatives from both my father's side and my mother's side as well as friends of mine who were having difficulties and had no home to live in while they were finishing high school. So I grew up really as a child among many, changing the siblings from time to time as they needed.

All of these additions to our family threw a great deal of financial responsibility onto my parents who were struggling even without such additions. Yet they handled it with such care and apparently so easily that I remember very little conflict and heard no talk of hardship.

My father was in turn a carpenter, a fine wood finisher of pianos, a landscape gardener, worker in the mill, worker on the railroad, salesman and, during the Depression, unemployed for a long period. My mother went back to school in the 1920s. She had graduated from high school and was a bookkeeper before she married. Now she finished requirements for her bachelor's degree in two years (by taking several examinations) and began teaching in the one- or two-room schools in the small towns about Jamestown.

Early Years

The year immediately following our move to Jamestown in 1908 marked the end of dreams and brought the death of my sister, Lucille; the beginning of my father's continuing search for work suitable to his health; and the onset of every childhood disease, which were packed into one winter. It was a year of despair for my mother. Although unaware of it at the time, I later learned that this was when my father began drinking heavily, which was the main cause of friction between my parents and almost destroyed the marriage.

One of my clearest memories of that disastrous year was of my lying in a white enameled iron bed with sides that moved up and down and my father bringing me a tiny white rabbit with pink ears, pink nose, pink eyes—a real live baby rabbit in a tiny grape basket. He brought it home to be my companion, and that rabbit was a playmate for many years. I look back on this as another way of my father telling me how much he cared for me. I know now that this was at a time when my mother had felt that she had little in life to live for, and my father and I were probably closest in that year.

Our next move was to a three-room house that my father built only a few blocks away. One of my happiest experiences was hearing him tell with pride that he and I had built the house. (I had sat on the plank or the two-by-four to keep it steady while he sawed.) Another strong memory is the Christmas when someone told me that there was no Santa Claus. I remember sitting on my father's lap in the living room, my mother beside us, while they together explained that there is a Santa Claus, that they were Mr. and Mrs. Claus, and that they gave me gifts because they loved me.

A third incident that seems significant in my early life was the experience brought to my mother by a door-to-door salesman. It seemed that I had a very active imagination and would come running in to tell my mother stories: that I saw a big bear in the front yard, or I saw a tiger run across the lawn, or I had seen fairies and birds on the ceiling of my bedroom. One day she was explaining to me that these things are not so and that I must not tell things that are not so. She was interrupted by a knock on the door and a man said, "Pardon me, ma'am. I feel that I have been eavesdropping, but I heard you scolding your little girl for telling things that are not true, and I wanted to say to you that my sister used to do the same. She had an active imagination and now she's writing short stories for magazines and publications, while I am delivering items from house to house. So, be patient with your little girl and encourage her imagination."

It seems important to note that my mother listened to the advice of the salesman and that, from that point on, she actively encouraged my imagination.

On the Farm—School Days

My parents sold the house my father had built to buy a farm, although my father had no experience as a farmer. He worked early and late with the help of my mother's father, Grandpa Dorn, who had a farm nearby. My father also contracted with a local creamery for buttermilk and developed a milk route in the neighboring town of Warren, Pennsylvania. He hoped this would supplement the family income.

My mother was my teacher before I went to school. I learned to read, to tell time, and to pick out notes on her organ. From her, I also learned to enjoy a thunderstorm, watching for the flash of lightning and listening for the roll of thunder. She taught me something about the stars. It was a wonderful place to star-watch. There were no lights to interfere. From my grandfather and my mother, I learned much about plants and flowers, and how they grew; fruit, orchards, and animals on the farm. I had a favorite colt whom I loved to romp with when he was small. He later partially ate an Easter hat of mine!

Our second year on the farm marked the beginning of my academic life. It was not until the January after I turned seven that my mother felt it time for me to go to school, which was a one-room schoolhouse about a mile up a steep hill from our house. I remember it as a time of some interest and excitement for me. At the end of June, I was promoted to second grade with the suggestion that I might skip a grade, but my mother opposed it.

During the following two years, children from neighboring farms gathered at the crossroads near our house and in good weather we walked four miles to a four-room schoolhouse. In wintertime, parents took turns loading us into a horse-drawn sleigh for the ride to school. It was on the long walk home in fall and spring that I stopped at my grandparents' farmhouse, where Grandma Dorn had an inexhaustible supply of sour cream cookies, milk, and custard pie.

In many ways, she was a remarkable woman. Her mother had died when Grandma was twelve, and she assumed responsibility for the household. Her father must have been unusual for his time, making it possible for her—the one girl in the family—to attend Oberlin College for two years. After mothering her younger brothers, she had seven children of her own, five of whom survived to adulthood.

I remember that in those days my mother often had what she called a sick headache and that she took medication—patent medicine, I suppose; I'm sure no doctor prescribed it for her headaches. She must have been under a great deal of strain through those years, although I never guessed it at the time. During those years, Grandma Dorn died at our house. My grandfather continued on his farm.

For me, the farm years were years of freedom and roaming the out-of-doors. My constant playmates were my rabbit and my dog, Dash. This black-and-tan short-haired shepherd, who had been patient enough to teach me to walk, went everywhere with me and my rabbit. We took my father and those who were working with him lemonade in the summer or their lunches, and we roamed freely through the pastures and orchards.

But a year of drought was followed by a year of torrential rains, in which crops could not be harvested, and finally a year of heavy frost, which killed the cash crop. The only time I saw my father cry was one morning in early fall when he looked out his bedroom window and saw the leaves and tassels from the corn hanging limp from a devastating frost. We moved again.

As I relive through memory the early part of my life, I again become aware that I have a strong visual memory, to an extent I can hardly believe. Yet I know it's true. As far back as two and three, I remember distinctly the floor plan of our first Jamestown house. I could draw it, I believe, almost to scale and would be willing to have it tested against the actual house if it still exists. The same is true of the three-room house that my father and I built, the farmhouse, and all the others. In fact, the same is true of every house in which I have lived, and of places I've visited. If I have stopped at a restaurant or hotel in my travels, I can easily find it again when I go back months or years later. I am including this in my story because I believe it is significant now that a severe vision problem has become a daily reality to me. My strong visual memory is very helpful in making the transition, more and more, from the visual sense to the auditory and the tactile.

Growing Up in Venturetown

We moved from the farm to a small oil refinery town, Venturetown, Pennsylvania, not far from the place of my birth and near Warren, the center of my father's business. During the years in Venturetown, my life shifted away from that of a carefree child unaware of the problems around me, with a great deal of freedom, few playmates, but free to roam and imagine and dream. A very adult part of my life now began.

By this time, my father was drinking quite heavily and often would come home from a day's work with little or no money. He would need to go to bed and sleep a lot. I was aware that my mother was worried and angry. She encouraged me to go with him whenever I was not in school, in the hope that my presence in the truck on the milk route would deter him from stopping too long at the hotel bars and restaurants that were his customers.

When I was nine or ten years old, I clearly remember occasions of driving the truck home from Warren to Venturetown—a distance of about five miles—and managing to get into the driveway and down a rather steep grade to the place where we parked it. I don't remember any special strain about it except that I was always a little bit scared that I wouldn't be able to reach the brakes or stop when I wanted to as I perched on the edge of the seat.

By childish inference, I began to assume that women are the strong ones and men are not dependable. Maybe they don't have the same kind of feelings that women have. My dream picture of my father began to fade. However, in his better days, he was still a charmer, the Pied Piper of the children in our neighborhood. Our house was always the center of the Fourth of July fireworks, and my father took great care ensuring that it was a safe celebration. In years when there was an oversupply somewhere, he would come home with a great amount of goodies: watermelon, cantaloupes, all kinds of other fruit, and perishable goods. We would feast and share the feast with our neighbors. That we could feed our friends but not always ourselves was a cause of great resentment to my mother. Although, with fine-tuned selectivity, I do not recall deprivation during those years. I assume my mother was a good manager. She was a good cook, and I felt well cared for and secure enough.

Years after my sister's death, the second tragedy of my life was the death of my loved dog, Dash. As I reminisce, I find it very interesting that I do not remember the physical pain of my illnesses, even of my bout with polio, but I do remember the pain of the death of my rabbit and the death of my dog.

My playmates at that time were the boys from my mother's Sunday-school class. (She had always taught such classes.) We used to play down at the refinery, get warm wax, make things with it, and chew it. Those days are for the most part pleasant memories.

It was then that my father gave me permission to invite anybody I chose to come to my mother's birthday party. I proceeded to write invitations and put them in the mailboxes of all the neighbors, inviting entire families. On the night of my mother's birthday party, my parents were completely overwhelmed. It was an exciting evening with a lot of lights and food, a lot of people, and a lot of laughter.

The two and a half years from age nine through eleven were truly growing up years. We lived in two different homes. I recovered from polio. I had my first lesson in male anatomy by playing doctor with my cousin, who was two years older. I learned from my mother that I was not to play that way any more, which threw a kind of mystery around the whole subject of sex and made it all the more interesting. To be sure, I told no one of my new interest.

Among all my experiences in those rapidly growing up years, one of the bitter disappointments of adult reality came from learning that although a barn that burns on more and more brightly through a whole afternoon is important and tremendously exciting, it is *not* a legal reason for being absent from school. It resulted in my first note from a teacher to my parents telling them that I had transgressed.

The sounds, the sights, the sensations of those years are so clear and alive in my memory that I find great difficulty in moving on. But I am about to enter a period of stability, moving into full-blown adulthood.

Coming of Age

It began when I was twelve years old and we made our final move to a house in Jamestown which my father and the local United Brethren minister remodeled from a storefront with a one-slant roof to a comfortable bungalow. Our home until I had finished college and begun to teach nearby, it was our eighth homeplace!

Adulthood first stirred during a conference with the minister, Reverend Hanks. I had considered being baptized, accepting the doctrine of the church, and becoming a member. I told him, "I'm sorry, but I cannot join this church because I do not believe in original sin. I do not believe that people are sinful, and I don't believe that they are born in sin." It was a genuinely adult conversation in which he confided that he too did not accept every part of the church's doctrine, but that it was a congregation of people generally of like mind and faith who were helpful to one another. Therefore, he had chosen to make it his life work. With that understanding I was baptized, joined the church, and became very active in the Sunday school and young people's activities. In my later teens, I was named a lay minister, which lasted until near the end of my college years. My social life in high school, which centered in the church, was rich, satisfying, and pleasant, although severely circumscribed by the accepted lifestyle of other church members. I had many friends, both among the young people with whom I worked and with the adults who were leaders in the organizations. I didn't attend dances, for example. I did go for sleigh rides, enjoyed the more informal kinds of activities, was on the debating team (the only girl on the team), and was coached by my Grandfather Dorn, who was living with us at the time.

At the same time, an older schoolmate introduced me in a limited way to the world of vaudeville. He wrote two or three acts for which he received a contract and in which I played the straight man. It gave me an opportunity for some experience in ad-libbing. It seemed like a very intriguing thing to do and not so different from the kind of support I had given my father when, on many occasions, I was his assistant in an evening of sleight-of-hand and magic. It was all done in the spirit of fun and I enjoyed it, but my parents objected. So I did not further pursue a vaudeville career, even for fun.

My Grandma Cooper, who lived with us for a short time after she retired as housekeeper for a prominent family in Jamestown, was a round, usually jolly woman with a Maine accent. She had a very quick temper and a very warm heart. When she laughed, she laughed all over. I always thought of her when I read the Christmas story about St. Nick, whose belly shook like a bowl full of jelly when he laughed. She was a comfortable woman whom I loved. She made the best New England baked beans I ever tasted.

It was from her younger daughter, my Aunt Nel, that I learned my father had been Grandma's favorite among her five children and therefore resented by the others. I never knew my Grandfather Cooper, who died before I was born. But a card that I still have announced him as "an eclectic physician."

During my fourteenth summer, my mother went back to school at a state college, working toward her teaching certificate. During one summer while she was away, I became the homemaker and wage earner for the family, with the help of my father's garden and my grandfather's small flock of chickens, which he kept in a barn nearby.

In my junior year of high school, we as a family realized we would need to find a college where I could get scholarship aid and loans, and my mother would need to qualify for a steady income. She went to the president of the major bank in Jamestown, whom she had known from previous business transactions, to ask for a loan for my first year of college. It seems like a shocking question now, but he asked, "Why is it important for your daughter to go to college with the financial situation you have?"

My mother's rejoinder was, "Is your son in college?" When he answered yes, she said, "My daughter is worth just as much as your son, and she has a right for the opportunity to go to college." She got the loan.

For two years following my high school graduation, I worked to save money and augment my mother's resources. I engaged in house-to-house selling of Real Silk hosiery. I remember how desperate I was for the job, which promised to pay even more than a school-teacher's salary for a good salesperson, possibly up to forty-five dollars a week. The trainer who was interviewing said to me, "You applied for this job? I advertised for a man, much less a kid of a girl." My anger flared. I kept it to myself, but I was determined that I would show the man I could sell. So, we had the interview and role-played a sales call. He worked for a very long time trying to "sell" me some Real Silk hosiery, and I was the "customer." I offered every objection I could think of to get every kind of answer I could from him until finally he said, "I give up. You have the job." And I was in. In my mind, it made the difference between going to college and not going to college.

My parent's graduation gifts were a beautifully bound Bible, a wristwatch, and a huge wardrobe trunk—the first tangible evidence that I was leaving home. A real tinge of sadness still persists as I remember that Grandpa Dorn did not live to see me go to college. It had been a great joy and hope for him. He had been one of the rare ones of his time who had completed the Jamestown Academy when few people did that. He confided to me in those last years that no matter how long a day he worked on the farm, he never went to sleep without first reading for an hour. He was one of the best-read persons I ever knew, and he was a purist in the use of the English language. He believed in honest work: that if anything was worth doing, it was worth doing well. This is part of the heritage he left my mother and me.

And so it was that on one night in September of 1926, a naive nineteen-year-old who had spent her entire life within a radius of twenty-five miles went to bed in the upper berth of a Pullman car and found herself the next day in a dormitory room of Lebanon Valley College in Annville, Pennsylvania.

The College Years

It was in this small church-affiliated college in a small town that I stumbled on a book that shook me loose from my narrow religious foundations and aroused my intellect. The book was Alfred North Whitehead's *Science and the Modern World*.[2] It was broad rather than narrow, inquiring rather than accepting; it was discovery. But it was my association with three classmates—two of them older men who had had some experience in world travel and in intellectual inquiry before they came to Lebanon Valley—that peaked my curiosity, stimulated my literary and artistic interests, and involved me in the production of the junior yearbook. Its theme was the Alhambra, and it was only many years later when I had visited the Alhambra myself that I could appreciate the excellence, the beauty of the photography, and the art work that distinguished our yearbook from any others I had seen or have seen since.

Meanwhile, its personality sketches of the faculty created a furor. Some faculty members took umbrage at their characterizations, which one of the four members of our group had written. Each was in the style of some prominent literary figure which we, the editors, considered suitable to the personality or characteristics of that faculty member.

As a result of the uproar and the discovery in their room of some of the works of Voltaire and other "dangerous" thinkers, two of our editorial staff were dismissed from the school. It is difficult to believe now that the Board of Trustees could have taken such drastic action in the summer, when most students were not on campus, without some protest developing from the student organizations when they returned in the fall, but such was the case.

My other colleague and I were warned but allowed to complete our four years at the college. My mother was most supportive of my right to freedom of expression and offered to help me find another college for my senior year if the necessity arose. These experiences take on added significance because I was moving farther and farther away from my freshman intentions of becoming a medical missionary.

Another valuable experience involved my favorite professor, Dr. Paul A. W. Wallace. I had the good fortune of being his student assistant during my junior year. Because I had been so busy with my various student activities, I had neglected to prepare for an important test in American literature. He gave me a grade of D, which was a failure in my opinion and which could not be changed by reexamination. I was humiliated and went to him with the plea of changing my grade to an E, which would mean that I could retest and erase the disgraceful grade. He refused to do it, "Because," he said, "Miss Cooper, you undoubtedly made the better choice by engaging in the activity. But you made your choice and it is important that you accept responsibility for that choice. I cannot change your grade." This lesson was a gift.

Venturing into a Profession

A guardian angel in some form must have been watching over me in the Easter vacation of 1930, for I returned to the campus having signed a teaching contract at a time when many classmates were entering the ranks of the unemployed. The following year, I settled in at Lakewood High School, within easy driving distance of my home in Jamestown, as a teacher of first-, second-, and third-year English.

Two years later, my parents separated. All three of us felt the pain of being wrenched free from the common soil that was our home, but my father stayed on at our house for some time until it was sold. My mother and I moved temporarily into a small apartment near my school while each of us was looking for a small apartment of our own.

During my second year of teaching, I became impatient with the Regents' curriculum and its strict requirements (which preceded the three-year Comprehensive English Examination for the State of New York), so I ventured into an experimental program in education. With the support of the principal and the school librarian, I established a classroom library which included multiple copies of the Regents' recommended titles plus poetry, fiction, biography, and drama, including Shakespeare. Choosing one third-year class as the experimental group, I encouraged students to read widely and then discuss their reading with others in the class. A more experienced teacher could have avoided some of the pitfalls of such a departure from the usual procedures, but I was generally satisfied in the end. The results were good and brought about some changes in all of the English classes, particularly in the last three years when I became chairman of the department.

Another innovation that brought me great pleasure was the reading, listening to, and writing of poetry with the use of color. At the beginning of the syllabus's unit on poetry, I provided each student in my third-year English class with a set of artist's colored pencils. I gave them time to browse through books of poetry and selections from a textbook, and to choose favorite poems that they could read aloud to the class. Some students chose several poems; others were unable to find more than one or two. I joined in by reading some of my favorites.

I asked the students to close their eyes as they listened to a poem, then to write its title in their notebooks, call up whatever colors they imagined, and record their images. Afterward, various students talked about and showed the ways they had used color to match their feelings and impressions as they heard the poem.

Some poems became known for the colors called up in people's imagination. For example, *The Vagabond Song* by Bliss Carmen evoked bright autumn colors, blue skies, and purple asters ("There's something in October sets my Gypsy blood astir, I must rise to follow her, When from every hill of flame she calls each vagabond by name").

Many of the students wrote their own poems, colored their words, and then shared their notebooks. Some students posted on the bulletin board "color poems" they had written outside of class. The district superintendent became interested in these experiments and brought many visitors to the class to observe the work I was doing.

Toward the end of my tenure at Lakewood High, I realized that I was spending a great deal of my time, particularly after school, in the counseling of students on various kinds of problems—academic and personal—and that if I were to be a good counselor, I would need to learn more about counseling. For some reason I chose Teachers College at Columbia University in New York and requested a sabbatical leave for further study. And, again, a person who had some authority over my action did what seemed at the time like a very cruel thing. The principal, Mr. Matthewson, refused to grant me a leave, saying, "Once you have gone to New York and done graduate work, you will not want to be tied to a contract in this little small town high school. So, burn your bridges."

New York, New York!

I burned my bridges, spent my sabbatical doing graduate work in New York, and found that Mr. Matthewson had been wise indeed. As transforming as the step from Jamestown to Lebanon Valley had been, it was minor compared to the leap from Lakewood to Morningside Heights.

By some chance and by great good fortune, I had arranged to live at International House while attending courses two blocks away at Teachers College. I had no idea that two important strands which would become a part of the tapestry of my life had their beginnings on that day in September 1936. One began at International House, the other at Teachers College. Three years later, I was to learn that Daniel Sanford, later my husband, had been the director of admissions at International House in an earlier period. So when we first met in 1939 at Teachers College, we had in common an interest in international living, a base at International House, and a real bond.

The other strand—which I realized many, many years later—was a common experience that Carl Rogers and I had by doing graduate work at Teachers College, where preparation for counseling was highly traditional. Surprisingly enough, both of us survived it without becoming traditionalists.

A practice at International House which has long since gone the way of many of the gentler courtesies of life was a double blessing to me that year. I was able to eke out a food allowance by becoming the hostess who greeted guests at the House and poured coffee during the breakfast hour. By so doing, I earned my breakfast, which became a major meal. I also came to know many people who were living in the House and developed a real love and enthusiasm for meeting and greeting new people.

From my savings I had paid in advance for the tuition and my room, which left me with a dollar a day for food. In addition to my experiences in the course work, I learned that it was possible to spend very, very little and yet find the best in entertainment in the city. I could go to the old Metropolitan Opera House and stand at the back; at the close of the first act, people who had sat in the orchestra would often leave and give their tickets to standees who were nearest the aisle. It cost very little to sit in the top balcony of theaters (later, when I first sat in a first-balcony seat, I was amazed at how large the stage and the actors were; it was a revelation).

As far as course work was concerned, no one at Columbia Teachers College censored my books or questioned my values and my religious commitment. During my first year of graduate study, I had the good fortune to meet Harry Kitson, an instructor whose field was vocational guidance—particularly testing. He taught me an important lesson from his own experience. He told my class that he had set out feeling that tests could be used as magic in learning about people and their talents, and in matching them with careers or jobs. Early in his practice, however, he had decided that "a test tests only what it tests." He urged that we use our common sense rather than always following the guidelines set down in our textbooks.

Later, as his assistant, I again ventured into new territory: preparing a script and a discussion guide for his weekly program at the American School of the Air. Radio was an exacting medium. The aim of the program was to help students think about their place in the world, their capacities, and ways they could use their abilities.

In a course called "Education and Society," Dr. William Heard Kilpatrick made a lasting impression on me. I recall his quiet digni-fied manner, his soft voice, his quick mind, and the great halo of lux-uriant white hair that was so dominant a part of his appearance. On one occasion, after a guest speaker had finished at one of the sessions, I remember Dr. Kilpatrick saying, "Dr. Begley and I are in about 98 percent agreement but the other 2 percent is very important."

It was later, when I met him on the street and engaged in a five- or ten-minute conversation with him, that I realized more of Dr. Kilpatrick's human qualities: his warmth, his interest in persons, his humor, and the twinkle that was characteristic of his eyes in such a situation. That was the year of his retirement, and it seemed to me that he was really pleased to have a former student stop him on the street, speak to him about the experience of being in his course, and talk with him.

Across the street from International House and one block away from where I was studying was Riverside Church, with Harry Emerson Fosdick as the minister. I remember the experience of attending services in that great cathedral-like building, looking down from one of the boxes along the side of the cathedral wall at the great organ and the stained-glass windows, listening to the carillon and hearing Dr. Fosdick's sermons—so very, very different from the kind of sermons I had heard in my childhood and in my college days.

At Sunday night suppers at International House, prominent people from different fields were invited to speak or to meet informally after supper with students in the Homeroom. Often we sat around on the floor or in comfortable chairs and just had a dialogue or conversation with some prominent thinker or writer. One of these speakers was Reinhold Niebuhr. After he had spoken, a philosophy student said, "But, Dr. Niebuhr, in thus-and-so book you made this statement, and tonight you said something which I believe contradicts it. Will you please explain?" Dr. Niebuhr listened very intently and then said, "My Lord, man, that was written five years ago!" He did go on to explain the difference, but his first response was a strong lesson for me about the fluidity and the openness of one's thinking.

Another speaker was Dr. Henry Pitt Van Dusen, also from Union Theological Seminary, whom I remember less well but nevertheless think of as one of the persons in theology who helped strengthen the individuality of values and judgments in religion and in personal life.

Another professor at Columbia Teachers College, whose name I do not recall, emphasized adjusting to life situations as the goal of counseling. I remember with clarity and some detail a debate that ran on through a large part of that semester—with myself and with others in the course and with the professor—as to whether the purpose of counseling was to help people to adjust. If it was helping people adjust to existing conditions, how then could we expect education to bring about societal changes? At the time, I was questioning an accepted value of the counseling profession. I have since realized it was a major step in the development of my own values and philosophy of education.

From financial necessity, I turned my attention from continuing my graduate work to finding employment for the following year. My mother joined me in New York, and I assisted her in establishing her own nursery school in nearby New Jersey.

To my deep regret, I lost touch with my father when I went to New York and returned only to arrange his funeral in 1944. Ironically, as I had moved away from the religious influences of fundamentalist Protestantism, my father had found in a Gospel Tabernacle, a community that gave him support and a friend in the Evangelist. As a result, he stopped his excessive drinking and died with the feeling that he had found a substitute family. All I could offer, in place of myself, was to adopt his little dog and, years later, to write an epitaph on his gravestone. It reads: "To a dancing spirit, you are loved." I hope that in some way he got the message.

Jobs were very scarce in the early summer following that academic year, and it seemed like a gift to find an advertisement in the paper for a college or graduate student to ghostwrite a book. A man by the name of Houser had been conducting a study of the needs and preferences of customers and the needs of employees at B. Altman & Company in New York, and the title of the book would be *What the People Want from Business.* I applied and got the job. It was a valuable experience, not only writing but also summarizing these opinion surveys and talking with the heads of various departments about the questionnaires and the opinions of the people in their departments. It also paid more money than most jobs of that sort, and I felt very fortunate. I returned to my mother's home in Jamestown, New York for the remainder of the summer.

The next episode affected the rest of my life. I received two job offers: one from the Office of the Secretary at Teachers College, the other from the YWCA in Portland, Oregon as director of their program. The salaries were not very different, and I wasn't sure about the one from Teachers College, which involved advising graduate students in certain departments of the university, responding to their applications, counseling them about their courses, helping them with financial arrangements, and providing other services.

When I received a telegram from New York asking for my decision, however, I accepted that afternoon. The next morning a telegram from Portland arrived, dated the evening before; but I'd already made my commitment.

Little did I know how far-reaching that decision and the delay of two hours would be in my lifetime. Had I not been in the Office of the Secretary at Teachers College, I would never have met Niel Sanford, and my life would have been quite different. He used to say jokingly, "If you had chosen Portland, you would have married a lumberman and been rich, and you would never have known me." I don't know that my brief career there was distinguished, but I did marry the most eligible bachelor around; and when I left in the summer of 1940, it was as the wife of the Dean of Instruction at Tampa University in Florida.

A delay of two hours in the delivery of a telegram had made the difference between Portland and New York. It seemed that a tenuous connection was holding together parts of my life. Such a delicate thread appeared again in the summer of 1940. We had planned our wedding for August 7. It was not until August 5 that we had a telephone call from the president of Tampa University in Florida, in response to Niel's application to become Dean of Instruction there. "Today my wife reminded me that you people are getting married," he said, "and that it was important that you have a formal confirmation of employment. Consider this the formal confirmation, and

I shall send a telegram that will make it final." We left for Florida a few days later.

Introduction to the World of Academe

In the early days, the University of Tampa was housed in what had been the old Tampa Bay Hotel, an elegant Victorian structure. It was easily converted to accommodate the needs of a young university during its formative years.

What was expected of the new dean was to become well known, get his name in *Who's Who,* join professional organizations, become the speaker at various occasions and different universities in the state, and help develop a reputation for the university. His wife was expected to be a social hostess willing to give lawn parties, entertain guests and faculty, stand endlessly in receiving lines at receptions, and be agreeable and gracious. I did not own a formal floor-length gown but found that that was the accepted social uniform, be it for afternoon or evening functions.

So it was that my excitement, my great joy in being the wife of a man whom I loved very much, of being a part of the faculty rather than the student body at a university, were met head-on and greatly tempered. The reality of being part of a Southern university was that social mores were quite different from those of New York. It was important, for example, that we have a black servant, at least part time, and that we pay her no more than the "going rate." Otherwise, the neighbors would complain that we were spoiling the "nigras." Photographers arrived to take my picture in my garden and to photograph my husband and me in a receiving line, along with the president of the university and his wife. All this was a strange and strained world for me.

To keep my brain alive, I sought out two women's organizations: one of them the American Association of University Women, and the other an international organization for career women. I attended and became part of their discussions. One day, when a Florida state senator visited one of these groups to speak, I felt the first stirrings of a feminist spirit. In the course of his address, which was to a small informal group, he said that there were three categories of persons in the state who could not legally be responsible parties in the signing of legal contracts. These were minors, the mentally incompetent (including the insane), and married women. When we questioned him, the senator responded with "Women! I have nothing against them. Bless 'em. I just want to protect them!"

I went home that evening furious that I had been included in such a list. In my own way, I became a part of the feminist movement. I have never marched in a parade. That is not my way of expressing myself. But I have, particularly since then, been conscious of the fact that I am first of all a person and a woman and that my mother's declaration to the president of the bank in Jamestown was a touchstone for me.

Our first home was a comfortable, roomy bungalow with extensive lawns and a flower garden where I earned my wings as a social hostess for the university. After a year and a half, Niel and I moved to the first floor of a larger, two-family house facing the great and beautiful Tampa Bay. A gorgeous red bougainvillea vine clambered over its brick chimney. The front porch was lined with fragrant lavender butterfly bushes and brilliant red hibiscus. In our back yard, which was small, we had a banana tree, an avocado tree, and two orange trees. We made it known we no longer needed a servant.

It was there that I became acquainted with the Gasparillas Celebration, which was a part of the city's recognition of the role of the pirate who had sailed into the bay, according to legend, and taken over the city in early years. Another one of the most pleasurable parts of our stay in Tampa was our participation in a book-and-supper club that met each month in the homes of different faculty members. One of the faculty described Niel as "a man without guile." Expressed as it was in the midst of the turmoil of university reorganization, this was a potent observation—and, to me, very true and well deserved.

Niel was under a great deal of strain during those three years. At the end of that time, by mutual agreement with the president, we left and returned north. For the most part, the strain for both of us was the result of conflict between Niel and the president. Niel had intense interest in and hope for developing a curriculum for the university that would acknowledge some of the social issues and help to encourage something of excellence in faculty and in the curriculum itself. The president seemed to look upon not only his own role, but that of the dean, as one of a public relations official.

It would be unfair to leave the impression that the three years in Tampa were unpleasant or disappointing. It was an easy place for pleasures. Both of us began to realize our interest in watercolor painting, and we traveled about different lakes and points of interest in Florida, camped on a small lake nearby for a vacation period, and had plenty of time to indulge our interest in painting. Niel did a rather fine one of the swamp cypress trees and the Spanish moss. I devoted considerable time sitting on our front porch at our bay house trying to capture the evanescence of the sky during the bright days with the clouds that seemed to pile high almost from the horizon to the zenith.

I remember, too, the fun of being a shopper in the downtown district of Tampa in the afternoon, when the usual shower suddenly appeared and even the most elegant women—finely coiffured and in the most modish of costumes—would take off their shoes and walk through the rivers in the streets caused by the sudden cloudburst, paying no attention to the others who were also carrying their shoes in their hands.

It was before the days of central heating and air conditioning, so each of our houses was heated only by a fireplace. In the wintertime it became very cold and damp in the house. On various occasions, we went on weekend trips to the southern part of Florida in the hope of getting warm. In the hot part of the year, the humidity was such that even ten minutes after taking a shower, we would be dripping with perspiration. So, this was another learning about living in a different place.

The most distressing of our experiences was the dawning awareness of life in a segregated society. Neil and I had never before been conscious of this—a mark of naiveté, perhaps; blindness is a better term. In retrospect, I am appalled that both Niel and I could have lived for years in Morningside Heights in New York, which is on the edge of Harlem, without becoming conscious of the cultural and racial segregation that was so blatant. We met and enjoyed black friends at International House. Niel was a man of international experience, having gone directly to China as a member of the Yale-in-China faculty in Changsha, Hunan Province, when he graduated from Yale University. Upon his return, he joined the faculty of Hampton Institute, a college for black students in Virginia, where he experienced various levels of his own feelings of discrimination. He used to talk about it quite freely. He had been the director of admissions at International House in New York City and had completed his graduate work at Teachers College, Columbia. During the time that we worked together in the Office of the Secretary, he was the advisor for students from other countries. Yet this issue of racial segregation apparently had never become real to him until Tampa.

Having experienced the reality of racial segregation in our daily lives, we were also sensitive to ethnic segregation evident in Ybor City, where most Spanish members of the Tampa community lived. People would go from downtown or residential Tampa along the bay to Ybor

City for special Spanish dinners, but socially there was a sharp line of division. Is going away from home requisite for looking at home with clear and seeing eyes?

A Door Swings Open—Maryland

Niel decided to leave administration and return to teaching psychology. He accepted a position as professor of psychology at Western Maryland College. In spite of my expectation and intention, a door to professional life swung open for me again during Niel's tenure there. I was invited to teach a course in counseling during the summer sessions. When I observed the lack of counseling for undergraduate students at the college, I was asked to initiate such services and to organize the college's first counseling office. We also served students from the theological seminary that was located on the same campus.

Another far more important door opened in Maryland. Our daughter, Mei-Mei, was born in 1947. It was an unusually cold January in Maryland, and during the thirty-mile drive home from the hospital, she developed a respiratory infection. Within the first week, she had to return to the hospital for treatment. The day after she was admitted, a case of infant diarrhea was reported in the hospital; two days after we brought her home, she was hospitalized again, this time for infant diarrhea. As we were leaving home, Niel said to her, "Come back to us safely, little Mei-Mei." As he spoke, she turned her gaze directly to him. That fixed her name as Mei-Mei, an affectionate name for a little girl in a Chinese family.

I shall forever be grateful to three fine doctors at Johns Hopkins Hospital for the work they did that following night. A patient in the hospital who was sitting in the corridor in the early morning hours told me she had heard one doctor say, "It's no use. We've done everything possible to keep her alive and bring her back to life, and we can't do anymore."

The other doctor replied, "What do you mean we can't do anymore? This baby is all these people have, and we've got to save her."

The next morning when we returned to the hospital, the doctors said that she was not out of the woods but they felt she had a good chance for survival. At the end of the week as we were leaving the hospital, Dr. Goodwin said to us, "Take her home and enjoy her. She's not as fragile as she seems."

She was an answer to our prayers, a hope long deferred, and a joy to the household—not only to us, her parents, but to both her grandmothers. Niel's mother was already living in a small apartment in Westminster, and my mother (who still had a nursery school in New Jersey) soon moved to the outskirts of Westminster. She established another nursery school there. Our family doctor assured us there was then no obstacle to our having another child or two, which we very much wanted. But it was not to be.

After the first month of her life, when her very existence hung on a fragile thread, Mei-Mei became a bright, active, happy little girl who was a constant source of delight. I have often wondered what impressions, what sensations, what feelings are somewhere buried in her memory of those first days, the first month of her life.

As I write this, she is a Fulbright scholar, completing her field work in Nigeria for her doctorate in anthropology and religion. She is an accomplished wood-carver and was a teacher of woodworking for several years in the Manhattan Country Day School in New York City. Very early, she showed verbal facility by saying poems to me (which I wrote down and have kept)—a facility she has not lost.

Crisis in Virginia

Problems related to Niel's health arose, and he accepted a position in Virginia as a member of the clinical staff at a hospital for retarded persons. While this promised to be less demanding during his period of recuperation, it was disastrous to his health. For three years we traveled from doctor to doctor, trying to discover the nature and cause of Niel's illness.

During this personal crisis and the financial crisis that followed, I was pushed to the brink of a decision between collapse and transformation. From my early years, I had learned to be conscientious and responsible, to be resourceful, to stay with a problem until I had worked it out. I had come to believe that I could do whatever needed to be done if I could find a way to do it. Although I had moved far away from the fundamentalist beliefs of my early years, I still held to the golden rule, which meant to me that one must be considerate of others. All these forces were brought to bear on the family situation in which we found ourselves.

Niel was unable to assume his usual part in family matters. Mei-Mei was small, about three or four years old. Both our mothers had come to be near us in Lynchburg and were eager to help us in any way they could. They had decided, in the interest of economy, to live in one apartment and discovered that they were not compatible.

We had exhausted our savings and had used most of a legacy that had been left for Mei-Mei's education. Mei-Mei had no playmates, except possibly one older girl. She was trying to puzzle out signs along the road and billboards and reading material at the house. I was very busy with household concerns and taking Niel to the doctor frequently—long trips sometimes. In the process of all this, I was trying to be a good wife, a good mother, a good daughter, a good daughter-in-law, trying to consider everyone and losing myself. No matter how hard I tried, nothing came right.

My temper was short. I scolded Mei-Mei for little bits of misbehavior that would have completely escaped me before. I was short-tempered with my mother and with Niel's mother. I was unhappy about the tension and the friction in the household, but I seemed unable to do anything effective about it. My life had become like a tangled skein of yarn: if I could find one end of that skein, that tangle, I might be able to untangle it. But I couldn't find that end. So, I wrote to my friend Sara in Pennsylvania, who was a psychiatric social worker, asking her if she could come and help me. I knew I had been feeling helpless, even hopeless, about finding my way out. And desperate.

Sara offered to spend one intensive week of therapy with me. We both understood that we could be risking our long-time friendship, but we also knew that the depth of our knowledge and understanding of one another would be a real help in the therapy.

Toward the end of the week, I awoke from an afternoon nap with a message in my mind as clear as any spoken words. "Protective! Protective! You have been protective of members of your family." Protective. What do I protect? I protect what I possess. I was shocked, devastated to realize I had been a possessive mother, wife, even daughter and daughter-in-law.

Sara, in her wisdom, brought to my attention that Mei-Mei had her own strength, even as young as she was. If I did less protecting, she would be able to use her own strengths and to develop them. I immediately made the connection with my husband. I had begun to untangle the tangled skein. It was only a beginning.

With the best intention, with love in my heart, I had been damaging the people I loved most. It was unthinkable. But, I protested, some responsible adult was needed to hold the family together in a crisis. True. Slowly, the realization came that it was not necessary to take care of every member of the family in order to hold the family together. That had been *my* need. In meeting my own need, not theirs, I had helped to create the tangle—a truth I did not want to hear.

I began to let in anger: anger first at myself, then at my mother for her intrusion and advice-giving, and Niel's mother for her intrusion and offers of support. It was not until much later that I realized my anger at my husband for being ill. But how does one express anger to a sick husband, to a little girl, to parents who are trying sincerely to help?

That is how the geyser, long capped, broke forth in tears of anger, grief, and guilt. Although it took place in the same house, there was never any evidence that other members of the family understood or were aware of the struggle that was going on. All my feelings, now loosed, reached back into my early years, and I felt anger that I had been expected to assume responsibility to be my father's keeper. I felt then guilt and grief at my anger and at the pain I now realized my parents had felt in those years long ago.

At the end of that intense and exhausting week, I emerged humbled and strengthened, encouraged by my friend's assurance that we had gone more deeply in one week than she had gone in more than two years of therapy—I would add, much to her credit, and to mine, and to our friendship.

I began months and years of learning new ways of nurturing and of caring. At the same time, I faced the necessity of becoming the wage earner for the family. This brought to light a new source of anger toward Niel. I had not intended to become a career woman. My expectations of married life left no room for becoming the wage earner for the family, as my mother had done. Through the winter and the following spring, I tried diligently to make peace with my conflict. The result was that, after obtaining a contract as a house-to-house sales representative—at which I had done well in my post high school years—I talked myself out of every sale for a month, although I saw prospective customers for hours every day.

My next attempt was requesting referrals from the employment office of Columbia University. After two interviews, I realized that again I was talking myself out of any prospect of being employed by being apologetic about seeking a position. Facing my own acts of sabotage and accepting them as real was not easy, but at the very next interview I signed a contract—a cause for jubilation.

To leave Lynchburg without noting the joys, the pleasures, and the comforts of our stay there would be neither fair nor honest. We were within only fifty miles of Charlottesville with its excellent medical center, where we at last found a diagnosis and the beginning of a successful treatment for Niel's illness. Charlottesville is also the site of Thomas Jefferson's home, Monticello. We made several visits there which are a very rich part of our memory of Virginia.

Our second home in Lynchburg was located on the outskirts of the city in a very comfortable brick home belonging to people who were pleased to have occupants while they were away over an extended period of time. We thus had a roomy, comfortable home, partially furnished, with lawns, well-kept shrubbery and hedges and shade trees, plenty of room for a child to play, and a porch where we could enjoy the warm days through most of the winter.

At the height of the tensions and anxiety, we made frequent day trips into the surrounding countryside, drove up to Washington, DC, and visited the home of the artist Dennis Morgan, who illustrated *Misty of Chincoteague* and *King of the Wind* and other wonderful horse stories which Mei-Mei loved. On shorter trips, we took the car out on Skyline Drive above Lynchburg. In fact, from one of our bedroom windows we could see the mountains, magnificent in the change of season and always a joy to watch.

After our experience in Tampa, we were keenly aware of indications all around us of racial segregation and deprivation. We talked with black friends and acquaintances about voting and about the poll tax, and saw for the first time how hopeless some of them felt, never to have a part in governing their own town.

During our last year in Virginia, Mei-Mei attended a church-related kindergarten class and was invited to a birthday party of one of her classmates which would not have been memorable except that the classmate lived in one of the houses built by Thomas Jefferson as a vacation retreat from Monticello. After Mei-Mei had attended the party, the family invited us to make a complete tour of the building, which was very interesting indeed, as was the folklore associated with it.

When Mei-Mei had been in the class for several days, she asked the teacher, "Why are there no black children in our class?"

The teacher replied, "Because there are no black children in the church."

"But I don't belong to this church, and I'm in the school."

The teacher said, "Well, that's the way it is." When Mei-Mei came home and told the story, she had her first lesson in the reality of segregated living.

In retrospect, the one experience with the most profound and far-reaching effect on the life of the family was the crisis in Lynchburg. It pushed me over the edge into self-awareness and openness to a new way of being with myself and with others. I believe that it marked a life-changing transformation, not only for me, but for other members of the family. Without it, Niel could have comfortably drifted into becoming a dependent invalid. Mei-Mei could have become a spoiled, dependent, and perhaps rebellious child. The simplest way for me to describe the change that took place within me is to quote a prose poem I wrote twenty-five years later, "Loving with an Open Hand."

This week as I talked with a friend I recalled a story which I heard this summer. "A compassionate person, seeing a butterfly struggling to free itself from its cocoon, and wanting to help, very gently loosened the filaments to form an opening. The butterfly was freed, emerged from the cocoon, and fluttered about but could not fly. What the compassionate person did not know was that only through the birth struggle can the wings grow strong enough for flight. Its shortened life was spent on the ground; it never knew freedom, never really lived."

I call it learning to love with an open hand. It is a learning which has come slowly to me and has been wrought in the fires of pain and in the water of patience. I am learning that I must free one I love, for if I clutch or cling, try to control, I lose what I try to hold.

If I try to change someone I love because I feel I know how that person should be, I rob him or her of a precious right, the right to take responsibility for one's own life and choices and way of being. Whenever I impose my wish or want or try to exert power over another, I rob him or her of the full realization of growth and maturation; I limit and thwart by my act of possession, no matter how kind my intention.

I can limit and injure by the kindest acts of protecting, and protection or concern overextended can say to the other person more eloquently than words, "You are unable to care for yourself; I must take care of you because you are mine. I am responsible for you."

As I learn and practice more and more, I can say to one I love, "I love you, I value you, I respect you and I trust that you have or can develop the strength to become all that is possible for you to become—if I don't get in your way. I love you so much that I can set you free to walk beside me in joy and in sadness. I will share your tears but I will not ask you not to cry. I will respond to your need, I will care and comfort you but I will not hold you up when you can walk alone. I will stand ready to be with you in your grief and loneliness but I will not take it away from you. I will strive to listen to your meaning as well as your words but I shall not always agree.

Sometimes I will be angry and when I am, I will try to tell you openly so that I need not resent our differences or feel estranged. I cannot always be with you or hear what you say for there are times when I must listen to myself and care for myself, and when that happens I will be as honest with you as I can be."

I am learning to say this, whether it be in words or in my way of being with others and myself, to those I love and for whom I care. And this I call loving with an open hand.

I cannot always keep my hands off the cocoon, but I am getting better at it!

Late in the summer of 1952, our family moved to Lakewood, New Jersey, where I had obtained a position as high school counselor. I also agreed to organize a counseling office with facilities for career information and resource materials. Because the principal believed that there should be no sharp division between teaching and counseling, I taught one class a day in the English department. Although it seemed difficult at the time, I believe it helped in establishing a completely new service in the high school.

The following summer, I attended a refresher postgraduate course at Rutgers University, taught by Bruce Shear, the chief of the Bureau of Guidance for the state of New York. It was a course on planning programs and facilities for counseling services. He recommended that I come back to New York and was helpful in securing my next position in West Hempstead.

When I left Lakewood in 1955, I left a thriving counseling program with a second counselor. With the approval of the principal and the Board of Education, my plans for new counseling facilities were included in the proposed new high school building. Professionally, the years in Lakewood had been satisfying, stimulating, even exhilarating at times.

The climate in our home had changed. Niel was recuperating, but not employed, so that he was home with Mei-Mei when she returned from school and during the time when I was working long hours and sometimes going back in the evening. The two grandmothers were also accessible for special occasions, but the climate was very different from Lynchburg. Mei-Mei did well in school and had playmates. She remembers the time with her father as being some of the very happy parts of her life, in which they learned to be good friends and companions.

It was I who was still in the throes of working out a way of being, shedding the old patterns of responsibility for others. During that tumultuous, intensive week in Lynchburg and the year that followed, what had been horrifying, devastating, and depressing was my inability to recognize the person I thought I was in the person I saw. I still had not completely reconciled these two opposing images of myself.

There were times when, again, I felt despair and was overwhelmed with guilt for what I perceived as the damage I had done and was capable of repeating. At times, I felt a real depression. One evening while walking in the woodland near our home, I prayed that God would strike me with a bolt of lightning so that I would be out of my inner struggle. The bolt did not strike. Gradually I began to find my way into this new inner world into which I had been pushed.

The prospect of returning to New York, particularly the vicinity of New York City, was quite alluring. Bruce Shear had followed his recommendation by offering to hasten the procedure necessary for obtaining my license in New York state and also had sent the names of school districts on Long Island that had openings for counselors. He said in a telephone conversation, "There's not much more I can do except to see that your papers are taken from the bottom of the pile and placed on top"—an interesting comment on one of the ways a bureaucracy can be made to function.

Our move back to New York seemed to bear out, partially at least, the observation of one Maryland friend that we spend half our lives getting away from home, and the other half coming back. We were coming home.

We could only intuit that we were stepping over the threshold into a more stable, productive, and creative part of our lives.

West Hempstead Years—Research and Experimentation

After three interviews for counseling positions on Long Island, I made my choice. I rejected the first because the only counseling available was college placement, which did not appeal to me; the second, because I felt the principal and I would not be able to work together productively. The third, West Hempstead School District, I recognized immediately as the place for me to be and to develop professionally.

Following the initial part of the interview with the Superintendent of Schools and M. Kimball Garrison, the principal of the junior–senior high school, Mr. Garrison suggested we walk through the building together to get the feeling of the place. As we walked, we talked about his philosophy of education. One statement is still very clear in my mind. He was interested in the professional background and the careful preparation of the job applicant, of course, but what he was primarily concerned about was the person's attitude toward education and toward children. He said he would prefer to choose a counselor who might not be quite as strong in some other aspects if that counselor really liked young people and wanted to work with them and their families.

Immediately I felt this was a man with whom I could work, and the very next day I accepted the appointment as a junior high school counselor. Along with James Moore, who later became chief of the Bureau of Guidance in Albany, I was to initiate a program of counseling services for junior high school students.

I knew who I was. I knew what I wanted to do. We had made some important decisions, and it seemed at last we were on our way. Within the week, Niel and I spent two days, at the suggestion of Mr. Garrison, searching for suitable houses in Seaford. On the evening of the second discouraging day, as we walked away from the last house on our list, Niel said, "This is our house." It still is. It was our eighth home since our marriage in 1940. It seems strange to me now that this is exactly the number of homes in which I lived up to the time of my leaving Jamestown, New York for New York City.

For our family—Niel, Mei-Mei, Mother Sanford, and my mother—this opened up new vistas for all of us except Mother

Sanford. We came here in September 1955, and she died on January 17, 1956; so she never had the pleasure of seeing the family unfold during the Seaford years. Granny Sanford was quiet, reserved, a very strong woman, controlled, generous. To Mei-Mei she was the storyteller, one who read fairy tales and Pooh books. So she was greatly missed, and Mei-Mei felt a great deal of pain when her Granny Sanford died.

My mother, resourceful woman that she was, put down new roots here and established herself as a teacher for the homebound children of neighboring towns. Her new career as director of her own nursery school, which she had begun in her sixtieth year, had been the most financially successful venture of her life. Now she made her home in a little apartment in our house for eleven years, until her death in 1967. We learned the pains and pleasures of having three generations in the same household.

My mother was always here when Mei-Mei came home from school. They were good companions, enjoyed reading together, and enjoyed each other's company. Yet my mother was also a disciplinarian, as she had been when I was growing up and she carried over her strong religious beliefs and tendencies.

Mei-Mei, from the beginning, seemed to be a strong-minded person in her own right, both at home and at school. There were confrontations and clashes. Mei-Mei chose the trumpet as her instrument in fourth grade because she liked the sound. Although she was the only girl in the trumpet section all through her elementary and high school years, she persisted. She then graduated from Bennington with a major in music; the trumpet was her first instrument, the piano was her second. She did exceptionally well in subjects she liked and which had meaning for her, was a voracious reader, and did passably well in subjects that had little or no meaning for her.

During our second year in Seaford, Niel found a doctor in New York City who was very helpful to him. He recommended Niel to the Department of Vocational Rehabilitation about becoming a rehabilitation counselor. In that position, Niel could work one-to-one without the strain of administration or of teaching. Finally he was in his element.

Niel studied for a year at New York University in vocational rehabilitation and became a rehabilitation counselor, the first one in New York state to counsel drug abusers. Until his mandatory retirement from the state system in his seventies, he became well known for his work in the field of drug addiction and received successive awards as Counselor of the Year in New York City, in New York state, and for the Northeast Region (which included all of the northeastern Atlantic states, Canada, and Nova Scotia). He went on to be nominated for Counselor of the Year in the United States. It was a time of real blossoming for him. It seemed at last he found the professional niche in which he was most productive and happy.

Being close to the open Atlantic Ocean seemed to have had both a figurative and a direct influence on the life of our family, bringing a fresh breeze. But the school system was highly traditional, which ran counter to the educational opinions of all three adults in our family. Two anecdotes may bring some clarity to the difference.

I received a call from the sixth-grade teacher who later became a counselor in the junior high school, asking for an appointment. During the conference he said, "If Mei-Mei doesn't do better in Math, she'll have to drop Band" (which was the love of her life at that time).

I raised the question with him, "If she doesn't do well in Band, must she then drop Math?" He was very angry and later gave Mei-Mei the impression that her parents didn't care whether she did well in school or not. Mei-Mei did not drop Band and she did not fail Math.

In eighth grade, parents were invited to come for a parent night. Niel and I attended. After listening to the English teacher, who had been explaining how much she took off for misspelled words, for errors in punctuation, and for incomplete sentences, Niel raised his hand and asked, "And how much credit do you give for a good idea?" I think we were not popular as parents in the district.

Meanwhile, when I appeared for pre-opening orientation at my new job, I discovered that the counseling offices I had seen in my earlier interview visit were for the senior high school. As yet, no offices had been prepared for us. Mr. Garrison and I walked through the building, looking for places for two counselors, and came upon what was known as Book Storage #5. It was unsuitable, inadequate, and uncomfortable, but it was the space that Jim Moore and I occupied during that first year. Due to the area's lack of oxygen, the alternate heat and cold, and the general airlessness, we barely survived physically. But we worked well together and were pleased with the response of students, parents, and faculty. We were building a junior high school counseling service for the first time ever in the West Hempstead School District.

When an opening appeared for the following year in the senior high school, Jim Moore decided to move up, as he called it. "Upward mobility," he quipped with his easy laugh. My choice was to remain in the junior high school, where I felt there was less pressure for goal-oriented activities and more opportunity for personal counseling with students and parents.

To my surprise, that decision met with the assumption that I would be remaining in Book Storage #5 the second year. Such was not my intention. When I talked with Mr. Garrison about it, he suggested that we take another walk, along with the Superintendent and a member of the Board of Education, to tour the building and find a better place. During that walk, someone in the group said, "I feel that there really is no other suitable location."

I made a very clear statement. "I certainly will not continue in Storage #5. If, after the work of this past year, junior high school counseling is seen as having so little value as to keep it in a completely unsuitable place, then I feel that I do not wish to remain at West Hempstead." We found more suitable temporary space. And when the junior high school wing was completed, I moved into the new counseling area which I had helped to design.

I became chairman of the junior high school guidance and counseling staff and worked directly with Alan Rothenberg, the principal of the junior high school. It was my association with him that brought much of the exhilaration and the feeling of accomplishment into my West Hempstead years. His creative imagination, his ability to subordinate administrative structure to human need, his high regard for the individual, and his great good humor made working with him a joy. Mr. Garrison's formula was to choose good people, trust them, and not get in their way. Together, these two people created a most favorable working climate. They built a strong, distinguished faculty.

Because I was well acquainted with junior high school students, I had been designated to represent the school district in statewide research, the Holding Power Project. Holding Power is the other side of the coin from the dropout problem. The design was to identify early indications of success or failure in school. We would search school records (for kindergarten through sixth grade) of the incoming seventh-grade students, and then follow them through twelfth grade. The anecdotal records kept by teachers in the elementary grades were a treasure trove of data. Together with the academic records, the grades, and the standardized testing, this gave a very detailed history of each child. With these data, it was possible to construct a parallel chronological pattern for each child's behavioral and academic development.

Reading the anecdotal records was like being part of an unfolding drama. I was intrigued and moved to ask, "What is it that dulls this sharp edge of curiosity, this desire to learn, with which children come into first grade and second, and begin to lose in grades three and four? What dulls that wonderful, bright, shining edge of curiosity?"

So I embarked on a research project that lasted with these same students until 1961. It was the first of a series of open doors that led me into serious research, locally as well as on the state level, and to experimentation in education.

At this point, I must invoke the definition of creativity that I very much like. Creativity is being open to experience and letting one thing lead to another. That is exactly what happened. Early in that year, I was invited by Bruce Shear and a member of his staff in Albany, New York, to design the final year of the Holding Power Project, which had involved fifty-seven school districts in New York state. I spent the summer in Albany working with the data, trying to determine which of the factors in the lives of the students had most affected the probability of their staying in school or dropping out. Of greatest importance to me was what could be learned from the records of students who would be entering seventh grade in our school system. These seemed to hold clues about their growth and development during the junior and senior high school years.

It was a summer of exploration and exhilaration in which I discovered my genuine interest in and excitement about research and what it could mean in education. I owe a real thank you to Harold Munson, who later became a professor of counseling and psychology at the State University of New York in Buffalo. He was my guide and my sponsor during that summer when I discovered my passion for research.

I had chosen 1962 to 1963 as my sabbatical year. Fresh from the Holding Power Project, I was fired with the fascination of what happens to that burst of energy in young children which is so creative. In this connection, I attended a lecture at Columbia by Dr. Jacob Getzels of the University of Chicago and arranged to meet with him at his office a month later when I attended a conference in Chicago. He had said he would be able to spare about an hour.

His small office was lined with books, and more books were piled on his desk. It was in the late afternoon, probably four o'clock. The sun was beginning to go down as we started to talk. By the time we finished, it was completely dark. Dr. Getzels had become interested in the research I was planning to do in West Hempstead. He gave me permission to use some of the instruments he had used in assessing, in some rough kind of way, the creative tendencies of the children in the schools in which he had worked.

I also arranged to meet with Donald McKinnon and to discuss the work he had done in the field of creativity. I read the work of Jerome Bruner, of Harvard, who had carried his study of children's activities into the playgrounds and all of the places in which children gathered.

In establishing correlations between creativity, intelligence, and achievement, I chose to study students from grades eight and eleven. We already had detailed school records. After consultation with Lawrence Kubie and with Elizabeth Drews of Michigan State University, who was consistently helpful in designing the EXP Program (as the students always referred to our Experimental Program), I devised instruments that would indicate degrees or levels of creative thinking, or of creativity in its many aspects. These tests were administered at the beginning of my sabbatical semester so they could be scored and much of the statistical work could be done by the time I returned. Modest but substantial federal and state grants were obtained to implement some of the findings in the classroom.

I was living on the edge of something really important. The possibilities were many. I could, during the sabbatical, go back to Columbia or elsewhere, take additional courses, and lay the foundation for a doctoral degree—or I could stay with the material with which I was working and use the semester to design a research project that would make possible some experimentation in my own school district. I chose to stay at West Hempstead for the fruition of my study about the nature and nurturing of creativity in a public school setting.

From 1955 to 1962, my responsibilities had ranged from being a junior high school counselor to being director of counseling for the school district (for grades seven through twelve). This included supervising a growing staff of counselors, orienting students from three elementary schools and, ultimately, supervising a new district from an adjacent town. My experience is best described in the following excerpt from *Freedom To Learn for the 80s*.

> This experiment in learning began with an almost desperate need to save myself. As a counselor with administrative responsibilities in a public school district, I had felt for some time that I was dying a little every day. I had begun to feel like a shock absorber, taking in the pressures, the anxieties and frustrations of students, parents, administrators, teachers, the Board of Education and the community, trying to be at the same time an

advocate for student growth and learning. It seemed to
me that everyone was losing, especially me. There had to
be a better way! Unless I could find one, my energies and
enthusiasms would ebb away and I would become
another drop-out from the educational system.

One of my strong points is, I believe, that once I
have gained an insight, I do something about it.

My first step was to apply for a sabbatical leave,
which I used for research.. . . The research grew the
following year into an experiment in education . . . the
purpose of which was to create a climate in which the
creative urge to growth and the excitement of learning
would be nurtured. Much to our surprise we found that
in the nurturing climate which we were striving to create,
we ourselves were nourished, and found within ourselves
a renewal of excitement in learning.

The next eight years were the most vital and
adventurous of my professional life—up to that time.

The purpose of our research was to identify students who were
potentially highly creative and to provide them an opportunity to use
their potential in a nurturing climate in the classroom. When we
administered various tests,[4] our findings indicated that highly creative
students are discriminated against when school grades and intelligence
scores are used as the criteria of selection for college admission.
Approximately two-thirds of the students with high creativity scores
would be eliminated by using tests of intelligence or school grade aver-
ages as indicators of potential. In general, school administrators tend
to use either or both of these measures in the selection of students for
college or classes for the gifted.

Creativity and getting on in school may also be related. An
inverse relationship apparently exists between the incidence of emotional problems severe enough to interfere with social or academic
success in school and the degree of creativity as measured by these
tests.

Finally, we noted a relatively high correlation between creativity in the low fifth of scores and intelligence in the low fifth. That is,

students who tested low for creativity were usually the same ones who tested low on the IQ test.

These findings led us back to the anecdotal records mentioned earlier. They helped us include not only students with high creativity scores, regardless of achievement or high IQs, but also those whose flame of enthusiasm for learning had gone out in grades three or four. Being aware of the need for a multidimensional approach to identify various kinds of ability leads to recognizing and interpreting the needs of these students.

These findings take on meaning in the light shed on the relationship between creativity and conformity by Dr. Richard S. Crutchfield of the University of California at Berkeley. "Conformity tends to destroy creativity by alienating the creator both from reliance on his own thought processes and from contact with basic reality," he says, and "Conformity pressures tend to elicit kinds of motivation in the individual that are incompatible with the creative process." He also makes the point that "high susceptibility by the individual to conformity pressures tend to be associated with certain personality traits which are detrimental to creative thinking."[5]

In 1986 when Carl Rogers read my paper on "Creativity and Intelligence," he commented, "Here are at least five doctoral dissertations"—none of which I have written.

Details of the experimental program that followed from the creativity study can be found in Carl Rogers' *Freedom To Learn for the 80s*. Briefly, the first step involved using research data to select students from grades 7, 8, 9, and 11 (ages 12 to 17) to be included in the experimental classes. With the exception of the seventh-graders, the EXP students had scored high on our measure of creativity or had been considered especially curious and alert in kindergarten and first grade.

While the selection process was going on, teachers who had volunteered to be part of the project met once weekly during one semester to prepare. The principal, who shared our enthusiasm for the project, helped create a schedule that made it possible for counselors, teachers, and psychologists to work together during their free or "prep" periods; and students were scheduled to accommodate double periods that allowed time for discussions, films, and special projects.

We were fortunate to find a core teacher, who was sometimes characterized as "the Renaissance man." He worked comfortably with students and was attuned to use of the *Living Textbook*, a source book of materials patterned after that of Dr. Elizabeth Drews, then of

Michigan State University. She was also a consultant in the use of her film series "Being and Becoming."

The *Living Textbook* was compiled from the writings of well-known authors and from current magazines, most of which were left incomplete to stimulate further inquiry. The materials were divided into four worlds: the natural world, the human/social world, the technological world, and the aesthetic world. Students were free to create an additional world of their own. The preface of the *Living Textbook* assured students that as soon as they made their first comment or change, the textbook was uniquely their own to add to or delete from as they wished.

For students with serious reading problems, a supplementary book was prepared by teachers—and by older students, as the project progressed.

The film series "Being and Becoming" upset stereotypes of occupations suitable for men or for women by presenting a woman doctor, a man artist, a woman lawyer, and a man naturalist. The film portrayed them not only as professional persons but as parents, husbands, and wives—at work and at play.

Together, these resources formed the base for lively discussions in class, all of which were taped for future reference and were available to members of the class. Both teacher and counselor assured the students of confidentiality, so that students were not hampered in expressing their opinions and values. We found that some students required a whole semester to establish trust in the presence of so much freedom after years of what they saw as manipulation by adults.

When a special question or problem arose, the teachers of math, science, social studies, literature, art, or music were invited to meet with the group. We met regularly once a week with the art and music teachers, who were involved in the program as special consultants.

We were surprised to find in all of this cooperative venture that members of the professional staff changed their attitudes toward teaching and were enriched beyond any expectation. A quotation that summarized a teacher's evaluation of the program was: "After my years in EXP, I'll never be the same again."

Parents and teachers not directly involved in the program and students were also involved in the evaluation process. Parents spoke of more lively conversations at dinner with less dissent and anger. Several parents asked to be included in evening sessions similar to EXP classes. Teachers found that students were more independent in forming opinions, less likely to make categorical judgments about issues in English and Social Studies classes, and more spontaneous in class participation. Student evaluations included such comments as:

> This is the first time in nine years of school that I felt I had a PLACE.

> This course did nothing for me—except to give me a few new ideas in education.

> Why is it that in this class with no teacher, I have learned more than in my other classes with regular teachers?

> This EXP has brought me nothing but trouble. When I have an idea now or disagree with someone, I speak up. Usually the teacher doesn't like it, especially if I disagree with the teacher.

Brief composites of the students' self-evaluations, along with those of teachers and parents, were included in the students' files in place of grades. Much to our surprise, these composite evaluations were welcomed by college admissions officers as more valuable in the selection process than the traditional grade.

Some of the unanticipated side effects of the program resulted from the close cooperation of teachers, parents, counselors, and psychologists. Counselors and psychologists began to understand that teachers who work with thirty or thirty-five students at a time need to be appreciated in their work. Teachers found that the more they met and exchanged their experiences and professional knowledge, instead of working separately, the more they could understand one another and work effectively with students.

Another unexpected benefit was that, as students experienced more freedom from regulations and more choice in what they learned, discipline problems diminished.

So a dream was realized. It was then time for me to move on. Although the program was not continued after my retirement, much to my disappointment, EXP is still going on in the lives of the students and others they have touched, including mine.

Retirement?

In 1972 I retired from the West Hempstead public school system. After one month, I was invited to be a supervisor of counselor-interns at the C. W. Post campus of Long Island University; discovered Alex Comfort's *The Joy of Sex;* tasted the pleasure of social dancing; attended a conference in San Diego where, for the first time, I heard Carl Rogers speak; participated in the La Jolla program and became a member of the before-breakfast Movement to Music Group of Bruce Meador, at which I discovered the joy of dancing; met Carl Rogers for the first time face to face; and became cofacilitator of the couples group in the La Jolla program. That was all before the end of July. It was a very good year.

As chairman of the counseling department at West Hempstead, I had reestablished my connections with Teachers College, Columbia University, through my contact with Professor Ruth DeLemos. She had invited me annually to meet with her classes in counseling to discuss the EXP Program and the research I had been doing. As a result, the Teachers College Department of Counseling had referred several graduate students to me at West Hempstead for their internship.

Ruth DeLemos spoke with the chairman of the Counseling Education Department at C.W. Post, with the result that I became an adjunct faculty member and supervised counselor-interns at the graduate school there. This involved traveling to schools the length of Long Island and even into some of the boroughs of New York City. I met with interns' on-the-job supervisors, visited interns in their workplaces, and met with them weekly at the college. This weekly group convened for the purpose of discussing the work they had done during the week preceding, to talk about problems that had arisen, to explore questions, and to devise ways of counseling with and helping one another. Each student prepared a weekly log which I returned the following week with my responses. This became a kind of ongoing dialogue with each counselor-intern.

It was an exhilarating time, in which I felt my perspectives broadened and my knowledge about the counseling process deepened. The students had the feeling, some of them for the first time, that a student and a professor can be partners in learning. I was also responsible for turning in an evaluation and a grade for each student at the end of the year, which I felt unable to do without the help of the on-the-job supervisor and the intern. This practice of sharing responsibility and freedom was very difficult for the interns. Evaluating oneself, as we had learned in EXP, is very difficult—but the on-the-job supervisors in the various school systems experienced an even greater problem. They felt in some way that it was my responsibility to do the work. It was a growing experience for all of us. Letters and sometimes visits still come from some of those interns. Their comments give evidence that they gained more from those classes than had been expected.

Learnings from the years in EXP had spilled over—forerunner of the way of working with graduate students in other classes at C. W. Post Campus and at Hofstra University in years to come.

The 1970s were years of adventure, expanding vision, new and varied activities, renaissance: I was involved on local and state levels in the structuring of new licensure requirements for psychiatrists, counselors, and psychologists in New York state; initiated and chaired a coalition of civic groups for the rejuvenation of downtown Seaford, a five-year project; wrote a weekly column, "As I See It," for *The Observer* newspaper; and enjoyed the new freedom to spend more time in my home and with my family.

It was a decade of fruition, and some of the fruits of recognition were sweet. Among them was an award from my alma mater for Outstanding Contribution in the Field of Education (I was the first woman to receive such an award), the Counselor of the Year award for outstanding contribution to schools and colleges in New York state, and the Peter Zenger award for excellence in journalism and community service. But sweeter and more enduring is knowing that my ability to work with others—neighbors in Seaford, students in the counselor-internship classes, editors of the newspapers—yielded some lasting change, part of which is visible, as on the streets of Seaford, and part of which is invisible and must be taken on faith.

Renaissance

During the seventies, our family indulged a yen for travel and international experience by visiting the Scandinavian countries, England, Spain, Italy, Greece, Egypt, and in 1975, Hawaii. There we were guests of Daniel S. K. Chang, a Yale-in-China friend and International House friend of Niel's who had invited us many times. On the return from our delightful summer vacation island-hopping in Hawaii, I remained in Oakland, California for a person-centered workshop, "Building of Community," at Mills College.

Facilitators from the Center for Studies of the Person had in advance divided the participants into small groups of approximately fifteen, at least for the beginning of the seventeen-day workshop. One member from each group was to draw from a hat the name of the facilitator for that group. By pure chance, my group selected Carl Rogers. For the first time, I knew him as a person. Our group met several hours daily, except for one weekend.

On the last day, in the midst of goodbyes, I realized I had not made reservations for a flight to San Diego, where I was to visit a friend from West Hempstead days. When I called the airline, I was told there was one seat available if I could get to the airport within the next half hour, which I did. I rushed onto the plane and was shown to the one empty seat. When I looked up, I discovered that my seatmate was Carl—again, by pure chance! A few weeks later, I received a request for permission to use part of my workshop experience in the chapter "A Person-Centered Workshop: Its Planning and Fruition" in *Carl Rogers on Personal Power*.[6] Thus began our correspondence.

The experience at the La Jolla program and Mills College, along with serious reading of Carl's work, had stirred my mind and my awareness. My way of thinking and being was compatible with the way of being about which Carl wrote. It was like finding a professional home. Two years later, I knew that the La Jolla staff was presenting a two-week workshop at Sagamore in the Adirondacks and that Carl would be present in late June and early July of 1977. So persistently were ideas and half-formed plans spinning about in my head that I called Sagamore to ask Carl if I could see him there. He had an hour free on the following Friday, 7/7/77. It became a memorable day in my life. I arrived at this cabin at the appointed time, told him that I had "a bee in my bonnet"—a homely expression which he understood—and we began talking about some of my ideas for bringing the person-centered approach to the East Coast in workshops facilitated by local people. I also told him of my dream of offering a course at C. W. Post campus in the person-centered approach to education and counseling.

Upon my return from the La Jolla program and the Mills College workshop, I felt isolated, because no one within easy reach of my home on Long Island had had the Mills College experience. My hope was to saturate the metropolitan and tri-state area with invitations to local workshops so that everyone who attended could find nearby a support group—or at least one other person—with whom they could share experiences and continue their growth. It would also, I believed, make possible the continuing community meetings of those who wanted to renew and refresh their person-centered experience.

He offered suggestions, was supportive and enthusiastic, but was unsure about the organizational details. "I don't know," he said, "what your experience is in organization and administration, but I will support you in any way I can, be of any help that I can in bringing these plans about." Through the years that followed, he kept his word.

He asked specifically how I would choose a staff for the first workshop with local facilitators. I told him that the only way I knew was to go to the dining room or elsewhere on the grounds there at Sagamore and to approach different participants in this workshop. If they got excited about the idea of a workshop on the Post campus the following year, I would invite them to a preliminary meeting so that we could plan a year-long preparation program. He laughed and said, "Well, I think that probably is as good a way as any." And we realized that it was already time for dinner. The afternoon had slipped away.

When I suggested that I would like to stay on the grounds or find a place in town to stay over so that I could meet and talk with more participants about my idea, he said there was a vacancy and I could stay, but he recommended that I not go to the community meetings, because it had been a very difficult workshop with a great deal of disagreement and contention. It was just beginning to come together, and he felt that I might have a painful experience if I placed myself in the community meeting. I heard his concern, both for the workshop participants and for me, but I had such a strong feeling that this was an important time that I went to the community meeting the next morning. When confronted, I thanked the person who had confronted me and said he had made it easier for me to explain my presence. There was no problem. Various people expressed consent, and we proceeded through the last two days of the workshop.

Early in the fall, I met with Carl and three members of the Center for Studies of the Person, in La Jolla, in Carl's home, to learn something about the logistics of planning the kind of workshop I had in mind. They were very helpful and Carl, true to his word, continued through the year to be a consultant.

Through monthly meetings during the fall, winter, and spring of the following year, some members of the original group persisted and became the staff of facilitators for the residential workshop on the Post campus, exactly one year later. Of the eight facilitators, including Carl, all but two had been recruited from the Sagamore workshop. An exuberant vitality ran through the work of that year, along with some deep differences and genuine struggle, but because we had a strong will to succeed, it carried us through to a powerful workshop in July 1978.

As a member of the adjunct faculty at Post, I was able to request a synthesis paper from participants in the 1978 and 1979 workshops. They could thus receive three units of graduate credit for their participation in the ten-day workshop. Already a ripple effect was beginning to show.

Curtis Graf, whom I had invited to become a member of the facilitating staff at Post, had begun work at a small center in nearby Port Jefferson. The following year, he and I became codirectors of the Center for Interpersonal Growth, with Carl Rogers as a consultant. Later, Peggy Natiello joined the Center staff, and we continued working together until April 1985.

During those years, the "Ongoing Learning Experience" became an important part of the program at the Center. We also sponsored various person-centered workshops in and around the metropolitan area. It was a time of activity, a great deal of vitality, with the three of us as staff members. Some of my hopes of 1977 were being realized! At times, participants assisted in offering workshops. Varying in length from one day to a "long week" (ten days), these were held at Fordham University, Fairleigh Dickinson University, Columbia University, and others.

We learned a great deal from our successes and our mistakes. Through all of this time, Carl kept his promise of support and, in addition to being a consultant to the Center, also attended one weekend session of the "Ongoing Learning Experience" each year as a guest staff member.

During these years and continuing through the 1980s until his death, our work together gained momentum. Carl and I were cofacilitators or cofaculty at more than forty intensive groups, workshops, and conference sessions in the United States, Mexico, South Africa, and the Soviet Union. We also were members of a larger staff for more than twenty workshops and training programs in the United States and Europe, including several "Cross-Cultural Communication" workshops organized by Charles Devonshire, who has devoted twenty years to workshops and training programs in Europe. With this kind of activity, my ties with the Center began to loosen. In early 1985, I withdrew from active association.

For me, the years from 1977 to 1981 are best characterized by electric energy and the anticipation and excitement of a new venture. There seemed to be no end of possibilities in the kind of work we were doing. This person-centered approach seemed to be an idea whose time had come, as Carl had said earlier in one of his acceptance speeches in Montreal.

But 1982 ushered in a kind of whirlwind of international activity and a period that to me felt like a renaissance—not rebirth but a new flowering, a bursting into bloom, the realization of potentials that had hardly been identified or guessed before. I was continuing my work at the universities and my activities with my family and local professional groups, but most of all I was realizing the extent to which my association with Carl was changing my professional life and, by impact, also much of my personal life. It came about in this way.

Late in 1981, I received a letter from Carl with this message: "I have been invited many times to South Africa and have refused to go because I did not want to be associated with any group sponsored by a white university. I insisted that when I went, it would be with sponsorship of all classifications of residents in South Africa. Last week I received an invitation from Len Holdstock, a former student, which promises that there will be representation from all four classifications, and I have wanted very much to go but I feel that I don't want to go alone and I have been sitting here mornings on my patio thinking about who might go with me. I have thought often of you but I know that you have family responsibilities and therefore probably are not free to go on a trip that might require four or five or six weeks. This morning I said to myself, the hell with holding back, I'm going to ask. And so, I am asking will you go?"

I was taken completely by surprise and my reaction was figuratively to look over my shoulder and say, "Who, me?" Then I read the letter to Niel and asked him how he felt about it—what were his thoughts? Without a moment's hesitation, he said, "Of course, you must go. You can't afford to miss such an opportunity." For some time we sat and discussed pros and cons of my staying or going and its effect on our relationship.

The following day I wrote a very brief response:

> Dear Carl,
> Yes!
> Ruth

So began a new part of my life.

Only weeks previously, Neil and I had engaged in a similar conversation about him. Following his final retirement from two agencies in New York City related to drug prevention, Neil had applied for the Peace Corps; now he had been accepted and given an assignment to Thailand. He would be away for two years. Over a period of time, we had worked through our feelings about such a venture and separation. We were on solid ground so far as being supportive of one another in seeking out that which would be most rewarding and satisfying in our lives. After retirement, the Peace Corps was very important to Neil, and I had supported him wholeheartedly. He reciprocated in full measure.

South African Experience

In South Africa, with the dedicated sponsorship of Len Holdstock and the warm hospitality of his wife Alida, our work became both productive and substantial at the University of the North, in Johannesburg and Cape Town, and at Stellenbosch University. We also worked in Zimbabwe and Kenya. Because Len had wide associations and deep sympathy with various traditional and tribal groups of the South African community, he opened the doors to Soweto, Cape Flats, Kwandebele, and other homelands. With almost no assistance, he carried out detailed plans and arrangements that made the visit not only fruitful but pleasant. He made it possible for persons from all parts of South Africa to participate, particularly in the Johannesburg intensive workshop.

We met in his home with *isangoma*, traditional religious leaders and healers, and learned of the native traditional forms of counseling which they call "throwing the bones." We were much impressed with the dedication and the respect for the individual with which these rituals were undertaken.

The way of working together that Carl and I evolved in Johannesburg is described in this chapter's prologue. I discovered a deep well of resources, some of which I had not been aware of.

The University of the North is a beautiful campus with a landscape of rolling contours and impressive buildings. Carl and I had a single two- or three-hour session with a student-and-faculty group in the auditorium, followed by a luncheon where we were able to meet and become acquainted with several faculty members (I still correspond with one of them). We were dismayed to learn that although the student population was 100 percent black, the faculty were less than 25 percent black. Of course, this raised the question: if qualified black professors could not be appointed to positions in South Africa's black universities, where could they be placed?

In contrast, when we visited Stellenbosch University south of Cape Town, a university with white students (most of whom, we understood, were being prepared for government positions), all the faculty members were also white. At the University of the North, we had not been shown any psychological resources and equipment; my assumption is that they had very little. But the Stellenbosch faculty were very proud of their psychology labs and equipment. They showed us around with a great deal of pride. It was there that Carl had an interview with a white South African, which thereafter was published.

Len and a friend had arranged a person-centered workshop to be held over a long weekend at the Hohenhort Hotel Conference Center, a little north of Cape Town. It was there that we did the longest and most intense work, outside of Johannesburg, in the 1982 visit. A more detailed description of our 1982 work in South Africa can be found in an article that Carl and I did together, "Journey to the Heart of South Africa."[7]

In Cape Town we also were guests in the home of a successful businessman whose main interest had been the mining industry and so encountered a very different point of view from that of most of the people we had met. He and his wife were most supportive of the position that the black peoples had not really used the land, that the white newcomers had really developed the land and it belonged to them. The black tribal members of the population should appreciate the opportunity that the white man had brought.

The very next evening we visited the home of a woman in Cape Flats, the Soweto of Cape Town. We were present as illegal visitors after dark in the black part of Cape Town and could have caused arrest for our hostess. In defiance of apartheid, she had declared herself at different times in her life as white, black, colored, and Indian. She had been imprisoned many times and was quite ill as a result; in fact, soon after we left Cape Town, she died. I still have a collection of poems that she wanted me to read and which her husband sent me after her death.

Again in 1986, Carl and I spent about five weeks in South Africa, dividing our time mainly between Johannesburg and Cape Town. We were disappointed not to visit Durban, but we did have a long weekend workshop at a Catholic convent in the vicinity of the University of the North and Pretoria. As we had done in 1982 and later in the United States and Mexico, we continued working in a spontaneous dialogue way with groups and cofacilitating smaller groups of twenty-five or thirty.

The wind blowing in 1986 felt different from the one we had felt in 1982. It seemed more hopeful, although in some ways the contrast and the clashes were sharper. In Johannesburg, we changed our plan to concentrate on smaller groups of participants who were interested in becoming facilitators of person-centered groups. We had a long weekend workshop that reached through Monday, then two or three days free. The following weekend, Carl and I facilitated a large meeting open to the public. The large group broke into smaller groups that were facilitated by participants from the previous week-end sessions. Later we reconvened in our original group, this time as a staff, and talked about our learnings, our questions, and our own feelings about both parts of our time together.

We used much the same format at the University of Cape Town and included a visit to the University of the Western Cape, a black university in which some members of our intensive group were faculty. The largely black faculty there were a most welcome shift from our experience with University of the North faculty in 1982.

In my opinion, we were closer to the heart of South Africa in 1986 than we were in our previous visit, partly because we were more open to the experience of South Africa as a result of our earlier visit, and partly because people were apparently more trusting, open, and willing to engage in sharp confrontations when the feelings arose.

A strong and beautiful woman from Soweto made a very telling comment to me as we left the last session of our residential workshop on the campus of Witwatersrand. She said, "Thank you for bringing us bitter medicine which we needed to take."

To Shirley Shochot goes the credit for the four years of careful groundwork in the environs of Johannesburg and Cape Town in the four years between our first and second visits. As evidenced by her careful planning with a committee for the preparation of cofacilitators, one of Shirley's strong points was her ability to bring others into the planning and the carrying out of those plans in a kind of ongoing committee. It seemed that everyone on the committee developed his or her own interest and expertise—a real credit to Shirley and her colleagues. Members of the Johannesburg and Cape Town groups have since been influential in organizing a South African Psychological Association which recognizes humanistic psychology as a significant part of the profession. Others have been influential in bringing this approach to human relationships into youth work, social work, and business, labor, and medical organizations, as well as arbitrating directly in violent conflicts in various communities.

Carl and I planned to return to South Africa for the third time in 1987. After his death on February 4 of that year, I returned to South Africa in the fall, continued the work in Johannesburg, and began what we had not been able to start in Durban. Most of my time was spent with smaller public groups and with the committee that had gathered around Shirley Shochot. At the University of Witwatersrand in Johannesburg, a Carl Rogers Center for the Person-Centered Approach had been organized. I am still in contact by telephone and correspondence with members of those groups and feel much enriched by their friendship.

Work in Mexico

Intensification of international work with Carl marked the beginning of 1982. In February we began planning for both the Guadalajara, Mexico work and our first visit to South Africa. We also agreed to take part in the first International Forum, organized by Alberto Segrera, which would be in Oaxtepec, Mexico.

Juan LaFarga, Alberto Segrera, and others made possible the largest person-centered conference to which we had been invited up to that time (and later exceeded only by the Conference on the Evolution of the Psychotherapies). Well planned on a very large scale, it was in Guadalajara in the fall of 1982. Carl and I met with sixteen to seventeen hundred people gathered in the municipal auditorium. With the help of translators, we spoke briefly and responded to questions and all points of view from the huge audience. It was a real test of communication to be able to respond, alternately or in any way we chose, to questions and comments from all over that great auditorium. A group of women had invited me to speak with them after the meeting; this never really materialized because there seemed to be not enough time, but I was pleased that they thought of it and invited me.

It was there I learned that the effectiveness of groups is not determined by their size. When we went to the university in Guadalajara for the remainder of the program, we found that participants had been separated into "small" groups—of 200 each! Later, in one of those groups where Carl and I were cofacilitating, Carl was responding to a question when his translator stopped him and said, "Please, I would like to translate before I forget what you've said."

As she proceeded to translate, I thought, "Well, it must take longer to express these opinions or feelings in Spanish."

Then she turned to Carl and asked, "How was that?"

Carl, with a little smile, said, "Oh, it was fine. And I liked *your* speech, too!"—a reply that almost broke up the meeting.

When Carl was ill one day, I found myself filling in for him— meeting with psychologists and conducting a demonstration therapy interview in a large auditorium. I was greatly relieved when he felt better and was able to reappear later in the day for the closing session.

Our third trip to Mexico occurred in 1984, at the invitation of Juan LaFarga and Alberto Segrera, this time at the Universidad Iberoamericana. As part of a panel of psychotherapists, we appeared before about two hundred university professors and students. The panel represented a wide range of approaches, from Freudian to Neo-Freudian to behavioral. Carl and I presented the person-centered approach.

Some of the panelists became involved in the discussion of fees, of the desirability of diagnoses, the desired or the optimum length of treatment, and the problems of maintaining a practice. A woman social worker who had worked with the underprivileged, the deprived of Mexico City, stood up and made an impassioned plea for some answer to the crying need of people who had no money for fees but whose very survival depended on the kind of psychological help which had been discussed. She called to our attention the fact that if every psychologist and psychiatrist in the city were to offer their services at no fees, there would not be enough professionals to take care of the problem. Then she directed a question at me. "What has the person-centered approach done to help those who can't afford the kind of therapy we've heard about today?"

I had not expected to be addressed, but within a few seconds of hesitation, these words came to my mind clearly. "Elitism—we must go beyond elitism." I called attention to the practice among person-centered therapists of determining fair fees jointly with their clients. I spoke briefly of the various ways in which people had been helped in large groups, in small groups, and by reading the work of Carl and others. I told how a young client of mine who had survived the nightmare of being in prison by holding onto a quotation from Carl's *A Way of Being:* "If I can be myself in the moment, I am enough."[8] I cited some other examples and came away with a new realization of the innovative and hopeful nature of the person-centered approach. Immediately after the panel, Carl gave a demonstration interview with a volunteer client, as was his wont.

A day or two later, we met with a group of undergraduate students at the University of Mexico City in what proved to be a most surprising response to the announcement of our presence there. When we went into the large auditorium, we found that all the seats were taken. Extra rows of seats had been arranged around the platform, in back of us and to either side, so that we were completely surrounded. It was an especially lively session, with a great deal of the vitality of younger students and their serious questioning. I recall one question particularly: "If a homosexual comes to you for counseling or therapy, how do you treat that client?"

I quickly volunteered to respond to that question, and when I said I would be with that client in the same way that I would be with any other client, there seemed to be a reaction of surprise and even some applause from various parts of the auditorium. I learned later that the question of homosexuality was a very provocative one, particularly at the university. The diversity of people's background and interests presented a welcome variety and challenge during our stay in Mexico City. Participants ranged from graduate students, faculty, and practicing professionals to undergraduate students. Regretfully, we had very little time to enjoy the city itself.

Inside the Soviet Union

During the spring and summer of 1985, Niel and I were making plans to visit the Soviet Union with a group of rehabilitation counselors and therapists under the title of Citizen Ambassadors. It happened that during that time I was also in La Jolla working with Carl on a chapter for the fifth edition of *The Comprehensive Textbook of Psychiatry*.[9] I mentioned to him that we were going to the Soviet Union and asked whether, if I found the opportunity, would he like to have me make some preliminary inquiries about our going there? He was immediately enthusiastic and said there was nothing he would like better, which opened the door for us to the Soviet Union.

I knew that Fran Macey was to be in the Soviet Union at the same time as our group, but I had no idea where he would be staying. Much of my time during the early days of our visit there was spent in trying to locate Fran, whom I knew would be the liaison person for any work that Carl and I might plan. Finally, I gave up my search. I joined with two or three psychologists in the rehabilitation group to arrange a meeting with one of the psychological institutes in Moscow. We went for our session, which was on one of the last days of our stay, only to find that an American group was running overtime with the director of the institute. We were ushered into the room where they were just saying their goodbyes. I found my way to the director's side and was about to comment about the shortness of time and the need to meet with her as soon as possible. When I spoke, the person talking with her turned around and I saw it was Fran Macey. It was one of those threads again, a very fragile connection. But it was a strong connection, as it developed.

We discovered that we were staying on the same floor of the huge Moskva Hotel, which covers a whole city block. That evening in Fran's room, with Tom Greening present, I talked about the possibilities of a visit to the Soviet Union by Carl and me. It was almost a year to the day later that Carl and I arrived, in late September 1986, to begin our visit of approximately four weeks. Later, in his review of the activities of those weeks,[10] Fran said over 2,000 enthusiastic Soviets were present at one or more of the sessions that Carl and I cofacilitated. He then wrote at some length of the impact of our work in Moscow and Tbilisi. Tom Greening wrote of a larger impact and quoted Michael Murphy of the Essalen Institute:

> Michael expressed admiration for what Carl had accomplished on his first trip and describes it as directly relevant to Gorbachev's *glasnost* campaign for greater openness and dialogue in Soviet society. Michael sees the person-centered process and the results Carl reported as introducing into the Soviet system a teachable practice that facilitates constructive airing of issues.[11]

Our major host was Alexey Matushkin, director of the Psychological Institute in Moscow and head of the psychological organization for the USSR. His assistant, Irina Kuzmacheva, was a translator for me and of invaluable assistance in carrying out the details of our various activities. Without the vision and the courage of Alexey Matushkin, our work could not have taken place. Several times we met with him, Irina, and other assistants in his office in the same building where our intensive four-day sessions were held. We also met there with the Scientific Council toward the end of our visit. During one of those meetings in Alexey's office, Carl raised a question about the kind of work we would be doing there, encouraging people to empower themselves, and said, "You know this could be dangerous."

Alexey said, "Why? How could it be dangerous?"

"Because when people get a sense of their own empowerment," Carl responded, "they may not work in the same way that they are expected to in a country accustomed to strong direction and leadership."

Alexey responded thoughtfully, "Yes, but it would be *more* dangerous not to."

Our time was divided between Moscow and Tbilisi. In Moscow we met with an intensive group over a four-day weekend. A public meeting at the auditorium of the institute attracted an audience that overflowed into a second room. Following the intensive group, we met with the Scientific Council for a half day of evaluation. The University of Moscow invited us to spend a day with students and faculty. When we arrived, we found an audience of about 900 students packed into an auditorium intended to hold 700 or 750. We were surprised to learn that about 85 percent of these students had read some paper or book of Carl's. It's worth saying that Alexey and others had planned in advance for our visit by having monthly meetings at which Carl's work was read and discussed among psychologists. This was the only country, I believe, in which we met such a concerted effort to lay groundwork for our visit.

In each of the public meetings, Carl did a demonstration therapy session with a volunteer from the audience as the "client." Together we did our easy four-way dialogue with ourselves and the group, which led to such a flood of questions and comments that people began sending written notes and questions to the platform. We did not have time to respond to all of them, but when we analyzed them later, we learned the diversity of interests represented in the questions. All of them were serious and probing, revealing a genuine interest in the principles and application of Carl's approach to psychology. I hope to use them, should I return to Russia.

As cofacilitators, Carl and I were interested, caring participants who made known from the beginning our wish to hear every person present who wished to speak. We also made clear that our time together during the four days belonged to the entire group—including Carl, Fran, and me but equally to all members of the group. It was not our intent to direct or control what they would do with their time.

We had assumed that the Moscow group might be cautious or reserved. We need not have been concerned. Rather than the limit of thirty participants which Carl and I had requested, forty-five had crowded into the room. Many others stood outside the door, wanting to come in. The group was clearly divided into two camps. Tensions were running high amid accusations and counteraccusations of favoritism, cheating, lying, and domination of one institution over the other. Carl and I were suspected of setting up the conflict in order to influence the group in some way. Trust was practically nonexistent in the room. Occasionally we captured the attention of the group to ask for a pause so that we might hear what was going on, what was being said, and to have time for translation as needed.

During the long day, Carl and I were importuned in the group, in the session, and in private during breaks, to step in and bring an end to this disorder, to make decisions, and to get the group in motion. Participants worried we would never accomplish anything in the four days. Carl and I steadfastly declined, feeling that the group would find its way to work out conflicts better than we could. We had agreed during the lunch hour to request at the close of the day that the group sit quietly for the last five minutes and then leave, without resuming the session. We did.

The next morning, the atmosphere in the room was very different. People began listening to one another. They began speaking to one another, even from opposite sides of the room, with some intent to listen. Gradually the trust began to build. The communication began to flow at times, and we felt the group beginning to pull together.

More than thirty of the participants appeared at the Scientific Council later that week, in response to an invitation to evaluate the intensive group experience. Only ten or twelve had an opportunity to speak. Others resonated when one of those speakers told of his own experience of the four days together. He said, "When Carl and Ruth came, I thought, yes, this is an approach that will work in the West and that they can do it, but it's not for us. I learned that it is true, we can do it ourselves."

In Tbilisi the groups were smaller, opening with a session at the Psychological Institute attended largely by professionals. Carl and I presented the person-centered approach and opened the discussion to anyone who wished to take part. Questions were penetrating, perceptive, sometimes questioning or critical. Carl offered to demonstrate a therapy session, and a young woman volunteered. She later attended the intensive group; in Tbilisi, it too was smaller.

The director of the Psychological Institute, along with several members of his staff, appeared at the first session of the intensive group. To our surprise, he requested the group to decide whether or not his presence would inhibit the openness of the sessions for members of his staff and others. After a frank and open discussion, he was accepted as a member of the group. Thus we began on a very different note from that sounded at the beginning of the Moscow meeting.

The opening discussion had created an atmosphere of congeniality, warmth, and trust in the room but as the session began, there seemed to be a kind of self-conscious holding back of personal feelings. However, as the first day proceeded, it became evident that this group was going to reach into deep places in their personal lives—in their relationships with other members of the group and with their families. This became particularly evident during what we called the empathy lab, in which we broke into triads. Within a given period of time, members of each triad became in rotation a client, a therapist, and an observer.

In a kind of rhythm, theoretical questions—some inquisitive, some critical, some purely provocative—alternated with disclosures of deep personal experiences. This pattern continued throughout the second day and into the third. I noticed that theoretical or philosophical questions were directed to Carl, never to me, which was quite different from all of our previous experience. That evening I spoke to Carl about my feeling of unease and expressed my feeling that I must make my uneasiness known in the group if I were to remain actively engaged, because I had sensed that I was withdrawing somewhat on the third day.

The following morning, I told the group how I had been feeling. I didn't know what it signified, I said, but I felt very much a part of the group at all times except when theoretical or philosophical questions came up. I wondered whether it was because Carl was a renowned psychologist, a person of prominence, or whether it was because he was a man. In Georgia perhaps the man was looked to for the intellectual, the factual, and the theoretical, rather than the woman. Whatever it was, I would be interested in knowing. I did not want anyone to make an apology, but I said, "It took me until late in life to appreciate my brain, that I have a brain, and I don't want to give that up. So, I feel now that I have been honest with you about my feeling. Now I can become more wholeheartedly a member of the group."

The reaction was the first really intense, involved discussion of men–women relationships that we had had in all of the Soviet meetings. At the end of our discussion, the director of the institute (who had requested permission to become a member of the group) spoke up very thoughtfully, saying he had not been aware of his lack of appreciation for the women on his staff, that he felt he had been holding within himself a double standard, and that he intended to pay more attention to the accomplishments, contributions, and work of the women of his staff. He said, "That includes my wife," who was present as another member of the group on that last day.

Again, as at many times in the past, I experienced the importance of being real, of communicating feelings such as those to a group. Quite often when I was able to do that, the group was able to move to a new place. I think this was one of the experiences of our working together that pleased Carl greatly, because several people have told me that he related that story with delight.

Reluctantly, I leave only these tiny fragments of our weeks in the Soviet Union because they mark the last time that Carl and I worked together in this way. When I returned with Fran Macey in 1987, women's groups became a part of the sessions in Moscow. Expectations of returning to Russia in 1993 to continue work in Moscow and perhaps other cities seem to be gaining substance. I look forward to meeting friends from past years and finding new ones.

A Quick Glance Back

In 1972, when I became acquainted with Carl Rogers and his work, the warm acceptance of the human condition, the intellectual stimulation of this philosophy and theory, the respect for rigorous research and a willingness to submit his work to the verdict of research, and the continuous demonstration of the self-actualizing tendency in his own life, beckoned me to a new part of my professional career and my personal life. I have tried to impart something of the extent, the intensity, and the flavor of our work together and of my work independently through the 1986 visits to South Africa and to the Soviet Union. I also continued with my return visits to the Soviet Union and to South Africa in 1987, but now there may be some sketches that should be filled in.

In January and February of 1986, we spent six weeks in South Africa and two weeks in Szeged, Hungary in a "Cross-Cultural Communication" workshop. Later we reported on our South African work at the Association for the Development of the Person-Centered Approach (ADPCA) and Forum Meeting in Chicago, in the first week in September. Finally, our last work together was from September 22 to October 19 in Moscow and Tbilisi.

In January 1987, we planned a return visit to South Africa for the spring and laid plans to begin researching the lasting effects of our earlier visit with the Cape Town groups. That visit was changed by Carl's accident and his death on February 4, 1987. I postponed my visit to South Africa until the fall of 1987.

During the first two weeks of July, I was a member of a "Cross-Cultural Communication" workshop in Sunion, Greece. It was the first workshop held after Carl's death and had a commemorative spirit.

In November, at a joint Forum and ADPCA Conference in Los Angeles, I assisted Gay Swenson in hosting Alexey Matushkin and Irina Kuzmacheva from the Soviet Union during their participation in the conference. Also in November, I participated with Tom Greening and others who had worked with Carl, in a commemorative meeting at the University of California at Los Angeles.

When we left the Soviet Union in 1986, Fran Macey, Carl, and I had hoped to return and to meet with members of the diplomatic service from the United States in the Soviet Union. We wanted to continue both our work with establishing communication across lines of difference as well as what we had done with professional participants in 1986. After Carl's death, Fran and I returned to spend time in Moscow and Tbilisi again.

At the ADPCA Conference at International House, New York, in May 1988, I participated in three sessions: congruence in the person-centered way of being, facilitation in large groups, and a follow-up report on South Africa, with Jane Gama from South Africa and Sylvia Gaines. Jane also joined the intensive week that was my annual graduate course at Hofstra University: "The Person-Centered Approach to Counseling and Education," during the first week in June. The graduate course at C. W. Post during August was my last professional activity for the remainder of 1988.

From August until Niel's death in January of 1989, my time was entirely devoted to being with him and with the family. I returned to professional work only in June, at the "Cross-Cultural" workshop in Sheffield, England, where I was one of the facilitators. The following week, at the request of Charles Devonshire, I conducted a three-day training program with students from France and Hungary.

One of the memorable experiences of 1989 was my four-week visit with my daughter, Mei-Mei, to Nigeria. She was preparing the way to begin her field work for satisfying requirements for a doctoral degree at Drew University in anthropology and religion. It was the first time either of us had visited Nigeria and the first time we had both been engaged actively in the same project for so long a time.

Mei-Mei's life style is very different from mine. She is one of my clos-est friends, one of my best teachers, and a vibrant and imaginative companion.

As I look back, I see that the form, the shape, even the directions of my life have been held together by what seemed like a tenuous thread of chance. But *was* it chance? There was the wonderment of the illusion that I built a house with my father; the salesman at the door who spoke to my mother; my mother's response to the banker who could have withheld a loan for my going to college; the telegram that came too late for me to go to Portland rather than New York City; that magic moment after seven years of marriage in which Mei-Mei was conceived; that awful night in which two doctors at Johns Hopkins held her fragile life in their hands; the unbidden cri-sis in Virginia that changed the tenor of my relationships with oth-ers; the almost desperate need for an infusion of energy for survival at West Hempstead, which led to the research and experimentation of one of the most exciting parts of my life; the drawing of Carl's name from a hat as leader of my group at Mills College; the pure chance that the last seat on the plane for La Jolla at the end of that conference was next to Carl.

As I take again this journey through my life, I find that what seemed earlier like the fragile gossamer threads of a spider web have become strong, like silken threads in a Chinese fabric—or even stronger, like the cord that holds the sky and the sand together and controls a kite in a good strong wind. Or perhaps you could call it a musical theme that gives symmetry and synchrony to the various parts and binds the whole together.

I am becoming acquainted with several of those cords. One is the assurance that I belong in this world. Another is that "the way it has always been done" is not necessarily the best way. That challenge first showed itself in my second year of teaching in Lakewood, when my interest in research and experimentation began. Subsequent years saw my involvement in the Holding Power Project, designing the final year of that project, and testing and establishing of correlations between creativity, intelligence, and achievement in the West Hempstead schools. Finally, I launched a seven-year experimental pro-gram in nurturing creativity in the classroom. The challenge persisted through innovative supervision of counselor-interns and teaching of graduate students in the universities, using the experiential pattern.

During the past six years, colleagues and I have been finding our way in person-centered qualitative research into "The Inner Process of Significant Change in the Individual."[12] In May 1992, at the annual conference of the Association for the Development of the Person-Centered Approach, Robert Barth and I presented our work of the previous five years. That paper has since been accepted for publication. I am also revising my 1990 paper, "The Theory of the Person-Centered Approach and the Theory of Chaos—A New Science: From Rogers to Gleick and Back Again."[13]

Even more significant to my personal life—and who knows the bearing that it had on my professional life—has been the thread of music, movement, and dancing. In 1934, when I was in my own apartment in Lakewood, New York, I had a dream that was sufficiently important to have remained in my memory with minute detail and clarity, even to this day. I was alone in a great grand ballroom with a dance floor as smooth and clear as glass. Dressed in a long, flowing, diaphanous gown such as dancers wear, I was dancing with abandon, my feet hardly touching the floor. Around and around and up and down that enormous space, I had such freedom as I had never felt before. It was a kind of ecstasy. That is all. There were no spectators. Eventually I woke up, with regret. I carried the glow about me for some time. The glow has continued over the years whenever I remembered.

There was only a taste of pleasure for me in social dancing after my retirement in 1972, followed that summer by my discovery of the joy in free movement in Bruce Meador's group in La Jolla. But it was not until 1974 that my dream was realized in a courtyard in one of the colleges within Yale University. At an alumni reunion for my husband's class, there was a small temporary wooden platform on the grass on a fine summer evening with good music. A classmate of Niel's asked me to dance. I became again that young woman in 1934 who knew nothing about ballroom dancing; but my feet, my mind, and my spirit knew what to do. We were the only dancers on the floor, and I shall never know for how long we danced. When the music stopped, my partner said, "My God, you're an exciting woman"—the first person, dance partner or other, who had ever said those words to me. It didn't matter whether they were true or not. I had experienced the excitement of the dance, and I had realized a dream of forty years.

In 1977 I had another such experience, shadow dancing with my daughter at a special celebration. When we finished, we heard that other guests at the celebration had been watching. We were, again, the only dancers on the floor.

One birthday message I remember was a message from Carl which said, "to a dancing spirit." Carl and I often danced, occasionally at one of the workshops but more often when we had finished our work in his La Jolla home. We often danced freely to the tunes of some of the classic musicals, as we did on that last night before Carl's accident. Early the next morning he broke his hip, which required surgery and led to his death a few days later.

Only weeks before Niel's death in 1989, he and I had such an experience dancing in the old Williamsburg Inn in Williamsburg, Virginia. It was the last time we had a vacation together.

When I am alone here at home, I still dance. Surprisingly, my confidence and my balance become much more sure. That is why I say that if I had grown up in a different religious climate, I might have been a dancer. The thought gives me pleasure. My experience in working with Carl over the years led me to speak of him as the Baryshnikov of communication: all the same attributes—the agility, dedication, responsiveness, and ability to enter the world of a dance partner—showed in his therapy and in our way of working together. Still, it is a comparison that probably would have elicited a droll comment from Carl.

I am moved to believe that I have some of those qualities. When I'm at my best with a client or a group, I experience again the intuitive sense that was present in me on that dance floor in 1974. Another connection that has persisted feels more like a kite string than a silken thread. Like the "insatiable curtiosity" of Curious George in the children's story of that name, it keeps me wondering: what comes next? What is just around the next bend? As I look back, I know that whenever I had passed through a kind of valley of gloom or near despair or discouragement or disappointment and could lift up my eyes, I had a vision of something ahead that could be really exciting.

Epilogue

This has been a longer journey that I expected when I began. To you who have journeyed with me through these years, I thank you for your companionship as we move back into the present. Were it not for your presence, I would not have written of this journey.

A Sanford family anecdote comes to my mind. A homespun philosopher-driver of the Sanford School in Connecticut used to say, "I always likes to come back the same way I went so that I can see where I was coming from." It seems appropriate at this point.

The perfect moment in making love, enfolding in your arms a child, conceiving a new idea, seeing a look of understanding in the eyes of a friend, feeling the lift of your spirit in recognizing the moment of creating something beautiful by yourself or with another—these are the moments when the past and the present come together in harmony and are to be savored with joy. So, for that nineteen-year-old girl who boarded a train for the first time in her life to go to Lebanon Valley College in 1926, I would say I couldn't have done it better if I had planned it myself.

As I said to a friend, with wonder, upon my return from the Soviet Union in 1986, "I don't even know yet what my potential is!" Capricorns *are* late bloomers.

Acknowledgments

The informal conversational tone of this story of my life is partly by intent and partly by necessity, given a sudden and severe loss of my vision during the past year. I am learning a new way of being, a new way of working, and a new way of writing. I wish to express my deep gratitude to Ed Bodfish, without whom this work would not have been completed; to Cheryl Desrosiers, for her careful transcription, commitment, and cheerful encouragement; to Mei-Mei, for her critical reading and helpful suggestions; and also to Denise Curran, Jeanne Ginsberg, Richard Elgart, and Robert Barth, for being my eyes in this endeavor.

References

[1] Carl Rogers and Ruth Sanford, "Client-Centered Psychotherapy," in Howard I. Kaplan and Benjamin J. Sadock, *Comprehensive Textbook of Psychiatry,* Fourth Edition. Baltimore: Williams and Wilkins, 1985.

[2] Alfred North Whitehead, *Science and the Modern World.* Glencoe, IL: Free Press, 1967.

[3] Carl Rogers, *Freedom to Learn for the 80s.* Columbus, OH: Merrill, 1983; p. 108.

[4] Our first step was to administer to all students in the grades selected the following tests: (1) Word Association—listing as many meanings as possible for commonly used words, such as *fire* or *date;* (2) Objects—listing as many uses as possible for common objects, such as brick; (3) Hidden Shapes—finding a simple figure hidden in complex figures; (4) Fables— writing an ending for fables left incomplete; (5) Problems—making up original problems which could be solved by the use of data given (no solutions necessary).

To minimize the handicap of nonreaders, in the administration of tests all paragraphs (Fables and Problems) were read aloud by teachers, and words causing difficulty were defined. Teachers were instructed to make sure that students understood the content. They did not assist in interpretation. All these tests were given in a relaxed atmosphere with only broad time limits.

5 Richard S. Crutchfield in Gruber, Terrel, and Wertheimer (Eds.), *Contemporary Approaches to Creative Thinking.* New York: Atherton Press, 1963; p. 125.

6 Carl Rogers, *Carl Rogers on Personal Power: Inner Strength and Its Revolutionary Impact.* New York: Delacorte Press, 1977; pp. 108-11.

7 Carl Rogers and Ruth Sanford, "Journey to the Heart of South Africa" (unpublished article).

8 Carl Rogers, *A Way of Being.* Boston: Houghton Mifflin, 1980; p. 153.

9 Carl Rogers and Ruth Sanford, "Client-Centered Psychotherapy," in Howard I. Kaplan and Benjamin J. Sadock (Eds.), *Comprehensive Textbook of Psychiatry, Fifth Edition.* Baltimore: Williams and Wilkins, 1989.

10 Fran Macey in *AHP Perspective,* February 1987, p. 10.

11 Tom Greening in *Journal of Humanistic Psychology* 27 (2), Spring 1987.

12 Robert Barth and Ruth Sanford, "Human Science and the Person-Centered Approach: An Inquiry into the Inner Process of Significant Change within Individuals" (paper presented at the Second International Conference on Client-Centered and Experiential Psychotherapy, Stirling, Scotland; 1991) in *Person-Centered Journal* 1 (2).

13 Ruth Sanford, "Theory of the Person-Centered Approach and the Theory of Chaos: From Rogers to Gleick and Back Again," to appear in David Brazier (Ed.), *Beyond Carl Rogers: Towards a Psychotherapy for the Twenty-First Century.* London: Constable (in press).

BIBLIOGRAPHY

Major Sources by and about Carl Rogers and His Work

Cain, D. (Ed.). *The Person-Centered Review.* Quarterly journal published from 1986 to 1990. Newbury Park, CA: Sage Publications.

Coulson, W. R. and Rogers, C. R. (Eds.). *Man and the Science of Man.* Columbus, OH: Charles Merrill, 1968.

Evans, R. *Carl Rogers: The Man and His Ideas.* New York: E. P. Dutton, 1978.

Farson, R. *Journey Into Self.* 16mm film. La Jolla, CA: Western Behavioral Sciences Institute, 1968.

Hart, J. T. and Tomlinson, T. M. (Eds.). *New Directions in Client-Centered Therapy.* Boston: Houghton Mifflin, 1970.

Kirschenbaum, H. *Carl Rogers: A Case Study of a Psychologist and Educator.* Unpublished doctoral dissertation, Temple University, 1974.

Kirschenbaum, H. *On Becoming Carl Rogers.* New York: Delacorte Press, 1979.

Kirschenbaum, H. and Henderson, V. (Eds.). *Carl Rogers: Dialogues. Conversations with Buber, Tillich, Skinner, Bateson, Polyani, May, and others.* Boston: Houghton Mifflin, 1989.

Kirschenbaum, H. and Henderson, V. (Eds.). *The Carl Rogers Reader.* Boston: Houghton Mifflin, 1989.

Lietaer, G.; Rombauts, J.; and Van Balen, R. (Eds.). *Client-Centered and Experiential Psychotherapy in the Nineties.* Leuven, Belgium: Leuven University Press, 1990.

Rogers, C. R. *Measuring Personality Adjustment in Children Nine to Thirteen Years of Age.* New York: Teachers College, 1931.

———. *The Clinical Treatment of the Problem Child.* Boston, Houghton Mifflin, 1939.

———. *Counseling and Psychotherapy: New Concepts in Practice.* Boston: Houghton Mifflin, 1942.

———. *Counseling with Returned Servicemen.* New York: McGraw-Hill, 1945.

———. *Client-Centered Therapy: Its Current Practice, Implications and Theory.* Boston: Houghton Mifflin, 1951.

———. A theory of therapy, personality and interpersonal relationships as developed in the client-centered framework. In Koch, S. (Ed.), *Psychology: A Study of a Science, Vol. III. Formulations of the Person and the Social Context.* New York: McGraw Hill, 1959.

———. *On Becoming a Person.* Boston: Houghton Mifflin, 1961.

———. Autobiography. In Boring, E. W.; and Lindzey, G. (Eds.), *A History of Psychology in Autobiography, Vol. V,* New York: Appleton-Century-Crofts, 1967.

———. *Client-centered therapy,* Film No. 1. In E. Shostrom (Ed.), *Three Approaches to Psychotherapy.* Three 16mm color motion pictures. Orange, CA: Psychological Films, Inc., 1965.

———. *Freedom To Learn: A View of What Education Might Become.* Columbus, OH: Charles Merrill, 1969.

———. *Carl Rogers on Encounter Groups.* New York: Harper and Row, 1970.

———. *Becoming Partners: Marriage and Its Alternatives.* New York: Delacorte Press, 1972.

———. *Carl Rogers on Personal Power: Inner Strength and Its Revolutionary Impact.* New York: Delacorte Press, 1977.

———. *A Way of Being.* Boston: Houghton Mifflin, 1980.

———. *Freedom To Learn for the 80s.* Columbus, OH: Charles Merrill, 1983.

Rogers, C. R. and Dymond, R. (Eds.). *Psychotherapy and Personality Change.* Chicago: University Press, 1954.

Rogers, C. R.; Gendlin, E. T.; Kiesler, D. J.; and Truax, C. B. (Eds.). *The Therapeutic Relationship and Its Impact: A Study of Psychotherapy with Schizophrenics.* Madison: University of Wisconsin Press, 1967.

Rogers, C. R. and Sanford, R. Client-centered psychotherapy. In Kaplan, H. and Sadock, B. (Eds.), *Comprehensive Textbook of Psychiatry/IV.* Pp. 1374–88 (100 typewritten pages). Baltimore: Williams & Wilkins, 1984.

Rogers, C. R. and Stevens, B. *Person To Person: The Problem of Being Human.* Lafayette, CA: Real People Press, 1968.

Rogers, H. A wife's eye view of Carl Rogers. *Voices,* 1(1), 93–98.

Thorne, B. *Carl Rogers.* London: Sage Publications, 1991.

Wexler, D. and Rice, L. (Eds.). *Innovations in Client-Centered Therapy.* New York: John Wiley, 1974.

About the Editor

Much of my life story is devoted to the many persons who influenced my life. My first five years were spent on the west side of Detroit, on a lower-middle-class street lined with the houses of my mother's entire family (except for her older sister). My grandfather, a rabbi and the first humanistic psychologist, taught me the logic of numbers when I was four. My father was an electrician and a semi-pro baseball catcher who took me to many games and helped me learn to use a baseball scorecard. My father's brother Sam was the symbol of the Uncle Sam who epitomizes the greatness of this country. Aunt Trudy, who personified effervescence and knew the words to every popular tune of the day, taught me how to sing and taught me some of those songs.

My cousin Ted, five years my senior, was a true leader and a socially conscious person from his early teens. Later, as president and chairperson for the board of a large U.S. conglomerate, he spent much of his time proving that a large, successful corporation could devote its energy to peaceful commodities rather than defense production. Ted's sister Nita (who is six weeks younger than I) has always taken turns with me in being the experienced learner for each other. Her mother, my aunt Blanche, is now 93 years old. She still drives to work one day a week, and she volunteers two days a week to entertain retirement-home residents—none of whom has reached her age.

Finally, my grandmother and mother were true models of matriarchy. During their lives they held our large family together and reflected the dignity and the commitment to lifelong learning that later became my mission.

I have spent much of my life connecting with like-minded people and trying to put into practice what I learn. In the sixth grade, I formed the Musketeers after reading *The Three Musketeers* by Dumas (and of course gave myself the character of Athos, the wise, mature one). In junior high, I helped form the Tokalons, a club of eighteen persons; fourteen of us are still in touch today, sixty years later.

Not all the influential events in my life have been so idyllic. I spent three years in the infantry during the Second World War, fighting with the Rainbow Division during the Battle of the Bulge. My company was the first to enter the main camp at Dachau as the war was ending. The pyramid pile of 3,000 bodies at the entrance will haunt me for the rest of my life.

When I was discharged, I married my high school sweetheart and moved to California, where my first son was born. I dropped out of the psychology department at UCLA, operated a gas station and then sold Fuller brushes, automobile seat covers, and kitchenware. Five years later, we moved back to Detroit, where my other son and my daughter were born. I sold automobile accessories and real estate before I finally realized that I wanted to be a teacher.

After graduating from Detroit's Wayne State University, I taught fifth grade in Ferndale, Michigan, and developed my philosophy of open education. At the first International Reading Association conference, I was called the "father of individualized reading."

This was a period when others influenced my development greatly. Scott Street, the principal of my Ferndale school, was a leader in progressive education. He did not believe in grades or corporal punishment, and he honored the separation of church and state. Minnie Burson, who was our kindergarten teacher, wrote *Kindergarten, Your Child's First Step,* and modeled humanistic education—as did Irene Lancaster and Joan Goldsmith, who developed learning centers and created an atmosphere for individualizing instruction.

In 1955, in graduate school, I took my first class with Clark Moustakas. For the next eleven years, I studied humanistic psychology and play therapy with Clark and his learning community. During this period I formulated the basis for my values in education and in psychology. Clark was the most influential mentor in my life. His learning community also included Dorothy Lee, Carl Rogers, Art Combs, Abraham Maslow, Ross Mooney, Sereta Perry, and many peer learners who came to study with Clark at Merrill-Palmer. Another key person for me was Earl Kelley, who chaired my doctoral committee at Wayne State.

Meanwhile, in 1959, some of us had a national year as educational innovators. After being feted for earning his doctorate, Scott Street was fired by the Ferndale school board. His dismissal as principal was based on complaints from the mother of a student in my fourth-grade class. She apparently accused me of teaching chess and helping students design mobiles rather than learning math, science, and English.

For the next five months, we were engaged in a battle with the school board and were front-page news in all three Detroit papers, as well as being featured celebrities in *Time, Newsweek, Life,* and other national publications. By the end of the year, I resigned and took employment in an adjacent school district, where I became an assistant principal in an elementary school with 1,100 children. I also spent time being the national director of the Evelyn Wood Reading Dynamics Institute, setting up centers all over the country.

When Scott returned from heading military schools in North Africa and southern Europe, he was appointed full professor at Eastern Michigan University. He headed their laboratory school and asked me to join him as an assistant professor. I spent the next two years teaching courses in education and psychology, and supervising student teachers at the laboratory school.

In 1964 I became the headmaster of Lesley Ellis School (attached to Lesley College) in Cambridge, Massachusetts. I also did some teaching at Harvard and helped design the first Headstart classroom. Concurrently, I was director of the Dearborn School for emotionally disturbed children and children in remedial courses.

John Goodlad invited me to complete my doctorate at UCLA, where I developed my theory of pluralism in education. The main idea is to allow students, parents, and teachers to select their own best learning style: self-initiated, eclectic, or directed. (Various school districts in Minnesota, California, and Alaska successfully adopted this model in the 1970s.)

John also asked me to be part of an innovative consulting program in southern California called The Institute for the Development of Educational Activities. My role was to be a supportive agent to school principals and staff as they explored innovation and change. The two schools assigned to me were located in Delano and Santa Monica. On my visits to Delano's Fremont School, I met Cesar Chavez and wrote a speech he gave at a California Education Association conference.

With the Office of Economic Opportunity, I helped administer a grant called the Advisory for Open Education. For nearly nine years, this grant helped parents and teachers create more open classrooms for very young children. We built adventure playgrounds around the country and created learning centers that let parents and teachers engage in artistic and creative activities with surplus industrial materials. This was to encourage them to stimulate similar openness and creativity in children under their care.

My move away from early childhood education, psychology, and administration evolved gradually. From 1967 through 1976, I was director of a Creative Environment Workshop, part of a federally funded project (through the Advisory for Open Education) in Watts. Simultaneously, I served as a project officer for parent–child centers (a pre-Headstart program for parents and children under three) in Detroit and in Lincoln, Nebraska. Until 1968 I also had a private practice as a child therapist and as an organization development leader.

Then, from 1968 through 1971, I taught at Pacific Oaks College, California State University at Northridge, and Goddard College in Plainfield, Vermont. On Goddard's core faculty, I helped design the country's first external master's degree program. From California, I served for eight years as a core faculty member and West Coast director for their external Master of Arts program, helping many learners complete degrees in an individualized structure.

In 1968 I also designed and administered the first University Without Walls, funded by the U.S. Department of Labor's Office of Child Development. The idea was to create an individualized forum for creative, imaginative learning that would be accessible to people whose schedules, aptitudes, locations, or academic backgrounds might otherwise exclude them from traditional higher education. Of the first twenty-five parents and teacher's aides who enrolled, twenty-four graduated from USC and received teaching credentials.

In 1977 I became president of UWW in California and served in that capacity for nine years. UWW expanded to include centers up and down the state: in San Diego, the greater Los Angeles area, Santa Barbara, on the Monterey peninsula, in San Francisco, and Sacramento. We established a master's and a doctoral program, and graduates became eligible for licenses in psychology and in Marriage, Family, and Child Counseling.

In 1974 and 1975, leaders or heads of psychology departments from eight accredited universities met monthly to deal with the restraints being imposed on graduates wanting to become therapists. With the encouragement of my colleagues, I founded the Association for the Integration of the Whole Person (AIWP), a nonsectarian religious organization. AIWP ordains persons committed to minister to the well being of self and others. In the ensuing years, AIWP has become a recognized spiritual institution that has made an important contribution to the field of therapy.

In 1986, I resigned as president of UWW because of a serious illness. After a two-year recovery, I joined five other pioneers in UWW history to form Summit University of Louisiana. I now serve as president and trustee of that institution, whose bachelor's, master's, and doctoral degrees are awarded for institutional as well as community-based learning.

Index